First published in 1975
by Methuen & Co Ltd
11 New Fetter Lane London EC4P 4EE
© 1974 Leszek A. Kosiński and R. Mansell Prothero

Printed in Great Britain by
William Clowes & Sons Limited
London, Colchester and Beccles

ISBN 0 416 78410 0 (hardbound)
ISBN 0 416 83000 5 (paperback)

Distributed in the USA by
Harper & Row Publishers Inc.
Barnes & Noble Import Division

People on the Move

*Studies on
internal migration*

edited by Leszek A. Kosiński
& R. Mansell Prothero

Methuen *&* Co Ltd
London

People
on the Move
Studies on
internal migration

J

Contents

Figures

Preface

Migration is recognized as one of the most important areas of contemporary research on population. Geographers, with their concern for spatially-expressed processes, are obviously attracted to the study of relocation of people. Recognizing this growing interest, the International Geographical Union Commission on Population Geography devoted its meeting in August 1972 to matters concerning internal migration. This Symposium, held at the University of Alberta, Canada, was attended by forty participants from nineteen different countries.

This volume is based on papers submitted and discussions held during the Symposium, but it is more than a report of the proceedings. Papers have been substantially rewritten, several contributions have been added and an introductory and linking text provided. The aim has been to provide a text on migration which will demonstrate the important contribution which geographers are making to the study of this human phenomenon.

The Editors' thanks are due to Richard Lawton, Gunnar Olsson and Wilbur Zelinsky for their assistance in helping to organize the Symposium, though they do not have papers in this volume. Financial aid for the Symposium and towards the cost of publication was received from the Population Council of New York and is gratefully acknowledged. Support of various kinds has come from the Departments of Geography at the Universities of Liverpool and Alberta, and all figures for publication were prepared at the latter under the supervision of Geoff Lester.

Both Editors have had the privilege of being associated with the Commission on Population Geography for long periods as present and former Chairman respectively. We are happy to see this book appear in the United Nations World Population Year and hope that this contribution by geographers will advance the understanding of human problems.

Leszek A. Kosiński
R. Mansell Prothero

Liège, August 1973

Introduction: The study of migration

There has been much discussion about migration in recent years from
students of population in various disciplines including geography. Although
migration is an especially attractive research area for a geographer, the
development of migration studies owes much to interdisciplinary efforts
and it is impossible to draw sharp lines between different contributions.
There are several reasons why geographers devote attention to the study
of migration. The territorial redistribution of population is an attractive
subject for a spatially-orientated discipline. Dynamic aspects have attracted
more attention and at the present time interest in spatial processes and
spatial interaction is of more concern in modern geography than a concern
with spatial patterns. This results in increased interest in migration studies.
More research into mobility is made possible by the availability of data
which are more detailed and more reliable and more regionally orientated
than in the past.

Concepts in the study of migration

Since 1885, when Ravenstein first formulated his 'migration laws', a substantial literature has appeared concerned with the spatial mobility of
population. A number of specific terms have been proposed and accepted.
The need to define various concepts used in population studies led to the
production of an international dictionary of terms (UN 1958), and the
present discussion follows closely terminology suggested by the UN and
developed later in other publications (UN 1970; Shryock *et al.* 1971).

The term *mobility* is perhaps the most general concept in migration
studies. It includes all kinds of territorial movements, both temporary and
permanent, over various distances (Zelinsky 1971). *Migration* is much more
restricted and relates to a permanent change of residence. An operational
definition of migration requires that both temporal and locational criteria
be more specifically defined. This operational definition may depend on
the type of research or type of data which are available, or both. Usually, a
migrant is defined as a person who moves from one administrative unit to
another. Sometimes moves between the lowest units in the administrative

hierarchy are omitted and only those between middle or higher rank units
are considered. On the other hand, a migrant is considered to be a person
who moves with the intention of establishing a new residence in a different
country or a region. If he later changes his mind he will be considered a
migrant again or, if he returns to the place of origin, a returning migrant.
Alternatively, the migrant can be a person who will stay in a new residence
for a minimum period of time, such as six months or one year. Some
researchers distinguish between *migrants*, those who move between political
units, and *movers*, those who move within them. Thus, at any given time,
the total population of a region can be divided into *migrants* and *non-migrants*,
movers and *non-movers*. This classification establishes the *mobility status*
of the population.

If there is interest in the direction of the move, the distinction between
inmigrants (inmigration) and *outmigrants* (outmigration) is useful. These
terms refer specifically to internal migrations, while for external migrations
the term *immigrant* and *emigrant* are used.

Migration takes place from an area of *origin* (departure) to one of
destination (arrival) and a group of migrants with a common origin and
destination is called a *migration stream* (sometimes a *migration current*).
Usually, each stream has a *counterstream*; the distinction between the two
is based on the size of the respective flows. The term *gross migration* refers
to the total number of inmigrants and outmigrants of an area and is sometimes referred to as the *turnover* for an area. If analysis is restricted to two
units connected by a migration stream, the total size of both stream and
counterstream is called the *gross interchange* between the two areas and
the difference between the two is referred to as the *net stream* or *net
interchange* between the areas.

If analysis is limited to a single unit, total moves affecting its population
(inmigration and outmigration) are referred to as *gross migration* or *volume
of migration* whereas the difference between the two streams would be *net
migration* or *balance of migration* (which may be positive or negative).
Sometimes more specific terms, *net inmigration* or *net outmigration*, are
used. By comparing net migration with gross migration *efficiency* or *efficacy*
of migration can be established.

In a study based on data concerning previous residence the term *migration
period* or *migration interval* has to be introduced. If the question asked
concerns the residence at a specific date (*fixed period migration*) this
period becomes a *migration interval.* If the concern is with *lifetime migration*,
then lifetime becomes synonymous with migration interval.

Although considerable efforts were made by internation organizations
to define and popularize terms in order to minimize misunderstandings,
degrees of flexibility still prevail and new terms are being introduced. The
above discussion includes only the most important terms about which there

is general agreement (UN 1970; Shryock *et al.* 1971; see also *Gould and Prothero*).[1]

Geographical or spatial mobility includes all sorts of moves both temporary and permanent. It differs from social mobility which refers to a change in socioeconomic status. However, increasingly these two types of mobility are treated jointly and this attitude is reflected in various definitions proposed. There have been various suggestions ranging from consideration of exclusively spatial criteria to those giving priority to social ones, and the following are examples:

> We define migration as the physical transition of an individual or a group from one society to another. This transition usually involves abandoning one social setting and entering another and different one. (Eisenstadt 1953, 1)

> Henceforth, we will use the term 'migration' for the change of residence of an individual from one parish or commune to another. (Hägerstrand 1957, 28)

> Human migration is the changing of the place of abode permanently or, when temporarily, for an appreciable duration as e.g. in the case of seasonal workers. It is used symbolically in the transition from one surrounding to another in the course of human life. (Weinberg 1961, 265–6)

> 'Change of community' as an index of migration affords a very rough gauge of the meaning to be assigned to such indeterminate words as 'permanent' or 'significant' in the usual definition of migration – the relatively permanent movement of persons over a significant distance. (Petersen 1969, 254)

> Migration is a relatively permanent moving away of a collectivity, called migrants, from one geographical location to another preceded by decision-making on the part of the migrants on the basis of a hierarchically ordered set of values or valued ends and resulting in changes in the interactional system of the migrants. (Mangalam 1968, 8)

> Genuine migration obviously means the perceptible and simultaneous shifts in both spacial and social locus, so that the student cannot realistically measure one kind of movement while he ignores the other . . . Ideally, we should observe shifts in both varieties of space in tandem but given the dearth of techniques and data for handling purely social movement, we are forced to rely solely on territorial

---

[1] Please note that references in the text which are in italic refer to papers which appear in this volume.

movements as a clumsy surrogate for total mobility. When a truly
serviceable index of mobility is fabricated, it will certainly be composite, bringing together measures of several dimensions. The problem
is comparable to that of gauging general socio-economic advancements;
no single number will do; a variety of indicators must be viewed
simultaneously. (Zelinsky 1971, 224)

If the definition of migration is narrowly conceived, it would exclude
various types of flows. For example, insistence on independence of decision
would eliminate forced migration from consideration. Since forced migration
has represented a considerable part of flows, especially between countries,
such an exclusion from the definition does not seem justified.

No attempt has been made to follow one uniform definition of migration
throughout this volume. Hence, a variety of concepts and operational definitions will be encountered in various papers depending on the requirements
of individual authors and the data at their disposal. This diversity reflects
the present state of migration studies.

Mechanism of migration

Migration takes place when an individual decides that it is preferable to
move rather than to stay and where the difficulties of moving seem to be
more than offset by the expected rewards. To explain the mechanism of
migration, we have to consider the decision-making process. The concept
which helps best to understand this mechanism is that of 'push and pull'.
Most individuals have a permanent residence and this is the normal state of
affairs even if each is involved in a number of circular moves around this
place. If, however, it is believed that needs can no longer be satisfied at this
place, then a move somewhere else may have to be considered, if psychological strain is to be avoided. Thus, a 'push' factor appears. Real life
examples are loss of employment; racial, religious or political persecution;
social, cultural or personal alienation from the community; social or natural
disaster. Otherwise, an individual can be satisfied with the present situation,
but new information may persuade that a move elsewhere will offer new and
attractive opportunities. This can be termed the 'pull' factor and examples
include better political, economic and social opportunities, and increased
amenities.

Each person is constantly exposed to factors at a place of residence some
of which inhibit movement and others which encourage it. By the same
token, there are numerous positive and negative impulses coming from
different potential destinations. The decision to move or not to move
results from the evaluation of all these factors (fig. 0.1). Such evaluation is
not carried out objectively but by exposure to various kinds of conditioning

and bias. The decision will thus depend on factors such as cultural and environmental conditioning – moving may be considered quite normal or most unusual; group reaction – decision may be prompted by conformity with community and peers rather than individually; state in life – graduates terminating education and persons changing marital or occupational status are more likely to move than others; other individual characteristics. Decisions may be modified by real or perceived obstacles which include costs and fatigue of move, personal anxiety which will result from change in the social and physical environment, legal restrictions.

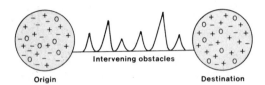

Origin   **Destination**

Factors at origin and destination

+   **attracting**   O   **neutral**   –   **repulsing**

Figure 0.1 Origin and destination factors and intervening obstacles in migration
Source: Lee 1966. Copyright © 1966 by the Population Association of America

The decision to migrate should not be identified with the decision to choose destination, although the two are closely related. In this respect the concept of 'place utility', defined as 'the net composite utility derived from the individual's integration at some position in space', can be helpful (Wolpert 1965). Perceived utility of a new place has to be greater than the utility (or disutility) in the old place for a migration to take place. If a better alternative is not available then a person would most likely remain in the same place, but unless his/her expectations are altered he/she will remain a latent migrant ready to move whenever opportunity presents itself. There is also the concept of 'migration elasticity' which concerns the amount of stimuli necessary to persuade the potential migrant to make a decision (Wolpert 1966).

A different approach to rural-urban migration is provided by Mabogunje who tries to conceptualize the problem within the framework of General Systems Theory. His approach 'enables consideration of rural-urban migration no longer as a linear, uni-directional, "push and pull" cause-effect movement, but as a circular, interdependent, progressively complex, and self-modifying system in which the effect of changes in one part can be traced through the whole of the system' (Mabogunje 1970, 16). The migration system is influenced by an economic, social, political and technological environment (fig. 0.2). The exchange between this environment and the migration system is open and continuous. Having received the stimulus, the potential migrant will be influenced by the rural control subsystem (family, local community) in his decision either to remain in the rural area or to make a move. The urban control subsystem (mostly related to housing and economic opportunities) can help the migrant to adjust to the new environment and eventually to become a true urbanite. Success or

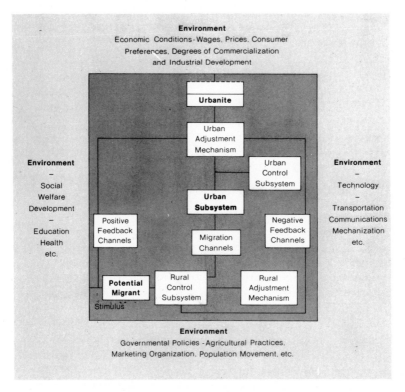

Figure 0.2 A systems schema for a theory of rural-urban migration
Source: Mabogunje 1970. Copyright © 1970 by the Ohio State University Press;
all rights reserved.

failure is constantly transmitting positive or negative feedbacks to the area of origin to influence subsequent migration. Although Mabogunje's concept is mostly related to Africa, it has some general relevance. 'It emphasizes rural-urban migration as a continuous process occurring in most countries all the time though at different levels of complexity. In this respect the systems approach also serves as a normative model against which one can seek to explain obvious deviations' (Mabogunje 1970, 16).

Typology of migration

The variety of moves classified as migration calls for a typology to attempt
to introduce some order to the apparent chaos. A number of classifications
have been suggested based on different criteria.

   An early classification (table 0.1) was based on the difference in the
level of culture and presence or absence of violence (Fairchild 1925) and
was later adopted by several researchers despite its shortcomings discussed
by Petersen (1958). Kant discussed various typologies especially concerned
with circular movements (pastoral nomadism and transhumance) suggested

Table 0.1
Typology of migration

Migration from	Migration to	Peaceful movement	Warlike movement
Low culture	High culture		Invasion
High culture	Low culture	Colonization	Conquest
Cultures on a level		Immigration	

Source: Fairchild 1925.

in the 1930s and 1940s. His own classification is based on areal units
between which a movement takes place. Thus, migrations are divided into
intralocal or intraregional and interlocal or interregional (Kant 1953).
Beltramone followed essentially the same line of reasoning and divided
migration initially into temporary and definitive and later into those
taking place within or without areal units (*extra-muros* and *intra-muros*)
(Beltramone 1966). George included only two classes: migration prompted
by economic factors and that in which the need or obligation to move is so
strong as to push economic considerations into the background (George
1970).

   The best known classification by Petersen used a variety of criteria, probably the most important being the distinction between migration which
is undertaken in order to change the way of life (innovative) and that
which helps to preserve it (conservative). Other criteria include the type
of interaction expressed by migratory force which results in classes and
types of migration (Petersen 1958) (table 0.2).

   A typology of migration should take into consideration various criteria
and the resulting classification can be thought of as a multidimensional
matrix with some cells empty and some occupied by distinguishable types.
The dimensions of such a matrix would be designated by: time (temporary,

Table 0.2
Typology of migration

General typology of migration			Migratory selection by type of migration							
			'Conservative'				'Innovating'			
Type of interaction	Migratory force	Class of migration	Type of migration	Destination	Migratory selection	Comments: Examples	Type of migration	Destination	Migratory selection	Comments: Examples
Nature and Man	Ecological push	Primitive	Wandering (Wandering of peoples / Marine wandering)	None	Survival of the fittest	Prehistoric migrations	Flight from the land	Move for land (or towns)	?	Malthusian pressure
			Gatherers and Nomads (Gathering Nomads)	Greener pastures	None	Migratory way of life				
State (or equivalent) and Man	Migration policy	Impelled	Flight	Place of safety	None or minority groups	Emigrés and refugees	Coolie trade	Site of work usually plantations	Young males	Large remigration
		Forced	Displacement	Any place	None or minority groups	Population exchanges	Slave trade	Site of work	Young males	Mercantile or industrial
Man and his norms	Higher aspirations	Free	Group	New lands	Dissident groups		Pioneer	Frontier lands	Young males	Individually motivated
Collective behaviour	Social momentum	Mass	Settlement	Rural areas	Young males predominate	Social momentum	Urban-ization	Towns	Young females predominate	

Source: After Petersen 1958.

permanent); distance (long, short); boundaries crossed (internal, external); areal units involved (between communities, counties, states); decision-making (voluntary, impelled, forced); numbers involved (individual, mass); social organization of migrants (family, clan, individual); political organization of migrations (sponsored, free); causes (economic, non-economic); aims (conservative, innovative). A further discussion of migration typology followed by a classification of mobility in Africa follows in a paper in this present volume (*Gould and Prothero*).

Migration laws

Following an extensive empirical enquiry on internal migration, first in Britain and later in twenty other countries, Ravenstein published two seminal papers in the 1880s in which he postulated his 'laws of migration' (Ravenstein 1885, 1889). He thus reacted to an earlier study of Farr who remarked that migration appeared to go without any definite law (Farr 1876). Ravenstein included five explicit and two implicit statements concerning patterns and distance of migration, migratory streams, migration motives, and characteristics of migrants. Recently, Lee has returned to the same theme and restated Ravenstein's laws in a series of hypotheses about the volume of migration under varying conditions, the development of stream and counterstream and the characteristics of migrants (Lee 1966, 295–7). On the volume of migration:

1. The volume of migration within a given territory varies with the degree of diversity in areas included in that territory.
2. The volume of migration varies with the diversity of people.
3. The volume of migration is related to the difficulty of surmounting the intervening obstacles.
4. The volume of migration varies with fluctuations in the economy.
5. Unless severe checks are imposed, both volume and rate of migration tend to increase with time.
6. The volume and rate of migration vary with state of progress in a country or in an area.

On the stream and counterstream:

1. Migration tends to take place largely within well-defined streams.
2. For every major migration stream, a counterstream develops.
3. The efficiency of the stream (ratio of stream to counterstream or the net redistribution of population effected by the opposite flows) is high if the major factors in the development of a migration stream were minus factors at origin.
4. The efficiency of stream and counterstream tends to be low if origin and destination are similar.

5. The efficiency of migration streams will be high if the intervening obstacles are great.
6. The efficiency of a migration stream varies with economic conditions, being high in prosperous times and low in times of depression.

On the characteristics of migrants:

1. Migration is selective.
2. Migrants responding primarily to plus factors at destination tend to be positively selective.
3. Migrants responding primarily to minus factors at origin tend to be negatively selective; or, where the minus factors are overwhelming to entire population groups, they may not be selected at all.
4. Taking all migrants together, selection tends to be bi-modal.
5. The degree of positive selection increases with the difficulty of the intervening obstacles.
6. The heightened propensity to migrate at certain stages of the life cycle is important in the selection of migrants.
7. The characteristics of migrants tend to be intermediate between the characteristics of the population at origin and the population at destination.

These hypotheses provide a general framework for research and are stated in such a way that they can be tested with current data. In some cases, data are not available and would have to be specially collected. A number of research projects have attempted to test these hypotheses. Together with other theoretical statements, especially concerning intra-metropolitan flows (e.g. search spaces in relation to awareness spaces, sectoral bias in migration) Lee has helped to refocus migration study from a purely descriptive to an analytical approach.

The role of migration in social change

A general framework for scientific enquiry into territorial mobility of population was recently provided by Zelinsky in the hypothesis of mobility transition. He suggests that 'there are definite, patterned regularities in the growth of personal mobility through space-time during recent history, and these regularities comprise an essential component of the modernization process' (Zelinsky 1971, 222). Zelinsky deals with mobility in a broad sense including migration and various forms of circulation. Mobility transition in his view parallels vital transitions (in fertility and mortality) since the two processes occurring simultaneously and probably interdependently affect the overall demographic and residential behaviour of society.

Five stages of mobility transition are postulated which are characteristic of five stages of socioeconomic development of a society. The pre-modern traditional society displays little genuine residential migration and limited circulation, sanctioned by customary practices; population size remains relatively stable. The early transitional society experiences sudden increase in fertility, accompanied by massive rural-urban migration, colonization of domestic and foreign frontierlands, possibly a small immigration of skilled personnel from abroad and increased circulation. In the late transitional society, when rates of natural increase gradually decelerate, traditional types of movement, such as rural-urban migration, colonization of the frontier and emigration, also slacken, but various forms of circulation increase in volume and complexity. In the advanced society, natural increase is limited as a result of reduced fertility and mortality, residential mobility levels off and oscillates at a high level, rural-urban migration continues but its volume and rate are considerably reduced, inter-urban and intra-urban mobility increases. Settlement frontier is likely to retreat; foreign migration is significant and includes the incoming of unskilled personnel and the exchange of highly trained migrants. Further increase of circulation takes place. The future super-advanced society may be characterized by a decline in residential migration which will be then be almost exclusively of inter-urban and intra-urban variety, and further changes in circulation with some types declining and others increasing. Mobility within and between countries will very likely be strictly controlled.

Zelinsky further suggests that each stage begins in an area which can be conceived as a hearth and later spreads outwards. Diffusion through time and space will display the well-known distance-decay effect except that distance should be measured in demographic rather than linear terms. Discussion on relationship between mobility and modernization has continued in geography (Pryor 1971) and the present volume provides further examples.

A different approach has been outlined by Mangalam who discusses social organizational theory of migration. Each society undergoes a social change which is the 'difference between social organization of a given society at two different points in time, comprising changes in any or all the three component systems, namely the culture, social and personality systems' (Mangalam 1968, 13). In the process migration takes place. Here migration is conceived as 'an adaptive process whose major objective is maintaining the dynamic equilibrium of a social organization with a minimum of changes and at the same time providing those members ways to overcome their deprivations' (Mangalam 1968, 14). Migration affects and is affected by social organization of the society of origin and destination. Also, the cultural values, norms and goals of migrants change in the process. The migration system includes all three elements – society of origin, society of destination and migrants themselves – in mutual dynamic interdependence.

Research orientations in migration studies

Migration research has been mainly concerned with four types of questions: who migrates? why? what are the patterns of flow and direction of movement? what are the consequences of migration? (Mangalam 1968, 15). Geographers were mostly interested in the third question but they have addressed themselves to other questions as well. Large numbers of empirical studies have been published over the years and it is impossible to discuss them all. A number of bibliographies have been published and are listed in an appendix of this volume.

Selection of migrants

It is assumed that migrants differ from non-migrants; their peculiar traits, characteristics and attitudes are of interest. Various methods and indices are used to measure selectivity of migrants and census data often enable comparison of migrants and non-migrants. It has been pointed out that a study of non-migrants or latent migrants can help to understand migrants, since if the reasons that keep people from moving are known then presumably the situation conducive to migration can be better understood. If this is the case, then future flows can be better predicted.

Reasons for migration

The causes for human migration are extremely diversified. Only rarely can a move be attributed to one cause since in most cases several reasons operate. However, various situations can be identified which stimulate migration decision.

According to Bogue three groups of variables can be identified: socio-economic conditions affecting migration (major capital investment, technological change, migration regulations, social welfare provisions etc.); migration stimulating situations (such as graduation, marriage, employment offer, natural disaster); and factors instrumental in choosing a destination (e.g. cost of moving, presence of relatives and/or friends, special employment opportunities, hearsay information) (Bogue 1959, 499–500).

Study of causes of migration can be based on direct questions put to migrants or to prospective migrants. Censuses, registers and special surveys carried out in many countries contain such questions. The answers have the advantage of coming directly from the persons involved and, if there is no reason deliberately to distort the truth, they can be most valuable.

However, there is always a problem of information recall if the survey
is taken a long time after migration has taken place; some people can
justify their actions *ex post* rather than give the real reasons operating at
the time; more important, assigning proper weights to various factors in the
multi-causal situation can be extremely difficult. Otherwise, correlation
analysis of migrations with other variables can imply causal relationships.
This method can and has been effectively used in migration research by
geographers when various factors areally associated with migration gains
were investigated (Kariel 1963).

Pattern of migration

Migration can be studied at different spatial scales and the analysis of flows
depends on the level of generalization. In any case there seems little doubt
that the friction of distance reduces migration contact between the areas
(Bogue and Thompson 1949; Stewart 1960; Olsson 1965; Claeson 1968).
Distance can be measured in linear terms but much more relevant is the
measure of distance expressed in economic, demographic or cultural terms
(Brown *et al.* 1970). The role of distance differs depending on characteristics
of migrants (Rose 1958). Obstacles intervening between origin and destination
influence the flow, as do the intervening opportunities; one of the best known
concepts in migration research deals with the role of intervening opportunities separating origin and destination (Stouffer 1940). The role of large
concentrations of population as magnets generating migrational flows has
been reflected in interaction models (Zipf 1946; Stewart 1960; Ter Heide
1963). In migration studies, comparison of 'expected' flows, predicted on
the basis of a gravity model, and actual flows can sometimes be more
instructive than analysis of flows themselves (Berry and Schwind 1969).

In studies of internal migration, the direction of flows has been of great
concern to spatially-orientated researchers who have tried to introduce
vectors as a measure and representation of both volume and direction of
migration (Tarver and Skees 1967). Directional bias of migrational streams
has been more recently studied by geographers interested in intra-urban
mobility (Wolpert 1967; Adams 1969; Whitelaw and Robinson 1972).
It is in relation to study of spatial patterns of flows that most models used
in migration study have been developed (Ter Heide 1963; Termote 1967).

Consequences of migration

This aspect of migration study has the greatest appeal to scholars oriented
towards application of their research and to politicians responsible for
making decisions affecting migrations (UN 1953). There is no doubt that
migration affects the society at origin, at destination, and migrants them-

selves (Mangalam 1968). The consequences can be observed and measured in economic, social, cultural, political and demographic terms. The researcher may try to predict as objectively and accurately as possible the likely consequences of migration so that politicians and planners can take decisions in full knowledge of what can be expected. One version of such policy-orientated research is the prediction of a future redistribution of population resulting from the unaltered continuation of present trends (Rogers 1966; Compton 1968). Another aspect of studies on consequences of migrations deals with assimilation of migrants (Eisenstadt 1953). Successful assimilation of a migrant can be said to represent the final stage of the process (Mabogunje 1970). Here the distinction between spatial and social aspects of moving becomes blurred and there is more involvement in the study of the sociological aspects of migration.

Conclusion

It is impossible within limited space to more than touch upon some of the major aspects of migration study. Discussion has inevitably been restricted and selective for the literature on migration is diverse and voluminous. Nonetheless, of the major components in population change migration is the one to which the least attention has been given. It is the most difficult component to conceptualize, measure and analyse. Some of the basic concepts and problems of measurement are considered in the papers which follow. They are both descriptive and analytical in their approach to the study of migration.

References

Adams, J. S. (1969) Directional bias in intra-urban migration. *Econ. Rev.* 45, 302–23.
Beltramone, A. (1966) *La mobilité géographique d'une population.* Paris. (Especially chapter 1 – Typologie des déplacement, 21–41.)
Berry, B. J. L. and Schwind, P. J. (1969) Information and entropy in migrant flows. *Geogr. Anal.* 1, 5–14.
Bogue, D. J. (1959) Internal migration, in Hauser, P. M. and Duncan, O. D. *The study of population: an inventory and appraisal*, 486–509. Chicago.
Bogue, D. J. (1969) *Principles of demography.* New York. (Especially chapter 19.)
Bogue, D. J. and Thompson, W. S. (1949) Migration and distance. *Am. Sociol. Rev.* 14, 236–44.

Brown, L. A. and Moore, E. G. (1970) The intra-urban migration process: a perspective. *Georg. Ann.* B, 52, 1–13.

Brown, L. A., Odland, J. and Golledge, R. G. (1970) Migration, functional distance, and the urban hierarchy. *Econ. Geogr.* 46, 472–85.

Claeson, C. F. (1968) Distance and human interaction. *Geogr. Ann.* B, 50, 142–61.

Compton, P. A. (1968) Internal migration and population change in Hungary between 1959 and 1965. *Trans. Inst. Brit. Geogr.* 47, 111–30.

Eisenstadt, S. N. (1953) Analysis of patterns of immigration and absorption of immigrants. *Pop. Stud.* 7, 167–80.

Fairchild, H. P. (1925) *Immigration: a world movement and its American significance.* New York.

Farr, W. (1876) Birthplaces of the people and the laws of migration. *Geogr. Mag.*

George, P. (1970) Types of migration of the population according to the professional and social composition of migrants, in Jansen, C. J. (ed.) *Readings in the sociology of migration*, 39–47. Oxford.

Haberle, R. (1951) Types of migration. *REMP Bull.* 4, 1–5.

Hägerstrand, T. (1957) Migration and area: survey of a sample of Swedish migration fields and hypothetical considerations on their genesis, in Hanneberg, D. *et al.* (eds.) *Migration in Sweden: a symposium.* Lund Stud. in Geogr. B, 13, 27–158.

International Labour Office (1960) *Why labour leaves the land: a comparative study of the movement of labour out of agriculture.* Geneva.

Kant, K. (1953) Migrationernas klassifikation och problematik. *Svensk Geografisk Årsbook.* 180–209. English translation: Classification and problems of migration, in Wagner, P. L. and Mikesell, M. W. (eds.) *Readings in cultural geography*, 342–54. Chicago.

Kariel, H. G. (1963) Selected factors areally associated with population growth due to net migration. *Assoc. Am. Geogr., Ann.* 53, 210–23.

Lee, E. S. (1966) A theory of migration. *Demog.* 3, 47–57.

Mabogunje, A. L. (1970) Systems approach to a theory of rural-urban migration. *Geogr. Anal.* 2, 1–18.

Mangalam, J. J. (1968) *Human migration: a guide to migration literature in English 1955-1962.* Lexington.

Morrill, R. L. (1965) *Migration and the spread and growth of urban settlement.* Lund Stud. in Geogr. B, 26.

Morrill, R. L. and Pitts, F. R. (1967) Marriage, migration and the mean information field: a study in uniqueness and generality. *Assoc. Am. Geogr., Ann.* 57, 401–22.

Olsson, G. (1965) Distance and human interaction: a migration study. *Geogr. Ann.* B, 47, 3–43.

Petersen, W. (1958) A general typology of migration. *Am. Sociol. Rev.* 23, 256–65. Later versions have been incorporated in two editions of the book *Population* by the same author (New York, 1961 and 1969).

Pryor, R. J. (1971) *Internal migration and urbanization.* James Cook University of North Queensland, Townsville.

Ravenstein, E. G. (1885) The laws of migration. *J. Roy. Stat. Soc.* 48, 167–227. Reprinted in the Bobbs-Merrill reprint series No. S-482.

Ravenstein, E. G. (1889) The laws of migration. *J. Roy. Stat. Soc.* 52, 241–301. Reprinted in the Bobbs-Merrill reprint series No. S-483.

Riddell, J. B. (1970) On structuring a migration model. *Geogr. Anal.* 2, 403–9.

Rogers, A. (1966) A Markovian policy model of interregional migration. *Reg. Sci. Assoc., Pap.* 17, 205–24.

Rose, A. M. (1958) Distance of migration and socio-economic status of migrants. *Am. Sociol. Rev.* 23, 420–23.

Rossi, P. H. (1955) *Why families move: a study in the social psychology of urban residential mobility.* Glencoe.

Shryock, H. S., Siegel, J. S. *et al.* (1971) *The methods and materials of demography.* Washington. (Especially chapter 21 in Vol. II).

Stewart, C. T. (1960) Migration as a function of population and distance. *Am. Sociol. Rev.* 25, 347–56.

Stouffer, S. A. (1940) Intervening opportunities: a theory relating mobility and distance. *Am. Sociol. Rev.* 5, 845–67.

Stouffer, S. A. (1960) Intervening opportunities and competing migrants. *J. Reg. Sci.* 2, 1–26.

Tarver, J. D. and Skees, P. M. (1967) Vector representation of interstate migration streams. *Rur. Sociol.* 32, 178–93.

Ter Heide, H. (1963) Migration models and their significance for population forecasts. *Milbank Memorial Fund Q.* 41, 56–76.

Termote, M. (1967) Les modèles de migrations. *Recherches économiques de Louvain* (Sept)., 413–44.

Termote, M. (1969) *Migration et équilibre économique spatial.* Louvain.

United Nations (1953) *The determinants and consequences of population trends.* Pop. Stud. No. 17. New York.

United Nations (1958) *Multilingual demographic dictionary.* English section. Pop. Stud. No. 29. New York. (Other linguistic versions are also available.)

United Nations (1970) *Methods of measuring internal migration.* Pop. Stud. No. 47. New York.

Weinberg, A. A. (1961) *Migration and belonging: a study of mental health and personal adjustment in Israel.* The Hague.

Whitelaw, J. S. and Robinson, S. (1972) A test for directional bias in the intra-urban migration. *N.Z. Geogr.* 28, 181–93.

Wolpert, J. (1965) Behavioural aspects of the decision to migrate. *Reg. Sci. Assoc. Pap. and Proc.* 15, 159–69.

Wolpert, J. (1966) Migration as an adjustment to environmental stress. *J. Soc. Issues* 22, 92–102.

Wolpert, J. (1967) Distance and directional bias in inter-urban migratory streams. *Assoc. Am. Geogr., Ann.* 57, 605–16.

Zelinsky, W. (1971) The hypothesis of the mobility transition. *Geogr. Rev.* 61, 219–49.

Zipf, G. K. (1946) The $P_1 P_2/D$ hypothesis on the intercity movement of persons. *Am. Sociol. Rev.* 11, 677–86.

Part One
Theoretical issues

Introduction

Three papers concentrate on the developing world where the study of migration at the present time is of intrinsic academic interest and of great practical significance for social and economic developments. In the introduction attention has been drawn to the recent hypothesis of a close relationship between changes in the nature and patterns of mobility and those of vital events (Zelinsky 1971). With reference to this hypothesis and other theoretical work on development *Pryor* explores relationships between migration and the processes of modernization, noting the complexity of their interaction at various scales. This overview for the developing world is followed with a further macro-consideration by *Gould and Prothero* of a typological framework within which the different forms of population mobility occurring in tropical Africa may be related to one another. Complementing and within the context of these two broadly based studies *Harvey and Riddell* focus attention more specifically upon development and urbanization in respect of stepwise migration in Sierra Leone.

Migration upward through the urban hierarchy is further pursued by *Hudson* in the first of three papers concerned with the developed world. The model of hierarchical migration which he outlines as applicable in the USA and possibly elsewhere emphasizes relationships with theories of population distribution and of growth. *Gale* discusses models of residential change at the micro-level with emphasis very firmly upon the theoretical base of investigation. *Johnson, Salt and Wood* complement this study with a paper concerned with theoretical considerations which have provided the background to an empirical investigation of the relationships between housing and the geographical mobility of labour in England and Wales.

These papers are not claimed to comprehend the vast body of theoretical issues associated with spatially-orientated studies of migration. They illustrate something of this range in the developing and developed areas of the world at a variety of scales.

1 Migration and the process of modernization[1]

R. J. Pryor

Introduction

One of the major problems underlying recent research into spatial mobility is a need to integrate individual behavioural and regional level studies. Geographers and others tend to take two broad approaches in studies of developing countries. The *first* approach focuses on micro-scale analysis and is derived from a 'man-environment paradigm' (Brookfield 1968; Chapman 1969) with more emphasis on the indigenous cultural setting and related endogenous variables affecting individual spatial behaviour. The *second* approach is at least implicitly based on a macroscale 'distance-decay paradigm' (Soja 1968; Gould 1970; Riddell 1970); here the emphasis is on aspects of the impact of the international and intra-national diffusion of Western-type capitalism and technology, and the operation of exogenous forces on the spatial structure and processes of countries of the Third World. A recent study (Pryor 1972) to some extent attempts to combine both approaches, the analysis of sample survey and other micro-level data on individual migrants being carried out in the context of (i) paradigms of urbanization and internal migration, and (ii) a description of the current levels and diffusion of economic development and modernization in the case of West Malaysia. This paper introduces the relationships between the degree of enconomic development, the spatial extent of modernization, and the spatial and structural characteristics of internal migration generated in phases II–III of the 'mobility transition' (Zelinsky 1971); the prime focus is on the developing countries.

[1] This paper is based on a previously published monograph, *Internal migration and urbanisation: an introduction and bibliography* (Pryor 1971). Reference may be made to the extensive bibliography.

The economic development context of migration

Economic development can be viewed in stages:

  (i) the centrifugal stage, with the establishment of the main settlement
       pattern and the opening up of potential economic bases;
 (ii) the centripetal stage, with increasing centralization and primacy, along
       with a process of 'cosmopolitanization'.

Alternatively, two parallel phases can be identified:

  (i) the extrovert phase with dependence on an international export
       economy, and
 (ii) the introvert phase of industrialization, often accompanying the rise
       of a self-conscious nationalism, and the desire for economic as well as
       political independence.

In spatial terms, the ideal-typical dichotomization of the centre (or core
region) and periphery (or hinterland) has stressed the bipolar structure
and functional interaction of developmental space. The economic interaction can be seen as the active penetration of the peasant system of
production by the capitalist, colonial one, and the 'trickling down' or
diffusion of development into the periphery on which the centre comes
to rely for its own expansion (Kuklinski 1972). One reason for adopting
the concepts of centre and periphery is the advantage of these over the
traditional urban-rural polarization. Cities may be export-oriented and
relatively monetized, without being 'urban'. Urban settlements can be
found in the periphery (secondary growth centres, planned agro-towns),
and rural settlements within the centre (squatter settlements, agricultural
enclaves). Although this conceptualization is not without critics, and while
developing countries tend to exhibit an increasingly complex hierarchy or
network of growth centres rather than a single primate centre, nevertheless
this spatial structuring has important implications for population redistribution and developmental diffusion (see fig. 1.1).

The modernization context of migration[2]

Rogers (1969, 14) defines modernization as

> the process by which individuals change from a traditional way of
> life to a more complex, technologically advanced, and rapidly
> changing style of life.

---

[2] Relevant concepts are further explored in Pryor (1971); important theoretical works
on modernization include Bernstein (1971), Dore (1969), Hagen (1962) and Lerner
(1958).

He also emphasizes: (i) modernization at the individual level corresponds to development at the societal level,[3] and defines development as

> . . . a type of social change in which new ideas are introduced into a social system in order to produce higher per capita incomes and levels of living through more modern production methods and improved social organisation (p. 18);

(ii) modernization is a multidimensional concept and, for instance, it cannot be operationally defined by a single variable; (iii) modernization is frequently though not necessarily equated with Europeanization or Westernization, and there is no implied value judgement as to its desirability.

These comments are accepted, with the proviso that the spatial extent of 'new ideas' (modernization) is not necessarily isomorphic with the spatial extent of 'higher per capita incomes' (economic growth). If the centre in fig. 1.1 is taken as the *development* space, it is not coincident

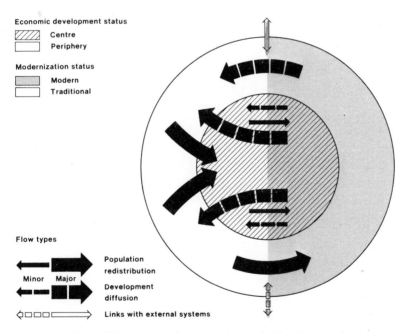

Figure 1.1 The spatial structure of urbanization: transitional stage of development

---

[3] Compare Pearse's (1971, 76) 'incorporative drive', the intensification of communication and exchange of goods, persons and ideas between the centre and periphery, providing a series of alternative behaviours and orientations; and Yalan's (1972, 10) emphasis on technological development.

with that space which has achieved modern status. Fig. 1.1 depicts the intermediate situation of developing countries; pre-industrial regions lie at the beginning of the modernization continuum, and industrial regions at the end, with, in theory, no traditional orientation at all.

The concept of modern and traditional sectors in developing countries provides a second example of ideal-typical dichotomization, supported in theoretical and empirical studies, but also generating a number of arguments[4] where some arbitrary (Western?) limitation appears to restrict the conceptually feasible 'destinations' of and analytical frameworks for social change. The modern sector of developing countries combines a 'Western-style' export-oriented economy with an upper-middle or élite social stratum. The traditional sector combines an indigenous market with petty trade among plantation and village workers, with a lower social stratum and a localized orientation. Social and economic dualisms have in many instances been crystallized as instruments of colonial policy, resulting in the fulfilment of the axiom that 'one may produce wealth without development', if development means improvement in peasant living standards.

The spatial extent of modern status overlaps both the centre and periphery, and conversely segments of traditional space are found both within the centre and, more especially, in the periphery. Both fulfil essential economic functions. Further, although the world or a nation may be divided into developed and developing regions, still

> Progress and tradition may dwell in close spatial proximity by simply fastening on different human groups and economic activities that exist side by side. (Hirschman 1958, 184)

Two examples spell out not only the non-parallelism of the centre/periphery and modern/traditional dualism, but also their dynamic interaction. Federal Land Development Authority schemes in West Malaysia, though located in the periphery, are far removed from the traditional peasant rice-cropping of nearby depressed rural areas. They are in fact highly capitalized 'agro-towns' with all the physical and many of the sociocultural trappings of urban life. The settlers, although their transformation is no doubt incomplete, have a *modern* rather than a traditional orientation, even though their social organization may retain some traditional elements (Pryor 1972). Secondly, in *Quiet crisis in India*, Lewis (1962, 53) discusses the traditional sector of the centre in terms of:

> The urban in-migrant who, instead of doing absolutely nothing, joins Bombay's army of under-employed boot-blacks or Delhi's throngs of self appointed (and tippable) parking directors. . .

[4] For example by Higgins (1956), Nash (1964), Gusfield (1966) and Bernstein (1971)

This and other work on the squatter settlements of the Third World leave no doubt as to the presence of a traditional sector within many primate cities. Finally, it is significant that at least two countries of Southeast Asia, Hong Kong in the context of census data-generation, and Malaysia in its current development plan, have dichotomized traditional and modern sectors.

Towards a paradigm of internal migration

To modify an ECAFE definition,

> A migrant in internal migration is an individual who within a given nation moves from one regional unit to another for a certain minimum period of time. This involves a change of residence from one community to another and usually the crossing of a specified kind of internal administrative boundary. (1967, 167)

It should be noted that internal migration is distinguished from intra-community *movement*, or 'partial displacements'; and the utilization of administrative boundaries has no conceptual significance but is merely a constraint normally imposed by data availability. Operational definitions of centre/periphery and modern/traditional unfortunately tend to be far removed from the theoretical constructs in current Third World census-taking.

From a theoretical viewpoint, an important extension of our understanding of the evolutionary nature of spatial behaviour has been made by Zelinsky (1971, 221–2):

> There are definite, patterned regularities in the growth of personal mobility through space-time during recent history, and these regularities comprise an essential component of the modernization process.

The hypothesis makes two contributions to our present discussion. First, it provides a dynamic framework, specifically in a spatial mobility context, with which to assess the interaction between migration, and urbanization in its economic development and modernization aspects. Secondly, it emphasizes the interaction between demographic transition and spatial mobility. The relationships between the 'socioeconomic transition' and Zelinsky's structural and spatial population transitions are summarized in table 1.1. Alongside the transition from pre-industrial and traditional society through varying degrees of industrialization and modernization, there is a parallel and closely interwoven transition in population characteristics. The transformation of the economic structure both causes and results from population redistribution. The demographic transition results

Table 1.1

Relationship between socioeconomic and population dynamics

Socioeconomic dynamics		Population dynamics	
Economic development status	*Modernization status*	*Demographic transition phase*	*Mobility transition phase*
Pre-industrial Independent, dispersed settlements Subregional agrarian enclaves	*Traditional*	A: High BR, High DR, Low NI	I: 0 RU ——C
Early transitional Centre/periphery differentiation commences; incipient industrialization	Initial diffusion of modernization from innovative node in the centre	B: +BR −DR +NI *or* 'Demographic relapse'	II: ++RU +RR ++E ——U +C
Late transitional Emergence of subdominant centres; major industrialization	Extensive diffusion of modernization from multiple nodes; upward social mobility increasing	C: −BR −DR −NI	III: −RU −RR −E +C
Advanced industrial Interdependent central place network; industrial maturation	*Modern* Maximum spatial diffusion; qualitative differences declining	D: Low BR Low DR Low NI	IV: ——RU —— *or* 0 RR ++UU +E? +I ++C
Post-industrial Industry declining as % of GNP. Interregional and international linkages dominant	*Neo-modern* Sociocultural convergence	E: Low BR Low DR Controlled NI	V: ++UU −I ++C Communications developments may modify migration and circulation

Notes:
1. Demographic transition: BR = Birth-Rate/Fertility, DR = Death-Rate/Mortality, NI = Natural Increase.
2. Mobility transition: RR = Rural-Rural migration (colonization), RU = Rural-Urban migration, UU = Inter/Intra-Urban migration, E = Emigration, I = Immigration, C = Circulation (reciprocal movements).
3. Direction and intensity of change: + Increasing, − Decreasing, 0 None, —— Minor, ++ Major.

Source: Pryor 1971; Zelinsky 1971.

in part from the diffusion of medical and family planning information, and partly from the rising socioeconomic aspirations and information availability which accompany economic development.

What then are the key structural, spatial and motivational characteristics of internal migration, and in what ways are they related to the spatial extent and intensity of economic development and social change?

Innovative/conservative migration

The main emphasis in what follows is on voluntary migration, and it is useful to quote Petersen (1958, 275):

> Some persons migrate as a means of achieving the new. Let us term such migration *innovating*. Others migrate in response to a change in conditions, in order to retain what they had; they move geographically in order to remain where they are in all other respects. Let us term such migration *conservative.*

While there are connotations here of aspiration contrasted with uncertainty reduction, and of the migrant's assessment of relative place utility, Petersen does not further elaborate this behavioural approach. In the context of the preceding discussion, and referring specifically to the transitional stage, there are two types of migrations. *Innovative migration* is postulated as spatial mobility from the periphery to the centre, and/or

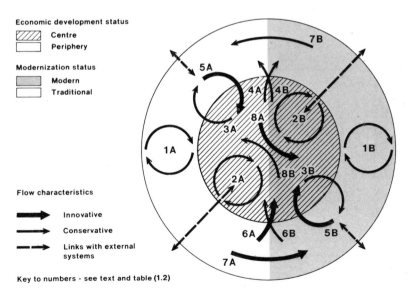

Figure 1.2 An internal migration paradigm: Mobility Transition Phases II-III

from the traditional sector to the modern sector. *Conservative migration* is spatial mobility within the centre, or the periphery, and/or within the modern sector, or within the traditional sector. It also includes movement from the centre to the periphery, and/or from the modern sector to the traditional sector. These patterns are shown in fig. 1.2; it should be noted that feedback (countercurrents) is associated with all flows, and the spatial dimensions of the figure are diagrammatic only. It should also be emphasized that both the areas of origin and of destination are structurally and functionally affected by the flows, and the individual migrant undergoes a number of partial changes of attitude and environmental perception.

Table 1.2
Patterns and characteristics of migration, Mobility Transition Phases II–III

Symbol	Directional pattern	Characteristic	Pattern details
1A; B	'Intra-rural'	Conservative	TT.PP; MM.PP
2A; B	'Intra-urban'	Conservative	TT.CC; MM.CC
3A; B	'Urban-rural'	Conservative	TT.CP; MM.CP
4A; B	'Urban-rural'	Conservative?	*TM*.CP; MT.CP
5A; B	'Rural-urban'	*Innovative*	TT.*PC*; MM.*PC*
6A	'Rural-urban'	*Innovative*	*TM.PC*
6B	'Rural-urban'	Conservative?	MT.*PC*
7A	'Intra-rural'	*Innovative*	*TM*.PP
7B	'Intra-rural'	Conservative	MT.PP
8A	'Intra-urban'	*Innovative*	*TM*.CC
8B	'Intra-urban'	Conservative	MT.CC

Notes:
1. T = Traditional, M = Modern, C = Centre, P = Periphery.
2. TT.PP – summarizes a migration stream, in this case from one part of the traditional sector to another and, at the same time, from one part of the periphery to another.
3. Italics in columns 3 and 4 indicate innovative migration.

In concise terms, innovative migration implies movement to a higher status (more industrial, more modern) space, and conservative migration involves movements within present status space or to lower status (less industrial, less modern) space (table 1.2). The symbols (column 1) are those used in fig. 1.2; the directional pattern (column 2) resorts to the urban/rural dichotomy avoided so far, 'rural' being taken as 'shorthand' for the periphery, and 'urban' for the centre; the need for this shorthand is demonstrated by the complexities of the alternative format in column 4. The (rare) cases of migration from the traditional sector of the centre to the modern sector of the periphery and vice versa are probably conservative in nature. Of the innovative moves, flows 5A and 7A are more typical of Mobility Transition Phase II, while flows 5B, 6A and 8A are more typical of

Phase III; other patterns are less common and of minor relevance to urbanization and the mobility transition.

The two types of migration flows are, to some extent, responses to what Mabogunje (1970; 5–8) calls *control subsystems*. An innovative migration flow results where control subsystems in the area of origin are conducive (either positively encouraging, or at least viewing migration as acceptable behaviour) to outmigration, while control subsystems in the area of destination permit (either positively attracting, or at least not restricting) inmigration. In the extreme cases of rigid controls against mobility, in the 'origin', 'destination', or both, migration will be minimal or non-existent. If it did occur it would deserve to be termed *innovative*! Alternatively, controls may operate to produce conservative flows, in that they only encourage or permit flows within the existing socioeconomic or cultural environment. However, control subsystems by no means always or fully determine flow characteristics. In many instances controls will be non-existent or neutral in influence, and whether migration is innovative or conservative will depend on individual motivation, and the respective importance given to what Lee (1966) terms *attraction* and *repulsion factors*, together with *intervening obstacles.* Innovative flows may further be identified with Hägerstrand's (1967, 132) *active* migrants, those who base their mobility on future prospects; conservative flows are related to *passive* migrants whose mobility is constrained by the more limited information available from previous migrants or of known environments. Further, conservative flows are unlikely to involve upward social mobility, although by widening horizons through expanding spatial experience they may pave the way for future innovative moves. On the other hand, upward social mobility is one possible concomitant of innovative migration, and even if it is not always the stimulus it is frequently the result, at least *in the course of time* and most dramatically so during Zelinsky's Phase II.

Migration flow patterns

Some additional comments can be made on the migration networks. While seasonal and other forms of temporary migration may fall within the typology proposed, its role is less clearly innovative or conservative. In Phases II and III it may be a method of introduction to urban life and values, and is often a significant source of exogenous income for communities in the periphery. Alternatively, it can be close to nomadism in its subsistence nature. It is unlikely that temporary moves will cross the traditional/modern boundary, though they may cross the periphery/centre frontier. In Phase IV, temporary moves are of a radically different nature, as the circulation of professional élites accelerates through the urban network. There is no necessity for the migrations to occur as single spatial displacements. Step migration has long been recognized in the migration literature, and may be divided into

> (i) *simple step migration*, whereby one person takes several moves to cover all or part of the rural-urban residence continuum, and (ii) *complex step migration*, in which for example, one person moves from a rural area to a small town, and another individual moves from the small town to a larger urban place. These two forms of step migration may occur simultaneously or consecutively. . . (Pryor 1969, 69)

Todaro (1969, 139) suggests that, in the context of Phase II-type rural-urban labour migration,

> The first stage finds the unskilled rural worker migrating to an urban area and initially spending a certain period of time in the so-called 'urban-traditional' sector. The second stage is reached with the eventual attainment of a more permanent modern sector job.

This view accords well with the present paradigm, and emphasizes the interaction between flow types whereby a migrant can move within the traditional sector but from the periphery to the centre, and in a second (or later) stage, move into the modern sector. In Phases IV and V, step-migration could be applied to certain interregional or international moves where urbanization differentials may exist on the macro-scale.

One form of innovative migration is that from the traditional to the modern sector of the periphery, and in stimulating this form governments or other institutions can make a significant contribution to development during the transitional stage of urbanization. As the Hackenbergs (1969, 19) state,

> . . . rural-to-rural migration, with attendant farm community reorganisation, might be a more compatible form for the economic redevelopment of former colonial areas.

Their evidence from the resettlement regions of eastern Mindanao, and the previously mentioned FLDA land schemes in Malaysia, certainly show this to be innovative migration, providing an impetus to both economic development and modernization. The creation of 'agro-towns', and rural infrastructure, and the stimulus to the growth of regional service centres, indicate the impact on settlement patterns as well. In the case of progressive, motivated individuals, freed even partially from traditional 'redistributive economics' and sociocultural ties, this may well pave the way for further upward social mobility, as well as spatial mobility to at least secondary centres if not the primate city itself.

Spatial interactions of migration

Apart from the obvious impact of migration on settlement, there are also effects on socioeconomic, political and demographic spatial patterns. Mangalam (1968) discusses the impact of migration on what he calls the culture, social, and personality systems. Previous, less holistic, approaches raise many problems. A migration flow, selective by having a high proportion of males, particularly those aged 20–29 years, searching for unskilled or semi-skilled jobs, and coming from a traditional village environment having definite mobility constraints as well as expectations of reciprocal benefits from migrants, must have an impact on the destination area, even if individuals keep a 'foot in both camps'. The effect is not confined to the destination, for the community of origin reflects the loss of migrants by differentials such as age, sex, occupation and sociopsychological traits. Institutions have a role both in attracting migrants, and as an adjustment mechanism, and their interaction with migration is heightened, for example, if migrants become involved in the urban political system.

Major initiating factors

Lee (1966, 50) summarizes the major factors which enter into the migration decision and action as being associated with the areas of origin and destination, and personal (individual perceptual and behavioural) factors. Mabogunje (1970, 10) suggests that stimuli to move are analogous to potential energy, as contrasted with the characteristics of the actual migration process analogous to kinetic energy. Both these approaches are useful in providing an alternative to the traditional push-pull model, though the latter has rarely been applied in the completely closed form suggested by some critics. Petersen (1958) distinguishes between four migratory forces: ecological push (primitive nomadism), migration policy (impelled or forced movement), higher aspirations (free movement) and social momentum (mass settlement or urbanization). These various approaches are restructured for this paradigm, and are generalized for the total mobility transition although some factors could be more characteristic of particular phases.

Different stimuli or initiating factors operate to produce autogenic and allogenic spatial mobility. The former is essentially voluntary and rational, in so far as 'boundedly rational man' is able to collect, evaluate and act on perceived information of varying quantity and quality. This may be contrasted with non-voluntary mobility initiated by a force outside the individual's (or the migration flow's) control. The following major factors contribute to autogenic spatial mobility.

Economic factors. Empirical evidence probably justifies describing this as the primary cause of migration, whether as the only method of achieving a *cash* income for personal needs or culturally-induced obligations; or in a more developed society (Phase IV?), migration based on (perceived) prospects for upward occupational/social mobility, or the location of particular job opportunities.

Institutional and political stimuli include mechanisms for uncertainty reduction regarding alternative locations. Mabogunje (1970, 8) cites a case where a *secondary* effect of a government's policy of disenfranchisement of farmers was to stimulate migration to cities. A more positive example would be agricultural development policies such as land schemes or marketing infrastructure.

Demographic stimuli include family size, the community sex ratio, an imbalance in marriageable ages, and age distributions with heavy dependency rates. Such factors are often linked with the economic demands of household budgets.

Sociocultural factors include the provision of medical and educational amenities attractive to migrants from deprived areas; the extent to which migration is expected/required behaviour; chain migration to link up with successful migrant kin; and the role of ethnic and other organizations in cushioning the problems of new migrants which can tip the scales in favour of making a locational change – the 'functional area of adaptation' (Mangalam 1968). Cultural factors can cause *out*migration, as with dissatisfaction with social amenities or cultural norms, and conversely the destination can be seen as providing these needs. Nevertheless, Mangalam stresses that migrants choose a destination as closely related as possible, in their perception, to the social organization in their place of origin.

Other behavioural or idiosyncratic factors cover the variety of complex personal motivations not readily included above, but which focus on the personality system as distinct from exogenous economic or other forces (while admitting that endogenous factors operate in an *open* system). Personal aspirations are one example, and the desire for a higher income can be contrasted with the desire to live in a rural idyll isolated from the rush of modern urban life. The concept of 'migration elasticity' and the behavioural application of the 'mover-stayer model' emphasize, in Mabogunje's (1970, 5) words,

> not so much the propensity to migrate but . . . how long impulses or stimuli from the environment must be transmitted to a potential migrant before he makes the desired move.

The following factors initiate allogenic spatial mobility.

Institutional and political forces which by executive decision, authority

and enforcement impel migration. Examples include population transfer
for ethnic/racial motives, wartime deportation and refugee flight; two
forms are discussed by Petersen, and Mabogunje quotes the Inclosure Acts
in Britain in the eighteenth and nineteenth centuries, and comparable
examples from modern Africa.

   Environmental factors such as flood, drought, bushfire and geophysical
hazards such as earthquakes and volcanic activity can cause outmigration
either temporarily or, in extreme cases, on a permanent basis. Soil-depleting
agricultural traditions introduce the interrelationship between technology
and some forms of physical environmental stimulus to migration.

Major integrating factors[5]

Human migration can be viewed as part of a more general evolutionary
process which Miller (1965, 371) refers to as *adaptive radiation* in which

> . . . systems may spread out, searching for space, food, raw materials,
> or new experience and so encounter other systems or environments
> they had not experienced before, to which they must make adjustments.

The concept, and even the terminology, are immediately suggestive for
migration theory. Individuals, or migrants as a 'collectivity' (as Mangalam
prefers to view them), are part of a vast interacting spatial system. They are
constrained by the system and must be selective and make adjustments, and
at the same time they inject new traits and demands so that the system
itself adapts as the network of migration develops in density and complexity.
The system, particularly through its socioeconomic, political and cultural
institutions, attempts to dominate the individual in order to adapt to the
total environment. Migrants for their part, by seeking positively assessed
place utility, or by seeking

> . . . ways to overcome their felt deprivations, but *without* giving up,
> as far as possible, the satisfactions they were enjoying at the place of
> their origin (Mangalam 1968, 10)

are forced to adjust by lowering their aspiration level, reassessing their
present location (and not moving?), or by migrating within explicit or
subconscious constraints.

   Information, all the varied components in the system which lead to
action, and the relationship between feedback and human behaviour, are
essential links between the individual and the developmental system within
which he migrates. Information, verbal, written, visually perceived, or com-

---

[5] Stimulated in part by R. A. Hackenberg, University of Colorado, and gratefully
   acknowledged (personal communication, November 1970).

municated through the mass media, influences individual evaluations and decisions, and also reflects the previous experience of others. Cash, or a length of cloth sent back to the village by a recent migrant to the city, provides information just as positive and motivating as a personal or written report. Individuals adjust by seeking new or ignoring old information, or vice versa, to fit the environment to their perception of it and their aspirations within it. The system at large may attempt to influence behaviour by the quantity and quality of information it diffuses, particularly in the post-industrial development stage.

Three concepts contribute to the integration of migration within the spatial system which is undergoing economic development and modernization, and while always present they will vary in importance according to specific location and phase in the mobility transition.

Individual adjustive factors which ensure the integration of migrants into the spatial system within a mover-stayer framework.

Institutional adaptive factors which ensure the integration of society as the donor-host matrix of human spatial behaviour.

Information diffusion, penetration and absorption, in all its shades and types, which links the system and the individual in a complex stimulus-response framework.

Conclusion

This paper commenced with a brief outline of the spatial spread and structural complexities of the joint processes of economic development and modernization. Population redistribution, internal migration, provide one key to understanding the organization and evolution of space in developing countries, as in the developed world. The suggested paradigm of internal migration, particularly in relation to Zelinsky's Mobility Transition Phases II–III, can be evaluated only in so far as it throws up relationships and explanations which are empirically measurable and verifiable in particular cases. It appears, however, to be crucial to an understanding of countries undergoing modernization. The radical transformation of human aspirations, life styles and spatial mobility are individual behavioural factors which are also reflected in the macroscale by changing settlement patterns, the emergence of a hierarchy of growth centres linked by increasingly dense communications networks, and by the diffusion of the ideas and artifacts of modernity.

References

Bernstein, H. (1971) Modernization theory and the sociological study of development. *J. Dev. Stud.* 7, 141–60.

Brookfield, H. C. (1968) The money that grows on trees. *Austr. Geogr. Stud.* 97–119.

Chapman, M. (1969) A population study in South Guadalcanal: some results and implications. *Oceania* 40, 119–47.

Dore, R. P. (1969) *On the possibility and desirability of a theory of modernization.* Communic. Ser. 38, Inst. of Dev. Stud.

ECAFE (1967) *Report on the Expert Working Group on problems of internal migration and urbanisation and selected papers.* Bangkok.

Gould, P. R. (1970) Tanzania 1920–63: the spatial impress of the modernization process. *Wld Pol.* 22, 149–70.

Gusfield, J. R. (1966) Tradition and modernity: misplaced polarities in the study of social change. *Am. J. Sociol.* 72, 351–62.

Hackenberg, R. A. and Hackenberg, B. H. (1969) *Secondary development and anticipatory urbanization in Davao, Mindanao.* Inst. of Behavioral Sci., Univ. of Colorado.

Hagen, E. E. (1962) *On the theory of social change.* Dorsey.

Hägerstrand, T. (1967) *Innovation diffusion as a spatial process.* Chicago.

Higgins, B. (1956) The 'dualistic' theory of underdeveloped areas. *Econ. Dev. and Cult. Change* 4, 99–115.

Hirschman, A. O. (1958) *The strategy of economic development.* New Haven.

Kuklinski, A. (1972) *Growth poles and growth centres in regional planning.* Paris.

Lee, E. S. (1966) A theory of migration. *Demog.* 3, 47–57.

Lerner, D. (1958) *The passing of traditional society.* New York.

Lewis, J. P. (1962) *Quiet crisis in India.* Bombay.

Mabogunje, A. L. (1970) Systems approach to a theory of rural-urban migration. *Geogr. Anal.* 2, 1–18.

Mangalam, J. J. (1968) *Human migration.* Kentucky.

Miller, J. G. (1965) Living systems: structure and process. *Behavioral Sci.* 10, 337–79.

Nash, M. (1964) Southeast Asian society: dual or multiple? *J. Asian Stud.* 23, 417–23.

Pearse, A. (1971) Metropolis and peasant: the expansion of the urban-industrial complex and the changing rural structure, in Shanin, T. (ed.) *Peasants and peasant societies.* Harmondsworth.

Petersen, W. (1958) A general typology of migration. *Am. Sociol. Rev.* 256–66.

Pryor, R. J. (1969) 'Laws of migration'? – The experience of Malaysia and other countries. *Geographica* (Univ. of Malaya) 5, 65–76.

Pryor, R. J. (1971) *Internal migration and urbanisation: an introduction and bibliography.* Townsville.

Pryor, R. J. (1972) *Malaysians on the move: a study of internal migration in West Malaysia.* Ph.D. thesis submitted to Univ. of Malaya.

Riddell, J. B. (1970) *The spatial dynamics of modernization in Sierra Leone.* Evanston.

Rogers, E. M. (1969) *Modernization among peasants: the impact of communication.* New York.

Soja, E. W. (1968) *The geography of modernization in Kenya.* Syracuse.

Todaro, M. P. (1969) A model of labor migration and urban unemployment in less developed countries. *Am. Econ. Rev.* 59, 138–48.

Yalan, E. *et al.* (1972) *The modernization of traditional agricultural villages.* Rehovot.

Zelinsky, W. (1971) The hypothesis of the mobility transition. *Geogr. Rev.* 61, 219–49.

2 Space and time in African population mobility

W. T. S. Gould and R. M. Prothero

Despite the important empirical and technical advances that have been made in the study of population movements in tropical Africa in recent years (see *Harvey*; Prothero 1968a), much remains to be done to clarify the complexity in space and time of mobility phenomena. This paper presents a typology of mobility that deals with all types of movements at a variety of spatial and temporal scales – from the one extreme of movements over very short distances several times a day to single intra-continental moves over several thousands of miles. The frame of reference therefore extends beyond the conventional demographic concept of migration as movement between two specific places over a specified period of time, such as can be enumerated for the usual forms of census. Many movements are not specific in place or time and therefore go unrecorded in census data. Furthermore, they have received little theoretical consideration and limited attention in empirical research. The typology identifies the basic geographical components of individual movements and makes it possible for these to be related to and compared with one another.

The spatial dimension

Space may be considered in terms of either distance and/or direction. Distance may be perceived and measured in physical terms as in Ravenstein's classic 'laws', in economic terms as in Stouffer's concepts of intervening opportunities, or as within or between administrative units as in Beltramone's typology. The last of these differentiates the distance continuum through administrative units (*'surfaces de référence'*), of successively larger scales from the 'commune' through to the national and international units. Such differentiation certainly has relevance for Africa and an example may be cited from the seasonal movements that take place within and from north-western Nigeria. Two types have been distinguished, movements over shorter distances to farm or to practise traditional crafts and movements over longer distances to wage employment. The former are essentially intra- or inter-village movements, the latter intra- and inter-district movements which in the past extended to being intra-national and international (Prothero 1957; Goddard *et al.* 1971).

The conventional distinction between movements which are international or internal is less appropriate in the case of tropical Africa than elsewhere. Many types of mobility in the continuum from rural or urban and from traditional to modern involve the crossing of international boundaries, but without reference to them since they either existed from a time before the boundaries were agreed and/or demarcated, or because even after demarcation no control over movement has existed or, for that matter, is possible.

Direction has been used in preference to distance in the typology. Physical distance is difficult to specify. On a distance continuum terms such as 'short' and 'long' are inevitably relative and are impossible to apply in comparative analyses. In addition there is virtually nothing known of how distance is perceived by those who move. Data which might be applied in a typology based on a hierarchy of administrative units are generally not available.

Direction may be most satisfactorily considered in terms of 'rural' and 'urban' relationships. While these terms differentiate what is in reality a continuum, problems of categorization may arise; but in practice it is usually possible to make an acceptable differentiation. The typology has been formulated to facilitate the study of population mobility in a continent of continuing social and economic change and where therefore the problems of rural and urban development are at the same time distinctive and related (Gugler 1969; Mabogunje 1970). The typology therefore considers space in four categories of rural/urban relationships – rural/rural, rural/urban, urban/rural and urban/urban.

The temporal dimension

Like that of space, the dimension of time in mobility may be considered in a variety of ways. In historical perspective three categories may be distinguished: movements that took place in the past but which have now ceased, movements which have been continued from the past into the present, and movements that have developed in recent times (i.e. within the present century) (Prothero 1968a). Or else in contemporary terms, movements are differentiated by their periodicity which may involve a continuum from the often repeated movements of a few hours' duration within a limited area to a permanent change from one place to another over greater distances.

The temporal dimension in the typology is formulated in contemporary terms since the concern is with present-day mobility phenomena. However, it is important to recognize that even in contemporary terms the nature and importance of various types of mobility are changing continually, both relatively and absolutely.

A distinction between migration and circulation is of fundamental importance. *Migration* is sometimes used in a broad general sense to include all types of movements (e.g. Jackson 1969); others recognize that migration is more limited in scope than mobility and specifically excludes such movements as of seasonal workers and tourists from their consideration (e.g. Lee 1966). Migration may be defined in a strictly operational sense as movements revealed in official statistics, as in the official definition of a migrant used by the UN. This sort of definition does not have any rigorous conceptual basis but rather is one of convenience. On this basis it could be argued that movements which are not included within the category of migration are those which are not revealed in official statistics, and this clearly is unsatisfactory. However, the use of more theoretically based definitions may be limited in practice by the need to depend upon official statistics.

Most definitions of migration include reference to permanent change of residence. Movements which are not within this category therefore are those which do not involve any permanent change but are of an oscillatory nature. Those movements where there is no permanent change can be most suitably designated by the term *circulation*, to include 'a great variety of movements, usually short-term repetitive or cyclical in character, but all having in common the lack of any declared intention of a permanent or long-standing change of residence' (Zelinsky 1971).

While the principal distinction between migration and circulation lies in the permanence of the former and the non-permanence of the latter, 'permanent' has been and may be defined in different ways to blur that distinction. For example, 'the period of time implied by the term "permanent" cannot be generalized in all instances of migration, but have to be considered individually in each case' (Mangalam 1968, 8). Petersen's view is similar (1968, 278): '. . . no broad specification of the duration of stay suits all purposes, and each individual analyst has to adapt the available data as best he can'. Hence the definition of the United Nations of migrations as those movements having a duration of more than one year has generally been ignored in practice in studies in Africa which have involved the collection of data in the field, but has been followed by statisticians and others relying on official African census data. Other discussions of permanence have considered the economic and social commitments of a mover to a destination compared with those to his home area (e.g. van Velsen 1963). There has been no universally accepted definition of permanence, which may in any case be impossible to achieve. We suggest that if there is a specific desire on the part of the individual or group of individuals who are moving to return to their place of origin, and when before leaving in the first place this intention is clear, then the movement may be considered as circulation rather than migration. However, some movers do not know either the timing or the direction of future movements, or both, and their movements could be considered as migration. These distinctions between circulation and migration are not directly related to the duration of each movement, for some circulatory movements may last longer than migratory ones, but are related to the long-term changes in the distribution of population that result. With circulation, changes in the distribution of population in the long-term are not significantly different from those in the short-term; with migration, changes in the long-term are very different from changes in the short-term. Circulatory movements may be subdivided according to the length of their cycles into several main categories.

The typology

On the bases of four categories of rural/urban relationships and differing time spans, generally but not invariably increasing from left to right, the typology may be framed as follows:

Population mobility in Africa						
Time						
	Circulation				*Migration*	
Space	*Daily*	*Periodic*	*Seasonal*	*Long-term*	*Irregular*	*Permanent*
Rural-rural						
Rural-urban						
Urban-rural						
Urban-urban						

Daily circulation includes the great variety of intra-rural and intra-urban movements that are sufficiently commonplace to require no detailed description. It should be noted however that daily intra-urban movements have become an increasingly important component in African mobility in recent years, associated with the rapid growth of towns and increasing personal mobility by various forms of transport (e.g. Demur 1972; Gould 1973; Ojo 1970).

Periodic circulation may vary in length from one night away (e.g. for a visit to a relative or a market), to one year, though it is more usual for periodic circulation to be shorter in duration than seasonal circulation. The latter is in fact a particular type of periodic movement, the period being defined by marked seasonality in the physical/economic environment. Seasonal circulation does not include local movements with a high seasonal incidence (e.g. movements of farmers to market their produce) but movements which involve individuals or groups being absent from their permanent homes through a particular season(s) of the year. Movements in this subcategory are particularly important in West Africa (Prothero 1957; Rouch 1957).

Long-term circulation involves absence from home for longer than one year. It includes important groups, particularly of wage labourers and traders, who despite long absences maintain close social and economic links with their home areas with the objective of eventually returning to them. Such movements occur throughout tropical Africa, but are particularly characteristic of East, Central and Southern Africa (Mitchell 1969).

The presence or absence of 'permanent' elements in movement is the basis for distinguishing between migration and circulation. However different interpretations of 'permanent' give rise to two broad types of migration. Permanent migration in the conventional use of the term, that is definitive movements with no propensity to return to the home area, is relatively uncommon in tropical Africa, though this is less so now than was the case in the past. Movements assigned to this subcategory are for example 'downhill' movements in parts of West Africa and elsewhere (Gleave 1966), movements to settlement schemes (Chambers 1969) and residential changes within cities (Roussel *et al.* 1968; Knoop 1971; Brand 1972). Irregular migrations are not wholly permanent in that further movement is likely in the future, but neither the time nor the direction of such movement is known. This subcategory includes the movements of some nomadic groups (Stenning 1957; Prothero 1968b; Gulliver 1969) and the movements of refugees (Hamrell 1967; UNHCR 1969).

All types of population mobility may be accommodated in the twentyfour categories of the typology. It should be noted, however, that among any one group of people more than one category of mobility may be identified.

The typology may be exemplified in respect of those who move from their homes for economic gain either in wage employment or to work on their own account. In towns there are many such people who as commuters are involved in daily circulation, but movements of longer duration and distance are widespread in Africa. These are commonly referred to as 'labour migration', though Mitchell (1969) suggests that the term 'labour circulation' is more appropriate in the Rhodesian case with which he is concerned. Certainly a large proportion of labour movements in Africa and in other parts of the developing world involves the individuals concerned returning sooner or later to their home areas, and alternating between these and places of employment several times in the course of their working lives. The majority of these labourers are involved in long-term circulation, moving either as individuals or increasingly, as a more stabilized work force evolves, with their families. Usually each individual is part of and functions in a larger group which has a permanent and identifiable economic, social and demographic structure in the place of employment. The group itself remains identifiable, though its composition may change (Cohen 1969). While members return home after a period of employment, others arrive. As time goes on, individuals tend to increase their average length of stay at work. Though they may retain a place in the social structure of their home communities, the long-term effect of increasingly longer absences may lead to a decline in the socioeconomic life of these communities (Allan 1965).

In contrast to such long-term circulation, the seasonal circulation of labourers, which is particularly common in the savanna lands of West Africa, has no comparable detrimental long-term effects. Workers leave home areas to work elsewhere in the dry season, and then return for the onset of the next wet season to practise agriculture. While they retain their place in the social structure in their home areas, as is the case in long-term circulation, they continue to function also in the economic structure of these areas (Goddard *et al.* 1971). Differences between the seasonal circulation and the long-term circulation of labourers over short and longer periods of time may be summarized as follows:

(A) *In the short run*

	Source areas	*Receiving areas*
Seasonal circulation	Net benefit; relief of pressure on local food supplies; supplementation of local income.	Net benefit; labour to meet demand primarily in agricultural production.
Long-term circulation	Net benefit; rise in *per capita* food production; supplementation of local income.	Net benefit; as above, but with greater importance for mining and industry.

Seasonal circulation and long-term circulation of labour involve both rural/rural and rural/urban movements. Rural/rural movements are of greater significance in seasonal circulation than they are in long-term circulation, the former often taking advantage of demands for agriculture labour occurring elsewhere at times when there is little or no such demand

(B) *In the long run*

	Source areas	Receiving areas
Seasonal circulation	Little social disruption; may inhibit rural economic development.	Beneficial; little permanent settlement.
Long-term circulation	Socially and economically disruptive.	Increasing contribution to economic development; permanent settlement.

in the home areas. However, there is also seasonal circulation of labour to mines and towns in West Africa. Conversely there is seasonal circulation of urban dwellers to rural employment at peak periods of agricultural activity. Other urban/rural mobility includes those who have moved from the countryside to towns with the intention of this being permanent, but who have become disillusioned with urban life or are unable to find work and move out from towns to rural areas other than those from which they originated (Hutton 1968), and the compulsory transfers by some governments of urban unemployed back to rural areas or to government-sponsored settlement schemes.

Extending the typology

The foregoing example illustrates how the typology aids appreciation of the geographical character of population mobility in Africa. It identifies movements which are widely recognized but also identifies movements of which relatively little is known (e.g. short-term and short-distance movements such as journey to work, to school, to market or to rural dispensary), but to which increased attention should be given in rational development planning since demands are great but resources are limited.

Typologies are by nature descriptive rather than explanatory. The two dimensions in the typology which has been outlined differentiate the nature of mobility and indicate its variety. Description may be enhanced by the consideration of other dimensions to reveal further complexity. The relevance of distance and historical time are indicated in the discussion of the spatial and temporal dimensions of the typology. There is need for more sophisticated insight and understanding involving socioeconomic and other criteria which are vital factors in the processes determining mobility, and some of these can be outlined in a simple diagram in which the totality of contemporary mobility is shown as being influenced by two major groups of factors – *economic* and *non-economic* (fig. 2.1). Since the former are the more important, the segment representing mobility influenced by non-economic factors is deliberately smaller, but the dimensions of the segments are intended to be indicative rather than absolute.

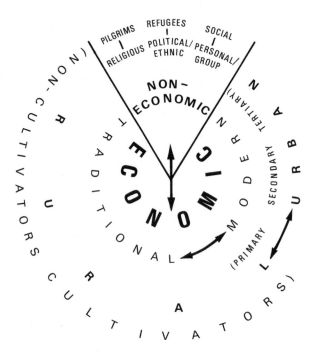

Figure 2.1 Factors affecting population mobility in tropical Africa

Mobility differentiated according to socioeconomic criteria may be related to the traditional and the modern sectors. Many forms of mobility associated with traditional economic activities continue in contemporary movements of pastoralists, fishermen and cultivators. Geographical patterns of individual and group movements are known to be extremely complex. Specific knowledge of these is limited and for the most part is available for pastoralists only (Johnson 1969). Patterns of movements in the traditional sector have tended to be associated with the economic mechanisms required to overcome or exploit ecological variations within the area occupied by the group, but it is increasingly clear that within the limitations of the natural environment flexibility is possible in the direction and periodicity of movement influenced by social considerations and individual decisions (Mabogunje 1972).

Movements into or within the modern sector inevitably attract greatest attention for these movements are related to and have an impact upon economic development and on rural/urban differentiation. Movements in the primary sector include those to resettlement schemes and movements of wage labourers to plantations or to other forms of cash-crop agriculture. Wage labourers in the secondary and tertiary sectors are rural/urban and urban/urban migrants. In all three sectors of the modern economy the prime motivation is the perceived opportunity of economic advantage. There is mobility involving trade which may be between rural and urban areas, or which may be entirely within the latter (Hodder 1961). There is mobility in urban areas of residential change and journey to work associated with populations which may have passed through the phase of rural/urban/rural circulation and have severed almost completely, if not entirely, the links which they may have had previously with the rural areas from which they originated (Peil 1972).

The second group of factors which are primarily non-economic give rise to three major categories of mobility. Religous factors promote pilgrimage (*Birks*), political and ethnic factors are responsible for refugee movements, and social factors for mobility associated with personal and group relationships (Lux 1971). The last produces the greatest amount of movement. Each of these three categories is influenced by economic factors and each category of mobility has economic implications. In Sudan, for example, the labour supply for cotton production, especially in the Gezira Scheme, is augmented by West African pilgrims en route to and returning from Mecca (Davies 1964). Each category may involve the range of rural/urban continuum.

Conclusion

Studies of population mobility in Africa must aim to combine the spatial/temporal dimensions outlined in the typology with the associated economic/non-economic factors. What have been indicated here are no more than frameworks into which existing knowledge may be fitted and related and for guidance in future work. While much has been accomplished in the study of mobility, perspectives have tended to be limited. Overall there has been very little consideration given to space and time and a limited appreciation of mobility primarily associated with non-economic factors. There has been an over-concentration on economically motivated rural/urban mobility which is important in the processes of modernization as defined in western terms. While rural/urban movements and urban growth are of major significance the majority of population lives in rural areas and will continue to do so for the foreseeable future. To promote successful development in rural areas and to introduce elements of modernization will require a much better appreciation of the patterns and processes of mobility occurring within them than have previously been available.

Acknowledgement

This paper is derived from work of the African Mobility Project, University of Liverpool, financed by the Social Science Research Council. Another version of this paper, but with different emphases, is to be published in *The populations factor in Africa* by R. Moss and R. Rathbone (in press).

References

Allan, W. (1965) *The African husbandman.* Edinburgh.

Brand, R. O. (1972) The spatial organization of residential areas in Accra, Ghana, with particular reference to aspects of modernization. *Econ. Geogr.* 48, 284–98.

Chambers, R. (1969) *Settlement schemes in tropical Africa.* London.

Cohen, A. (1969) *Custom and politics in urban Africa. A study of Hausa migrants in Yoruba towns.* London.

Davies, H. R. J. (1964) The West African in the economic geography of the Sudan. *Geogr.* 49, 222–35.

Demur, C. (1972) Les transports urbains à Abidjan, in Vennetier, P. *La croissance urbaine en Afrique Noire et à Madagascar,* 501–23. Paris.

Gleave, M. B. (1966) Hill settlements and their abandonment in tropical Africa. *Trans. Inst. Brit. Geogr.* 40, 39–49.

Goddard, A. M., Fine, J. C. and Norman, D. W. (1971) *A socio-economic study of three villages in the Sokoto close-settled zone. Land and people.* Ahmadu Bello Univ., Inst. for Agricultural Research, Samaru, Miscellaneous Paper, 33.

Gould, W. T. S. (1973) Secondary school provision in African cities. The case of Addis Ababa. *Tn. Plan. Rev.* 44, 391–403.

Gugler, J. (1969) On the theory of rural-urban migration: the case of sub-Saharan Africa, in Jackson (1969) 134–55.

Gulliver, P. H. (1969) Nomadism among the pastoral Turkana of Kenya: its natural and social environment, in Rigby, P. (ed.) *Society and social change in Eastern Africa,* 30–41. Kampala.

Hamrell, S. (ed.) (1967) *Refugee problems in Africa.* Scandinavian Inst. of African Studies, Uppsala.

Hodder, B. W. (1961) Rural periodic day markets in part of Yorubaland. *Trans. Inst. Brit. Geogr.* 29, 149–59.

Hutton, C. (1968) Nyakashaka. A farm settlement scheme in Uganda. *Afr. Affairs* 67, 118–23.

Jackson, J. A. (ed.) (1969) *Migration.* London.

Johnson, D. L. (1969) *The nature of nomadism: a comparative study of pastoral migrations in south-western Asia and Northern Africa.* Univ. of Chicago, Dept of Geography, Research Paper No. 118.

Knoop, H. (1971) The sex ratio of an African squatter settlement: an exercise in hypothesis building. *Afr. Urb. Notes* 6, 19–23.

Lee, E. S. (1966) A theory of migration. *Demog.* 3, 47–57.

Lux, A. (1971) A network of visits between Yombe rural wage-earners and their kinsfolk in Western Congo. *Afr.* 41, 109–28.

Mabogunje, A. L. (1970) Systems approach to a theory of rural-urban migration. *Geogr. Anal.* 2, 1–18.

Mabogunje, A. L. (1972) *Regional mobility and resource development in West Africa.* Toronto.

Mangalam, J. J. (1968) *Human migration.* Lexington.

Mitchell, J. C. (1969) Structural plurality, urbanization and labour circulation in Southern Rhodesia, in Jackson (1969) 156–80.

Ojo, G. J. A. (1970) Some observations on journey to agricultural work in Yorubaland, south-western Nigeria. *Econ. Geogr.* 46, 459–71.

Peil, M. (1972) *The Ghanaian factory worker: industrial man in Africa.* Cambridge.

Petersen, W. (1968) Migration: social aspects. *Internat. Encycl. Soc. Sci.* 10, 286–300.

Prothero, R. M. (1957) Migratory labour from north-western Nigeria. *Afr.* 27, 251–61.

Prothero, R. M. (1968a) Migration in tropical Africa, in Caldwell, J. C. and Okonjo, C. *The population of tropical Africa,* 250–62. London.

Prothero, R. M. (1968b) *Public health, pastoralism and politics in the Horn of Africa.* Sixth Melville J. Herskovits Memorial Lecture. Evanston.

Rouch, J. (1957) Migrations au Ghana. *J. de la Société des Africanistes* 24, 33–196.

Roussel, L., Turlot, F. and Vaurs, R. (1968) La mobilité de la population urbaine en Afrique Noire: deux essays de mesure, Abidjan et Yaoundé. *Pop.* 23 (3), 333–52.

Stenning, D. J. (1957) Transhumance, migratory drift, migration: patterns of pastoral Fulani nomadism. *J. Roy. Anthrop. Inst.* 87, 57–73.

United Nations High Commission for Refugees (1966) *Refugees in Africa.* Geneva.

Van Velsen, J. (1963) Some methodological problems of the study of labour migration, in *Urbanization in Africa*, 34–42. Univ. of Edinburgh, Centre of African Studies.

Zelinsky, W. (1971) The hypothesis of the mobility transition. *Geogr. Rev.* 61, 219–49.

3 Development, urbanization and migration: a test of a hypothesis in the Third World

M. E. Harvey and
J. B. Riddell

Introduction

In most areas of the Third World the distribution of population is essentially influenced by social, historical and environmental factors. Change in this landscape is initiated and affected either by internal structural changes in the economy or by the superimposition of these changes by an alien society. In these situations the economic basis for population concentration at advantageous locations is created by a marked division of labour and occupational specialization, together with the existence of a well-developed and organized exchange mechanism. At least in part, such internally induced change was true of the industrial revolution in Britain, while alien imposition has been characteristic of most countries which have experienced a history of colonial rule.

Before the colonial division of Africa in the late nineteenth century only a few areas in West Africa contained distinct urban nodes within what was an otherwise rural settlement matrix. These included the savanna belt, at the points of contact of centuries of trans-Saharan trade, and isolated pockets in the forest zone, such as Yorubaland, which reflected indigenous cultural traits. Elsewhere, the settlement pattern was typically one of scattered and small population clusters, widely dispersed at varying densities across the countryside.

While the colonial period had certain economic and social evils associated with it, it must be conceded that it did initiate the forces which altered the socioeconomic landscape of much of the continent. Characteristics of this period were the introduction of a centralized administrative system over heterogeneous entities, the establishment and gradual diffusion of medical and educational facilities, of postal services and a monetary system of exchange, of cash-crop production and mining, and above all the construction of railways and roads. The propagation of these impulses has been studied under the rubric of modernization, diffusion and social change (Riddell 1970a).

Aggregatively, these innovations caused many sequential changes in the traditional systems upon which they were melded. First, political stability considerably reduced internecine fear and suspicion; people could move through, and live in, areas where they were formerly regarded as strangers. Secondly, the concentration of educational, administrative and medical facilities in a few nodes induced the beginnings of agglomeration, the accelerated growth of some centres, and the initiation of an urban hierarchy where none previously existed. Finally, mining and cash-crop production, coupled with the development of rail-road networks, caused the emergence of new urban centres, the mercurial growth of certain existing nodes, and the decline of some not located upon a transportation artery.

The net effect of these three structural changes was the marked concentration of employment, education and services in a few nodes or regions which eventually became focal points or destination areas for inmigration. The attraction of such places was complemented by certain push forces in the rural areas – population pressure, environmental hazard, the lack of cash income and social conservatism.

From the account of migratory forces so far presented, it would appear that in tropical Africa man behaves as 'an economic being', able to assess the cost/benefit structure of the entire region, and thus relocate so as to maximize some objective utility function. However, in a less economic and more behavioural framework, we would contend that within the developing continent of Africa migration is essentially an adaptation to perceived differences in opportunity (Gould 1964). Such a process of selection relies heavily upon the prospective migrant's mental map of his environment, a composite map reflecting the processing of information collected from various information channels, from interpersonal communication and from personal observation.

The effect of distance and information on the migration of individuals through successively higher-order nodes has been discussed elsewhere (Riddell and Harvey 1972). This paper concentrates on empirically testing the notion that hierarchical migration is an important mobility process in developing countries. Thus, the paper emphasizes an operationalization of the concept of hierarchical migration, the derivation of migration hierarchies from empirical data, and the testing of certain hypotheses regarding such hierarchical migration.

Chain and stepwise migration

In the literature on interregional or internodal mobility, chain and stepwise migration, depicting migration literally up the steps of an urban hierarchy, although in a geographical sense similar, have been differentiated. The former has implied either of two processes: that while the higher-order urban centres draw their population from intermediate centres, these places are, in turn, receiving migrants from lower-order centres (Hägerstrand 1957); or, in a sociological context, when one member of a family has migrated there is a very high probability that some of his relatives will also move to the same destination subsequently (Caldwell 1969). The notion of the stepwise migration, which implies a migration by stages or steps from a rural environment via lower-order centres to higher-order places, is an interesting concept but one that has been difficult to test empirically because of the paucity of data describing individual moves (Wendel 1953).

Hierarchies

Given a data set describing migration flows between a group of regions within a country it is possible, by considering the preferences expressed in this movement, to define a hierarchy based upon the observed movements of migrants. The resultant hierarchy will indicate both a number of discrete levels and the location of each of the original regions within this hierarchical arrangement (fig. 3.1a). Regions in the lowest level will send the majority of their migrants to places in the next highest level which, in turn, will send to the next highest, and so on. If this association exists a perfect hierarchy is formed. However, often such a perfect hierarchical arrangement is not defined by the migration data; the levels may not be discrete and certain circular associations may be present. In this case an overlapping hierarchical arrangement is described (fig. 3.1b). The derivation and the conditions for the existence of hierarchies are not the primary concerns of this paper. It is sufficient to indicate that such a hierarchical arrangement implies subordination of lower-level places to higher-order places (Whyte *et al.* 1969).

The notion of the criterion for the derivation of the hierarchy is of primary concern to our analysis. In general, there can be two broad categories of criteria, endogenous and exogenous. When the criterion is derived directly from the data set itself (as in the study by Nystuen and Dacey 1961) then we say that it is endogenously computed and an autonomous hierarchy is formed. In exogenously computed systems, where the criterion is defined externally to the data set, the hierarchy evolved may be termed a conditioned or a dependent hierarchy.

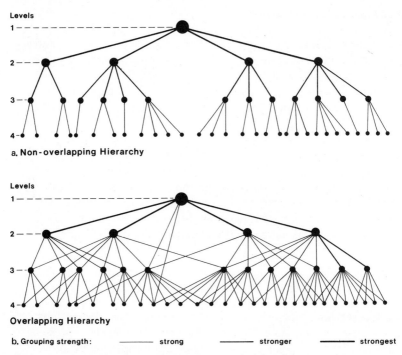

Figure 3.1 Settlement hierarchies based upon migration flows

The distinction between such autonomous and conditioned hierarchies has interesting empirical implications, and these are the major findings which lead to the conclusions of this paper. The former represents a hierarchy based upon a within-system grouping and reflects the existing, real world conditions. The latter can be employed as a simulation procedure to test certain criteria which are suspected to have affected the relationship described by the autonomous system. In this case, such a comparison provides a manner of testing hypotheses about the factors which are assumed to have conditioned the types of migration movements found in the real world. Specifically, if an urban hierarchical criterion is employed in the conditioned hierarchy, a test may be performed as to its role in affecting the overall migration patterns described by the interaction matrix.

Such a comparison can be conducted in several ways. The first involves the notion of similar subordinations in the two hierarchies and entails a comparison of the locations of individual regions in the two hierarchies. This can be performed by developing a k x k contingency table (where k is the number of levels in the hierarchy) which compares the status of the two systems. Secondly, the analysis can be based upon the aggregate flows from all the nodes at one level to those at the other $(k - 1)$ levels. These collapsed interaction matrices allow a comparison between the elements of the two matrices and within either. As the levels in these collapsed matrices are ranked, the study of their lower triangles will indicate the allocation process among the ordered set of regions. In a similar sense, the upper triangles represent flow down the hierarchical ratchet, or return flows of circular migrants (Elkan 1967). The hypothesized distribution of probabilities describing migrant flows is illustrated in fig. 3.2 on p. 61. Thirdly, the mean first passage times (MFPT) derived from these collapsed matrices represent a measure of proximity between levels. The elements of such a matrix are abstract measures of the lengths of time an individual takes to migrate from level to level in the hierarchy. Indeed, the matrix of MFPT will reflect the overall ordering among the different levels of the hierarchy. A one-to-one comparison of the elements of the MFPT matrices for the aggregated autonomous and dependent hierarchies will be useful in assessing the contrasts between the two systems. In this context, the associated equilibrium vectors will enhance the analysis because they make possible the comparison of the probabilities of being in any state (Kemeny and Snell 1969).

Development of the hierarchies

One of the basic difficulties about mobility research, particularly in developing countries, relates to the gross scale of aggregation of the flow data, if such exists, and the large calibration of the time scale as reflected in the birthplace data which tends to be the only source generally available. In this particular research these difficulties are partly overcome because the study area, Sierra Leone, West Africa, covering an area of 27,800 square miles, is divided into 148 administrative regions, a rather fine areal detail. For these, a 148 x 148 birthplace-residence matrix was compiled from the 1963 national census. Such a matrix describes long-term inter-area population movement and constitutes the data base for this study. One basic data problem that cannot be overcome, however, is the fact that the data available describe movement between the administrative regions of the country (chiefdoms) and not between urban places. In some instances an urban centre is synonymous with the region, while in others it is numerically dominant. It must be stressed though that administrative regions (each with an urban focus of varying size) are here equated with urban centres. Likely this is an advantage as it provides a continuum of areas from urban to rural.

For the development of the autonomous and conditioned hierarchies a modification of the Nystuen–Dacey graph theory algorithm is employed.

Specifically, let [M] be the n x n origin–destination (birthplace–residence) matrix. From it a criterion vector [v] may be derived, such that:

$$V_j = \sum_{i=1}^{n} m_{ij} \quad (j = 1, 2, \ldots, n)$$

Then [M] may be transformed into the matrix [A], such that:

$$a_{ij} = m_{ij}/Max\ v_j \quad (j = 1, 2, \ldots, n)$$

$$and \quad 0 \leqslant a_{ij} \leqslant 1$$

The elements of this scaled matrix [A] represent a measure of direct connectivity between the regions in the system, in this case as defined by long-term movement patterns. A powering of this matrix [A] describes the indirect connections among the regions (Gould 1964). Thus, matrices [A], $[A]^2$, $[A]^3$, . . . , $[A]^k$ together describe the direct and indirect associations among the regions. Thus:[1]

$$[S]^k = \sum_{k=1}^{r} [A]^k$$

To analyse the structural associations between the regions in the system, the largest destination j for an origin region i is identified. The superordinate-subordinate relationships are determined by the scores of i and j respectively upon the criterion vector [v]. Thus:

If $v_i - v_j$ $\geqslant 0$ then i is an independent node

< 0 then i is subordinate

When all of the independent nodes have been identified and their associated subordinates identified, the independent regions are extracted from the [M] matrix. To produce the next and higher level of the hierarchy a new, collapsed [M] matrix is constructed with rows and columns being the independent regions and the elements the migration between them. The analysis is repeated and a continuation of this process eventually produces a single or a few dominant regions at the apex of the hierarchy. In this case, the criterion vector was weighted by the number of regions subordinate to each independent region.

Besides developing an autonomous system, a comparable system based upon a criterion vector of the level of urbanization in each of the 148 regions was also computed. Hence these autonomous and dependent hierarchies could be compared, and the important point in this comparison is that the

---

[1] A basic problem, of course, is the selection of the size of k. Here, the matrix is powered until the difference between $[S]^{k-1}$ and $[S]^k$ approaches zero.

dependent hierarchy represents the hierarchy which would occur if migration were solely conditioned by the urban system, while the autonomous hierarchy reflects actual movement. In other words, such a comparison provides a test of the notion of migration being conditioned by and reflecting the urban system. It might be argued that the dependent hierarchy is based upon urban conditions at a fixed point in time while the autonomous hierarchy is derived from movements which have taken place in a prior period of indefinite length. However, as it has been shown that in large part the spatial pattern of the urban system has been recursive, this argument has little apparent strength (Riddell 1970a).

Empirical analysis of interregional migration

When the positions of the individual regions in the autonomous and exogenous hierarchies were assigned, a 4 x 4 contingency table was generated (table 3.1). If the urban-based hierarchy completely reflects the endogenously generated system then the off-diagonal elements of table 3.1 should be zero. In the cases of the second and third levels of the autonomous hierarchy there was some discrepancy with the urban-based system which might be

Table 3.1

Changes in nodal levels between autonomous and urban-based hierarchies – Sierra Leone

		Urban-based				
Ranks		1	2	3	4	
Autonomous	1	1	–	–	–	1
	2	–	4	2	2	8
	3	–	2	4	7	13
	4	–	1	4	121	126
		1	7	10	130	148

Note: For statistical analysis, rank 1 was ignored, and 2 and 3 combined. Therefore, with one degree of freedom, $X^2 > X^2_{.01}$, that is $50.17 > 6.635$.

important because of the relatively high ranking of these regions. However, despite this dissimilarity between the two ordered relationships, an X^2 contingency test indicated that the two hierarchies were not dissimilar; that the assignments of the 148 regions to various levels of the hierarchy are highly related at the more than .01 level of confidence. Here we find some support for the statements made above. This finding has both methodological and empirical implications. As regards the former, it shows one manner in which the algorithm can be employed for hypothesis testing. Empirically, such a conclusion implies that since the main channels of migration in a developing country are highly related to the existing urban system, modification of such a locational matrix for purposes of reorganizing space so as to induce local growth and reduce excessive interregional migration may affect changes in the space economy. The pleas for the creation of many intermediate-sized cities in the Third World appear justifiable (Johnson 1970; Grove and Huszar 1964; Harvey 1972), although other forms of analysis have indicated otherwise (Riddell 1970b).

For analysing aggregate movement between the various levels of the hierarchies, the 148 x 148 interaction matrix was collapsed into two 4 x 4 arrays representing movements between the levels of both the autonomous and conditioned hierarchies. Before aggregation, the diagonal elements, which represent the number of non-migrants in each region, were set to zero. The migration probabilities of the two arrays, under the different assumptions, are reported in table 3.2. The diagonal elements where $t_{ii} > 0$ represent the amount of interaction between regions at a specific level of the hierarchy; zero values in the diagonal indicate that there is only one region at that level of the hierarchy. Certain interesting observations are evident from an investigation of these diagonal elements. First, the aggregate interaction between regions at the lowest level in both hierarchies is most

Table 3.2

Transition probabilities between the various tiers in the hierarchy

(a) *Autonomous*

		With $t_{ii} > 0$					With $t_{ii} = 0$			
		1	2	3	4		1	2	3	4
Rank: Highest	1	.000	.089	.124	.787	1	—	.089	.124	.787
	2	.078	.093	.186	.643	2	.086	—	.206	.709
	3	.057	.101	.145	.697	3	.067	.118	—	.815
Lowest	4	.120	.084	.131	.665	4	.358	.250	.392	—

(b) *Conditioned*

		With $t_{ii} > 0$					With $t_{ii} = 0$			
		1	2	3	4		1	2	3	4
Rank: Highest	1	.000	.038	.078	.884	1	—	.038	.078	.884
	2	.032	.012	.102	.853	2	.032	—	.104	.864
	3	.107	.057	.094	.742	3	.119	.062	—	.819
Lowest	4	.114	.033	.083	.770	4	.497	.143	.360	—

Source: Calculated by the authors.

Table 3.3

Mean first passage time matrices for the autonomous and dependent hierarchies

(a) Autonomous

		With $t_{ii} > 0$				With $t_{ii} = 0$			
		1	2	3	4	1	2	3	4
Rank: Highest	1	10.050	28.144	12.105	1.147	5.414	5.994	3.963	1.277
	2	9.747	28.839	11.822	1.186	5.045	6.556	3.711	1.366
	3	9.096	27.588	11.917	1.314	5.054	5.821	4.431	1.247
Lowest	4	9.018	28.264	12.057	1.279	4.242	5.427	3.347	2.288
Limiting vector		[.099	.035	.084	.782]	[.185	.152	.226	.437]

(b) Dependence

		With $t_{ii} > 0$				With $t_{ii} = 0$			
		1	2	3	4	1	2	3	4
Rank: Highest	1	10.390	11.499	7.439	1.313	3.918	10.947	4.709	1.138
	2	9.708	11.432	6.981	1.511	3.089	11.367	4.607	1.162
	3	9.878	11.346	7.286	1.436	3.551	10.735	5.121	1.208
Lowest	4	9.279	11.549	7.395	1.473	2.824	10.302	3.999	2.167
Limiting vector		[.096	.087	.137	.679]	[.255	.088	.195	.461]

Source: Calculated by the authors.

marked. Since the regions at this level are largely rural, the magnitude of mobility at this level reflects the relative importance of such rural-rural movement despite the current growth of urban places. Secondly, with increasing diversification of the economic base of regions, and also with the expansion of their associated contact fields, lateral mobility between regions at the same level of the hierarchy is reduced relative to the lowest level. The importance of lateral migration at the lowest level is also well demonstrated by the diagonal elements of the computed matrices of mean first passage time (table 3.3). We would expect, however, that as modern conditions spread to wider parts of the countryside and significant changes occur in the rural areas, rural-rural migration will relatively diminish and vertical mobility up the hierarchy will slowly supersede lateral mobility among regions at comparable levels of development.

Analysis of the lower triangular elements (tables 3.2 and 3.3), especially with $t_{ii} = 0$, shows that the mobility pattern in Sierra Leone approximates the hypothesized model for a small country with extreme primacy. Visually, the hypothesis appears to be more validated by the transition probability matrix of the autonomously derived hierarchy, where for each level the next most important level is more preferred than the highest level centres. Thus within the mobility system itself there is a strong tendency towards an ordered asymmetrical relationship. Intuitively, a perfect ordering may have occurred if the country were not so small that even its elementary transport network brings people within a day's journey of the major city.

Unlike the autonomous system, examination of the lower triangular elements of the imposed hierarchical structure indicates that for the lower order tiers, the highest order region is the most important destination. This situation probably reflects the interesting fact that an urban-based criterion vector tends to accentuate the importance of the highest order regions and forces many of intermediate status into the lowest level of the hierarchy.

This apparent difference between the two hierarchies has interesting process implications. Increased national development tends to enhance the importance of regional growth poles while at the same time causing the decline of many lower and intermediate order regions. It may be inferred, therefore, that if the autonomous interaction pattern at time t describes the present Sierra Leone case, then at t + 1 it may tend towards the exogenously derived, urban-based pattern. In terms of temporal process, with the integration of geographic space over time, a perfect stepwise mobility pattern is superseded by a short-circuiting of the system which tends to bypass the intermediate centres. As transportation and communications improve and lead to a gradual transformation of the space economy, such a short-circuiting will take place. At that time, the most important centres become the most attractive to migrants from all types of lower order regions (fig. 3.2).

Analysis of the upper triangles of both the matrices of transition probabilities and the mean first passage times shows the strong preference of returning migrants for the lowest order regions (table 3.2). Comparison of these upper triangles for both the autonomous and imposed hierarchies shows that in the latter situation the attraction of the lowest ranking regions is greater than in the former. This observation, coupled with Wendel's

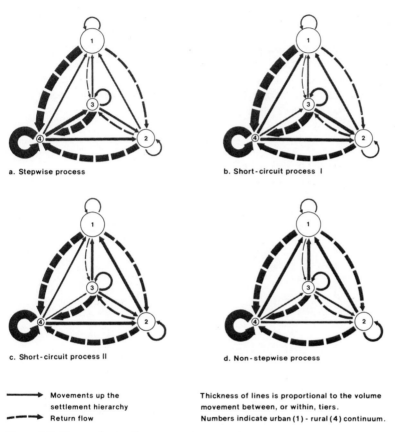

a. Stepwise process

b. Short-circuit process I

c. Short-circuit process II

d. Non-stepwise process

	Movements up the	Thickness of lines is proportional to the volume
	settlement hierarchy	movement between, or within, tiers.
	Return flow	Numbers indicate urban (1) - rural (4) continuum.

Figure 3.2 Types of migration processes

findings on the importance of return migration (Wendel 1953), shows that in both developed and developing countries the returning migrant does not move down the hierarchical ratchet.

Differences between the two systems of mobility hierarchies in terms of lateral movements, vertical migration up the hierarchical ratchet and counter-migration have been identified and discussed. An analysis of out-migration from each of the 148 individual regions would also be fruitful to test the notion of movement through the urban systems. It would be expected that movement patterns in the urban-based system will be less hierarchical than in the autonomously derived system. To test this proposition, migration from each node may be considered separately and then classified according to the main direction of movement with reference to the hierarchy of regions. In the four-tiered Sierra Leone system, an analysis of the direct and indirect movement patterns indicated that thirteen types were sufficient completely to describe the migration patterns (table 3.4). A preference ranking of 1-2-3-4 indicates a perfect stepwise pattern with persons from a low-order region being most likely to move to a region of the next highest order, then on to the next and finally to the highest. More common, however, is the 1-3-2-4 pattern which indicates a partial short-circuiting (fig. 3.2) with people bypassing intermediate centres and moving more directly to the larger places.

Table 3.4

Preference ranking in a four-tiered system

Rank of levels				Autonomous system	Dependent system
1st	2nd	3rd	4th		
1	2	3	4	46	44
1	3	2	4	53	48
1	4	2	3	13	22
1	4	3	2	18	17
1	2	4	3	7 { 4	7 } 12
1	3	4	2	{ 3	5 }
2	3	1	4	1	2
2	1	4	3	4	—
3	2	1	4	2	—
2	4	3	1	11 { 1	1 } 5
3	1	2	4	1	—
2	1	3	4	2	1
2	4	1	3	—	1
		Chiefdoms		148	148

Note: Tabular value of $X^2_{.05}$ for five degrees of freedom is 11.0705. Computed X^2 is 6.2006. Thus, accept H_0 at the .05 level of confidence.

The patterns described in table 3.4 have empirical expression and can be mapped. Here only the autonomous system is presented (fig. 3.3), but the dependent is roughly similar. The perfect stepwise pattern, 1-2-3-4, occurs in the regions along the southern coastal area and in the remote livestock-rearing regions of the interior Koinadugu-Kono plateau area of the northeast.

Characteristically, these areas are sparsely populated and poorly connected. The simple short-circuit pattern, 1-3-2-4, is largely related to the areas of arboriculture and alluvial diamond mining. In these areas, proximity to large

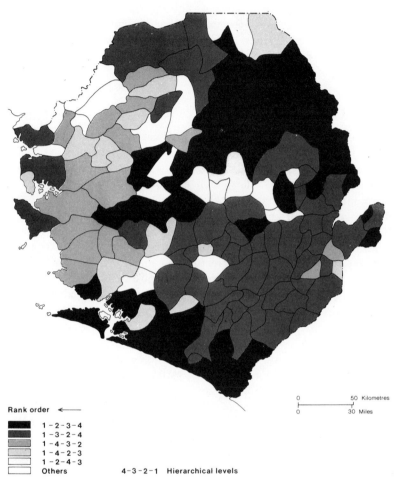

Rank order ⟵

- 1 − 2 − 3 − 4
- 1 − 3 − 2 − 4
- 1 − 4 − 3 − 2
- 1 − 4 − 2 − 3
- 1 − 2 − 4 − 3
- Others   4 − 3 − 2 − 1 Hierarchical levels

Figure 3.3 Migration preferences in Sierra Leone

towns such as Bo, Kenema and Kailahun, and important mining centres such as Panguma and Barma, coupled with the relative remoteness of the capital, produced this type of migratory pattern. The short-circuiting of the second level in the system is directly the result of many proximate centres of non-primary activity. Although Freetown, the capital, is undoubtedly the most attractive region as regards employment and social amenities, its pull is considerably reduced by both the attenuating effect of distance and the presence of nearby employment centres and regional capitals. Where the pull of Freetown as a first step migration destination supersedes that of more local destinations, the preference ranking is essentially 1-4-3-2 or 1-4-2-3. The general distribution of chiefdoms with this type of preference scale is largely conditioned by proximity to the capital and by historical ties between the two areas. Thus, these regions are found along the railway, especially in the west, and in chiefdoms located along the riverine routes extending inland from north of Freetown.

Conclusions and implications

The findings of this study have far-reaching implications for planning and national development. They show that the study of migration in developing countries should essentially be part of an analysis of the general modernization process and that changes in the geographic structure are intimately related to behavioural change. To restructure geographic space and man's mobility vectors in that space requires an isolation of the major components which affect the aggregate behaviour patterns in that environment. Thus a meaningful approach to population mobility research is to appraise the effect of new inputs on the *status quo*. In this context, the association established between state of development and type of migration pattern deserves further research. Such analyses would help in ascertaining, for example, the effects of rural modernization and the creation of intermediate cities on the subsequent pattern of human interaction.

Of a purely methodological value, this paper has demonstrated how, given interaction data, the effect of an exogenous variable on the system can be assessed. For long-term development planning, this implies that the behaviour of the entire system under different conditions can be examined and then decisions can be made regarding the best strategy for achieving the desired goals. In effect, the impact of various criterion vectors on human relocation patterns can be appraised.

Empirically, evidence of the existence of a stepwise movement of population through the urban hierarchy in Sierra Leone has been demonstrated. As well, it is evident that as the process of modernization continues and expands spatially such a movement pattern will be short-circuited and direct country-city moves will increase in relative importance. As distance effects are overcome, the reach of the large city with its employment opportunities and bright lights can extend and overcome the basic sociocultural differences between the city and the countryside that the stepwise pattern has served to ease.

Acknowledgements

The support of the Canada Council and the assistance of John AuWerter are acknowledged.

References

Caldwell, J. C. (1969) *African rural-urban migration.* New York.

Elkan, W. (1967) Circular migration and the growth of towns in East Africa. *Internat. Lab. Rev.* 581–9.

Gould, P. (1964) On the geographic interpretation of Eigen-values. *Trans. Inst. Brt. Geogr.* 42, 53–86.

Gould, P. (1972) On mental maps, in English, P. W. and Mayfield, R. C. (eds.) *Man, space, and environment.* Toronto.

Grove, D. and Huszar, L. (1964) *The towns of Ghana.* Accra.

Hägerstrand, T. (1957) Migration and area, in Hägerstrand, T. and Odeving, B. (eds.) *Migration in Sweden: a symposium.* Lund.

Harvey, M. E. (1972) The identification of development regions in developing countries. *Econ. Geogr.* 48, 229–43.

Johnson, E. A. J. (1970) *The organization of space in developing countries.* Cambridge.

Kemeny, J. G. and Snell, J. L. (1969) *Finite Markov chains.* Princeton.

Nystuen, J. D. and Dacey, M. F. (1961) A graph theory interpretation of nodal regions. *Pap. Reg. Sci. Assoc.* 7, 29–42.

Riddell, J. B. (1970a) *The spatial dynamics of modernization in Sierra Leone.* Evanston.

Riddell, J. B. (1970b) On structuring a migration model. *Geogr. Anal.* 2, 403–9.

Riddell, J. B. and Harvey, M. E. (1972) The urban system in the migration process: an evaluation of stepwise movement in Sierra Leone. *Econ. Geogr.* 48, 270–83.

Wendel, B. (1953) *A migration schema: theories and observations.* Lund.

Whyte, L. L., Wilson, A. G. and Wilson, D. (eds.) (1969) *Hierarchical structures.* New York.

4 Some observations on migration theory for an urban system

J. C. Hudson

The migration experience of the United States population in this century can be characterized by two facts of particular importance. The first is that net migration flow has been upward in the urban hierarchy. Persons born in small places are likely to be living in substantially larger places by the time they reach middle age. Second, this net upward migration has been cushioned by the spillover of large city dwellers into the surrounding suburbs and metropolitan fringes. By tracing age groups in the process, it is also clear that the suburbanization process was experienced several decades earlier by those born in the larger metropolitan areas. Their 'places' were filled by persons born in smaller metropolitan areas and by those born on farms and in small towns and cities. Only in recent decades has this latter group contributed appreciably to the flow of population to the major metropolitan fringes.

This suggests a model of hierarchical migration that is applicable in the United States and perhaps some other countries. The model resembles a fountain whose flow is upward until it spills over into the available space. There is substantial public and governmental awareness that this is a major characteristic of migration in the United States. Awareness has now reached the point of governmental action to treat some consequences of the process, namely depopulation of the non-metropolitan hinterlands and urban sprawl.

Apart from Ravenstein's early speculations, traditional migration theory offers few observations on hierarchical migration processes. This paper proposes some models that may prove useful in this area. In an earlier paper (Hudson 1970) a very general model for population growth and migration processes was introduced. Before presenting some extensions of this model for urban-system migration, its major characteristics are briefly reviewed.

Growth and migration models

Assume a closed, two-region system in which all population is classified as belonging either to a metropolis (M_1) or to its non-metropolitan hinterland (M_2). Each region can grow in two ways: by natural increase or by net migration received from the other. If each region attracts migrants in proportion to its size, as gravity models of migration usually postulate, and is characterized by a constant balance between the crude birth and death rates and the rate of outmigration, the growth rates of the two populations can be expressed as the linear differential equations

$$\frac{dM_1}{dt} = a_{11}M_1 + a_{12}M_2,$$

$$\frac{dM_2}{dt} = a_{21}M_1 + a_{22}M_2. \tag{1}$$

In more compact notation

$$M' = a \cdot M$$

where

$$\begin{bmatrix} M_1' \\ M_2' \end{bmatrix} = \begin{bmatrix} a_{11} & a_{12} \\ a_{21} & a_{22} \end{bmatrix} \cdot \begin{bmatrix} M_1 \\ M_2 \end{bmatrix}.$$

This type of ordinary differential equation model has been widely studied in economics, population genetics and animal ecology as well as in physics. Solutions of the system (1) that involve various configurations of the signs and values of the constant coefficients yield various insights into how theoretical populations (animals, stocks of goods, people) behave in time.

Particular interest attaches to the stability properties of such a system. For example, under what conditions do the populations remain stable or within some size range? Do some populations explode while others become extinct? Practically, this asks which populations become very large and which become very small. Two kinds of stability are usually mentioned. *Global stability* refers to the total properties of the system and considers growth paths passing through any point, meaning some vector of population sizes. The system possesses global stability if all growth paths converge in time to some equilibrium vector of finite sizes. If there is more than one such stable point, the system is said to have *local stability.*

It is sometimes the case that such equilibria are present. These are configurations for which point the growth vector, M', equals zero. Some equilibria are stable; once the system arrives in this state, it remains there or will return if the system is disturbed to a limited extent. Others are unstable. In such a case only a momentary equilibrium situation occurs and the system is highly unlikely either to be in such a state or to return to it, once there.

Returning to the example mentioned above, the stability properties may be investigated by computing the roots of the characteristic polynomial (eigenvalues) of the matrix, [A].

The time paths of population change in the two regions are

$$M_1(t) = c_{11} e^{\lambda_1 t} + c_{12} e^{\lambda_2 t}$$

$$M_2(t) = c_{21} e^{\lambda_1 t} + c_{22} e^{\lambda_2 t}.$$

(2)

λ_1 and λ_2 are the characteristic roots of [A] and the c_{ij}'s are constants, depending on initial population sizes.

Applications

There are two kinds of information necessary to specify a growth model of the type shown in (1). Hence, there are two sources of error which can creep into predictions made by such a model. First, it may be that the equation system is an incorrect representation of the process. One source of error would be that age-specific instead of crude rates are necessary for an accurate description of natural increase. It may be that the balance between crude birth and death rates is not a constant in time, as in the case of a demographic transition. Also, cities do not necessarily attract migrants in proportion to their sizes; there is evidence suggesting this for certain ranges of the city-size distribution. These errors are combated by securing better descriptions of how populations behave in time and space. They relate to how to write the system of differential equations describing growth and migration.

The second source of error is in estimating the constant coefficients in the model. Even if the equation system is of the right form, numerical predictions will be in error if incorrect constants are imposed. Although simultaneous-equation estimation of these parameters from available data may yield accurate predictions over a given interval of time, it is not necessarily true that these values will remain constant, even on the average.

If one is concerned with applications to questions of migration policy, the importance of these issues becomes almost reversed. If a migration scheme is imposed, say, one designed to redirect net population flow from congested to sparsely settled areas, then the configuration of the growth equations might not be considered problematic. Instead, it remains a question of how to select policies that will produce the desired distribution. The practical impact of this problem is that of specifying the range of values of natural increase and migration in the matrix, [A], which will yield growth and distribution patterns consistent with planning goals.

General model

The usual 'bookkeeping' equation for population growth in a region is simply to write

$$\Delta_t(M) = B_t - D_t + I_t - O_t$$

where the indicated quantities are respectively the number of births, deaths, inmigrants and outmigrants during the interval, Δ_t.

The corresponding instantaneous rate of change of a population is a differential equation,

$$\frac{dM_i(t)}{dt} \equiv M_i'(t) = (b_i - d_i)M_i(t) + \sum_{j=1}^{n} \frac{\partial M_i}{\partial M_j} - \sum_{j=1}^{n} \frac{\partial M_j}{\partial M_i},$$

expressing the rate of change of a population, M_i, in terms of its own natural increase, plus the balance between in- and outmigration flows.

Assuming all coefficients of migration and natural increase constant, then

$$M_i'(t) = (b_i - d_i)M_i(t) + \sum_{\substack{j=1 \\ j \neq i}}^{n} a_{ij}M_j(t) - M_i(t) \sum_{\substack{j=1 \\ j \neq i}}^{n} a_{ji}.$$

The system of growth equations will then be written

$$M_t' = AM_t, \text{ or}$$

$$
\begin{bmatrix} M_1' \\ M_2' \\ M_3' \\ \vdots \\ M_n' \end{bmatrix}
=
\begin{bmatrix}
\alpha_1 - \sum a_{j1} & a_{12} & a_{13} & \cdots & a_{1n} \\
a_{21} & \alpha_2 - \sum a_{j2} & a_{23} & \cdots & a_{2n} \\
a_{31} & a_{32} & \alpha_3 - \sum a_{j3} & \cdots & a_{3n} \\
\vdots & \cdots & \cdots & \cdots & \cdots \\
a_{n1} & a_{n2} & a_{n3} & \cdots & \alpha_n - \sum a_{jn}
\end{bmatrix}
\cdot
\begin{bmatrix} M_1 \\ M_2 \\ M_3 \\ \vdots \\ M_n \end{bmatrix}
\quad (3)
$$

where $\alpha_i = (b_i - d_i)$ is the crude rate of natural increase in the i-th population, and the a_{ij}'s are friction-of-distance coefficients.

Since the system of n subregions is closed, then necessarily

$$\sum_{i=1}^{n} M_i'(t) = \sum_{i=1}^{n} \alpha_i M_i(t).$$

There is no migration in or out of the system, so the sum of the growth rates at any point in time is simply the growth due to natural increase. This property is easily verified by summing each column of [A].

The rest of the paper discusses properties of the system (3).

Hierarchical migration

In terms of population growth and migration theory for a system of urban places, the configuration of constants in the matrix, [A], can be arranged to produce almost any system of population flows that is desired. Hierarchical flows are easily treated in this fashion.

Assume that {M_i} is a set of urban places on which there is defined some hierarchy of migration flows. If the hierarchy is strictly ordered according to size of place, with all flows moving upwards, then a necessary condition on the eigenvalues of [A] provides an easy solution to the time behaviour of the system.

If people migrate only to larger places, then the size of every place is potentially a function of the size of every smaller place, as well as its own size, but no others. The matrix, [A], is upper-triangular, with $a_{ij} \geqslant 0$ when $i \leqslant j$, and $a_{ij} = 0$ for $i > j$. The eigenvalues of such a matrix consist entirely of the values in the main diagonal. Hence, the growth equations for every place M_1, M_2, . . ., M_n are representable as a sum of one to n exponential functions similar to (2) and the exponents λ_1, λ_2, . . ., $\lambda_{k \leqslant n}$ are the differences between crude rates of natural increase and outmigration rates in the respective populations. This says that if migration flows are strictly ordered by size of place (or, in fact, by any other criteria, provided the flows are in one direction), then the balance between the natural increase and the sum of the outmigration rates describes the future growth of the system.

Although this characteristic of upward hierarchical flow through the city-size distribution is only an observed trend and not an absolute as the above result necessitates, it is possible that because it is so important, explanations of urban concentration based on factors of sheer population growth are as relevant as explanations based on migration preferences.

Stability properties

Because most available theory about city sizes argues that a hierarchy and gradation of sizes having a particular frequency distribution is to be expected, there is little theoretical interest in devising migration models that would 'flatten' this distribution. The city-size distribution itself must necessarily come about as a result of net migration, since natural increase alone could not produce such pronounced place-to-place differences in population. What is of interest is to conceive of migration processes that preserve a particular size distribution but do not result in further net redistribution.

This amounts to finding a coefficient matrix, [A], and values of M_t such that $M_t' = A \cdot M_t = 0$. This defines an equilibrium point in the system since net redistribution is not occurring; stability properties of the equilibrium are of interest.

An important theorem about the behaviour of linear systems with constant coefficients, such as (3), states that if all eigenvalues of [A] have negative real parts, then every solution of $M'_t = A \cdot M_t$ approaches zero as t approaches infinity. Without losing generality, the zero solution can be treated as the equilibrium point and the vector of population sizes will represent deviations from the equilibrium. Perturbations within some specified area of the equilibrium will result in an eventual return to equilibrium if it is stable.

Are there any realistic population processes which fulfil this condition? Intuitively, the imposition of zero natural population growth conditions on all n populations would seem to produce such stability. This condition is clearly an equilibrium with respect to growth. Does it preserve the size distribution of places?

Associated with every square matrix, [A], is a quadratic form $M^T AM$, where M^T denotes the transpose of M. Whether or not [A] is symmetric, if the quadratic form $M^T AM < 0$, then [A] is said to be negative definite, if this condition holds for all M except M = 0. Furthermore, [A] is negative definite if, and only if, the determinants of the n, principal minors of [A] alternate in sign, viz.:

$$a_{11} < 0; \qquad \begin{vmatrix} a_{11} & a_{12} \\ a_{21} & a_{22} \end{vmatrix} > 0; \qquad \begin{vmatrix} a_{11} & a_{12} & a_{13} \\ a_{21} & a_{22} & a_{23} \\ a_{31} & a_{32} & a_{33} \end{vmatrix} < 0,$$

and so on. If [A] is negative definite, then for all associated $\lambda_1, \lambda_2, \ldots, \lambda_{k \leqslant n}$, $\lambda_i < 0$. This is the stability condition.

If $\alpha_i = 0$ for all i, i.e. zero population growth, then for any a_{ij} in the i-th row of [A],

$$a_{ij} = - \sum_{\substack{k=1 \\ k \neq i}}^{n} a_{kj}$$

and the i-th row is equivalent to the negative of the sum of the other n − 1 rows, hence [A] is singular. If [A] is singular, then | A | = 0 and [A] cannot be negative definite, hence not all eigenvalues are necessarily negative, and the equilibrium is unstable.

A condition of zero natural increase is therefore not enough to maintain a population spatial distribution arbitrarily close to some equilibrium, although the population sizes are bounded. If for just one population $\alpha_j < 0$ while $\alpha_i = 0$ for all $i \neq j$, indicating a natural decrease, then [A] will be non-singular, $M^T AM < 0$ and $\lambda_i < 0$, for all i. This is a stable equilibrium.

Is it possible to maintain the equilibrium if just one population is growing by natural increase while others are declining? In this case, there would exist an $\alpha_i < 0$ and $\alpha_j > 0$ such that for some time, t_0,

$$\sum_{k=1}^{n} \alpha_k M_k^2(t_0) = \alpha_i M_i(t_0) = M_{t_0}^T MM_{t_0} < 0.$$

Then for some $t > t_0$, $M_i(t) < M_i(t_0)$ and $M_j(t) > M_j(t_0)$. Since $0 \leqslant M_k \leqslant \infty$, $M_i(t)$ approaches zero and $M_j(t)$ increases without bound and eventually $M_t^T AM_t > 0$, for all successive values of t. This shows that the equilibrium is unstable.

The implication of these results for questions of migration theory is that growth control is of more importance than migration control in order to produce stability in population distribution. Even if there is zero natural growth in all n regions, any perturbation of the system will move it away from equilibrium. Such perturbations would include factors such as stochastic fluctuations in population replacement rates and are realistically included in this kind of model. No matter what migration rates are imposed on the zero-total-growth system, no single set of rates will produce stability in the long run. If population is declining by natural decrease in one (or more) of the regions, and is not growing elsewhere, the equilibrium is stable regardless of the magnitude of interregional migrations.

Conclusions

This paper has considered properties of an urban-system migration process that may be developed from the theory of linear systems of ordinary differential equations. This theory seems to be a natural one to employ if the time path of population distribution in a set of regions is to be investigated. The growth equations can be specified in a variety of ways, but in their simplest form they are no more complicated than the usual formulation expressing population growth in terms of rates of natural increase and those expressing migration via gravity-potential formulae.

One question of particular interest for population geography concerns what kinds of population growth and migration flows result from the imposition of certain rules on the system. This often amounts to studying the stability properties of the set of equations. In case after case these properties depend strongly on the diagonal values of the coefficient matrix, which in this model represent the balance between natural growth and outmigration. This emphasizes the very strong dependence between theories of population distribution and theories of growth.

References

Brauer, F. and Nohel, J. A. (1969) *Qualitative theory of ordinary differential equations.* New York.

Hudson, J. C. (1970) Elementary models for population growth and distribution analysis. *Demog.* 7, 361–8.

Keyfitz, N. (1968) *Introduction to the mathematics of population.* Reading, Mass.

Lewontin, R. (1969) The meaning of stability, in *Diversity and stability in ecological systems.* New York.

Rogers, A. (1969) *Matrix analysis of interregional population growth and distribution.* Berkeley.

Taeuber, K. E. (1965) Cohort population redistribution and the urban hierarchy. *Milbank Memorial Fund Q.* 43, 450–63.

5 More on models of residential change

S. Gale

Introduction

A central issue in many urban planning situations is the estimation and explanation of changes in the characteristics of populations. An understanding of the processes underlying residential changes within urban areas, for example, has implications for planning a wide variety of public services, but until recently there has been very little interest in this problem. This seems to have been a result of social scientists' preoccupation with aggregated data (such as from a decennial census) and with a restricted view of the problem of developing appropriate conceptual frameworks and associated formal models.

By utilizing existing aggregate data as the basis for inferences about the process of residential change, current methodological orthodoxy has promoted the reification of the ecological fallacy in human geography in a manner reminiscent of the adoption of classical mechanics as a paradigm by social physicists. But, more importantly, the failure to take seriously the two-way relationship between philosophical and methodological issues has given this reification the status of deification. Methodology has been assumed to be a set of *a priori* unified principles and the questions we ask about empirical phenomena have been forced to conform to it. (See Gale 1972a for more detailed discussion.)

At the heart of this problem is the manner in which we conceive of the concept of 'model' and its implications for the process of explanation. What is required is a formal framework within which data can be structured in such a way that it provides a basis for constructing a reasonable understanding. Several attempts have been made to provide some justification for a modelling strategy which, at various points, has been called a 'patternist', 'informationist', 'structured inductive', and a 'transparent-box' approach to an explanatory model of human population movements (Gale 1969, 1971, 1972d, 1973a; Gale and Katzman 1972; Olsson and Gale 1968). The idea has always been quite simple and is, in fact, part of a rather long tradition of empiricism based on inferences from longitudinal data structured in terms of conditional probability statements. It is the process of discerning patterns (e.g. stationarities, interactions) in cross-classified information on changes in individual behaviours. At present, however, even though there is a general recognition of the importance of developing such models, the operational procedures for developing them nevertheless remain only partially specified (Ginsberg 1972a, b). It is apparent that the general model will involve the use of a time-dependent contingency table framework, but at the same time it is not at all clear how theories are to be developed and tested within this. Similarly, although there seem to be extremely good grounds for basing the parameter estimates of the models on disaggregated longitudinal data, there have been difficulties in developing guidelines for specifying, collecting, classifying and representing these data. In general, there seems to be a set of methodological questions relating to the interplay between model, theory, and measurement which require examination before we can proceed with the analysis of data. The few empirical studies employing these methods have been relatively interesting, but limited in scope for precisely these reasons (e.g. Gale 1969; Gale and Katzman 1972; Thernstrom and Knights 1970).

This paper continues the investigation of the rationale for this methodological strategy. It draws quite heavily on several earlier papers and, in particular, from a recent discussion of micro-analytic models of occupancy shifts for households in specific classes of dwellings (Moore and Gale 1973).

Models of theories and models of data

Several recent papers attempt to demonstrate the impact of the interdependence of philosophical and methodological positions on the design of scientific research (e.g. Gale 1971, 1972a; Olsson 1969; Suppes 1962). Neither philosophical outlook nor choice of methodology can be treated as independent of the nature of the questions to be answered. The questions are taken as the epistemologically primitive realizations of an inquiring mind; the range of potential answers (the theories) and the strategies for providing answers (the methods) follow directly as context-specific methods. Although a general formulation of the logic of such a dialogue for scientific investigations has not yet been devised (say, in terms of what has been called erotetic logic, e.g. Åqvist 1965, 1972; Belnap 1963; Prior and Prior 1955), insights into the procedures for investigating special classes of problems have been advanced (e.g. Gale 1972c; Mitroff *et al.* 1970; Murakami 1968; Pörn 1971; Przelecki 1969; Suppes 1959, 1962, 1965; Suszko 1965; Zadeh 1972).

The issue here may be regarded as a specific case of the problem of developing empirical theories and, as such, it is also closely related to the process of model building, in which the general idea of a *model* is regarded

very simply as 'a means to state something in a different way'. Clearly, this
'restatement' is constrained by the necessity for retaining the important
properties of the objects and their relationships. (See Conant and Ashby
1970 and Suppes 1960 for a more detailed discussion of this issue.) However, the point of the restatement is quite simple: the idea is to use an
analytically more tractable language for describing and examining otherwise complicated problems (Gale 1972b; Przelecki 1969; Suppes 1959,
1965; von Wright 1971). Note that this conceptualization differs from that
of Chorley (1964) in that it is interpretation rather than technique oriented.

To give this idea a more concrete basis, consider the following characterization of the abstract notion of a model. The development is an adaptation
of Suszko's (1965) treatment although the term 'model' has been applied
in a somewhat unorthodox manner. First, let a *model*, M, be defined by
$M \stackrel{\text{def}}{=} \langle S, O \rangle$ where S designates the properties of the subject (or mind)
which conceives of and thinks about the area of interest and O designates
the properties of the object world. S and O can themselves be further de-
composed as a triple $S \stackrel{\text{def}}{=} \langle L, A, T \rangle$ and on n + 1-tuple $O \stackrel{\text{def}}{=} \langle U, R_1, \ldots, R_n \rangle$
(Przelecki 1969; Suszko 1965). L is thus the language in which the subject
thinks about (or formalizes) his ideas about O (which may include natural
language); A is a set of axioms (postulates, assumptions) employed in specifying these ideas; T is the set of ideas (or theories in the above-mentioned
sense) the subject has about O; U is a non-empty set of individuals (or
individual objects); and $R_1, \ldots, R_n$ is an n-tuple of relations on U. Note
that where the usual form of logical empiricism is employed in the scientific
process, the n + 1-tuple $\langle U, R_1, \ldots, R_n \rangle$ is the usual intension of the term
model with respect to empirical theories under a given language, L (Przelecki
1969). However, since this implies that a two-valued, truth-functional,
descriptive and inferential language is employed (usually the first-order
predicate calculus with identity), a line of reasoning is followed that was
developed in several earlier papers (Gale 1972a, b, c; Olsson 1970) which
characterizes models by the slightly broader definition employed above.

It can be shown that by using this extended formulation of the concept
of a model, a quite flexible means is available for developing and interpreting alternative models of social phenomena. In particular, by allowing
L to range over modal, deontic and n-valued, truth-functional, logical calculi,
it can be demonstrated that a quite powerful set of tools (e.g. for developing
prescriptive theories) can be made available to social scientists (Gale 1972b, c,
1973b; Körner 1969; Olsson 1970). For the present purposes, however, this
increased flexibility in the specification of models is important only in so far
as it illuminates its diverse components and the considerations which are
important in the model-building process. It is at all times assumed that L is a
two-valued, truth-functional language and that the set of individuals and

their observable properties are distinct and discrete. The questions in mind relate instead to the concomitant problems of specifying the related properties of T and A and providing a reasonable set of relations and measures for O such that T can be evaluated and interpreted within the context of a particular set of observations.

Consider now the problem of specifying and building a model of residential relocation processes, recognizing that the properties of S and O are not independent. More specifically, consider two kinds of models, M_D and M_T, where the former is a model which is developed to describe the observed properties of the individuals (e.g. their status or behaviour) and their environment (e.g. housing quality and area of residence), and the latter is a model which has been designated to represent some particular theory of residential mobility (e.g. Hägerstrand's 1967a theory of spatial interaction; McGinnis' 1968 'axiom' of cumulative inertia; Rossi's 1955 life cycle theory; or Smith's 1964 and 1970 filtering theory). Clearly, except in the case of a highly formalized theory where the observation language of the theory is (to a very high degree) the same (such as in classical mechanics), we would not expect that $M_D \equiv M_T$, *a priori.* But this is precisely what we desire in descriptive (as opposed to normative) investigations: a single model, M, in which the theories and assumptions accurately represent the properties of the observations. The question is, 'How do we go about constructing such a model?'

The use of micro-analytic models which employ highly disaggregated data is crucial in the developmental stages of a science, and this form of empiricism requires an interplay between a hierarchy of model types. The former point is of particular interest since it leads immediately to the assertion that the usual ecological models do not provide an adequate basis for studying localized population shifts. The next section, therefore, focuses specifically on the rationale for micro-level approaches to model development.

Micro-level data and models of residential change

The use of micro-level data in the social sciences has become fairly common in the past decade. There has, for example, been a growing realization that gross indicators of observed behaviours (e.g. marginal distributions) are ineffective as a foundation for explanatory theories. Similarly, these same indices have not permitted the construction of accurate predictive models for any except the most simple social situations. As an alternative, a sort of coarse methodological individualism has thus been invoked. Even though social phenomena have come to be regarded as something other than precisely definable observational units (e.g. Gale 1972c; Georgescu-Roegen 1971), the pressure for immediate solutions to social problems has led researchers to employ highly disaggregated indicators of individual behaviour in the hope that they will lead to an understanding of small-scale social interactions. This, for example, has been the basis of the work of Cyert and March (1963), Katona (1951) and Orcutt *et al.* (1961) in economics as well as a wide variety of mobility studies in sociology (e.g. White 1970).

The argument for the use of micro-level data in the investigation of residential mobility goes well beyond the simple invocation of a reductionist principle. First, the kinds of research questions which are asked often contain presuppositions about dispositional behaviour and unless these macro-level data (say, of population aggregates) represent homogeneous units, inferences consistent with these presuppositions will be inaccurate. Secondly, the current availability of alternative sources of data on the residential behaviour of individuals obviates the usual claim for the efficacy of aggregate data. Data do not simply exist; they are collected with particular ends in mind. By relying on ecological theories of behaviour, data were in effect created for the expressed purpose of supporting and evaluating those theories. Finally, the level of explanation and prediction of models which employ ecolgical data has been so poor as to make the continued use of such theories dubious.

Another way of looking at this same issue is in terms of the distinction between black-box (or phenomenological) and translucid-box (or representational) models. Black-box models may be represented as macro-level models of data wherein descriptive mathematical functions are used to relate inputs to outputs in aggregate systems (Turner 1967, 240). However, 'a black-box theory may provide a logically satisfactory explanation and prediction of a set of data, in the sense of their *derivation* from the theory and specific information. But it will fail to provide what the scientist usually calls an interpretation of the same data' (Bunge 1964, 248). A translucid-box approach attempts to fill in this gap by providing not only the basis for predictions, but also an interpretative foundation which permits an investigator to focus on the interrelationships, mechanisms and contingent interactions of the elements of the system. In short, the aim is to exploit the low-level descriptive properties of certain classes of models by constructing representations of complex systems in which the classificatory procedures, measurements, relationships, and mechanisms of change are all visualizable functions of the *individual properties* of the observable units. Clearly, at the early stages of research, this then provides a basis for developing primitive (e.g. relational) explanatory models.

What mathematical form might a representation model of migration take? In several recent papers (Gale 1971, 1972d, 1973a; Olsson and Gale 1968) it has been noted that the conditions of specificity and identifiability in models of social behaviour are most easily provided by the usual properties of multi-way contingency tables and their probabilistic counterparts. Similar conclusions have also been presented by Fisher (1960), Ginsberg (1971), Goodman (1962), MacFarland (1970), Moore (1972), Nordbotten

(1970), Spilerman (1970) and others in somewhat different contexts. In particular, the following conditions (relating particularly to migration behaviour) were seen as providing grounds for this choice: (a) migration is a function of individual decisions and a detailed, classificatory model is initially required to represent that pattern of residence changes; (b) social and locational data often yield only nominal measurement scales; (c) residence change decisions are themselves functions of a multitude of social and psychological conditions (where each of the influences on the individual decision-maker can, in turn, be conceived of as a conditional predicate in a contingency-type model); (d) in general, the relationship of each of these contingent factors in the decision process changes over time; (e) the information represented is usually incomplete and uncertain; and (f) an intercomparable set of measures is required for examining the properties of systems of different sizes. In short, the conditions suggest that a family of stochastic models of the type which have earlier been called K^N models (Gale 1972d, 1973a) provides a well-grounded characterization of a general model for representing the migration process. The K^N model is a two-valued, truth-functional model (Gale 1972d).

Clearly, the use of contingency tables is a standard research procedure. Properties of individual units are identified, classifications are defined, and frequency tables computed. What is perhaps unusual in the present treatment is the possibility of including spatial and temporal predicates, and the interpretation of the normalized frequencies as conditional probabilities, but even these are conceptually simple extensions. It is, however, the relationship of these tables to the epistemological framework of what has been called the patternist model of explanation theory which provides insights into the inferential and theoretical power to be gained (Gale 1973a; Gale and Katzman 1972).

The representational-patternist approach to model building in the social sciences emphasizes the organization and interpretation of disaggregated data so as to make clear the internal structure and mechanisms of change of social phenomena. Detailed descriptions of the interconnections within systems are provided in such a manner that explanations may be obtained by relating specific conditions to other (perhaps more general) patterns. Given these considerations, the methodological advantages of a contingency table formulation should be readily apparent. Micro-level observations of the social system may be easily tabulated, and, when temporal and spatial predicates are included, descriptions of the relationships between individuals and groups as well as the mechanisms of change are provided as sets of intercomparable probability measures. These measures, moreover, may be treated alternatively as state descriptions or as evolutionary laws (Gale 1971). By further synthesizing these observational statements and testing for specific conditions (such as interaction among states and stationarity) more condensed explanatory propositions can be advanced. As Goodman (1962, 1965, 1969, 1971) and others (e.g. Fienberg 1970; Madden and Ashby 1972) have demonstrated, eventually these syntheses can provide the foundation of a general understanding of a pattern of interrelationships. Finally, the results of this inferential process can be integrated with more general information (such as changes in the physical and economic structure of the overall community) in order to provide interpretative explanations.

Model building

Even if multi-way contingency tables are taken as reasonable models for representing the properties of residential relocation data, this nevertheless leaves unanswered a number of problems relating to what is meant by building a model, M, such that $M \equiv M_T \equiv M_D$ within this framework. Contingency tables are simply a means for representing certain *ceteris paribus* and measurement conditions; the association between the properties of the model and the analogous properties of theoretical models (say, as provided by an application of the methods outlined by Goodman) is left unspecified.

Recalling the previous discussion of the relationship between theories and models, it needs to be demonstrated, first, that current theories of residential mobility can be stated in terms such that they can be compared and evaluated with K^N models of data and, second, that the range of questions for which the theory is developed can be answered in terms of the given model form. The first point has been examined in several recent papers (Gale 1972d, 1973a; Ginsberg 1971, 1972a, b; Moore 1972) and, at least for the range of theories investigated, it was shown that the K^N model could be used as a quite general model for expressing ideas and information on residential mobility. It remains to describe the nature of the questions which arise in this same context and to investigate the connections among models of theories and models of data in the process of model building.

Drawing in part from Suppes' (1962) earlier work, it seems appropriate to begin by considering the process of model building in terms of a hierarchy of questions which can be answered by examining associated model forms. Under a given language, this results in a hierarchy which may be illustrated as follows:

(I) $\qquad\qquad M$

(II) $\qquad M_T$ ---------- M_D

(III) $\qquad M_{T_\mu}$ ---------- M_{D_μ}

(IV) $\qquad M_{T_\sigma}$ ---------- M_{D_σ}

As before, M is a general model which expresses both properties of a theory as well as properties of data, M_T is a model of a theory, and M_D is a model of observations (or model of data): M_{T_μ} and M_{D_μ} are the models of measurement, classification and definition associated (respectively) with a model of a theory and a model of data; M_{T_σ} and M_{D_σ} are the corresponding models of *ceteris paribus* conditions.

Associated with each of these classes of models are sets of questions which they can treat. In the present context, these include:

(I) expressing empirically grounded conceptions of the residential mobility process (e.g. causal theories);
(II) questions of homogeneity, stationarity and independence;
(III) questions of classification, definition and measurement scales;
(IV) expressing grounded conceptions of relationships among properties of the data (e.g. *ceteris paribus* conditions).

Note that none of these classes of models can be developed independently of any other class. Each model is constructed with a view not only toward properties of models on the same level, but also in terms of what is done on the other levels of the hierarchy. *Ceteris paribus* conditions are invoked, for example, because it is believed that a particular theory is appropriate, because it is believed that certain properties will give an accurate picture of any underlying interactions or stationarities, and because reasonable measurement and classifications procedures can be provided for those properties. Of course, there are also similar relationships among all the other classes of models.

Consider now the translation of this abstract conceptualization of questions into the specific questions of describing and evaluating population changes in local areas. Corresponding to the classification described above (and omitting questions of level I since there are no grounded theories as yet), the following issues can be identified as being relevant:

(IIa) Critical to any long-run efforts to improve forecasts of change is the development of a better understanding of the nature of the temporal homogeneity of movement processes. Existing models have usually used the simplest assumptions regarding stationarity (as in Wolfe's 1967 study, for example, which assumes the simple stationarity of Markov chains to describe the condition ageing of structures). At the outset, many questions concerning time homogeneity may be phrased in an empirical form and the structure developed should be responsive to these questions. (See Gale 1972e for a further discussion of the problem of stationarity.)

(IIb) In a broader sense, time homogeneity is part of a general concept of parameter independence and dependence. Most existing studies assume that the probability of changing condition class of a housing unit depends only on the attributes of the dwelling and not on the characteristics of, for example, the occupant household. Similarly, the urban simulation model developed by the National Bureau of Economic Research (1971) assumes that the propensity to move is purely a function of the attributes of the household and is independent of a large segment of its occupancy history, the type of dwelling it occupies, and so on. For a comprehensive picture which can yield suitable interpretations, the analytical structure constructed to examine neighbourhood change should thus be able to deal with such questions concerning the independence of different sets of specific attributes.

(III) The modelling framework should obviously be designed so as to be consistent with the types of data that can reasonably be expected to be available within the next few years. It may be expected, for example, that such data will contain a considerable amount of discrete, qualitative information, that they will permit the identification of individual households and dwellings in successive data files, and that these files will continue to be constructed at regular time intervals rather than be of a continuous nature.

(IV) The model should permit detailed questions to be asked regarding the structure of change in small areas as this relates to a wide range of housing and household characteristics, e.g. movers and non-movers, rented and owned, single and multiple family, etc. Note that, because our understanding of the mobility process is substantially incomplete, this class of questions is particularly important at the early stages of research. For example, many of the questions relating to change in residential patterns which arise in the context of level II have been expressed solely in terms of the differential characteristics of inmigrants and outmigrants for a given area; however, in many cases, the demographic, economic and social changes experienced by non-movers also form a major component of those changes of interest (witness, for example, the changes experienced by an ageing suburb characterized by low mobility).

These are the principal kinds of questions which are of current concern in the development of a model of residential change. From the discussion two points should be clear. First, although many types of models can treat questions of class IV, the questions in class III require a formal model which is able to handle qualitative, discrete and contingent data in such a way as to preserve a great deal of information. Secondly, given the nature of these data, the model must also be capable of permitting hypotheses related to the questions of class II to be tested; that is, it must allow inferences to be made which relate to questions of homogeneity and independence in multi-variate, contigent data. The argument of the preceding section has suggested that the K^N (or multi-way contingency table) model provides a reasonable model for such data; moreover, it was also pointed out that methods are currently available for testing hypotheses related to homogeneity and independence. Within the context of the classes of questions which have been outlined (i.e. II, III and IV), it thus appears that we can employ this same model as a framework for answering the kinds of questions which arise in the study of residential mobility.

As an illustration of these points, consider the problem of building a model of residential change, say, with the K^N model as a foundation. In terms of a model of data, M_D, this usually involves only the expression of frequencies of occurrences of individuals in prespecified categories and the theory explicit in the model refers only to the *ceteris paribus* assumptions and the measurement procedures employed; of course, there is always some general theory implicit in its extension. Similarly, models of theories, while explicitly representing potential answers to questions, also implicitly specify a form of the data for the model.

For example, Hägerstrand's (1967a, b) rather simplified model of residential change begins with a population distributed at discrete locations on a finite plane. Each of the locations (or cells) is regarded as connected, i.e. in that information (or people or goods) can flow between all of them; the extent of the connections between the cells is derived from disaggregated observations on the actual flows. Hägerstrand designates these patterns of individual behaviour as *private information fields*: given some point (x, y) as the origin, for example, the private information field indicates the number of contacts (telephone calls, migrations, etc.) each person at (x, y) has with every point on the plane. Clearly, for each individual and for each purpose, the pattern of shopping behaviour is not likely to be the same as for recreational movements, residence changes or telephone communications. Spatial anisotropies further distort the patterns.

For Hägerstrand, the synthesis of this diversity (i.e. the model-building activity) is provided by defining a mean or composite information field (MIF). The construction of the MIF has already been described on a number of occasions (Hägerstrand 1967a, 179-89; 1967b; Marble and Nystuen 1963; Morrill and Pitts 1967). Briefly, it involves recording the observed contacts between all pairs of locations in the space (in some small interval of time, $t_r - t_{r-1}$) and synthesizing or averaging – what Hägerstrand terms 'the technique of centering' (Hägerstrand 1967a, 179-89) – these interrelationships, subject to the following (theoretical) constraints: (a) the population is assumed to be uniformly distributed over discrete locations on a finite plane; (b) the average frequency of contact between any two locations is the same for all locations separated by an equal distance (i.e.

the contact array is symmetric); (c) the expected frequency of contact is higher for nearer locations than for more distant ones; and (d) the contact array is constant over time. These constraints (or conditions) are, of course, not random assumptions; investigations of several types of contacts have suggested that (a) to (d) are useful inductive generalizations. And while there has not as yet been enough detailed empirical research to verify these relationships, they nonetheless also reflect the current state of much of human interaction theory.

In general, the MIF for any spatial process is defined by a similar set of frequencies, based on observed contacts, and depicted on a 5 x 5 grid. The neighbourhood effect – the notion that the frequency of contact is higher for physically adjacent cells and that only a 5 x 5 grid is required to express all the relationships – is regarded as an inductive theoretical consequence of these observations. Moreover, since the frequencies of both temporal and spatial contacts are averaged, the same 5 x 5 grid applies to every location (origin) on the plane, at each point in time. In this respect, the MIF is treated as if it were an isotropic operator – as if it represented a temporally as well as a spatially homogeneous process.

Hägerstrand's formulation is a good example of what has here been called a model of a theory, but a model which retains certain very important properties of a model of data which is constructed from the observable properties of the interacting phenomena. It explicitly represents an (albeit simplified) potential answer to a set of questions about residential mobility, but at the same time it is designed with properties of the data in mind. This has been discussed in a recent paper (Gale 1972d) in which it was pointed out that Hägerstrand's model is really a special case of the general K^N design and that the theoretical conjectures within it could be quite easily tested with available methods.

A number of very important problems nevertheless remain with respect to the development of models of residential change. To a certain extent, the requisites of data collection and measurement imply the use of something on the order of the K^N model as a model of data for the description of migration phenomena. Similarly, it appears that models of theories can be developed in correspondence with the properties of this same formal model. As was noted previously, however, even the procedures for analysing properties of generalized contingency tables are only partially specified (i.e. for answering the kinds of questions described in category II). It is also an open question as to the circumstances under which we would expect M_T to converge to M_D (and vice versa); a reasonable approach might be to apply functional analysis (e.g. fixed point theorems) to determine the kinds of measures and classificatory schema which would result in reasonable contraction mappings (e.g. Hewitt and Stromberg 1965, 78). In Körner's terms (1969, 84) this implies that 'the conditions which any suitable identification has to fulfill will depend on the theory in question, as well as the context in which the theory is employed'. Perhaps most importantly, however, it is in terms of giving answers to questions of class I (which includes such problems as identifying the causal structure of the residential mobility process and the possible consequences of alternative policy actions) that our abilities are most severely limited. For example, the basic interrelations between the various elements of the urban system are so poorly understood that we can seldom do more than make educated guesses as to the outcomes of different actions; the theories we possess are so inadequately grounded in empirical evidence that they inspire little confidence as the basis for either explanations or predictions. Even the methods of analysis appropriate to questions of this type are only now being developed (e.g. Goodman 1972).

Although at the present time it cannot be demonstrated that cross-classification models and their associated evaluation procedures provide the best framework for modelling the process of residential mobility, it may be maintained that they are sufficient. Not only is this a reasonable formal basis for expressing the properties of models of residential movement data, but, at least for several very important classes of questions, methods for testing various classes of hypotheses are currently available. The model is thus not a model in the usual social scientific sense, but rather it is a framework for asking and answering questions which can lead to such models; it is, in effect, a model of data from which a general model of residential mobility can be synthesized.

Conclusions

At the beginning of a particular line of scientific inquiry, as in the case of research on residential mobility, the issue is not so much one of, *a priori*, developing the *right* (i.e. verified or corroborated) model. Our understanding is quite weak and there is no reason to expect that our intuitions will lead immediately to good theoretical models. Similarly, we cannot expect data collection procedures to result in clearly specified explanatory and predictive models. Without an explicit recognition of the complementarity between all classes of the hierarchy of models, particularly between models of theories and models of data, we probably will never obtain the desired results. What is required is an understanding of the kinds of theories implicit in each model and the relationships between all these classes of models.

These programmitic conclusions have, however, been based on several assumptions about the ontology of observables and the structure of descriptive and normative inference. The assumption that L is a two-valued, truth-functional language, for example, explicitly leads to the choice of a rather limited set of descriptive models and inference procedures: the residential categorization of the K^N model is Boolean as are all the other related classification procedures. Similarly, the truth-functional property ensures that the theories are constructed only in terms of existential qualities rather than the kinds of external prescriptive judgements which have been shown (Arrow 1966 and others) to be required in evaluating questions about social welfare (Gale 1972a, b, c). The conclusion thus goes beyond the suggestion that research on residential change should embody the principles discussed in this paper. If we wish to construct models which not only lead to valid inferences (in the classical sense), we must also investigate those models which, under alternative languages, can lead to far richer insights into existing questions and, perhaps, answers to whole new classes of questions as well.

Acknowledgements

This paper was supported by the National Institute of Mental Health, PHS Research Grant No. 1 R0e MH20403-01 from the Center for Metropolitan Studies and the Research Committee of Northwestern University. Professors Eric G. Moore and Thomas Morin commented on the first draft of this paper.

References

Åqvist, L. (1965) *A new approach to the logic of interrogatives. Part I: Analysis.* Uppsala.

Åqvist, L. (1972) On the analysis and logic of questions, in Olson, R. E. and Paul, A. M. (eds.) *Contemporary philosophy in Scandinavia.* Baltimore.

Arrow, K. J. (1966) *Social choice and individual values* (2nd edn). New York.

Belnap, N. D. (1963) *An analysis of questions.* Santa Monica.

Bunge, M. (1964) Phenomenological theories, in Bunge, M. (ed.) *Critical approach to science and philosophy*, 234–54. Glencoe.

Chorley, R. J. (1964) Geography and analogue theory. *Ann. Assoc. Am. Geogr.* 54, 127–37.

Conant, R. L. and Ashby, W. R. (1970) Every good regulator of a system must be a model of that system. *Int. J. Systems Sci.* 1, 89–97.

Cyert, R. M. and March, J. G. (1963) *A behavioral theory of the firm.* Englewood Cliffs.

Fienberg, S. (1970) The analysis of multi-dimensional contingency tables. *Ecol.* 51, 419–33.

Fisher, F. M. (1960) On the analysis of history and the interdependence of the social sciences. *Phil. Sci.* 27, 147–58.

Gale, S. (1969) *Probability and interaction: a stochastic approach to intraregional mobility.* Unpublished thesis, Univ. of Michigan.

Gale, S. (1971) *Evolutionary laws in the social sciences.* Paper presented at the 4th Internat. Congr. on Logic, Methodology and Phil. Sci. Bucharest.

Gale, S. (1972a) On the heterodoxy of explanation: a review of David Harvey's *Explanation in geography. Geogr. Anal.* 4, 285–322.

Gale, S. (1972b) Remarks on the foundations of locational decision-making. *Antipode* 4, 41–79.

Gale, S. (1972c) Inexactness, fuzzy sets, and the foundations of behavioral geography. *Geogr. Anal.* 337–49.

Gale, S. (1972d) Some formal properties of Hägerstrand's model of spatial interaction. *J. Reg. Sci.* 199–217.

Gale, S. (1972e) Stochastic stationarity and the analysis of geographic mobility, in Adams, W. P. and Helleiner, F. M. *Internat. Geogr., 1972,* 901–4. Toronto.

Gale, S. (1973a) Explanation theory and models of migration. *Econ. Geogr.* 49, 257–74.

Gale, S. (1973b) *A resolution of the regionalization problem and its implications for urban political geography and distributive justice.* Mimeo., Dept. of Geography, Northwestern Univ.

Gale, S. and Katzman, D. M. (1972) Black communities: a program for inter-disciplinary research, in Rose, H. (ed.) *Geography of the ghetto: perceptions, problems, and alternatives,* 60–86. De Kalb.

Georgescu-Roegen, N. (1971) *The entropy law and the economic process.* Cambridge, Mass.

Ginsberg, R. B. (1971) Semi-Markov processes and mobility. *J. Math. Soc.* 1, 233–63.

Ginsberg, R. B. (1972a) Critique of probabilistic models: application of the Markov model to migration. *J. Math. Soc.* 2.

Ginsberg, R. B. (1972b) Incorporating causal structure and exogenous information with probabilistic models: with special reference to choice, gravity, migration and Markov chains. *J. Math. Soc.* 2.

Goodman, L. A. (1962) Statistical methods for analyzing processes of change. *Am. J. Sociol.* 68, 57–78.

Goodman, L. A. (1965) On the statistical analysis of mobility tables. *Am. J. Sociol.* 70, 564–85.

Goodman, L. A. (1969) How to ransack social mobility tables and other kinds of cross-classification tables. *Am. J. Sociol.* 75, 1–40.

Goodman, L. A. (1971) The analysis of multidimensional contingency tables: stepwise procedures and direct estimation methods for building models for multiple classifications. *Technometrics* 13, 33–61.

Goodman, L. A. (1972) A modified multiple regression approach to the analysis of dichotomous variables. *Am. Sociol. Rev.* 37, 38–46.

Hägerstrand, T. (1967a) *Innovation diffusion as a spatial process* (transl. A. Pred). Chicago.

Hägerstrand, T. (1967b) A Monte Carlo approach to diffusion, in Garrison, W. L. and Marble, D. F. (eds.) *Quantitative geography,* Part I, 1–32. Evanston.

Hewitt, E. and Stromberg, K. (1965) *Real and abstract analysis.* New York.

Katona, G. (1951) *Psychological analysis of economic behavior.* New York.

Körner, S. (1969) *What is philosophy?* London.

MacFarland, D. D. (1970) Intra-generational social mobility as a Markov process: including a time stationary Markovian model that explains observed declines in mobility rates over time. *Am. Sociol. Rev.* 35, 463–76.

McGinnis, R. (1968) A stochastic model of social mobility. *Am. Sociol. Rev.* 33, 712–22.

Madden, R. F. and Ashby, W. R. (1972) The identification of many-dimensional relations. *Internat. J. Syst. Sci.* 3, 343–56.

Marble, D. F. and Nystuen, J. D. (1963) An approach to the direct measurement of community mean information fields. *Pap., Reg. Sci. Assoc.* 11, 99–108.

Mitroff, I., Betz, F. and Mason, R. O. (1970) A mathematical model of Churchmanian inquiring systems with special reference to Popper's measures for the 'Severity of Scientific Tests'. *Theory and decision* 1, 155–78.

Moore, E. G. (1972) *Residential mobility in the city.* Assoc. Am. Geogr. Commis. Coll. Geogr., Resource Pap. No. 13. Washington.

Moore, E. G. and Gale, S. (1973) *Comments on models of occupancy patterns and neighborhood change.* Working Pap. No. 1, Progr. of Res. on Intra-metropolitan Planning Problems. Evanston.

Morrill, R. L. and Pitts, F. R. (1967) Marriage, migration and the mean information field: a study in uniqueness and generality. *Ann. Assoc. Am. Geogr.* 57, 401–22.

Murakami, Y. (1968) *Logic and social choice.* London.

Nordbotten, S. (1970) Individual data files and their utilization in socio-demographic model building in the Norwegian Central Bureau of Statistics. *Rev. Internat. Stat. Inst.* 38, 193–201.

Olsson, G. (1969) Inference problems in locational analysis, in Cox, K. R. and Golledge, R. G. *Behavioral problems in geography: a symposium.* Evanston.

Olsson, G. (1970) Logics and social engineering. *Geogr. Anal.* 2, 361–75.

Olsson, G. and Gale, S. (1968) Spatial theory and human behavior. *Pap., Reg. Sci. Assoc.* 21, 229–42, 14–34.

Orcutt, G. H. *et al.* (1961) *Microanalysis of socioeconomic systems: a simulation study.* New York.

Pörn, I. (1971) *Elements of social analysis.* Filosofiska Studier, No. 10, Uppsala Univ.

Prior, M. and Prior, A. N. (1955) Erotetic logic. *Phil. Rev.* 64, 43–59.

Przelecki, M. (1969) *The logic of empirical theories.* London.

Rescher, N. (1970) *Scientific explanation.* New York.

Rossi, P. (1955) *Why families move.* Glencoe.

Smith, W. F. (1964) A review of the filtering controversy, in *Filtering and neighborhood change,* chapter 1. Res. Rep. No. 24, Center for Real Estate and Urban Economics, Univ. of California, Berkeley.

Smith, W. F. (1970) *Housing: the social and economic elements.* Berkeley.

Spilerman, S. (1970) *The analysis of mobility processes by the introduction of independent variables into a Markov chain.* Discussion Pap., Inst. for Res. on Poverty. Madison.

Suppes, P. (1959) Measurement, empirical meaningfulness, and three-valued logic, in Churchman, C. W. and Ratoosh, P. (eds.) *Measurement: definitions and theories,* 129–43. New York.

Suppes, P. (1960) A comparison of the meaning and uses of models in mathematics and the social sciences. *Synthese* 12, 287–301.

Suppes, P. (1962) Models of data, in Nagel, E., Suppes, P. and Tarski, A. (eds.) *Logic, Methodology and philosophy of science: proceedings of the 1960 International Congress,* 252–61. Stanford.

Suppes, P. (1965) Logics appropriate to empirical theories, in Addison, J. W., Henkin, L. and Tarski, A. (eds.) *Theory of models,* 364–75. Amsterdam.

Suszko, R. (1965) Formal logic and the development of knowledge, in Lakotos, I. and Musgrave, A. (eds.) *Problems in the philosophy of science,* Vol. 3, 210–22. Amsterdam.

Thernstrom, S. and Knights, P. R. (1970) Men in motion: some data and speculations about population mobility in nineteenth century America. *J. Interdisciplinary Hist.* 1, 7–35.

Turner, M. B. (1967) *Philosophy and the science of behavior.* New York.

von Wright, G. H. (1971) *Explanation and understanding.* Ithaca.

White, H. C. (1970) *Chains of opportunity,* Cambridge, Mass.

Zadeh, L. A. (1972) *Outline of a new approach to the analysis of complex systems and decision processes.* Memo. No. ERL M342, Electronics Res. Labor., Univ. of California. Berkeley.

6 Housing and the geographical mobility of labour in England and Wales: some theoretical considerations

J. H. Johnson, J. Salt, and P. A. Wood

Moves of home and moves of job: the general background

Of the various types of population mobility in England and Wales, movements involving both a permanent change of residence and a permanent change of job are particularly important because of their implications for regional contrasts in population growth and economic activity. In this paper, movement of this kind will be called labour migration. Unfortunately there is little firm information about the number of such moves. The 1966 census recorded over 5 million residential moves in Britain during the year before the enumeration; and during the five years from 1961 to 1966 the number was 16 million, virtually one-third of the total population (HMSO 1969). But many of these moves were made for reasons unconnected with employment, and many movers must have changed homes more than once. Even less is known of the number of people who change jobs in any given year, although a Ministry of Labour estimate in 1966 suggested that over 8 million people in Britain change their employer every year (Ministry of Labour 1966, 379). Again, as some individuals will have changed more than once, the figure does not represent 8 million different people, but in relation to a total labour force of 25 million it at least permits the conclusion that a remarkable volume of job-changing does take place. Confirmation of this estimate comes from an OECD report on labour mobility made in 1965, which estimated a labour turnover of about 30 to 40% per annum (OECD 1965, 51).

Many of these moves of homes or jobs were independent of one another, since they took place over a limited distance, when a move of job did not necessarily demand a change of home or vice versa. One-half of the residential moves recorded in the census were within the same local authority area; and, similarly a sample study showed that almost 80% of residential moves were of less than ten miles (Harris and Clausen 1967, 12). Nevertheless the absolute number of people moving longer distances is large; between 1961 and 1966, for example, gross interregional movement was over 2 million people and it seems reasonable to think that many of the longer moves were stimulated by job reasons. For example, for migrants who moved over ten miles, the most frequent reason for moving was because of a job, and the proportion moving for this reason increased with distance (Harris and Clausen 1967, 17).

These longer-distance movements have implications for national economic and social policy, reflected in the somewhat disjointed series of measures adopted by government and employers to influence the movement of population. The 'work to the workers' policy, for instance, has attempted to stem the flow of labour from the depressed areas (Richardson and West 1964) with an emphasis more recently on steering industry to growth zones within development areas. These policies have been complemented by attempts to assist the geographical movement of labour to those areas where it is needed. Subsidies from both national and local government are available for families moving to live and work in the new and overspill towns through the Industrial Selection Scheme (Ruddy 1969). In addition, the Department of Employment operates three adult transfer schemes for which grants and allowances are available to cover travel costs and to assist with house sale and purchase. Numbers aided by these schemes are few in comparison with the total amount of labour mobility: currently the total number of beneficiaries is only about 7,500 per annum, the majority being aided by the Resettlement Transfer Scheme which is designed to help unemployed workers.

Policies to assist the geographical mobility of labour are also operated by individual employers. The growth of corporate organizations with spatially dispersed production and administrative units frequently leads to transference of labour within the firm from one location to another. In such cases the costs of mobility are usually borne by the company. Although executive grades are most affected by these moves, this is not always the case. Thus, for instance, the National Coal Board will assist the movement of all its workers from pits that are closing to areas where coal production is still expanding. Between 1962 and 1970 over 14,000 miners were moved between coalfields under official NCB schemes. Other employers will often arrange the transfer of skilled workers to a new locality in order to facilitate the commencement of production when a new factory is being opened (Salt 1967, 256).

Despite the existence of these policies and the high level of mobility in general, it is clear that major barriers to labour migration remain. The sheer money costs involved, in terms of fares and removal expenses of various kinds, probably prevent movement in many cases. Distance and social disruption undoubtedly deter many would-be movers for whom community and family ties are too strong to be easily broken. Lack of information about job opportunities in other areas also results in stability rather than movement.

Housing is often assumed to act as one of the most important barriers to population mobility. A seminar on manpower policy claimed that in Britain '. . . the principal obstacle to geographic mobility is generally agreed to be the shortage of suitable houses' (OECD 1964, 64). A similar comment was expressed by the Confederation of British Industries in 1968 on '. . . the general discouragement of movement resulting from current housing policy' (CBI 1968, 11). A situation was created in which the shortage and price structure of housing aggravate the shortage of skilled and trainable labour by deterring movement and thus contributing to high labour costs. A pool of housing at a wide range of price levels was regarded as an essential prerequisite to increased mobility and an essential to the sound growth of the economy. Similar observations have been made by others (Stone 1970, 280; HMSO 1966).

Despite unanimity of opinion on the connections between housing and labour mobility, the actual relationship is far from clear and the evidence conflicting (Cullingworth 1969, 67). A popular view is that owner-occupied homes allow more labour mobility, and that publicly-owned and rent-controlled housing is associated with much less movement of population. When long-distance moves between the broader regions of the country are distinguished from local intra-urban moves some evidence seems to emerge that home-ownership facilitates interregional migration, that the inhabitants of local authority houses have a low interregional migration rate, and that those people who live in privately-rented accommodation are more commonly involved in short-distance moves (Willis 1967; 1968, 31). At the same time home-ownership may act as a further deterrent to movement among those people who have other social and economic characteristics which inhibit migration in any case.

What does emerge clearly is that the actual situation is much more complicated than can be explained by a simple correlation of mobility with any one factor. Housing is a complex phenomenon when regional differences in the housing market, the preferences of various social classes and their differential accessibility to housing finance are all considered. Movements of population are equally complex when they are disaggregated to reveal the different socioeconomic and demographic attributes of the people involved, the distances moved and the varying characteristics of origin and destination areas. Hence, even if it were possible to demonstrate some kind of statistical association between housing and labour mobility, it would not follow that the two phenomena are directly connected. It may be, for example, that the people who are attracted to new owner-occupied housing are largely selected by their financial prospects and family structure and would tend to be mobile anyway, whatever the nature of their housing. Similarly, the average resident in local authority housing estates may be less inclined to move long distances to a new job for reasons which have little to do with accommodation.

The construction of a theoretical framework

As a result of these complexities there is a need for more detailed empirical investigation into the association between the geographical mobility of labour and the housing characteristics of migrants. Much of the evidence at present available is derived from general household surveys in which only a small proportion of the respondents were migrants (Donnison *et al.* 1961; Gray and Russell 1962; Cullingworth 1965; Woolf 1967). There have been no studies directly concerned with the housing characteristics of migrants, nor is there any clear view of the key relationships between housing and labour mobility. An essential preliminary for any research in this field is the construction of a theoretical framework to serve as a basis for the development of hypotheses. The remainder of this paper presents a tentative outline for such a framework by weaving together some of the relevant strands that appear in the separate literatures on labour migration and housing to form a coherent pattern which has particular reference to conditions in England and Wales.

We have defined labour migration as involving the simultaneous change of employment and of home. This particular kind of population movement is assumed for simplicity to be largely motivated by the attraction of a new job or at least conditional upon the availability of suitable employment in the destination area. Hence it can be interpreted as part of the labour market mechanism which matches the supply and demand for particular occupation groups, each with its own short-term elasticity of supply. These elasticities are low for occupational categories which involve long periods of training and are high for unskilled and semi-skilled jobs. Thus the occupational structure of the workforce is determined by 'barriers' to movement between different occupational categories, largely based upon training and formal admission requirements to certain occupations. These barriers are relatively fixed, in so far as early education, training and skill strongly determines the subsequent role of an individual in the labour force (Hunter and Reid 1968, 93).

Second only to the degree of training required, the most universally important barrier to the ready attraction of suitable numbers of workers to a point of employment demand is the geographical location of this demand in relation to sources of supply. Conversely, from the point of view of the individual worker, the location of his residence also limits his choice of job. The location of job opportunities and of the places of residence are mutually linked in space by the commuting 'tolerances' of workers, given the location of workplaces in centralized nodes. In the same way, given the location of residence, the workers in a household seek employment opportunities over an area again defined in terms of commuting tolerance.

It may be easier for many workers to move to a similar job in a different local labour market area (thus producing labour migration) than to change their occupations of skill groups in the same local labour market. Hence from the point of view of increasing the flexibility of the national economy through providing appropriate labour supply conditions, a knowledge of the constraints on the locational readjustment of the labour force is as important as an understanding of the educational and training requirements of the workforce. Access to housing probably forms one of a number of key factors in determining the mobility of workers between different geographically defined labour market areas.

It has been argued that the concept of the local labour market is no longer useful because of increased personal mobility and the willingness of people to travel longer distances in order to obtain a satisfactory residential environment (Cullingworth 1969, 14). In the British context this argument has most force in and around Greater London and the larger conurbations, since here local labour markets are grouped tightly together and general statements about the journey to work conceal many counter-flows in the daily pattern of movement. On the other hand sample studies of some more independent local labour markets suggest that the concept still has validity (Johnson *et al.* n.d.).[1] In addition, if the difficult problems of delimiting local labour markets on a comparable basis throughout England and Wales is set aside, it remains true that this is the scale at which the interaction of housing characteristics and the geographical mobility of labour can be most reasonably studied. Whatever the validity of the local labour market concept, however, the area over which an individual household operates without moving home is clearly related to the journey-to-work distances which the members of that household find acceptable. It thus seems apparent that the definition of labour market areas needs to be more closely associated with the behaviour of particular social and occupational groups.

---

[1] Analyses of the changes of home of all migrants were undertaken in the preparation of the sample of labour migrants interviewed in a housing and labour migration study.

Occupational and spatial mobility

The close interdependence of occupational and spatial barriers in the free allocation of workers to jobs has been emphasized, since one cannot be considered without reference to the other. Because of this there are probably strong contrasts in the motivation and behaviour of labour migrants from different occupational groups and from different types of places (classified by their location and by their socioeconomic attributes). For example, a survey of 550 labour migrant households in 4 different labour market areas in England during 1970–1[2] indicated the high degree of participation in this type of move by the non-manual occupation groups, especially those people in managerial and professional occupations (Johnson *et al.* n.d.). Table 6.1 shows this bias very clearly. The motivations for moving

Table 6.1

Summary statistics of labour migrant sample according to socioeconomic groups

	1–4 Professional and managerial	5–7 Other non-manual	8–9 Skilled manual	10–11 Semi-skilled and unskilled	18–20 Students and unemployed
Percentage of total occupied population in England and Wales	14	20	28	20	9
Percentage of total labour migrants in sample of 4 towns, 1970–1	35	30	12	6	12
Percentage of those in sample moving primarily for reasons of employment	44	30	10	3	14
Percentage of those in sample moving primarily for 'other' (housing and personal) reasons	26	29	15	9	10

also showed marked socioeconomic contrasts. Those moving primarily for reasons associated with employment changes included 44% in professional and managerial jobs (over three times their national representation) and 30% in other non-manual groups. The smaller proportions of manual

[2] This survey was carried out amongst households which had moved into High Wycombe, Chatham, Northampton and Huddersfield during the year before November 1971.

workers engaged in a simultaneous change of home and workplace were more likely to have moved for other reasons, including the search for better housing and for social reasons (such as moving back to their home town). Between the extremes of socioeconomic status, the intermediate groups of non-manual and skilled manual workers show more mixed patterns of motivation.

The interdependence of occupational and spatial mobility can be illustrated by considering the factors influencing potential labour migrants. People are attached to particular locations partly because they have a job there, but also because the social and economic costs of movement elsewhere (assessed in the broadest terms) may be too great in relation to the likely returns they can perceive. As well as assessing the gains to be made by moving to a new job in a different area, the cost of housing there and the expense of moving, potential migrants may also be attached to the particular facilities offered by their present house, they may enjoy their social contacts in an area and they may value local amenities. At the same time they have imperfect knowledge of the possibilities of obtaining similar facilities elsewhere. Thus, even if there are definite job opportunities elsewhere, potential labour migrants make a calculation of the comparative net advantage to be derived from either staying in an environment which they know or moving to an alternative which will be a relatively long distance away, and where they are unlikely to have detailed information about the housing market. In our 1970–1 survey of labour migrant households, 70% of households indicated that they had experienced appreciable difficulties in moving, in spite of the fact that in this survey the households questioned had already overcome these problems. About half of the problems mentioned involved the acquisition of accommodation (including the finding of temporary housing), while another 40% were concerned with the personal and family upheavals of long-distance moves. Only 5% found difficulties with their jobs once the move had been made.

Information about certain kinds of job opportunities may also be localized in character, so that potential migrants may be unaware of employment possibilities in other places. In addition, many types of jobs are fairly ubiquitously available (at least in a condition of rising demand) and people in these occupations have little stimulus to move to another town. High-level managerial and professional employment, on the other hand, is often found only in large cities, while some highly skilled manual or technical workers may be able to find suitable work only in certain specialized industrial regions. Generally speaking, large urban-industrial centres offer greater opportunities than smaller centres for all types of worker to change employment without having to migrate elsewhere.

In extreme cases the various factors influencing the mobility of a particular socioeconomic group tend to combine to produce a pull in one particular

direction. More highly educated workers, for example, are less attached to
particular places by social ties. They are better informed about employment
opportunities and the jobs that they seek are, in any case, often advertised
nationally. Their jobs are of a kind in which to change an employer will
often require a relatively long-distance move; but financially they are able
to undertake such moves quite readily, since they are deemed to be credit-
worthy by building societies and insurance companies. Alternatively, their
paths of promotion within an individual large firm will demand the periodic
relocation of their homes, in which circumstances it is likely that the financial
(if not the social) costs of moving will be borne by their employers. Half of
our sample, for instance, received financial aid in moving to the new area,
mainly from their employers, and two-thirds of these aided households were
in the managerial socioeconomic groups, already earning over £1,500 per
annum. Thus to complement the relative scarcity and inelasticity of supply
of these skilled occupational groups, a higher level of geographical mobility
is usually found among them.

Unskilled workers, on the other hand, are usually recruited locally and scan
much more restricted horizons for job opportunities (except where single
men and women may migrate over long distances early in their working lives).
Because the kinds of jobs they fill are often available in a wide range of locations they tend not to be involved in long-distance migration between jobs.
Their lower incomes make the financial costs of moving a more significant
item of expenditure. They depend on council housing or on cheap, rented
accommodation, to which access would be difficult in a new area. Last, but
not least, until migration is first undertaken the households in traditional
working-class communities are enmeshed in a social network characterized
by high connectivity but limited geographical extent, features which are
normally associated with low levels of outmigration. Thus in extreme cases
their housing, their sources of information, the pattern of location of suitable
jobs and their social networks all combine to reduce their propensity to
migrate.

From a practical point of view it may be argued that the forces encouraging
or discouraging mobility in these extreme cases are so strong that little can
be done to bring about change, even if this were thought desirable. There
remain, however, 'intermediate' occupational groups which emerge as of
particular interest as a result of this theoretical discussion of housing and
labour mobility, since less is known about them and their behaviour is more
open to influence by government decisions. This group is very large: the
1966 census shows that 48% of the population of England and Wales falls
into socioeconomic groups which might be classified in this way.[3] Skilled

[3] Here the 'intermediate' groups are taken as socioeconomic groups nos. 5–9, as defined
in the census: HMSO (1966) *Census of population,* Household Composition Tables,
table 11, 149.

manual, technical, 'middle' managerial, lower-paid professional and trained clerical workers are enormously varied in their characteristics, but regrettably they have been little studied in the sociological literature. There is reason to think that shortages of such skilled workers form a key problem in the modern labour market situation in Britain (although this obviously applies more to some groups than to others). Following our line of reasoning, it may be suggested that in general these workers are occupationally 'fixed' by their training, and that on this basis their geographical mobility might be expected to be relatively high. These intermediate groups occupy either council housing or relatively low-cost, privately owned houses. Thus, in changing jobs over long distances, housing availability might be expected to be particularly critical for them compared with the mobile but relatively well-off professional and higher managerial groups, or the immobile unskilled and semi-skilled groups. In the case of council-house dwellers there are often considerable difficulties in exchanging a council house in one local authority area for a similar house elsewhere, particularly when moving to areas of high labour demand and housing shortage. Again, in the private housing market, prices in high labour-demand areas tend to be above those in the other regions, from which the 'middle-group' workers might be expected to be recruited, thus providing a similar check to movement. An indication of this situation is given in Harris and Clausen's survey of migration, which found that although there was a fairly close correlation between higher educational qualification and greater *actual* mobility, this was not necessarily so in the case of *willingness* to move (Harris and Clausen 1967, 26). It was those with intermediate qualifications, such as the Ordinary National Certificate and General Certificate of Education, Ordinary Level, who were most willing to move, rather than the more highly qualified. This suggests that many people in the intermediate groups wish to move but are frustrated in their desire to do so.

Conclusion

Labour migration, involving a simultaneous move of home and job, has tended to be regarded as a symptom or index of other socioeconomic forces, rather than as an important factor of change in itself. Thus economists regard it as a mechanism which allows the reallocation of labour resources either to facilitate economic growth or in the service of some longer-term economic equilibrium. Geographers, on the other hand, have tended to use long-distance migration as a symptom of geographical disparities of wealth or opportunity. Both of these views, of course, are crystallized in the various policy measures which have been adopted in many countries, either to discourage or encourage migration.

The origins of many of these policy measures are often to be found in pre-war reactions to economic decline in certain industries and regions.

Forty years on, in the 1970s, it should be expected that the validity of these rather simple views of labour migration will have changed. There can be little doubt that increasing labour mobility is a fact of modern life and, in a broader context, should be regarded as an important aspect of the geography of opportunity. In an increasingly mobile society those factors which constrain mobility where it is beneficial to individual households may become increasingly regarded as socially harmful.

When labour migration is examined as an important social process in itself its complexities become rapidly evident. This paper has simply sketched the nature of the key relationships between occupational training and aptitudes and geographical mobility, suggesting the range of conditions experienced by contrasted social groups. It has also highlighted those groups for which one widely recognized constraining factor, housing, might be particularly critical. Our analysis provides no more than a framework for the elaboration of the forces affecting labour migration. It is clear from our survey of labour migrant households that income, occupational structure, family structure, stages in the family cycle and family goals as well as housing are all factors which need to be taken into account in explaining labour migration. It is also quite evident that the relative importance of these factors varies greatly in different geographical locations. This makes it more important that research must focus at the most appropriate geo-graphical scale. Past analyses of small local authority areas or of over-large regional groupings of counties have tended to create artificial difficulties of interpretation.

Acknowledgement

The Housing and Labour Mobility Study was supported by the Rowntree Memorial Trust. The authors wish to thank particularly Nathalie Hadjifotiou, Richard Herne and Hilary Robinson, who contributed ideas on labour migration to this paper.

References

CBI (1968) *Regional study, regional development and distribution of industry policy.* (Duplicated typescript.)

Cullingworth, J. B. (1965) *English housing trends.* Occasional Papers on Social Administration, No. 13. London.

Cullingworth, J. B. (1969) *Housing and labour mobility.* Paris (OECD).

Donnison, D. V. *et al.* (1961) *Housing since the Rent Act.* Occasional Papers on Social Administration, No. 3. Welwyn.

Gray, P. G. and Russell, R. (1962) *The housing situation in 1960.* London (COI, HMSO).

Harris, A. I. and Clausen, R. (1967) *Labour mobility in Great Britain, 1953-1963.* London (HMSO).

HMSO (1966) *Scottish economy, 1965-1970.* Cmnd. 2864. Edinburgh.

HMSO (1969) *Census of population.* Sample Census 1966, Migration Summary Tables, Part 1, table 1. London.

Hunter, L. and Reid, G. (1968) *Urban worker mobility.* Paris (OECD).

Johnson, J. H. *et al.* (n.d.) *Housing and labour migration in England and Wales* (forthcoming).

Ministry of Labour (1966) *Gazette* 74.

OECD (1964) *International management seminar on active manpower policy.* Paris.

OECD (1965) *Wages and labour mobility.* Paris.

Richardson, H. W. and West, E. C. (1964) Must we always take work to the workers? *Lloyds Bank Rev.* 35-48.

Ruddy, S. A. (1969) *Industrial selection schemes: an administrative study.* Univ. of Birmingham Centre for Urban and Regional Studies, Occasional Paper No. 5.

Salt, J. (1967) The impact of the Ford and Vauxhall plants on the employment situation of Merseyside, 1962-1965. *Tidjschr. voor Econ. en Soc. Geogr.* 58.

Stone, P. A. (1970) *Urban standards, costs and resources.* NIESR.

Willis, J. (1967 and 1968) *Mobility and the North: population growth and movement.* North Regional Planning Council, Centre for Environmental Studies, Working Paper No. 12.

Woolf, M. (1967) *The housing survey in England and Wales 1964.* Government Social Survey. London (HMSO).

Part Two
Data

Introduction

The availability of data, their nature and their quality, are of importance in all studies of population. The problems of data are of particular concern in the study of migration. In the past the study of migration has been hampered by difficulties in obtaining satisfactory source material. It is therefore appropriate to give consideration to some of these problems.

General aspects of sources of data for migration research – their nature, the problems of collection and of comparability – are considered by *Kosiński*. They are also dealt with both directly and indirectly in subsequent papers in the volume, both the empirical and comparative studies and those which deal with the migrations of specific groups. The studies of interregional migrations illustrate the widely varying opportunities that are offered by the kinds of data available in different parts of the world, and underline the problems of international comparability with which the central and regional statistical agencies of the United Nations have tried to grapple over the last two decades.

Kosiński goes on to outline various means for measuring migration which have been devised. They are by no means capable of application in all parts of the world, depending as they do upon the availability of differing kinds of data.

Perry's review of sources for the study of migration in southern Africa focuses at a subcontinental level upon the nature of movements which occur and upon data which are available for their assessment. There are important contrasts between less developed and more developed countries in both these respects. Furthermore, the Republic of South Africa illustrates how political decisions relating to various elements in its multiracial population may influence movements and the availability of data. However, these political attitudes also influence the extent to which access to data may be restricted even when data are known to be available.

Reference has been made earlier and recurs subsequently to the aggregate nature of most data which can be used in migration studies. Even for the smallest units used in census enumeration the data refer to a sum of moves, masking their spatial and temporal individuality, the socioeconomic characteristics of movers and the factors influencing decisions to move. At the individual level little is known of these and the paper by *Chapman* is therefore of particular interest as an example of data collection at the micro-scale, in respect of individuals concerned and the environment in which their movements occur.

7 Data and measures in migration research

L. A. Kosiński

Introduction

Much migration research in the past has been concentrated on international flows and only recently has the emphasis shifted to the study of internal movements. This change in emphasis is reflected in the types of data and methods of collecting them. More questions on migration have been included recently in national censuses, special surveys have been undertaken, and the resulting data tabulated in a finer regional breakdown to allow more detailed analysis of internal flows. In most recent years, particularly in developed countries, interest has concentrated on intralocal migrations, especially within urban and metropolitan areas (Heberle 1955; Bogue 1969; UN 1970; Shryock and Siegel 1971).

Data collection

In general the amount of migration that is measured will relate to the size and shape of the units for which data are collected. The smaller the unit the relatively greater chance there is that its boundaries will be crossed and a movement recorded. However, data relating to migration may not be available for the smallest units. In India, for example, the smallest unit for which census data relating to migration are available is the *district*: for the country as a whole the average area of a district is 9,000 km² and the average size of population is in excess of 1.5 million.

Data on internal migration may be derived from different sources and the choice of the method of analysis depends to a large degree on the nature of the source. The most common sources of information on migration are population censuses and sample surveys. However, for some countries current registration is very important. Increasingly, other sources are also being used (table 7.1).

Migration data are collected on a complete or on a sample basis (as a supplement to the basic census questions). In some very limited censuses in less developed countries some measure of migration can be derived only from surrogate data relating to age and sex and to ethnic affiliation. None of these is time-specific, and in the case of sex balance in a population, for example, may be influenced by differential mortality for which no allowance can be made if no data on it are available. Otherwise migration data are collected on the basis of various direct questions. These include place of birth, which permits an estimate of lifetime migration between birth

Table 7.1

Sources and types of migration data

	Census	Survey	Population register or migration register	Other sources
Direct information				
Place of birth	+	+	—	+
Last previous residence	+	+	+	+
Residence at specific previous date	+	+	—	+
Duration of residence	+	+	—	+
Indirect information				
Present and previous population of an area (by age and sex)	+	—	—	+
Characteristics of migrants	+	+	+	+
Characteristics of nonmigrants	+	+	—	+
Reasons for moving	+	+	+	+

date and the time of the census; immediate previous residence, which is also unspecific as far as time is concerned; residence at a specific previous date, which includes as migrants only those who moved between this date and that of the census; duration of present residence and date of last move. Very often a combination of two or more questions is included. Similar information can be obtained from surveys either specifically concerned with migration or including migration questions with others. Census data have a number of advantages including the possibility of comparing information on migrants with that of non-migrants, with comparable data available for large areas. The most important limitation of a census as well as of a survey is the fact that they provide only retrospective data on migration for those alive at the date of observation, and consequently miss all those who actually moved but have died or who have left prior to the time of enumeration. It may be possible to make some adjustment for the effects of mortality. On the other hand, census data will include those born into migrants' families after migration has taken place.

Surveys conducted by government organizations (often census agencies) or private researchers can be much more specific and ask more penetrating questions than those included in a national census. Since they are usually based on a limited sample a fine spatial breakdown is often impossible. It is also difficult to establish time trends of migration moves. There are also problems in a sample survey of deciding whether the *de facto* or *de jure* population should be involved, since this will involve resident persons and those temporarily present or absent. In a sample it is necessary to include enough migrants to ensure statistical validity, but at the same time take into account the possibilities of geographical and/or occupational concentrations of migrants. An extended questionnaire may be used in the case of migrants identified in a sample, and/or special surveys undertaken where concentrations occur.

In some countries, population registers are maintained where all vital, residential, occupational, social and family events are currently registered. In some other countries only change of residence is centrally registered. These two types of registers are used for tabulation of current change of residence. In addition to this basic information, current registration normally provides data on characteristics of migrants, and very frequently reasons for moving. The basic advantage of migration data obtained from population or migration registers is the fact that they provide complete information of all the moves for a given country on a continuous basis. However, they are expensive and cumbersome to maintain and, no matter how detailed, omissions are always possible. By definition registration data should be complete, and since information is collected when moves take place there should be no problems of recall. However, the data relate only to people who are moving and for the total population at risk data are only available from the census. It is difficult to relate these two sets and therefore to study migration differentials from registration data.

Register data are available for a limited number of countries only (e.g. Sweden, the Netherlands, the Federal German Republic and most East European countries). Records in Sweden go back over a considerable period of time, but in most countries they are comparatively recent, in Eastern Europe largely since the Second World War. Registration was introduced on a limited scale in the USSR in 1923, but a common system was not established until 1953. In this system short-term moves are excluded, but in others a wide range of information is collected. Generally speaking, register data are not available for the less developed parts of the world. Thailand is one exception, it being a legal requirement to report to local administrative authorities within two weeks of any permanent change of residence. Comprehensive data are available at a local district level over a considerable time span, but like all register data these are difficult to handle for analysis. Day (1972) expresses the view that registration of migration is best suited to small, highly cohesive, or to highly organized, societies, or to readily distinguished groups in a population, but not to population in general.

There are a number of other sources that can be used for migration studies. They include records of religious denominations; birth, death, and marriage certificates where place of birth is usually recorded; school records; social or health insurance registers; electoral lists; tax registers; factory and plantation records; public utilities files; telephone directories; military records, and such like. Normally, these records are incomplete since they refer to specific categories of population only. Their usefulness for research is often limited since they are not freely available for research.

International organizations have long tried to standardize migration statistics. Previously, when the emphasis was on international migration, a series of recommendations was made, all focusing on current registration as the main source of information. For example, discussions took place in 1932 at the International Conference on Migration Statistics (International

Table 7.2

Topics related to migration investigated in latest national census of eighty-four countries: 1955–64

Topics	Total	Europe[a]	Asia and the Far East[b]	Africa[c]	America[d]
Total number of reporting countries	84	20	19	26	19
Question relating to migration					
Place of birth	71	11	18	23	19
Duration of residence	26	–	–	11	15
Prior place of residence	26	9	3	–	14
Whether refugee	2	2	–	–	–
Year of immigration into country	1	–	–	–	1

Notes: According to the reviews conducted by regional agencies:

[a] Economic Commission for Europe, Conference of European Statisticians.
[b] Economic Commission for Asia and the Far East, Working Group on Censuses of Population and Housing.
[c] Economic Commission for Africa, Conference of African Statisticians.
[d] Inter-American Statistical Institute.

Source: UN 1965.

Table 7.3

Migration and residential statistics: recommendations for 1970 population census

A. *Topics to be enumerated*

Topics included as basic in regional programmes of:

Recommended* and other useful topics	Conf. of African Stat'ns	Conf. of Asian Stat'ns	Conf. of European Stat'ns	Inter-Amer. Stat. Inst.
* Place where found at time of census and/or	+[a]	+	+[b]	+
* Place of usual residence				
* Place of birth	+	+	+[c]	+
Duration of residence	−	+	−	+
Place of previous residence	−	−	+[d]	+
Place of work	−	−	+	−
* Locality (derived)	+	+	+	+
* Urban and rural (derived)	+	+	+	+

B. *Tabulations to be prepared*

	Subdivision by:		
Recommended (first priority)**	Rural-urban	Major div.	Minor div.
1. ** Population of civil divisions by urban/rural residence and sex	+	+	+
2. ** Population in localities by size-class, locality and sex	Size of localities	+	−
3. ** Population of principal localities and their urban agglomerations by sex	n.a.	Individual	
10. ** Foreign-born population by country of birth, age and sex	−	+	−
11. Native population by major civil division of birth, age and sex	+	+	−
Other useful tabulations			
30. Population by duration of residence in locality and major civil division, age and sex	+	+	Principal locality
31. Population by place of usual residence, place of previous residence, and sex	−	+	+
32. Population by country of citizenship, age and sex	−	+	−

Notes:

[a] Priority given to first question.
[b] Priority given to second question.
[c] Recommended topic is 'country of birth and/or citizenship'.
[d] Recommended topic is 'place of residence at prior reference date'.
Source: UN 1969b.

Labour Office 1932). The United Nations made provisional recommendations on migration statistics in 1949 and later in 1953. Experience has shown that it is extremely difficult to collect comparable data and the present view seems to be that only field inquiries such as census and sample surveys, the latter in particular, can provide adequate, comparable and reliable data on both international and internal migration (Day 1972). Appropriate recommendations are presently being made by the statistical services of the UN.

The United Nations have also been involved in establishing recommendations for censuses and questions pertaining to changes of residence have been suggested (UN 1958). It appears that place of birth has been most frequently asked in the 1960 censuses, followed by duration of residence and prior place of residence (UN 1965) (table 7.2). Recommendations prepared for 1970 were modified by various regional bodies (UN 1969a, b). Place of birth has retained its position as the most frequent question from which migration information can be derived (table 7.3).

Geographers very frequently rely on data provided by government agencies in their studies and have to adjust their methods of research and scale of study to the available data. However, very frequently they are interested in a much more detailed regional breakdown than is provided by the statistical agencies. In such cases, as well as those when official data are not readily available, special field inquiries are conducted and data collected. In the present volume there are examples of such inquiries (see especially *Chapman*).

Migration rates

The general rate of mobility is similar to that used in other fields of demographic inquiry (Hamilton 1965). It is the ratio of the number of movers in an interval of time to the population at risk during that interval or

$$m = \frac{M}{P} \cdot k \tag{1}$$

where m is the mobility rate; M is the number of migrants; P is population at risk; and k is a constant, usually 100 or 1,000. In practice, the rate of mobility is usually computed for smaller areas or particular streams of population, such as inmigration into an area or outmigration from that area. In this case, M has to be replaced by another concept and symbols such as I for inmigration or O for outmigration. If net migration is to be computed, M is replaced by a difference, $I - O$; for gross migration $I + O$ will be used and the formulae become respectively

$$\text{Net } m = \frac{I - O}{P} \cdot k \quad \text{or} \quad \text{Gross } m = \frac{I + O}{P} \cdot k \tag{2, 3}$$

Migration rate can be also conceived as a probability rate and the proportion M/P gives a measure of the probability of a person moving at least once during a given migration interval. Obviously

$$\frac{M}{P} + \frac{N}{P} = 1 \qquad (4)$$

where N is non-migrants and P is total population exposed to the risk of migration.

Population at risk has to be defined depending on the requirements of the study and/or type of data available. Sometimes it is population at origin, sometimes population at destination; sometimes population at the beginning of the period, sometimes at the end of the period, most often in mid-period (Hamilton 1965; Thomlinson 1962; UN 1970). For example, in a study of a particular migration stream from i to j the population at risk will be defined as that residing in i at the beginning of the period. The formula then becomes

$$m_{ij} = \frac{M_{ij}}{P_i} \cdot k \qquad (5)$$

By comparing net and gross migration an index of efficiency (or efficacy) can be computed (Shryock 1959; Borejko 1968):

$$e = \frac{I - O}{I + O} \cdot k \qquad (6)$$

A large number of rates and indices have been devised and used in migration study such as indices of redistribution, indices of migration differentials and selectivity, index of preference, index of velocity, index of effectiveness, migration preference index (Shryock and Siegel 1971).

Measures of migration

According to the source of migration data, the resulting methods used are usually classified as direct or indirect (Das Gupta 1959; Haenszel 1967). Direct measures can be used if data are derived from population registers (or registration of migration) or from the replies to direct questions in censuses or in surveys. Direct census questions (table 7.1) are increasingly asked in modern censuses, and recent thinking among UN statisticians will most likely contribute to more frequent use of this source (Day 1972). Advantages and limitations of data depend on the type of question asked. A birthplace question is not specific as far as the time of movement is concerned. Usually it does not provide information on the type of place of origin when the move was made, though in India in 1961 population was classified as rural or urban for place of birth and place of enumeration. It does not take into consideration return migration and repeated moves (including those foreign-born but migrating subsequently within the country). This measure can also be influenced by cultural traditions. For example, if women return to their native village to give birth their children will be counted migrants even though they may not move subsequently from the parental village.

Table 7.4

Measures of migration

	Census	Survey	Registration
All moves registered	−	−	+
Direct measures of migration			
Lifetimes	+	+	−
During specific period	+	+	+
Vital statistic method	+	−	−
Survival ratio method	+	−	−

Intercensal net migration can be estimated when birthplace information contained in two subsequent censuses is compared (Zachariah 1967).

$$\text{Net } M = (I_{t+n} - I_t) - (O_t - O_{t+n}) \tag{7}$$

where O_t, I_t is total number of life outmigrants (life inmigrants) at time t, and O_{t+n}, I_{t+n} is total number of life outmigrants (life inmigrants) at subsequent time t + n. This estimate ignores the impact of mortality during the intercensal period.

Questions concerning last previous residence have similar limitations as those concerning lifetime migration in that they are not specific as to the time when migration occurred. Unlike birthplace information, which can include the effect of several moves, the question on last previous residence identifies all those who moved the last time.

Residence at a fixed previous time allows measurement of gross and net migration between areas during a fixed interval. Accuracy of data depends much on the point in time selected for analysis. Generally speaking the longer the interval the greater the problem of recall, unless the date was very easy to remember (outbreak of war, major natural disaster, etc.). Using this method the number of frequent (repeated) moves will be underestimated. Data for a very short migration period (one year or less) can be more reliable, but on the other hand they can be affected by seasonal movements or unusual events of short duration. They also exclude some long-term movers. This measure does not take into consideration return and repeated migration, migrant children born within migration intervals, and deceased migrants. By comparing migrants with non-migrants one can compute the ratio of stability of population (8) and the ratio of dispersal (9).

$$S_i = \frac{P_{i,t+n} - I_i}{P_{i,t+n}} \tag{8}$$

$$D_i = \frac{O_i}{P_{i,t}} \tag{9}$$

where P_i is population of the area (i) at the beginning ($P_{i,t}$) and at the end of a period ($P_{i,t+n}$); and I_i, O_i is total number of inmigrants in an area (i) or outmigrants originating from an area (i). The same measures can be used with birthplace statistics.

Information on duration of residence if combined with last previous residence can provide data on migration. Migrants can be classified according to the length of residence, synonymous with the time of migration.

In the absence of direct data, several indirect measures can be used which are based on census information. One condition for their successful application is stability of administrative units so that census data in subsequent enumerations apply always to the same area units; otherwise tedious adjustment is necessary before these measures can be effectively applied. Indirect methods normally allow an estimate of net migration only for a given area without differentiating between internal and international moves. Methods are collectively known as 'residual' (Shryock and Siegel 1971) and include *vital statistics method, survival ratio method* and *national growth rate method.*

The *vital statistics method* is also sometimes called the residual method. By comparing results of two censuses, total population change can be computed. Further comparison of this change with natural increase (difference between births and deaths) leads to estimation of apparent net migration.

$$\text{Net M} = (P_{t+n} - P_t) - (B - D) \tag{10}$$

where P_t, P_{t+n} is population at time t and t + n, and B, D is number of births and deaths during the interval. Vital statistics methods can only be applied if the number of births and deaths can be obtained from national registration. The results are limited to net figures and no information on total turnover, direction of flows, their composition, and reasons for moves, are available (Siegel and Hamilton 1952). However, if registration of vital statistics provides data on births and deaths by age, sex or other ethnic, occupational or social characteristics, then this method can be used to estimate net migration for respective groups (Hamilton 1967).

The *survival ratio method* does not require vital statistics. However, census data should be classified by age and sex at the time of two consecutive censuses. In addition, survival ratios must be available. The latter can be obtained either from life tables (*life table survival ratio method*) or by comparing two consecutive censuses (*census survival ratio method*). In either case the expected population by age and sex which is estimated with the help of survival ratios is later compared with the population actually enumerated and the difference is attributed to net migration.

$$\text{Net } M_A = A_{t+n} - (A_t \times S_A) \tag{11}$$

where M_A is estimated net migration of a cohort A over the migration interval; A is age cohort at the beginning (A_t) and at the end (A_{t+n}) of a period; and S_A is survival ratio for a cohort A. Depending on whether survival ratio is forward or reverse, different assumptions are implied with regard to the treatment of mortality and the time of migration. This method makes it possible to detect the impact of migration on different age and sex groups. It often happens that individual cohorts are more affected than the total population and in fact a cancelling effect can reduce total net migration to O despite the fact that various age groups experience net migration gains or losses. Survival ratios can also be used for estimating net migration if birthplace data or data on previous residence are directly provided from two consecutive censuses.

$$\text{Net } M = (I_{t+n} - O_{t+n}) - (S_I I_t - S_O O_t) \tag{12}$$

where S_I, S_O are survival ratios for outmigrants and inmigrants (life migrants or period migrants); O_t, O_{t+n} are outmigrants during two consecutive censuses; and I_t, I_{t+n} are inmigrants during two consecutive censuses. This measure is more exact than (7) in taking into consideration the impact of mortality upon migrants during the intercensal period. However, the accuracy of results will depend on the accuracy of the census and the appropriateness of survival ratios. If the estimate concerns a small population the chances of error may be quite considerable (Price 1955; Zachariah 1962; Hamilton 1966; Stone 1967; Wunsch 1969).

The *national growth rate method* can be used when census data do not allow the use of more complex methods. A difference between the rate of growth in a given area compared with a national average is interpreted as the result of migration.

$$\text{Net } M_i = \frac{P_{i,t+n} - P_{i,t}}{P_{i,t}} - \frac{P_{t+n} - P_t}{P_t} \tag{13}$$

where P is the national population at the beginning (P_t) and at the end of a period (P_{t+n}), and P_i is the population of an area (i) respectively at two censuses $(P_{i,t}$ and $P_{i,t+n})$.

Conclusion

All these measures and techniques can and have been used successfully in geographical studies of areas of different order ranging in scale from intra-urban to interregional migration. However, geographers are interested not only in describing migration trends but also in interpreting the spatial patterns of mobility. Consequently, the analysis of migration trends involves study of covarying factors which can explain emerging spatial patterns. This usually involves the use of regression and correlation techniques. Correlation cannot be identified with causation and consequently other means and methods are necessary. With increasing interest in the behavioural approach, geographers conduct surveys and ask direct questions aimed at a better understanding of the decision-making process. There is no doubt that purely statistical measures especially helpful in earlier stages of analysis have to be supplemented by others if meaningful results are to be obtained.

Acknowledgements

Professor Karol Krotki, University of Alberta, critically reviewed the first draft of this paper; Dr R. M. Prothero not only edited the text to read more smoothly but also made valuable comments and proposed major additions.

References

Bachi, R. (1967) Analysis of geographical data on internal migration. *Wld Pop. Conf. 1965* 4, 475–82. New York.

Beltramone, A. (1962) Sur la mesure des migrations intérieures au moyen des données fournies par les recencements. *Pop.* 17, 703–24.

Bogue, D. J. (1969) *Principles of demography.* New York. (Especially chapter 19.)

Borejko, W. (1968) Study on effectiveness of migrations. *Geogr. Polonica* 14, 305–12.

Das Gupta, A. (1959) Types and measures of internal migration. *Internat. Pop. Conf. Vienna 1959* 619–23. Vienna.

Day, L. H. (1972) *The newly-proposed UN recommendations for the improvement of migration statistics.* Manuscript circulated at the IGU Commission of Population Geography meeting, Edmonton.

Eldridge, H. T. (1964) A cohort approach to the analysis of migration differentials. *Demog.* 1, 212–19.

Haenszel, W. (1967) Concept, measurement and data in migration analysis. *Demog.* 4, 253–61.

Hamilton, C. H. (1965) Practical and mathematical considerations in the formulation and selection of migration rates. *Demog.* 2, 429–43.

Hamilton, C. H. (1966) Effects of census errors on the measurement of net migration. *Demog.* 3, 393–415.

Hamilton, C. H. (1967) The vital statistics method of estimating net migration by age cohorts. *Demog.* 4, 464–78.

Heberle, R. (1955) Migration mobility: theoretical aspects and problems of measurement. *Proc. of the Wld. Pop. Conf. 1954* Vol. 11. New York.

International Labour Office (1932) *Statistics on migration. Definitions – methods – classifications.* Geneva.

Price, D. O. (1955) Examination of two sources of error in the estimation of net internal migration. *J. Am. Stat. Assoc.* 50, 689–700.

Schwarz, K. (1969) *Analyse der räumlichen Bevölkerungsbevegung.* Hanover.

Shryock, H. S. (1959) The efficiency of internal migration in the United States. *IUSSP Conference, Vienna 1959* 685–94. Vienna.

Shryock, H. S. and Siegel, J. S. (1971) *The methods and material of demography.* Washington. (Especially chapter 21 in Vol. II.)

Siegel, J. S. and Hamilton, C. H. (1952) Some considerations in the use of the residual method of estimating net migration. *J. Am. Stat. Assoc.* 47, 475–500.

Stone, L. O. (1967) Evaluating the relative accuracy and significance of net migration estimates. *Demog.* 4, 310–30.

Taeuber, K. E. (1966) Cohort migration. *Demog.* 3, 416–22.

Thomlinson, R. (1962) The determination of a base population for computing migration rates. *Milbank Memorial Fund Q.* 40, 356–66.

United Nations (1958) *Principles and recommendations for national population censuses.* Stat. Pap., Ser. M, No. 27. New York.

United Nations (1965) *Report on the 1960 world population census program.* Report of the Secretary-General, Population Commission, Thirteenth Session. New York.

United Nations (1967) *Documents of expert working group on problems of internal migration and urbanization* (Bangkok, 24 May–5 June 1967). Economic Commission for Asia and the Far East.

United Nations (1969a) *Principles and recommendations for the 1970 population censuses.* Stat. Pap., Ser. M, No. 44. New York.

United Nations (1969b) *European recommendations for the 1970 population census.* Conference of European Statisticians, Statistical Standards and Studies, No. 13. New York.

United Nations (1970) *Methods of measuring internal migration.* Pop. Stud. No. 47. New York.

Winkler, W. (1967) Some new measures of aimed spatial mobility. *IUSSP – Contributed Papers* 762–6. Sydney.

Winkler, W. (1969) *Demometrie.* Berlin. (Especially chapter 21.)

Wunsch, G. (1969) Le calcul des soldes migratoires par la méthode de la 'population attendue' – caractéristiques et évaluation des biais. *Pop. et Famille* 18, 49–62.

Zachariah, K. C. (1962) A note on the census survival ratio method of estimating net migration. *J. Am. Stat. Assoc.* 57, 175–83.

Zachariah, K. C. (1967) Estimation of return migration from place-of-birth and duration-of-residence data. *IUSSP – Contributed Papers* 615–22. Sydney.

8 Sources for the study of migration in southern Africa[1]

J. W. B. Perry

Introduction

The search for work is the most important motivation for migration in southern Africa, mainly involving movements from rural to urban areas. Most of these movements are of Africans from Botswana, Lesotho and Swaziland to the Republic of South Africa, and of those within the Republic. They are motivated by economic duress, rural areas are over-crowded due to rapidly growing populations whose agricultural technology has not adapted sufficiently to the demands of increasing numbers, and there are demands for labour in the mines and industries and on the farms in South Africa. These external movements cross international boundaries but are otherwise comparable to labour migration which occurs within the Republic.

Government policy in the Republic of South Africa is directed ultimately to removing all Africans from White areas to the predominantly rural 'homelands' (Bantustans), where as yet only 46% of the African population is permanently resident. There are therefore compulsory urban to rural movements of Africans in accordance with the 'accepted Government policy that the Bantu are only temporarily resident in the European areas of the Republic, for as long as they offer their labour there' (Desmond 1971). Conversely, to meet labour demands there is a large-scale temporary migration of Africans from the economically-deprived Bantustans to the White areas. This policy was confirmed by the Deputy Chairman of the Bantu Affairs Commission in the House of Assembly in February 1968: 'We are trying to introduce the migratory labour pattern as far as possible in every sphere, that is in fact the entire basis of our policy as far as the White economy is concerned.'

[1] This includes Botswana, Lesotho, Swaziland and the Republic of South Africa. Information on Namibia is not available.

Data sources and limitations

The principal data sources for migration in all the countries of southern
Africa are the national censuses, but in all of these the information available
is limited. The Republic of South Africa, which is in the process of acquiring
detailed direct data, is exceptional.

Records of official organizations such as national health services or
employment registers do not exist. Even the largest labour recruiting agency,
the Mines Labour Organization, does not keep records of the engagement
of labourers from the individual Bantustans. Indirect sources all have
limitations, one of the most important being their inability to identify the
time and direction of migration flows.

In countries where seasonality in agricultural activity is important, as in
Botswana where many people move out from their permanent villages to
cultivate land which may be many kilometres away, the timing of the census
may be significant. The introduction of a question on tribal allegiance which
has been used in other countries as an index of migration (Hirst 1969; Southall
1961) was proscribed for political reasons in the Botswana census.

Data available for the study of migration are influenced by the administrative and/or political units for which they are collected. The kinds of movements that can be studied are limited since these are determined to no small
extent by the nature of the data units. Comparisons of data between
censuses are complicated by continually changing enumeration units, definitions and assessment methods, problems which may not be shared to the
same degree by more developed countries. The 1966 censuses of Lesotho
and Swaziland and the 1971 census of Botswana were based on enumeration
units, definitions and methods which differed from those used in the 1956
and 1964 censuses respectively. The 1966 census in Lesotho, for example,
was based on 1,056 enumeration areas, whereas that in 1956 was based on
202 'diptank' areas which had been originally demarcated for a campaign to
eradicate sheep scab in 1926. In the same country the definition of 'absentee'
changed from 'males or females temporarily absent for work or other purposes outside Basutoland . . . who are expected to return' in 1956 (Taylor
1958) to 'persons who were absent from the country for less than 5 years'
in 1966 (Kingdom of Lesotho 1969). The 'assembly' method of enumeration
of 1956 was replaced by individual enumeration in 1966.

The principal data sources from censuses and sample surveys provide
information on the qualitative characteristics of movement on a very general
level only. They tend to reveal only quantitative change and qualitative
information can only be obtained from intensive field studies which are
limited in size and scope by resources available and have the inevitable dis-
advantage of being time-specific. Ideal data sources, from specifically

designed studies which might for example follow the movements of individuals from rural to urban areas and back again, are obviously limited by cost and complexity. No major surveys of this type are known to have been undertaken in southern Africa.

Botswana

Of movements which may be classified on the basis of place, time and purpose, data exist only on the first of these. There is a significant movement of people from rural or semi-rural areas to the five principal towns – Gaborone, Lobatse, Francistown, Orapa and Selebi-Pikwe – a form of labour migration, though whether permanent or temporary and to what employment is not yet known. Rural-urban drift is illustrated by the rapid growth of the new-planned capital of Gaborone where the population increased from 3,855 in 1964 to 18,436 in 1971 with the development of a squatter settlement of Naledi on its fringe which houses 23% of the total population (Republic of Botswana 1972). Rural-rural movements, from villages to 'agricultural lands' and cattle posts, at the beginning of the wet season, may extend to between 30 and 50 kilometres. Because of these increasing distances some of these rural-to-rural movements are becoming permanent. This is leading to a redistribution of the national population on which very little data exist.

The 1971 population census contained some indirect data on population movements derived from a question on 'village of allegiance', generally interpreted as the village to whose headman people regarded themselves as owing allegiance and to which they felt they 'belonged'. However, 'belonging to' is not synonymous with 'living in'. Furthermore, there is no single agreed definition of what constitutes 'a village'. For this variety of reasons the question was answered in a highly subjective fashion. There are large discrepancies between the *de facto* population enumerated for a village, the numbers regarding it as their home, and the estimate by means of a pre-census house-count of the number of people that a village could contain. For example, in 1971 Serowe, the capital of the Ngwato, had a *de facto* population of 15,723; 43,186 persons in Botswana said that they 'belonged' to that village; 28,244 living in the same district said they 'belonged' to the village; and the estimate of the maximum potential population in the pre-census house-count was 27,000. From these data between 11,300 and 12,500 persons could be regarded as temporary migrants, either because empty, habitable houses exist to contain them or because they say they 'belong' to that village, and the remaining 15,000–16,000 have to be classified as having migrated permanently outside the district within Botswana.

An estimate of rural-urban migration to the main towns was tabulated at district level. Of the total population of 54,416 in these urban areas,

41,349 appear to have moved from the rural districts. Because of the complexity of tabulation and cost in relation to value derived, the 'allegiance' of the population of other settlements and the present residence of the absent population of the various settlements were not tabulated.

At district level a rough measure of internal migration was obtained from the 'village of allegiance' data and it was found that under one-half of the population was enumerated where they 'belonged' and nearly a fifth of the population was enumerated in a different district from that in which they 'belonged', implying that there must have been internal migration within the last twenty or thirty years.

Both quantitative and qualitative data on rural-rural and rural-urban movements were obtained by a UNDP project in the Shoshong area of eastern Botswana covering about 8,300 km² and 10,600 people with data on sex, age, occupation and place of birth. These showed, for example, that at Shoshong 10.3% of the population lived 'permanently' on the 'lands', though whether the movements are truly permanent, their rate and the reasons for them are not known (Syson 1972). Seasonal movements to the 'lands' also take place but the numbers involved are not known.

The nomadic population, mainly bushmen and Bakgalagadi, were not enumerated in the census because it was felt that their small numbers did not justify the cost of the effort that would be involved. However, an estimate of 10,550 nomads not enumerated in the census was made in 1971 and compared with an estimate of 11,650 made in 1964 (Republic of Botswana 1972). The only data on reasons for absence are contained in a study of migrant labour undertaken twenty-five years ago (Schapera 1947). No other direct data on population movements within Botswana are known.

Lesotho

Lesotho has the least data on migration, though rural-urban and rural-rural movements take place. The seasonal transhumance of flocks and herds is the most conspicuous of the latter. Some permanent movements from the lowlands to the mountain valleys may also be taking place as a result of population pressure in the former, but there are no data on them. The only data relating to migration in the 1966 census were limited to a question on presence or absence at the time of enumeration, and persons who had been absent continuously for five years or more were excluded from the count. Internal and external migration were not differentiated. Of the *de facto* male population in the 15–64 years' age group, 56.2% was recorded as absent, the majority presumed to be working in South Africa. Gross monthly figures of the numbers of migrants are obtainable from the Labour Department which collects them from the agencies which for the most part recruit for the mines. These agencies have complete migrant histories but these are normally confidential.

The principal data source on rural-urban movements is the Urban House-hold Budget Survey covering the seven lowland towns, which was undertaken in 1971-2 but which has not yet been analysed. It includes data on place of birth, duration of residence and last place of residence which were sought for urban planning purposes. With such limited data and since population movements are of such vital concern, the Government of Lesotho has sub-mitted a request to the United Nations Fund for Population Activities for an Integrated Multi-Subject Survey which may include studies of the magnitude, direction and characteristics of population movements, both internal and external, and regional variations in these.

Swaziland

Rural-urban movements are probably the most important in Swaziland, though rural-rural movements such as the settlement of the Vuvulane irrigation scheme in the northeast also occur. While most of the census data for Botswana and Lesotho were published only in generalized administrative district tabulations, the population of each enumeration area in Swaziland was listed by age and sex for those present and by sex for those absent for less than three years. However since other data, such as on ethnic group and birthplace, were tabulated only in terms of the four major administrative districts and the two principal urban areas, Mbabane and Manzini, the information that can be extracted about types of movements is very limited.

In the population census a question on birthplace was introduced to check ethnic groups and provide 'incidental useful information on migra-tion and population mobility'. Two tables were constructed to show 'the percentage distribution of the locally born African population of each district of enumeration by district of birthplace', and 'the converse picture of how the population born in each district is now distributed throughout the country by district of enumeration. . .'. From these it is possible to determine the main lines of internal migration in space, but neither the number of moves nor the period during which they occurred can be assessed (Jones 1968).

Age and sex ratios of the internal migrants were tabulated and compared with those of the non-migratory population, and the percentage distribution of the Swaziland-born migrant African population inside Swaziland was further analysed by district of birth. No explanation was found for the remarkably even balance in the sex ratio of internal migrants compared with that of the non-migrant population, but as might be expected the proportion of male migrants in the age group 15-49 years was high.

Direct data are completely lacking in Swaziland. No field studies are known which would provide detailed information but a multi-round sample survey of vital events is in the planning stage and will include questions on population movements.

The Republic of South Africa

The Republic is exceptional compared with the other three territories considered. Population movements are well documented as a result of the implementation of the policy of 'separate development'. A wholesale redistribution of non-Whites is taking place despite the demand for labour in White industrial areas and despite the need for work of Africans in the Bantustans. One of the most significant movements is urban-rural. This is of Africans 'endorsed out' of the urban areas or from White farms and repatriated to the Bantustans for not complying with all the technicalities of residence regulations, though they may have been born and spent all their lives in those urban areas or on those farms. Statistics of the numbers involved are released periodically by the Ministry for Bantu Affairs in response to parliamentary questions, but these are given in aggregate and not in detail.

Though the Department of Statistics says that no statistics on internal migration within South Africa are available, the questionnaire form for Whites, Coloureds and Asiatics in the 1970 population census asked for 'usual place of residence' which would provide some means of estimating movement in space. The census form for Africans requested birthplace by magisterial district which also records one movement though without information on any intermediate movements. The data from the census have not yet been completely tabulated and made available.

Temporary controlled rural-urban labour movements of Africans take place between the Bantustans and the White areas in enforcement of the policy of 'influx control'. Data on these movements exist in the 'Reference Book' which every adult African must carry outside the Bantustans; this records *inter alia* the name and address of his employment, the date of his engagement and discharge and the monthly signature of the employer. As any dependent African who is resident in an urban area outside a Bantustan has to have a lodger's permit, there is a continuous complete data source on the place and time aspects of all African movements between the Bantustans and the White areas. The Bantu Affairs Department, which is largely responsible for the control of movements of Africans into the urban areas by means of the system of registration, thus possesses a considerable amount of potential information on the rural-urban movement of this population group. However, this is not available since the Bantu Affairs Administration Act, No. 45 of 1971, which provides for 'control of most matters pertaining to Africans in urban areas to pass from local authorities to Government-appointed Bantu Affairs Administration Boards [and] makes it an offence for a member or a person serving the Board to disclose any information acquired by him in the course of his duties, without either the expressed permission of the Board or a directive from the Minister' (Wilson 1972).

For White, Coloured and Asian people a new identity document was introduced in February 1972 under the Population Registration Amendment Act, No. 29 of 1970, which include *inter alia* the holder's address and the constituency where he is registered as a voter. When the holder changes his address his card must be returned and a replacement obtained. A continuous direct record of the spatial and temporal aspects of movements of these population groups is therefore being kept, except that the last movement is recorded in the document held and is therefore not accessible.

Significant long-term, and usually permanent, movements of Whites from the farms to the larger urban centres has been taking place for several decades. Only data of absolute changes at district level have been recorded in censuses with no indication of direction or precise time of movement, though application of the 'survival ratio method' might give some indication of its extent. With the implementation of the 'Border Industries' policy there are daily or weekly commuting movements from the Bantustans to industries established just outside their borders in White areas. There are also daily commuting movements, as in most large metropolitan areas, by Whites from their residential suburbs and non-Whites from their townships, but no specific data on these are known to exist.

Other sources of information are regional or local studies carried out by universities, research units or individuals. For example, the Institute of Planning Research has recently published two local population studies, one containing data on rural-urban and intra-urban movements (Du Toit 1970), the other including the migratory history of local residents involving place of birth and former place of residence (Phillips 1971). The Institute of Social and Economic Research has also done some work on migrations of Whites (Watts 1966).

Conclusion

For southern Africa in general the migration data most available on a national level are on spatial aspects, in particular on rural-urban movements. Despite their economic significance, at present data are almost non-existent on seasonal rural-rural movements in Botswana and Lesotho, and on the daily commuting movements in the major urban areas of southern Africa. Data on the reasons for population movements are limited to the compulsory transfers of Africans within the Republic of South Africa. As a result of the extension of registration documentation to all South African citizens, the Republic of South Africa will have a valuable data source for research on population movements in space and time, but it is doubtful if the relevant government departments will be prepared to release it.

Data sources of population movements within Botswana, Lesotho and Swaziland are very limited and mainly indirect. The principal data source is still the national population census. Tremendous pressures for migration are generated in the process of modernization and these are rapidly developing in these countries. To understand them and to deal with them, the need for reliable data, qualitative as well as quantitative, at both national and local levels, is becoming more and more pressing.

Acknowledgements

Thanks are due to Paul Devitt and L. G. A. Smits for comments and criticisms of earlier drafts of this paper.

References

Desmond, C. (1971) *The discarded people.* Harmondsworth.

Du Toit, A. S. (1970) *Housing and population study of the European population of Uitenhage.* Inst. for Plan. Res., Univ. of Port Elizabeth, Research Report No. 5.

Hirst, M. A. (1969) Net migration patterns over Tanzania. *E. Afr. Geogr. Rev.* 7, 25–36.

Jones, H. M. (1968) *Report on the 1966 Swaziland population census.* Mbabane.

Kingdom of Lesotho (1969) *1966 population census report.* Maseru 1, Part II.

Phillips, B. D. (1971) *The Coloured population of the Port Elizabeth/ Uitenhage region: a socio-economic study.* Inst. for Plan. Res., Univ. of Port Elizabeth, Research Report No. 7.

Republic of Botswana (1972) *Report on the population census 1971.* Gaborone.

Schapera, I. (1947) *Migrant labour and tribal life: a study of conditions in the Bechuanaland Protectorate.* London.

Southall, A. W. (1961) Population movements in East Africa, in Barbour, K. M. and Prothero, R. M. (eds.) *Essays on African population.* London.

Syson, L. (1972) *The population of the Shoshong Area.* Unpublished UNDP Tech. Note No. 27, Surveys and training for the development of water resources and agricultural production. Botswana.

Taylor, D. H. (1958) *Basutoland population census 1956.* Maseru.

Watts, H. L. (1966) *South African town.* Occasional Paper No. 8, Inst. of Soc. and Econ. Res. Grahamstown.

Wilson, F. (1972) *Migrant labour in South Africa.* Johannesburg.

9 Mobility in a non-literate society: method and analysis for two Guadalcanal communities

M. Chapman

The interest, during the 1960s, of a small group of American demographers in a longitudinal approach to migration analysis has 'unlocked a number of doors' (Shryock and Larmon 1965, 592). They and others note that comparison of successive national censuses brings us closer to the time series of residential mobility, but freely admit that more dramatic advances are hampered by the absence of continuous records for the United States as a whole. As one slides along the scale of socioeconomic change such difficulties of data availability magnify until, for some non-literate societies,[1] there may not even exist a total count of their territorial population. This paper focuses upon the mobility data collected for one such people in Melanesia, the technical and methodological traps in such an attempt, and the conceptual rewards that arise from the collection of such fine-grained information.

The actual fieldwork, undertaken between October 1965 and February 1967, considered the reasons for the people's considerable mobility and, more specifically, the interplay of social and economic factors (Chapman 1969, 1970, 1971). It was designed to test the notion that considerations other than economic are far more significant than has often been recognized in migration research, particularly in non-Western societies; and that, in a process as complex and dynamic as a people's mobility, single-factor explanations are simplistic distortions of reality. A detailed investigation

[1] Throughout this paper the adjective 'non-literate', as for population or society, is used in the sense conventional in social anthropology: peoples for whom information was customarily transmitted by word of mouth and for whom there was no tradition of reading and writing.

was made of a coast and a peripheral bush village, Duidui and Pichahila respectively, on the Weather (south) Coast of Guadalcanal, British Solomon Islands Protectorate (fig. 9.1). On 1 March 1966, the former community had a *de jure* population of 221 residents in 40 households; on 1 October 1966, the latter contained 110 persons in 18 households.

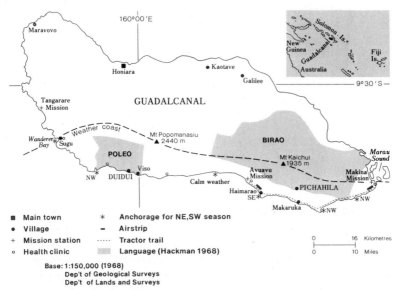

Figure 9.1 General map of Guadalcanal

Conventions – helpful or not?

In some prefatory comments to a study of population, land use and employment in three rural districts of Western Samoa, Pirie and Barrett (1962, 64) note:

> Most males, it was assumed, were born, learnt the ways of Samoan life, worked in the plantations under the direction of their *matai*, received the gift of many children, became titled and old, and died at last – all within one *aiga*, itself a permanent part of one Samoan village. For females the pattern was sometimes varied by migration at marriage if this was made outside their village. The peripatetic ways of the Samoans have been frequently noted, but it was believed that their journeys were temporary, mainly for reunions with their relatives, and that their migrations were for social reasons.

Even though this customary perspective was not sustained upon detailed investigation, it points to difficulties for research into the mobility of non-literate populations.

In the 1959 area-sample census of the British Solomon Islands Protectorate, as is standard for a *de jure* count, the population 'usually present' in
any village was defined as those who had been resident for the previous
year or whose absence was not expected to exceed more than one year
(McArthur 1961, 6). If this definition, rather than what is locally conceived
as 'usually present', is imposed upon the field census data for Duidui and
Pichahila, then the former's population is reduced from 221 to 214 and
that of the latter from 110 to 104. Expressed conventionally, the migration
rate for Duidui during the twelve months preceding the village census was
3.2% and for Pichahila 5.5%.[2] From this standpoint the people are quite
immobile, in precisely the same way the Samoans appeared to be at the
outset of Pirie's and Barrett's research on Upolu and Savai'i.

That such a statistic does not necessarily convey the mobility experience
of local communities is demonstrated by problems encountered with the
1959 census. Since year-long contracts on plantations were much more
numerous then than nowadays, there was some confusion about whether
absentees belonged, for enumeration purposes, to their home village or their
place of work. The final tabulations showed a marked deficiency of males
aged between 20 and 24, which 'suggests that there may have been inadequate provision in the sample for persons absent from their village for
periods longer than a year, and that the uncertainty about the intentions of
some of the plantation workers may have led to their omission from their
home schedules' (McArthur 1961, 14). The unexpected magnitude of
mobility for wage-labour and other assorted reasons thus probably contributed to both a faulty sample design and under-enumeration.

Whilst this dilemma will not be resolved by a territorial census that
invokes standard definitions of population movement, one little-used
alternative is to collect field data for which prior classification is minimal.
In both villages a mobility register was kept for five months[3] to record any
individual who either left or stayed in the community for twenty-four hours
or more. This time-span was chosen because it entails an overnight stop and,
consequently, a conscious decision, it also implies such preparations as
checking the supply of tobacco, betel nut and lime, taking a change of
'calico' (clothing) and, sometimes, even carrying a bedroll. For every entry,
information was obtained on the date of the inward and outward shift,
the name of the persons involved, their origin or destination, how and with

---

[2] This assumes, incorrectly, that the population exposed to migration at the midpoint
of the twelve-month period in question was identical to that at census date. In fact,
the net excess of births over deaths for both communities would slightly inflate the
rates quoted, but the small numbers involved do not warrant further refinement for
such a simple illustration.

[3] For Duidui, from 1 December 1965 until 31 May 1966, but excluding the month of
April; for Pichahila, between 1 July 1966 and 30 November 1966.

whom the move was made, over what time period, and for what reasons (table 9.1).

Table 9.1

Entry from population register, Pichahila, 12 August 1966, inward move

Name	Origin/Destination	Method of move
Jim (see 10 August)	Buturua–Pichahila	Walk with Paura about 9 hours, because went slowly; hunted opposum in bush [secondary forest]; stopped half-way at garden house (Nakoga). Arrived 6 p.m. Slept in single men's house.

Reasons for move

Returned from unsuccessfully trying to catch pig with Michael, Hesikibo, Mario (see 10 August entry) for feast for John's father who died in February at Palulu. Did not return with others for was raining then and did not want to catch cold. (Length of absence: $2\frac{1}{2}$ days.)

For ten months between December 1965 and November 1966, entries from this register total 1,478, range from 83 to 243 per month, and in only 2 instances are less than 100. About one-quarter and four-fifths of these moves were undertaken by persons not resident in Duidui and Pichahila or were directly or indirectly influenced by the fieldworker and his family (table 9.2). If the ebb and flow of outsiders through each study community

Table 9.2

Moves* for selected months 1965–6, Duidui and Pichahila

	Duidui	Pichahila
Total moves	746	732
Village residents	416 (55.8%)	582 (79.5%)
'Aliens'	321 (43.0%)	103 (14.1%)
Influenced by fieldworkers	9 (1.2%)	47 (6.4%)

* For twenty-four hours or more, but excluding those influenced by the fieldworker and his family.

is disregarded, the resultant tallies over ten months can be projected for twelve months and compared with the migration rates calculated earlier. Thus extrapolated, during 1966 every man, woman and child in Duidui made 2.3 moves and in Pichahila 6.4 moves, whereas for the same period only 1 villager in 31 (Duidui) and 1 in 18 (Pichahila) was away sufficiently long to be categorized as a migrant. In these terms the people of Duidui and Pichahila are highly mobile, one manifestation of which is the frequency of overnight absence from their households. The crucial question now becomes whether such contrary results and interpretations depict actual patterns of behaviour or represent merely the numerical artifact of conspicuously different definitions.

The problems implicit in this last question were overcome by two complementary strategies followed during the collection of data. First, for each village census 'absence' was defined as twenty-four hours or more – the same as for the mobility register and for identical reasons – and 'usually present' by the people themselves rather than according to some external convention. Second, the information about presence and absence obtained by the field census for a moment in time was deliberately augmented by continuous records that spanned varying periods. As well as revealing the customary but unexpected relocation of villages (Chapman 1969, 131–2), the completed census is a logical referent from which to consider the structure and magnitude of mobility experienced by a small nucleate population. To this view of the local community as a complex of movers and stayers can be added more detailed but more selective information from the mobility register, a two-year record of absences for wage labour (1965–6), conjugal histories for all married or formerly married persons, and a handful of migrant life-histories (Chapman 1971, 10–20).

Characteristics of movers

At census date, at least 1 member was away from 3 households out of 4 in Duidui and 5 out of 6 in Pichahila. Absentees per household varied from 1 to 5, for an average of 2.2 (Duidui) and 1.9 (Pichahila), and accounted for 30% of their village populations (Duidui, 67 out of 221, or 30.4%; Pichahila, 34 out of 110, or 30.9%).

Amongst those away, males considerably outnumbered females (Duidui, 46:21; Pichahila, 21:13) and their differential age structure suggests both the places to which they went and their reasons for doing so (fig. 9.2). For both communities, only one woman (Duidui) aged more than 29 was not resident in her household during enumeration, whereas absent males vary in age from less than 1 to 59 (Duidui) and in Pichahila, with one exception, from 7 to 43. Such a range of years conceals two distinct but contiguous groups: independent children[4] of both sexes and younger adult males.

[4] By 'independent child' is meant one who is learning and/or performing such specific tasks as gardening or fishing but who is not married and has never been away to work. Girls and boys between the ages of 7 and 17 are viewed as being at this stage, but the former tend to both reach and leave it two to three years earlier than the latter. In this sense and in this society, 'independence' carries none of the Euro-American connotation of material or financial independence.

As might be expected from these patterns, the predominant reasons for such absence are schooling and wage labour (table 9.3). There are, in addition, journeys to visit kinsmen or obtain medical treatment and longer absences for 'permanent' employment[5] or vocational training, but such are minor and collectively account for less than a quarter of the non-residents of either community (Duidui, 13 out of 67; Pichahila, 4 out of 34). If, following Petersen (1969, 290), a distinction is made between 'active' and

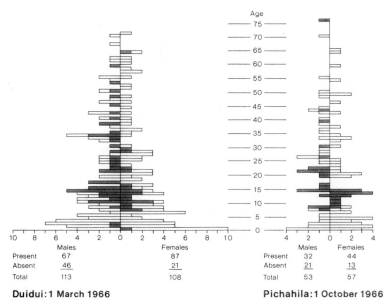

	Males	Females		Males	Females
Present	67	87	Present	32	44
Absent	46	21	Absent	21	13
Total	113	108	Total	53	57

Duidui: 1 March 1966   **Pichahila: 1 October 1966**

Total de jure population
⬚ Present
▬ Absent

Figure 9.2 Age-sex structure of *de jure* population (1966) in Duidui and Pichahila

'passive' migrants, then out of 101 individuals only 1 young woman and 3 dependent children from Duidui did not initiate the move they had undertaken prior to the census.

The results suggest that absence from the home community is for mainly economic and post-contact reasons; that independent, albeit related, indivi-

---

[5] By 'permanent' employment is meant some task to which there has been a continuous commitment for at least one year and the remuneration for which is not from a business enterprise undertaken on one's own account. Since sense of commitment is more crucial than the number of hours worked each day or the actual monetary return, 'permanent' positions embrace those with the central government, the various missions and the island council as well as situations in which kinsmen furnish the payments received: for example, a cutter builder or village preacher.

duals rather than family groups are involved; and that males predominantly travel (by sea) for more than a day and consequently beyond the language boundary (fig. 9.1).

Table 9.3

Reasons for absence, by sex, Duidui and Pichahila 1966

Duidui, 1 March 1966	Male	Female	Total
Active migrants			
Schooling	20	11	31
Wage labour	19	–	19
Visit kinsmen	1	6	7
'Permanent' position	3	–	3
Medical	1	2	3
	44	19	63
Passive migrants			
Accompany other persons	2	1	3
Born outside village	–	1	1
	2	2	4
Total number of migrants			
Active	44	19	63
Passive	2	2	4
	46	21	67
Pichahila, 1 October 1966			
Active migrants			
Schooling	11	13	24
Wage labour	6	–	6
Vocational training	3	–	3
Medical	1	–	1
	21	13	34

Time span of mobility

A solitary census contains little information of direct utility to assess whether particular kinds of movement fluctuate over time. In both Duidui and Pichahila a continuous record was developed of all persons away at school or wage labour for one or more months during the years 1965–6, the distinct seasonality of which soon became apparent. Only those Duidui children (15 out of 31 in 1966) at a junior primary school six hours' walk to the west return home during the school year, and a few, because of the policy of some missions to hold back pupils over the annual vacation either to look after gardens and buildings or to ensure their continued presence, only once every two years. None of the Pichahila children (24 in 1966) visits his parents during the year since Makina (Roman Catholic) Mission (fig. 9.1), which they attend, is almost a two-day journey. For the majority of pupils, going to and from school consequently follows ten- to eleven-month cycles.

Most of the wage-earners do not enter into twelve-month contracts with the various plantation operators or sign the shorter six-month agreements for unskilled labour favoured by government departments in the main town of Honiara (fig. 9.1). Instead, for the two years 1965–6 they were absent for varying periods of one to twelve months: an average of six months from Duidui (59 men, 7 women) and three from Pichahila (40 men: fig. 9.3). This ebb and flow, predominantly of married males aged between 25 and 44, fits with the planting of yams and taro in August–September and January–February, and permits the replacement of leaf on houses during the sunniest months, September to March.

Whatever the reason, departure from one's household is more likely to entail temporary residence under the auspices of some establishment or institution – in the school settlement,[6] the mission station or on the plantation – rather than with kinsmen in another village (Duidui, 46:21; Pichahila, 33:1).

Every year children leave for school and come back to their village; likewise adult males go away to earn money and later return to their households. Summarized in this fashion, the preceding results create an image of piston-like regularity in local mobility patterns that tends to be reinforced by the magnitude of absence for wage labour and schooling revealed through the field census. The population register permits a more precise test of this impression by taking as the unit of reference the two study villages rather than either households or individuals, by identifying all persons – whether residents or visitors – who pass into, out of or through those settlements, and by distinguishing between 'initial', 'completed' and 'transit' moves: respectively, where a person leaves the home village; where that same person returns to the home village; and where Duidui and

---

[6] By this is meant an independent settlement that results from a primary or secondary school being sited beyond the boundaries of a mission station or an established village. This ensures that primary schools in particular do not become enmeshed in the daily activities of any village in which they are located. It further enables head teachers to enforce rules that visiting parents may not stay overnight on the school premises but must sleep and eat in nearby villages.

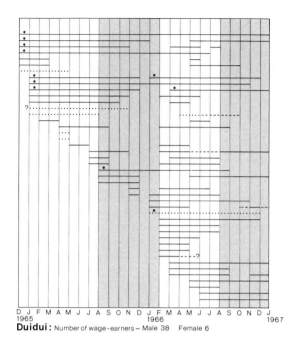

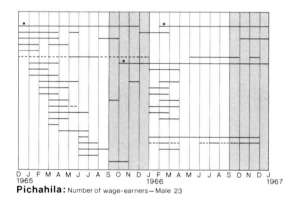

Duidui: Number of wage-earners – Male 38   Female 6

Pichahila: Number of wage-earners – Male 23

Gainfully employed
——— Male
······ Female
----- Absent but temporarily unemployed
* 'Permanent' position
░░░ Season of yam and taro planting

Note: 1.For convenience, all departures and returns have been assigned
     to the first of the month
    2.Any wage-earners absent for less than one month have been omitted

Figure 9.3 Migrant workers from Duidui and Pichahila
between December 1964 – 1 January 1967

Pichahila are merely passed through, as points of neither origin nor ultimate destination.

Whether residents, aliens or both are considered, the ratio of initial to completed moves is virtually identical for both communities, whereas transit moves account for about 2% of the ten-month totals (Duidui, 15 out of 737; Pichahila, 12 out of 685). Weather Coast people, in other words, seldom travel on foot to any locality that is so far distant from their household as to require an overnight stay in yet a third place. Previous results also have suggested that only rarely is the home village permanently forsaken for another domicile, and the fact that departures about equal arrivals for both residents and aliens provides additional evidence. Viewed through village lenses, mobility may not have the machine-like constancy conveyed earlier but it assuredly involves a continual transfer of people across its boundaries. As Hägerstrand demonstrates for a rural parish in southern Sweden, an area like the Weather Coast can be conceived as a 'fixed system of stations [here communities] which is run through by a flow of individuals, single or in groups' (Hägerstrand 1963, 65).

Objectives of mobility

Research which attempts to deduce reasons by indirect methods reflects, at least in part, the way in which census data not meant to reveal such information was originally collected; 'reasons' become an omnibus category into which various levels of information are fitted. To suggest such 'reasons' are 'causes' of mobility is a transition in migration research that is rather too comfortably and frequently, yet erroneously, made. One solution to these problems is to invert customary procedures so that the dependent variable becomes not the type of movement – for example, inward or outward – but rather statements about its occurrence made by the participant. This strategy in turn demands that the resultant wealth of information be collapsed and ordered in some logical fashion without violating its inherent character.

Declarations about the decision to move are not susceptible to analysis unless some distinction is made between the destination, the objectives – the activity pursued or intended to be pursued – and the underlying reasons why a physical transfer happened at the particular moment in question.[7] 'I am going to stay in my garden house', remarked one recently married male, 'because there are no yams on the Pichahila side and the women are afraid to cross the [Alualu] river when it is running. It is not fit for the women to cross the river to get food when it runs.' Such a comment is both complex and contingent. If the roles performed by an individual before and at the time of departure are adopted as the basic

[7] Defined as within seven days of the event (if known) that spurred the move.

criterion for assessment, then the above statement embodies one destination, two objectives and two underlying reasons. Specifically the destination is 'garden house'; the objectives 'live in garden house' and 'collect food'; the underlying reasons 'river stopped flooding' and 'able to go to gardens again'.

A painstaking survey of the entire register yielded a list of 162 objectives which were grouped into 9 clusters. Although a further 97 objectives were identified during a long period of coding (1968–71), not one of them altered the inherent character of nor required any addition to this original and intuitive grouping. Consequently these objective-clusters become the referent for the succeeding analysis.

In Duidui, residents and aliens made 737 moves in pursuit of 1,132 objectives during five months between December 1965 and May 1966; over a similar period, July to November 1966, the bush community of Pichahila experienced 685 moves undertaken for 1,221 objectives (tables 9.2, 9.4 and 9.5). For both communities, the number of objectives per move ranged

Table 9.4

Objectives of specified moves,[a] *Duidui and Pichahila 1965–6*

Collapsed objective[b]	Pichahila (July–October 1966)	Duidui (December 1965– March, May 1966)	Chi-square[c] (df = 1)
Return home	396	255	28.82*
Relatives/kinsmen	309	312	N.S.
Gardening	285	31	214.38*
General visiting	98	139	11.74*
Work/church	46	124	45.23*
Administrative	33	38	N.S.
School	30	155	102.37*
Medical	11	32	12.13*
Other	13	46	
Total	1,221	1,132	

* Chi-square significant at 0.01% level.
N.S. Not significant.

Notes:

[a] For twenty-four hours or more, but excluding those influenced by the fieldworker and his family. Compare table 9.2.
[b] Ordered according to the frequencies for Pichahila, the least acculturated of the two study communities.
[c] Each objective was compared with the total of all other objectives for both communities to test whether the observed differences were significant.

Table 9.5

Objectives of move, by residents and aliens, Duidui and Pichahila 1965-6

Duidui (December 1965–March, May 1966)

	Return home	Relatives/ kinsmen	Gardening	General visiting	Work/ church	Adminis- trative	School	Medical	Other	Total	Number of objectives per move
	(1)	(2)	(3)	(4)	(5)	(6)	(7)	(8)	(9)		
Residents	147	102	12	108	112	12	147	19	34	693	1.7
Aliens	108	210	19	31	12	26	8	13	12	439	1.4
Total	255	312	31	139	124	38	155	32	46	1,132	1.5
Percentage	22.5	27.6	2.7	12.3	10.9	3.4	13.7	2.8	4.1	100	

Pichahila (July–November 1966)

	(1)	(2)	(3)	(4)	(5)	(6)	(7)	(8)	(9)		
Residents	333	250	263	62	43	28	22	11	13	1,025	1.8
Aliens	63	59	22	36	3	5	8	0	0	196	1.9
Total	396	309	285	98	46	33	30	11	13	1,221	1.8
Percentage	32.4	25.3	23.4	8.0	3.8	2.7	2.5	0.9	1.0	100	

* Objectives for this and table 9.6 are ordered according to the frequencies for Pichahila, the least acculturated of the two study communities.

from 1 to 8, with averages of 1.5 (Duidui) and 1.8 (Pichahila). A single activity is therefore normally not sufficient to lure a villager away from his household, and analysis of the underlying reasons embedded in the movers' statements would even further emphasize this result.

Objectives that manifest the needs of the family or the social relationships amongst tribesmen far outweigh those that derive from the still peripheral impact of a colonial administration or metropolitan commercial interests. Journeys undertaken for activities associated with gardening, relatives and kinsmen, and local visiting comprise 65.1% (Duidui) and 89.1% (Pichahila) of 2,353 recorded objectives, whilst those concerned with wage earning, Christian religion, formal education, medical services and the district administration account for the remainder (tables 9.4 and 9.5). The pre-eminence of the undifferentiated category 'return home', first out of 9 clusters in Pichahila and second in Duidui, underscores previous assessments of a conspicuously mobile people. It also conclusively demonstrates the pertinence of viewing the village as both the place of origin and place of ultimate destination of completed moves.

These broad similarities conceal intriguing differences. In terms of frequency, gardening ranks third for Pichahila but last for Duidui, a statistically significant result that reflects a fundamental contrast in bush and coast lifestyles. Household groups leave Pichahila for up to five days at a time whenever horticultural tasks require more than a day's continuous effort, when the secondary bush needs to be heaped and burned, the various root crops planted, the previous season's produce harvested, or preselected tubers cut and dried for replanting. This long-standing practice has no parallel in Duidui, for even though garden houses are frequently maintained they are seldom used overnight. Indeed, the sole Duidui entry refers to a woman who, when in labour, discovered that a Solomon Island midwife was in the vicinity and fled to her garden shelter to ensure that unwanted professional help would be avoided!

To crystallize this and other contrasts, the undifferentiated clusters 'return home' and 'other' have been set aside and the remainder designated 'pre-contact' (gardening, relatives/kinsmen, general visiting) or 'post-contact' (work, church, administrative, schooling, medical: table 9.6). Such a procedure not only tests the initial hypothesis about the relationship of economic to non-economic factors in the mobility of a non-literate population but also admits the inappropriateness of descriptive labels derived from external models and alien contexts. To what extent going away to school means the fulfilment of an economic or a non-economic objective is not only an awkward question: to the people of Duidui and Pichahila, more crucially, it is an irrelevant one.

Whether the 1,643 objectives are grouped according to residents, aliens or total movers, activities that predate European contact dominate for all except Duidui residents (table 9.6). In these 5 out of 6 instances, further-more, the ratio of pre-contact to post-contact objectives is appreciably greater for Pichahila than for Duidui. Features common to both communi-ties, like a social organization based upon exogamous matrilineal moieties (Hogbin 1938), long occupance of the windward side of a high island, and an intimate knowledge of the foothills' ecology, clearly will not yield an explanation: at some time or another divergent forces have been at work. Pichahila's site (fig. 9.1), whilst only one and a half hours' walk inland, means that its inhabitants are somewhat isolated from the prevailing lines of communication and have fewer village-generated sources of cash than Duidui (Chapman 1969, 128–9). In addition, they belong to a more

Table 9.6

Proportion of 'pre-contact' to 'post-contact' objectives,* Duidui and Pichahila 1965–6

	Duidui		Pichahila	
	Total	Percentage	Total	Percentage
Pre-contact	482	58.0	692	85.2
Post-contact	349	42.0	120	14.8
Total	831	100	812	100
	Residents (61.6%)	Percentage	Residents (83.6%)	Percentage
Pre-contact	222	43.4	575	84.7
Post-contact	290	56.6	104	15.3
Total	512	100	679	100
	Aliens (38.4%)	Percentage	Aliens (16.4%)	Percentage
Pre-contact	260	81.5	117	88.0
Post-contact	59	18.5	16	12.0
Total	319	100	133	100

* 'Pre-contact' objectives are gardening, relatives/kinsmen and general visiting; 'post-contact' objectives are work, church, administrative, school and medical. The objectives 'return home' and 'other' have been omitted since it is not possible to differentiate them in this fashion.

locally-oriented Catholic order. Whilst the bush community appears nowadays to retain greater pride in and more satisfaction with its heritage,
attitudes in coastal Duidui are somewhat ambivalent. Throughout the past
generation all these influences have reinforced one another to ensure that
Pichahila approaches innovations within the context of customary behaviour,
whereas for Duidui new and old ways tend to be regarded as alternatives.
This revealing difference is most succinctly expressed in the marginal
dominance of post-contact objectives for the ebb and flow of Duidui
residents. Likewise, the overwhelming significance of pre-contact activities
and orientations for Pichahila mobility distils the manifold ways in which
values and attitudes translate into actual behaviour; result in local differentials
even when certain elements are constant; and carry through to such features
as the duration of completed moves, their origins and destinations, the
time consumed in travelling, the age and sex of movers, and their relatedness
to people with whom they journeyed (Chapman 1970, 151–66).

Taken overall, absences to earn money, go to school, attend church, utilize
medical or district administration facilities, constitute little more than one-
quarter of the total (469 out of 1,174: table 9.6). Such a statement is no
more than a paraphrase of the original contention that non-economic
reasons are far more important than often appears from migration research.
That result contradicts, however, the impression gained from the field
census that villagers are apparently responding to post-contact and predominantly economic goals. This difference, illuminating rather than
spurious, tends to confirm a growing suspicion about conventional
analyses of the reasons why people move. Given the definitional constraints
associated with census data that have been collected across rather than
through time, and given the analytical strategy of explanation by inference,
generalizations that 'economic' forces are primarily responsible for internal
migration seem unwittingly tautological.

In retrospect . . .

Considering the various technical and conceptual difficulties outlined here
it is no surprise that, of the three components of population change,
mortality and fertility have traditionally commanded greater attention from
formal demographers. During the late 1960s, mobility research gained
some technical impetus from Eldridge's (1964) transfer of longitudinal
cohort analysis from fertility to migration, but this breakthrough has still
to diffuse beyond a small disciplinary audience. For, as the sociologist
Reissman (1967, 211) correctly observes, 'The study of migration exerts a
noticeable attraction for those social scientists who are confronted with
the complex phenomena of development and change. For one thing . . .
migration is an appealing index of the development process; it is a clearly

relevant metric in an area of scientific concern where valid statistical indicators are scarce.'

Unfortunately, as Reissman takes care to emphasize, this appealing prospect is clouded by an untidily complex reality: 'It is rather more likely that migration is a behavioural result of a complex set of decisions that are rational and irrational, conscious and unconscious, deliberate and impulsive' (Reissman 1967, 212).

It was in an attempt to escape this bothersome dilemma that the present enquiry focused upon a bush and coast community in South Guadalcanal. The tactic of a micro-study was purposely adopted because, as Brookfield (1970, 20) cogently argues, 'It is in [this] that the system model, and especially the adaptive system, acquires the closest orthomorphism with empirical fact.' Examination of such a fragmentary slice of the real world, rather than being an exercise in the unique or the exotic as so often happens in human geography, reflected the desire to sharpen the cutting edge of technique and analysis, to focus upon mobility from the stand-point of the village in all its ongoing complexity, to yield definitions that are locally relevant rather than predefined from external conventions, and, finally, to generate inductive models based upon a specified nucleate population.

Over the years this field research also has crystallized larger questions. First, the cultural specificity of the conventions of population movement, for example 'migration', and the need to elucidate ones that are locally relevant but reported in ways that still permit cross-cultural and inter-national comparison. Second, our ignorance about the range of mobility experienced by a particular society and the refinement of available tech-niques necessary to identify them, one remedy for which might be the maintenance of a population register by semi-literate villagers when the academic is thousands of miles away! And, third, the need for more imagination in data collection, analysis and subsequent reporting to foster (a) identification of the logical links in the decision to move; (b) a sharper distinction between the different kinds of information contained in territorial censuses and sample surveys, movers' statements and field-workers' observations: and (c) field investigations and analyses that proceed at three levels: the objective, the normative and the psychosocial (Germani 1965). Paradoxically, this last distinction remains largely ignored in migration research, yet is perhaps the most crucial advance during the past decade.

Acknowledgements

The field study was funded by an International Development Fellowship from the East-West Center, Honolulu, and coding and processing of data by the East-West Population Institute and the Intramural Research Fund, University of Hawaii. My greatest debt is to the people of Duidui and Pichahila, and in particular to my interpreters and two outstanding 'big men'. Since 1968, a succession of research aides has battled with the mobility register; for their painstaking efforts this paper represents some belated recognition. Thanks are due also to Gary A. Fuller for statistical advice.

References

Brookfield, H. C. (1970) *Dualism, and the geography of developing countries.* Presidential address delivered to Section 21 (Geographical Sciences), Australian and New Zealand Association for the Advancement of Science. Port Moresby.

Chapman, M. (1969) A population study in South Guadalcanal: some results and implications. *Oceania* 40, 119–47.

Chapman, M. (1970) *Population movement in tribal society: the case of Duidui and Pichahila: British Solomon Islands.* Unpublished Ph.D. thesis, Univ. of Washington.

Chapman, M. (1971) *Population research in the Pacific islands: a case study and some reflections.* E.-W. Pop. Inst. Working Paper 17. Honolulu.

Eldridge, H. T. (1964) A cohort approach to the analysis of migration differentials. *Demog.* 1, 212–29.

Germani, G. (1965) Migration and acculturation, in Hauser, P. M. (ed.) *Handbook for social research in urban areas*, 159–78. Paris.

Hackman, B. D. (1968) *A guide to the spelling and pronunciation of place names in the British Solomon Islands Protectorate.* Geogr. Names Cttee., BSIP Lands and Survey Dept. Honiara.

Hägerstrand, T. (1963) Geographic measures of migration: Swedish data, in Sutter, J. (ed.) *Human displacements: measurement, methodological aspects*, 61–83. Monaco.

Hogbin, H. I. (1938) Social organization of Guadalcanal and Florida, Solomon Islands. *Oceania* 8, 398–402.

McArthur, N. (1961) *Report on the population census of 1959, British Solomon Islands.* Honiara.

Petersen, W. (1969) *Population* (2nd rev. edn). London.

Pirie, P. and Barrett, W. (1962) Western Samoa: population, production and wealth. *Pac. Viewp.* 3, 63–96.

Reissman, L. (1967) The metrics of migration. *Pac. Viewp.* 8, 211–12.

Shryock Jr., H. S. and Larmon, E. A. (1965) Some longitudinal data on internal migration. *Demog.* 2, 579–92.

Part Three
Empirical and comparative studies

Introduction

These studies range widely in area and in themes considered. There has been no attempt to achieve global coverage, but papers on interregional migration are concerned with North (*Lycan*) and South (*Geiger*) America, Western (*Fielding*) and East-Central (*Kosiński*) Europe, tropical Africa (*Harvey*), India (*Gosal and Krishan*) and Southeast Asia (*Ng*). Data and other information on migration are available for these major areas to varying degrees. The Soviet Union is regrettably the one major area for which there is such information that is not represented. Clearly data problems are much greater for some areas (India) than they are for others (Western and East-Central Europe).

Authors have adopted various approaches to interregional migration. Some give particular attention to patterns and flows (*Fielding, Gosal, Ng*); others emphasize motivations (*Geiger*) and factors and determinants (*Lycan*). Migration is viewed in the broader context of regional differentiation (*Geiger*), the influence of political factors (*Kosiński, Ng*), and the attraction of major urban centres (*Lycan, Gosal and Krishan*). *Harvey* provides historical perspective on interregional movements in tropical Africa, while *Fielding*, in view of present trends in Western Europe within the European Economic Community, looks to the future and reflects on whether the traditional notions of what constitutes internal migration will continue to be relevant.

Models of interregional migration are discussed in a number of papers (*Fielding, Harvey, Lycan*) with particular reference to factors of distance, considered in social as well as in physical terms (*Lycan*). The studies of interregional migration on continental and subcontinental scales are complemented by two papers for areas of much smaller scale. Both of these have problems of marginality in respect of economic development. *Lamont and Proudfoot* are concerned with migration, particularly rural depopulation, in relation to changing settlement patterns in the Canadian Province of Alberta. *Hansen's* study of the marginal areas of Norway considers urban growth with concomitant permanent migration and periodic commuting to urban centres. These movements are viewed in the context of the general demographic situation, both present and projected, with some comparisons between northern Norway and similar areas in the northern parts of Sweden and of Finland.

These studies at larger and smaller scales are illustrative of regional studies of population movements being undertaken by geographers, with particular reference to spatial characteristics and to the wider context of regional development of which mobility is one aspect.

10 Interregional migration studies in tropical Africa

M. E. Harvey

The long history of man in Africa has meant that centuries of population shifts and readjustments have occurred. The reasons for population relocation have changed as man's outlook on resources, technology and sociocultural ties has been modified. In addition, the patterns, structure and intensity of mobility in the African continent have also changed. This paper attempts to isolate historically the motives for interregional migration in the continent, to note the nature of studies which have been made, and to identify areas for future research.

Historical patterns of migration in Africa

In historic times, three patterns of interregional migration can be identified: the *tribal-based, traditional state-based*, and the *colonial-type*. Each of these has distinctive input variables that were the main inducements for relocation and general population shifts. As most independent African states have largely continued the colonial pattern of development with excessive concentration in a few nodes (or regions) and a dendritic marketing system, a post-colonial type of interregional migration has not as yet evolved (McNulty 1972).

The tribal-based phase

Although recent archaeological findings in Africa have indicated that interaction did exist between the various Neolithic communities, the different groups in Africa before the growth of Ghana about AD 700 can be conceptualized as spatially discrete subsets under isotropic conditions. In these, technology essentially remained invariant and a quasi-equilibrium existed between population and resources. The structure of this stability was 'a function of the techniques that . . . [were] perfected or adopted by each of these societies, and of the degrees to which they . . . [were] adequate to the environment' (Tricart 1970). Under such conditions, a homeostatic process tended to maintain the balance between population density and available resources (Wynne-Edwards 1967). Exceptionally favourable periods, however, often resulted in increased productivity and hence accelerated population growth. Deteriorations in climate and the general ecosphere or outbreaks of epidemics tended to institute a new homeostatic process by either Malthusian checks or by migration. In other instances attempts at stabilizing population to food supply sometimes entailed infanticide and spacing of births. Migration in such societies involved either a tribe or group of lineages. Although migration as a gradual diffusion process was sometimes common, warfare and coercion were often an essential prelude: 'warfare was frequently associated with slave trading and in the general pattern of events weaker tribes were displaced or enslaved by stronger and more warlike neighbours. Tensions and pressures were thus built up which set in train population movements that involved successive groups of people' (Prothero 1964). For example, theories about Bantu migration are very divergent though there is a compromise theory that this group dispersed from an original heartland around the headwaters of the Congo and the Zambezi rivers, first spreading west and east to reach both the Atlantic and Indian Oceans, and finally moving north into the Lake Victoria area, and south into South Africa (Oliver 1966).

In general, accounts of migrations during the traditional tribal-based phase are scanty. Further archaeological, historical and linguistic research is essential for a detailed understanding. Only then can questions about migration loci, duration, and motives during that era, be adequately answered.

The traditional state-based phase

The introduction of new technology or a new economic base resulted in sequential variables that eventually altered the system and gradually effected the processes of spatial integration. In pre-colonial Africa such changes were related to the increased use of iron tools and the extraction of minerals. These generated long-distance trading, increased population densities at advantageous geographic locations, and ultimately caused the growth of towns. In many instances a new centralized political system replaced that based on kinship. The rise of the Axumite kingdom of the Horn of Africa was in response to trade in the Red Sea; whereas in West Africa, trade in gold and forest products like kola nuts on the one hand and salt and manufactured goods on the other was paramount in the evolution of the savanna states.

Within the framework of centralized and non-centralized states, migration in post-eighth-century Africa was essentially induced by trade, population pressure and regional economic disparities, the continuous fission and fusion of states, and the Islamization process. The first generally resulted in internal migrations and the gradual extension of the tribal domain. In the last ten centuries, for example, the Somali of northeast Africa have migrated southwards to the northern fringes of Kenya (Prothero 1969). One of the best examples of large-scale migration and colonization is that of the Lwo-speaking peoples of East Africa during the fifteenth to eighteenth centuries. In a series of waves these groups migrated from the Nile valley into the Bantu-speaking section of Uganda (Oliver 1963).

The defeat of states and the emergence of new ones usually caused massive migrations of the defeated groups. Unlike the pattern of mobility described in the last paragraph, this migration usually resulted in the development of new spatially disparate communities. For example, the influx of Mande tribesmen of the savanna state of Mali ultimately led to the colonization of the area around the present Sierra Leone/Liberian border. Although Islam had some foothold in West Africa around the ninth century, it was in the eleventh that it made big advances into the savanna states of the region. It resulted in bitter conflicts between those who had accepted the faith and those who had not, causing internal population shifts and the expansion of territorial land (Davidson and Buah 1967).

Viewing population relocation as a diffusion process, the migration motives discussed are largely different. One which creates a rigid continuous surface is an example of an expansion-type diffusion. Migration due to the disintegration of states generally caused a discontinuous human response surface with minimal feedback between the newly established system and the former states. This is an example of diffusion by relocation.

The colonial epoch

The decline of the savanna kingdoms coincided with the development of forest states, a disruption of trans-Saharan trade and the inception of coastal-based trade in tropical products and slaves with Europe and Asia. The new trade orientation and the general change in the nature, intensity and direction of modernizing forces were finally institutionalized by the latter part of the nineteenth century. Though the colonial pattern of trade had started before this time, the mechanics of colonial rule in Africa were not laid down until then. Within the continent, the modernizing agencies – schools, communications, hospitals, Christianity – of the colonial period, reinforced by physical and climatic variations, introduced modifications in the resultant human response surface. Locational forces altered the space economy and caused unconformities in the socioeconomic surface, with urban/rural schisms and the prosperous/non-productive regional disparities. The result has been massive migration within and between countries.

In a simplified model, neoclassic economic theory postulates that movement from i to j is a result of geographic disparities in the productivity of labour. Under the assumption of labour homogeneity, it contends that migration tends to equalize marginal productivity among migrants and among regions. Maximization of differences in the comparative place utilities of i and all possible j destinations finally influences the choice of destination. In the colonial period such schisms occurred with the development of plantations, urbanization and on a limited scale the application of improved technology to agriculture. Over the continent, the uneven distribution of medical facilities, types of education and administrative services did increase growth and economic viability in the midst of tradition, illiteracy, diseases and subsistence agriculture. For example, in Sierra Leone, economic and employment differences between the diamond mining triangle of Kenema–Koidu–Bo, the iron ore mining centre of Marampa, the commercial rice cultivation region of the coastal northwest and the cash-crop belt of the east on the one hand, and purely rural areas with delicate ecological balances like the northern livestock area and the coastal mangrove swamp belt on the other hand, instituted internal migration. In these instances, the classic push-pull hypothesis is implicit.

Site and situation contrasts have caused massive migration in colonial Africa; however, at the individual level migration decisions are usually affected by the potential migrant's mental map of the country's opportunity surface. Whether this reconstruction is based on travel or information, vertical exaggerations in the surface, reflecting either over- or underestimation of an area's potential, are inevitable, Because of possible information gaps, the potential migrant may not be aware of the economic and social opportunities in certain areas which tend to fall outside his contact field. The importance of information about opportunities in the whole or part of a system considerably affect mobility patterns. In essence, migration is a lag response (Greenwood 1970).

Contemporary migration types and processes

In Africa the processes discussed in the last paragraphs have instituted many kinds of migration. This review, however, is concerned only with regional mobility, which includes '. . . only those movements of individuals and groups of individuals that take place across ethnic or national boundaries' (Mabogunje 1972). In terms of length of move, we can identify short-, intermediate and long-distance migrations. In a time framework, there are also three terms: short, intermediate and long. Thus in a time/distance dimension we have theoretically nine classes of interregional migrants:

Distance	Time (Term)		
	Short	Intermediate	Long
Short	A	D	G
Intermediate	B	E	H
Long	C	F	I

Within the African context, types A, D and G have not been studied to any great extent. Migration types B and C constitute what has so often been studied as seasonal migration. Prothero (1957, 1959), Mitchell (1961) and Southall (1961), for example, show seasonal migrants to be largely males who migrate either to urban areas or to economically more advanced agricultural regions and stay for about four to six months. The study of migration between Ivory Coast, Ghana, Upper Volta, Niger, Togo and Dahomey in 1958–69 revealed that of the 400,000 to 500,000 people involved, about 80% of all migrants stayed for less than a year, 59% made between two and four trips, and 14% made more than four trips per year (CCTA/CSA 1961). Prothero (1965) described the seasonal mobility pattern in West Africa: 'Migrants leave home to seek work between late September and November, at the beginning of the dry season after the harvest has been taken; they return home again in the following April and May to cultivate their farms with the onset of the rains. The distinct seasonal variations in climate between one part of the year and another thus permit migrations to be integrated into the annual cycle of activity.'

Mobility types E and F consist of short-term migrants who leave home for a specified period; usually between six months and two years. In terms of numbers, fewer people are involved in these types of migration. The study of migration between Ivory Coast, Ghana and adjacent countries showed that only 7% stayed more than a year but less than two.

Types H and I involve permanent or long-term migrants. Such migrations often occurred either by a leap-frog process or, especially in more recent times, by the direct relocation of individuals and/or families. One of the best examples of the former is the movement in Ghana of Krobos into Akim territory, the cocoa growing belt. Hunter (1963) analysing their mobility pattern reported that initially a Krobo would purchase a plot in the forest about a day's journey from his present home, would cultivate it and then reinvest in a second plot farther west. This process of progressive reinvestment finally brought many Krobo families into Akim territory. An example of the latter is the migration of the Kikuyu, Embu and Meru from the Kenya Highlands, Central Nyanza and the coastal belt to major cities such as Nairobi and Mombasa.

The typology of migrant types in terms of distance and duration of stay may be unreal and oversimplified. Observations have shown that in certain cases, seasonal migrants have become short-term or permanent migrants. This implies that the contrasts may be conceptualized as different responses to both the push forces at origin and the individual's allegiance to family, tradition and agriculture.

Although the literature on African interregional migration is rather limited, there is consensus that for any of the distance/time types identified above, migration reflects the individual's desire to maximize a utility function involving many economic and sociocultural variables. Prothero (1959), studying migration from Sokoto Province of Nigeria, clearly showed the importance of economic maximization and pay-off in migration. Of those involved in this seasonal relocation, 52% went to 'seek money', and another 24% claimed that trade was their primary motive. This economic motive is also evident in the results from the analysis of a Ghanaian national sample survey (Caldwell 1968, 1969). For Sierra Leone, Harvey, Dow and Benjamin (1973) showed that 72% of the explained variance in interregional migration was due to regional economic and informational disparities. Economic considerations have also been noted by Southall (1961) for Kikuyu migrations into plantation areas and important regional centres, in the analysis by Polly Hill (1963) of migrant labour into the cocoa growing areas of Ghana, and in the analysis of interregional mobility in Sierra Leone by Forde and Harvey (1969). Employing multivariate statistical methods Beals, Levy and Moses (1967) on Ghana, Hirst (1969, 1970) on Tanzania, Riddell (1970) on Freetown, Sierra Leone, and Harvey (1972) on the chiefdoms of Sierra Leone, have also emphasized the importance of economic factors in African interregional migration. The last paper specifically tested the proposition that internal migration in Sierra Leone tends to be from areas at a low level of development to relatively more economically advanced regions. A corollary to this posited that migration also occurs between units at comparable levels of economic development.

The importance of information prior to migration has also been identified as a very significant contributory factor in population relocation. Operationally, distance has been regarded as a very good surrogate for information flow. In all such cases its attenuating effect on mobility has been very significant indeed (Caldwell 1968; Forde and Harvey 1969; Riddell 1970). A few other studies have distinguished between information flow and distance. Harvey (1972) assessed the relative importance of economic motives, distance and information on ethnic mobility; the latter being calibrated as the percentage of the dominant ethnic group of i in destination j. The results showed that for smaller ethnic groups the information factor was most important. For the largest groups the single most important factor was economic differential. In all cases except the largest group, the friction of distance was significant at more than the .01 level of confidence.

Besides purely economic motives certain politico-sociological, medical and educational factors have also induced interregional migration. National boundaries cut across the historical migration routes of nomadic peoples who had to make readjustments in their long-established institutionalized behavioural patterns. For example, the Zande were partitioned into three by the establishment of boundaries between colonial territories. This problem, coupled with the imposition of forced labour and a hut or head tax payable in cash, created an atmosphere conducive to migration (Hance 1970). Labour migration to the Firestone plantation in Liberia, to the copper mines of Katanga and to the diamond and gold mines of South Africa all reflect these colonial machinations.

The second non-economic inducement to migration in the colonial era was the growth of education and the uneven distribution of educational and medical facilities. These became strong, attractive forces, especially after it was realized that good health and a good education meant non-agricultural jobs and escape from the traditional social norms (Caldwell 1968, 1969). For detailed development planning more empirical studies assessing the effect of education, educational institutions and other modernizing variables on national migration channels and development are essential.

A third aspect of the colonial impact on migration was the reduction of internecine warfare so that individuals had a larger potential area for mobility; furthermore, energy was diverted from warfare to agriculture. This latter factor, coupled with improved medical facilities, caused increased population pressure on resources, and hence migration. Adult males in the overcrowded areas of eastern Nigeria 'migrate seasonally to work on hired firms, or even as farm labourers, in the timber or tree crops areas farther south, and in Mid-West and Western Nigeria, sending home various remittances' (Dema 1968). In Sierra Leone the decline of intertribal warfare and the disruption of the general ecosystem in the cattle areas of the north reduced the potential capacity of the land, and outmigration to the diamond mining areas, the plantations and the urbanized regions has been increasing at an alarming rate.

Selectivity of migration as regards sex and cohort group has also been observed. The dominance of young adults, especially males, in the migration process is not surprising. In terms of other attributes such as literacy and vocational preparedness, however, conclusions have been divergent. Whilst Caldwell (1969) observed that many migrant labour groups in Ghana were essentially better trained and educated than their counterparts in the destination node, Harvey (1968) in Sierra Leone found the opposite. The study of interregional migration between Ghana, Dahomey, Togo, Upper Volta, Niger and the Ivory Coast also supported the latter's observation: about 75 to 80% of all the migrants (400,000 to 500,000) were illiterate. Of the remainder, about 10 to 15% were literate only in Arabic. Here there is need for further research.

This brief review of the factors influencing interregional mobility in Africa south of the Sahara shows that in spite of the paucity of studies and the rather unsatisfactory nature of most of the data, the limited literature shows that education, economic opportunity and information availability are all important attractive forces. On the other hand, persistence of traditional systems, the balance of the population/land ratio in rural areas and climatic vicissitudes all encourage population relocation. The friction of distance and age/sex differentials are also important variables in African interregional migration.

Empirical and analytical tools utilized in African migration studies

One of the basic excuses against using sophisticated techniques on African data is either their large margin of error or their extreme level of aggregation. Hence most of the empirical researches have been purely descriptive. Though they provide valuable information on the interaction processes in Africa, their contributions to the development of good empirical and analytical models have been very limited indeed.

In the last decade, attempts have been made to apply statistical and mathematical techniques to African mobility. Caldwell (1968, 1969) on Ghanaian migration is an example of the application of inferential statistics. Although no information is given of what type of statistical test (parametric or nonparametric) was employed, the degree of reliability of various associations is stated in terms of levels of significance and is a great help in assessing the relative importance of relationships. Hunter (1965), using the sex ratio of the economically active population (15–44 years) as a surrogate for migration, is another example. Based on a high correlation between immigration and sex ratio in Ghana, he concluded that 'the sex ratio may to this extent be regarded as indication of trends in population growth and migration'. Using the sex ratio he identified local councils of net in- and outmigration in the country. Although it was an attempt at overcoming some of Africa's data problems, it is an oversimplification of a very complex process. Clearly variability in sex ratio reflects other operational factors like differential fertility and mortality, and other less tangible factors. Male excess in a locality is either the result of excessive male inmigration or extreme female outmigration.

Hirst (1969) attempted a multivariate modification of Hunter's mobility/ sex ratio relationship. Using principal component analysis on six variables that are supposedly indicative of net migration trends, he extracted a net migration dimension as the basis for identifying net in- and outmigration areas in Tanzania. The assumption that migration is only a function of some ethnic index, persons per tribe, children per 100 adults, male children per 100 male adults, total sex ratio and the adult sex ratio is unjustifiable. Unlike Hunter, Hirst gives no indication of the relationship between the independent variables and immigration, which throws serious doubts on the validity of the whole exercise. Calibration of the variables may also be queried. For example, the ethnic index, computed as the 'number of tribes divided by the percentage in the dominant tribe (multiplied by 100 for convenience)', would surely exhibit a bias for large ethnic groups. Furthermore, no justification is presented for including both total child/adult and male child/adult male ratios. It is very difficult for the reader to find the relationship between a purely random process like number of male children and migration. The empirical and analytical usefulness of such studies is reduced by not including actual migration processes in the analysis.

Another application of principal component analysis is the study of immigration to Freetown, Sierra Leone (Riddell 1970). In testing the hypothesis on the relationship between *per capita* rates of migration, Y, to Freetown and a set of fifteen socioeconomic variables, $X_1, X_2, \ldots, X_{15}$, Riddell first used a multiple regression format:

$$Y = a + a_1 X_1 + \ldots + a_{15} X_{15} \ldots \tag{1}$$

60% of the variance in migration. In assessing the relative importance of the independent variables, he wrote: '. . . the strongest variables when considered in combination are the distance from the diamond fields, the date at which the area was connected to the transport system, and population density. The other variables are relatively insignificant.' To reduce multicollinearity among the variables they were subjected to principal component analysis with orthogonal rotation. The four extracted independent dimensions were then used as the explanatory variables. Thus (1) becomes:

$$Y = x + s_1 F_1 + s_2 F_2 + s_3 F_3 + s_4 F_4 \ldots \tag{2}$$

where s_1, s_2, s_3, s_4 are the factor scores for the chiefdoms. This new model increased the explained variance from 60 to 62%. Riddell demonstrated how (2) can be represented in the form of (1), thus enabling the researcher to assess the contribution of the original input variables. Although the methodology is sound and the conclusions are quite interesting, one

wonders whether a set of fewer independent variables might not have produced similar results. Because of the large number of independent variables
involved, the predictive values of this model are very limited.

Principal component analysis was used by Harvey (1972) as a filtering
tool to appraise the relationship between levels of economic development
and migration. For each of the 148 administrative units in Sierra Leone,
20 variables designed to reflect levels of development were collected and
subjected to a principal component analysis. The results showed that 5
factors accounted for 82.3% of the total variance. A multivariate grouping
algorithm, the Ward H-Group, was used to identify 5 levels of economic
developments. For the 96 chiefdoms for which 96 x 96 matrix of birth-
place-destination data was available, a Markovian mean first passage time
matrix (MFPT) was computed. Using the same grouping algorithm, 5
destination-types and 5 economic levels, a table of cross-tabulations
showed that there is some relationship between the level of economic
development of a locality and its relative attraction to migrants. A criticism
of this formulation is the absence of some statistical test to assess the
strength of the relationship between levels of development and migration
patterns. Elsewhere, however, using a combination of stepwise regression,
centrographic methods and point biserial correlation, 3 related hypotheses were tested: differences in ethnic propensity to migrate, directionality
in migration and the relative importance of economic factors, friction of
distance and information flow in structuring mobility patterns (Harvey 1972).

Probably one of the most extensive multivariate studies on interregional
migration patterns in Africa is that on Ghana (Beals *et al.* 1966). It
attempted 'to determine the relation between migration and the levels of
regional income and development in Ghana. The effects of transportation
investment on population movements, agricultural output and interregional
trade are of particular interest'. Using a multiple regression model (see
equation 1), they investigated the relationship between migration and
regional contrasts in education, degree of urbanization, the cohort structure
and income. With explained variances of more than 90%, the computation
showed that migration is responsive to regional wage levels, that distance is
a great deterrent to interregional mobility, and that migration is positively
affected by urbanization or population density. Although this study shows
how model building and hypothesis testing can be applied to an African
situation with interesting results, it had several shortcomings: '. . . the gross
regionalization of the data base and thus the ecological fallacy; . . . the
distance measures are no more than estimates for regions of such sizes;
many of the explanatory variables are only crude surrogates; and multicollinearity effects may bias the interpretation of the regression coefficients
and thus the interpretation of the model and the data' (Riddell and Harvey
1972).

Besides these empirical researches, there are analytical models on African rural-urban migrations. Todaro (1969) in a rural-urban labour migration model assumed that due to migration, the percentage change in the urban labour force in any time period is conditioned by 'the differential between the discounted streams of expected urban and rural real income . . . expressed as a percentage of the discounted stream of expected rural real income'. In a more recent two-sector analysis model (Todaro and Harris 1970), the two sectors are identified in terms of production and urban components: 'the urban sector specializes in the production of a manufactured good, part of which is exported to the rural sector in exchange for agricultural goods. The rural sector has a choice of either, using all available labor to produce a single agricultural good, some of which is exported to the urban sector.'

Future research

The paper has attempted to review works on interregional migration in tropical Africa. Because of the size and complexity of the area it does not pretend to be comprehensive. It shows that more research is required to test hypotheses, and explain processes. Such studies should aim at developing ways of utilizing the present scanty information on interregional mobility for prescription and prediction. Process-oriented research designed to understand how individuals and groups migrate over time and space is essential for any regional planning aimed at reducing rural depopulation and accelerated rural/urban migration. In such studies, models should be developed that would be capable of assessing the effects of alternate inputs at time t on the migration pattern at time t + 1. Because of the present data scarcity, more detailed fieldwork by scholars from various social sciences is essential if the future development of man and resources in Africa is to be efficiently planned.

References

Beals, R. E., Levy, M. B. and Moses, L. N. (1967) Rationality and migration in Ghana. *Rev. Econ. Stat.* 49, 480–6.

Beals, R. E., Levy, M. B., Menzes, C. F. and Moses, L. N. (1966) *Labour migration and regional development in Ghana.* Evanston.

Caldwell, J. C. (1968) Determinants of rural-urban migration in Ghana. *Pop. Stud.* 22, 361–72.

Caldwell, J. C. (1969) *African rural-urban migration: the movement to Ghana's towns.* Columbia Univ.

CCTA/CSA (1961) *Study of migrations in West Africa.* Joint Project No. 3, MIG (61) 2 (mimeographed).

Davidson, B. and Buah, F. K. (1967) *The growth of African civilization: a history of West Africa 1000–1800.* London.

Dema, I. S. (1968) Some reflection on the nutritional problems of dense farm populations, in Caldwell, J. C. and Okonjo, C. (eds.) *The population of tropical Africa.* New York.

Forde, E. and Harvey, M. (1969) Geographical analysis of migration to Freetown. *Sierra Leone Geogr. J.* 13, 13–27.

Greenwood, M. J. (1970) Lagged response in the decision to migrate. *J. Reg. Sci.* 10, 375–84.

Hance, W. A. (1970) *Population, migration and urbanization in Africa.* Columbia Univ.

Harvey, M. E. (1968) Implications of migration to Freetown – a geographical study of the relationships between tribes, housing and occupation. *Civilization* 10, 247–67.

Harvey, M. E. (1971) Social change and ethnic relocation in developing Africa: the Sierra Leone example. *Geogr. Ann.* B, 53, 2, 94–106.

Harvey, M. E. (1972) Levels of economic development and patterns of internal migration in Sierra Leone, in Ominde, S. H. and Ejiogu, F. (eds.) *Population growth and economic development in Africa.* London.

Harvey, M. E., Dow, T. and Benjamin, E. (1973) in Caldwell, J. C. (ed.) *Social and economic development in West Africa* (in press).

Hill, P. (1963) *The migrant cocoa farmers of southern Ghana.* Cambridge.

Hirst, M. A. (1969) Net migration patterns over Tanzania. *E. Afr. Geogr. Rev.* 7, 25–36.

Hirst, M. A. (1970) Tribal migration in East Africa: a review and analysis. *Geogr. Ann.* B, 52, 153–64.

Hunter, J. M. (1963) Cocoa migration and patterns of land ownership in the Densu Valley near Suhum, Ghana. *Trans. Inst. Brit. Geogr.* **33**, 61–88.

Hunter, J. M. (1965) Regional patterns of population growth in Ghana, in Whittow, J. B. and Wood, P. D. (eds.) *Essays in geography for A. Miller.* London.

Mabogunje, A. L. (1972) *Regional mobility and resource development in West Africa.* Montreal and London.

McNulty, M. L. (1972) African urban systems, transportation networks and regional inequalities. *Afr. Urb. Notes*, 6, 56–66.

Mitchell, J. C. (1961) Wage labour and African population movements in Central Africa, in Barbour, K. M. and Prothero, R. M. (eds.) *Essays on African population.* London.

Oliver, R. (1963) Discernible developments in the interior c. 1500–1840, in Oliver, R. and Mathew, G. (eds.) *History of East Africa*, Vol. 1. Oxford.

Oliver, R. (1966) The problem of Bantu expansion. *J. Afr. Hist.* 7, 361–76.

Prothero, R. M. (1957) Migratory labour from Northwestern Nigeria. *Afr.* 37, 251–61.

Prothero, R. M. (1959) *Migrant labour from Sokoto Province, Northern Nigeria.* Kaduna.

Prothero, R. M. (1964) Continuity and change in African population mobility, in Steel, R. W. and Prothero, R. M. (eds.) *Geographers and the tropics: Liverpool essays.* London.

Prothero, R. M. (1965) *Migrants and malaria.* London.

Prothero, R. M. (ed.) (1969) *A geography of Africa.* London and New York.

Riddell, J. B. (1970) *The spatial dynamics of modernization in Sierra Leone.* Evanston.

Riddell, J. B. and Harvey, M. E. (1972) The urban system in the migration process: an evaluation of stepwise migration in Sierra Leone. *Econ. Geogr.* 48, 270–83.

Southall, A. W. (1961) Population movements in East Africa, in Barbour, K. M. and Prothero, R. M. (eds.) *Essays on African population.* London.

Todaro, M. P. (1969) A model of labour migration and urban unemployment in less developed countries. *Am. Econ. Rev.* 138–48.

Todaro, M. P. and Harris, J. R. (1970) Migration, unemployment and development: a two-sector analysis. *Am. Econ. Assoc.* 60, 125–41.

Tricart, J. (1970) Physical environment and population pressure, in Zelinsky, W., Kosiński, L. A. and Prothero, R. M. (eds.) *Geography and a crowding world.* Oxford and New York.

Wynne-Edwards, W. C. (1967) Self-regulating systems in population of animals, in Dohrs, F. E. and Sommers, L. M. (eds.) *Physical geography: selected readings.* New York.

11   Interregional migrations in Latin America

P. P. Geiger

The significance of the regional approach

In studies of migrations keenest interest has tended to centre on the motivations of and socioeconomic implications for the migrants and the problems created at the foci of inmigration. Regional statistics represent relatively high levels of aggregation; even in regions that are true 'self-organizing systems' the population is too complex to share common motivations to migrate. On the other hand in geographic space it is common for point units to attain a significance of their own in the migratory process, especially as foci of attraction. The conditions that make the city of Brasília a pole of inmigration have nothing to do with the features of the homogeneous region of the Central Plateau in which the city is inserted. The same may be said of Ciudad Guayana or Monterrey.

Migrations have been concerned more especially with inter-urban, rural-urban, stepwise and other characteristics. Very often problems of urban socioeconomic content and city growth have been confused with migratory problems. Little has been done, for instance, in terms of analysis of the effects of migrations on regional 'convergence' or 'divergence'.

In certain situations the migratory process acquires striking areal expression, with characteristics related to regional environmental variables. Examples are to be found in the outmigration from the semi-arid Brazilian northeast, and in the inmigration to many pioneer fringes throughout the continent. Hyperurbanization around a national metropolis or regional primate cities is present in nearly all the countries of Latin America. Around the city of São Paulo, however, there stretches more than a simple metropolitan agglomeration; rather is it an urbanized region with tentacular extensions representing the expansion of a process of urban concentration.

In reality the decision to migrate is ultimately an individual response to total environment, but scientific and practical interest lies in the search for similarities and generalizations. These can be established from various points of view (Thomas 1970, 10), amongst them the regional one. For each system there will be significant variables for the spatial or regional examination of migrations.

Recently concern about interregional migrations and their comparison with intraregional flows has developed in response to the growth of interest in the relations between economic process and organization of national space. The regional approach is valid not only because migrations enter into the structuring of regions and of their projection in space, or because inmigration shares in the build-up of regions and outmigration influences evolution or involution. This approach is necessary for a more profound, dialectic or systemic comprehension of the migratory process. 'Characteristics of migrants reflect the conditions and changes in their social and spatial environment and therefore need to be evaluated in a community context. Ideally, both individual differences and group differences need to be analysed with regard to spatial behavior' (Wilkie 1972). The study of migration by city size, or according to the rural-rural or rural-urban character, may afford as high a level of aggregation. Cities of a given size are usually not homogeneous, often varying according to the regions to which they belong. This is all the more valid for the developing countries, with their regions at contrasting stages of development. It becomes necessary therefore to disaggregate any urban grouping, according to the regions in which the cities are found (Cornelius 1971).

The geographical approach relates the macro-, meso-, microregional and local levels. Problems arise as to regional definition, choice of regional hierarchical level to be used in the observations, and the scale of the regions. In Argentina, Brazil or Mexico, a mesoregion may be larger than an entire country of Central America. In a nested national regional system, it is of interest, for each area, to observe at which level or levels the most striking aspects of migration appear. What is interregional at one level becomes intraregional at a higher one.

Decisions that influence the development of migrations will also have different hierarchies; the decisions of the Brazilian federal government to build Brasília, to subsidize the industrialization of the northeast or to drive highways through Amazonia will naturally have greater repercussion than ones taken by local authorities. The strategies followed in government planning may include the handling of migratory movements. It is necessary, however, to understand the behaviour of the populations if the initiative taken is to yield worthwhile results (Schwind 1971, 117).

Finally, the regional approach encounters the problem of spatial data collecting units. It is desirable to have statistics available for the smallest unit from which it is possible to aggregate to levels of a higher order.

General aspects of interregional migrations in Latin America

Latin American countries have experienced massive internal migration since World War II, a process stimulated by improved transportation and communication, increasing social mobility, cultural emancipation and concomitant rising expectations, the growing demographic pressure on traditional rural areas and the widening gulf between developing and retarded regions within the country. (Wesche 1971, 251)

The results of increasing accessibility are apparent everywhere. Settlements have experienced an exodus of residents who were formerly more isolated and deep-rooted; 'frontier regions', formerly practically unsettled, have grown rapidly in response to the inflow of population.

The concentration of modernization in certain areas creates contrasts with stagnating regions, thereby originating migration. Contrary to the trend in the United States, where the mainstream flows are from the denser, more highly organized and industrialized regions of the northeast to the south and west, in Latin America the prevailing movement is directed toward the more extensively urbanized regions with the highest industrial concentration. Nevertheless, in some countries there has been a relative increase in migration to new farming regions.

In Mexico in the 1950s, for instance, there were 382 *municipios* with a positive migration balance as compared with 1,387 with a negative one. Of the former, 344 had a combined surplus of 536,000, and the remaining 38 a total inmigrant balance of 1,940,000 (Stevens 1968, 72).

A preliminary examination based on a 1.3% subsample of the 1970 census has been made recently by the Instituto Brasileiro de Geografia e Estatística of characteristics of the Brazilian population, according to ten macroregions. The data show that in one of those macroregions, the state of São Paulo, there reside 32.6% of all the people not living in their county of birth and whose last migratory shift was from one macroregion to another. This concentration is due mainly to urbanization, but the development of an urban system in the state of São Paulo is linked to the expansion of the non-industrialized region surrounding the metropolis, which accounts for 44% of the state population and 57% of its urban population. Of the 2,522,000 persons entering 'directly' (not including those who, though born in other states, made their last migratory move from one São Paulo county to another), 2,233,000 (88%) found their way into the urban framework, 1,543,000 moved from other cities and 690,000 from the rural milieu.

The creation of 'new regions' by the settlement and development of spaces hitherto empty of population is a continuous process. In South America, in this context, migrations from one country to another are now starting to build up, as between Brazil and Paraguay and between Brazil and Venezuela (Valladares and Gaignard 1971, 397).

In spite of industrial dominance in the GNP in several Latin American countries (Argentina, Venezuela, Chile, Brazil, Mexico, Peru) some of these still show an absolute increase of rural population. On account of the prodigious growth of the population and the fact that technological changes in farming do not strike very deep (Gonzalez 1971), the pressure on arable land resulting from migration to these recently cleared regions is enormous.

Migrations to new regions or industrial areas have a broad interregional character, tending to increase in absolute terms. In certain countries such as Brazil, however, with the growth of intraregional migration in the most developed regions and the role of the big cities in other regions, a relative decline has recently set in.

The preliminary data of the 1970 Brazilian census show that of the total persons migrating from one macroregion to another, 23.5% made their latest shift in the last 2 years; of those that last moved into the interior of the same macroregion, 26.1% did so within the last 2 years. The ratio between the total persons making their last migratory movement within the macroregion and the total persons shifting from one macro-region to another when they last moved was as follows: 1.66% for those who last moved more than 10 years ago; 2.27% for those moving 6 to 10 years ago; 2.89% for those moving 3 to 5 years ago; 2.76% for those moving 1 and 2 years ago; and 2.89% for those who moved within the last year (fig. 11.1).

There are some that look upon increasing migration as a matter of concern, in that it reveals 'push' forces. Their claims for measures to dynamize the depressed regions are opposed to interregional migration. Present urban growth is held by them to be excessive, inasmuch as it is out of proportion to the absorption of manpower in industry, and food prices are rising. The problems of underemployment and unemployment affect the population of town and country, places of outmigration and inmigration, and not strictly the migrants themselves. Frankman (1971) stresses the contradiction of complaining of industrialization with intensive capital while refusing to accept expansion of the primitive tertiary sector in the cities.

The supporters of migration point to positive correlations between development and migration. In Brazil, working with 10 macroregions, it has been observed that the variable of 'migrant entries in the last 5 years' has its highest index of correlation with that of the 'number of persons with a monthly income of 85 dollars or more'. The correlation was found to be .75 (Geiger 1972) (table 11.1).

The percentile relationship between difference of population in a Brazilian region i (a_i) and the population not born in the counties where they reside (e_i) in that region, and the Brazilian population in that same region, stands at 50.7% for São Paulo, the most developed region

$$\left(\frac{a_i - e_i}{a_i} \times 100 = 50.7 \right).$$

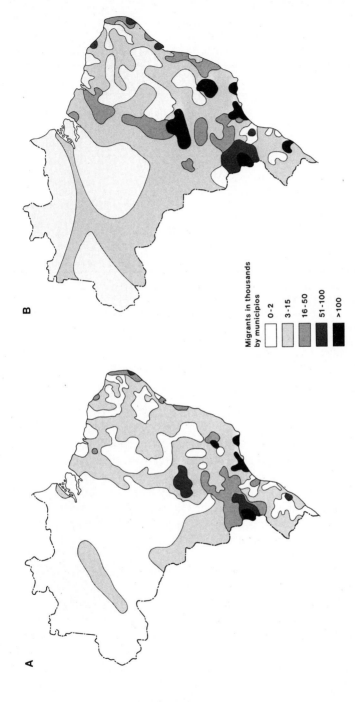

Migrants in thousands
by municipios

0 - 2
3 - 15
16 - 50
51 - 100
>100

B

A

Figure 11.1 Migrants in Brazil (1970) residing in a *municipio*: (A) less than a year; (B) 6–10 years

Source: L. C. Gomes, N. do Valle and A. C. Olinto (1972) *Recuperação de Informação e Migração*, Fundação IBGE, Rio de Janeiro (mimeographed)

Table 11.1

Correlation matrix of variables used for analysis of ten Brazilian regions

	1	2	3	4	5	6	7	8	9	10	11
1											
2	.59										
3	−.08	.56									
4	−.32	.48	.78								
5	.59	.68	.29	.07							
6	.43	.54	.33	.11	.59						
7	.06	.50	.25	.08	.69	.66					
8	.63	.78	.44	.15	.85	.70	.86				
9	.68	.65	.21	−.13	.81	.67	.91	.95			
10	.64	.71	.33	−.56	.83	.69	.90	.97	.97		
11	.63	.81	.47	.19	.85	.70	.91	1.0	.94	.96	
12	.75	.67	.16	−.14	.83	.62	.86	.95	.98	.97	.95

Variables: 1 – Direct entries within last 5 years. 2 – Person who changed counties of residence in the interior of the region within last 5 years. 3 – Direct exits within last 5 years. 4 – Personnel in crop and stock farming, forestry, vegetable extraction and fisheries. 5 – Personnel occupied in industrial activites. 6 – Personnel occupied in trade services and social work. 7 – Personnel in public office. 8 – Women in labour force. 9 – Personnel with 12 to 13 years of schooling. 10 – Personnel with 6 to 12 years of schooling. 11 – Total persons gainfully employed. 12 – Persons with monthly incomes of 500 cruzeiros or more.
Source: Based on data from *Tabulaçóes Avauçadas* (1971), Fundação 1BGE, Rio de Janeiro.

It is 79.8% in the traditionalist macroregion of the northeast, and 81.2% in Amazonia. Strong interregional migration affects this percentage in São Paulo. The ratio $h_i/a_i \times 100$, where h_i represents the non-native population in the counties where they reside, but residing formerly in region i, and a_i the total population of region i, may be taken as an indicator of intra-regional movements; the ratio works out at 31.5 for São Paulo, 19.1 for the northeast and 12.0 for Amazonia. This shows that in more traditional regions there is less mobility.

There are those who would be in favour of encouraging outmigration from depressed areas, as an element of regional balance, by creating greater accessibility. Urbanization, on the other hand, would lead inevitably to modernization of farming and incorporation of new areas under crops.

It has not yet been proved, however, that migration alone can promote regional balance, making other strategies for sustaining depressed regions unnecessary. There is another stand in favour of internal migrations related to the acceptance of regional 'imbalance'. 'Pursuit of regional balance as a means may frustrate the process of development if it is to be achieved at the expence of the most rapidly growing nuclei . . . regional balance might best be pursued through improvement in the transportation and distribution network in order that the national market may be effectively integrated' (Frankman 1971, 350).

The formation of new regions on the agricultural frontier enables new agrarian structures to be instituted, whereas transformation is difficult in the more traditional areas (table 11.2). It also serves to relieve excessive concentration in the more developed areas and superurbanization. Others find that it would be more worthwhile to intensify modernization and to raise the density even further in the more developed regions, than to expand spaces of low economic density. Bearing in mind demographic pressure, spatial reorganization operating in accordance with the growth of the modern nucleus adjusted to the von Thünen model, a differentially developed society and other aspects, it would seem logical to admit the concomitance of the two processes: expansion of new regions and accentuation of modernization and concentration in the more developed regions.

Table 11.2

Population growth, income and education in Brazil, 1970

Region	Rate of growth of population 1960–70 (%)	Average income per capita (cruzeiros)	Years of schooling Median of population
1 Amazonia (Amazonas, Pará and territories)	38.5	84.5	1 year
2 Middle north (Maranhão and Piauí)	24.6	51.5	Less than 1 year
3 Northeast (Ceará, Rio Grande do Norte, Paraíba, Pernambuco and Alagoas)	26.2	62.4	Less than 1 year
4 Bahia (Bahia and Sergipe)	24.5	70.6	Less than 1 year
5 Minas (Minas Gerais and Espírito Santo)	19.2	81.5	1 year
6 Rio de Janeiro (Estado do Rio de Janeiro and Guanabara)	34.0	192.7	4 and 5 years
7 São Paulo	37.0	181.8	3 years
8 Paraná	68.8	92.8	1 year
9 Extreme south (Santa Catarina and Rio Grande do Sul)	26.1	110.7	3 years
10 Centre (Goiás, Mato Grosso and Brasília)	68.8	94.0	1 year

An interesting avenue of investigation is concerned with the consequences of interregional migrations on the cultural patterns of the population. More homogeneous areas that have not received any recent inmigration (for example in the south of Brazil) may be contrasted with areas showing more active assimilation of new strains. As a whole, interregional migration may be assigned a role in the shaping of national self-realization of awareness through initiating contact between populations originating in different geographical units which were hitherto isolated (Martínez 1968).

Regional differences

Non-dynamic regions

Non-dynamic regions may present a population concentration in certain big cities due to intraregional migrations, while at the same time out-movements of population are proceeding interregionally.

Besides gathering masses of the regional population, the large cities act as steps of migration to even larger ones. The problem worsens as the large cities of the region lose members of their élite by outmigration, while there is an inflow of less qualified people as a result of easier accessibility. The increase in accessibility of these centres has intensified the flow from the more remote areas of their spheres of influence. In the city of Natal, capital of the Brazilian state of Rio Grande do Norte, the proportion of migrants originating from within a radius of 50 kms declined from 55.7% prior to 1930 to 22.8% in the period 1960–9. The decline over a radius of 100 kms was from 72.7 to 38.1%, while in the area 100 to 250 kms the proportion rose from 4.8 to 33% (Geiger 1972). In this 'northeast' of Brazil, a region that has lost spontaneous dynamism, the interregional migration of 'notables' (persons with a certain social standing) involves 37.6% of the migrants originating from small cities, while in the 'south' (São Paulo included) it is 29.9%. In middle-sized cities the percentages are respectively 64% and 26.2%, while the big cities are down to 46.7% and 13.7% (McDonough 1971).

In Monterrey, Mexico, the qualification of the migrants has declined steadily through the years (Browning and Feindt 1971). The growth of the so-called marginal sectors of the city under the effect of 'push' forces affecting the populations of the deepest hinterlands has caused some writers to use the term 'ruralization' of the cities.

The greater accessibility of the leading cities, however, is related to government efforts to make them into centres of modernization, basically by promoting infrastructure and services. The growth of these cities (generally state or provincial capitals) is geared to the expansion of the government sector, this being highly influential in the development of a series of activities, such as education and health. The big city acts as a disseminator of education, teaching the children of the migrants to read and write. In the northeast as a whole, 50% of the population 10 years of age and over are illiterate; but in a city like Natal with its 250,000 inhabitants, the rate falls to 14.5%. In Natal, only 4.1% of the population from 10 to 14 years of age is illiterate, rising to 12.7% in the 20- to 29-year-old sector, and 22% in that of 45 to 49 years.

Participation in the social life of the city is a function of the level of education rather than of the condition of the migrant (table 11.3).

Table 11.3

Education and participation in the social life of the city

Origin	Complete secondary education	Membership in a trade association		Membership in a club or other social or recreational association	
		Members (%)	Non-members (%)	Members (%)	Non-members (%)
Born in Natal	With	20.9	79.1	35.8	64.2
	Without	11.5	88.5	10.8	89.2
Coming from outside Natal	With	27.6	72.4	35.7	64.3
	Without	11.4	88.6	7.7	92.3

The urge to acquire education has been a factor in movements of population, mainly to central places for secondary education. Education, it is true, favours the exodus of persons from non-dynamic regions. In Brazil, the correlation of high-school graduates to intraregional migration is figured at .71, and .64 with respect to interregional 'entries'. Where university education is concerned, the indices stand respectively at .65 and .68. Nevertheless, though the university does qualify students for outmigration, a high proportion of graduates remain in the city (Sahota 1968). The expansion of a modern sector in these regional centres begins to attract qualified men and women from the larger metropolises. In the Brazilian northeast a certain return flow occurs of young people who, after studying elsewhere, come back to government office, to positions in the liberal professions and to fill chairs in the university. This helps to increase the number of students and renew the cultural life of the city, enabling is to play a major role in reactivating regional development. In the city of Natal, for instance, there has been an increase over the last few years in the relative participation of migrants originating in larger cities, such as Recife or Rio de Janeiro. Channelling the increasing stream of urban-urban and rural-urban migration from their areas of influence, these big cities attenuate the interregional outflow in relation to the intraregional movement. Considering changes of *municipio* dating back eleven years or more, the ratio of persons making an intraregional move to those moving interregionally was 1.6 in the northeast. This index rose to 2.1 for migrations of one and two years' standing. In Peru, where 24% of the population was made up of interregional migrants, a relative slackening of the outmigration was also observed in a study of the Northern Region in favour of the big local cities (Delavaud 1971, 248).

More highly developed regions

In large countries like Brazil or Mexico, quite highly developed regions emerge around a powerful industrial urban nucleus. There, as in the case of the state of São Paulo, the rural population tends to dwindle, in the absolute sense, accompanied by a technological advance in regional agriculture. The growth centre formed by the urban-industrial nucleus expands gigantically, absorbing the greater part of the migration, which is overwhelmingly urban-urban. In Buenos Aires, 50% of the migrants were born in cities with more than 20,000 inhabitants (Germani 1961). Sampling in Greater Santiago in 1962 showed that 63.5% of the male inmigrants originated in localities of more than 5,000 inhabitants, 30.4% in smaller localities and in rural areas, and 6.1% abroad or unspecified. In the Guanabara-Rio de Janeiro State region, 69% of the interregional inmigrants represented an urban-urban flow and 26% a rural-urban flow. Only 5% were attracted to a rural setting.

The fact that the developed regions continue to receive the greater part of the interregional currents (in Brazil, São Paulo, Guanabara and Rio de Janeiro were the magnets that drew 1,525,000 out of the total 3,250,000 who made an interregional move from one *municipio* to another within the last five years) is partly due to the high correlation between migration and established urban industrial centres, and the strong tendency of industry towards concentration. The correlation between industrial workers and interregional entries was no more than .59 in Brazil, because new non-industrialized farming regions also received flows. The index for intraregional movement was .68.

The intense internal currents characterized the developed regions, including those that feed the growth of new satellites around the expanding metropolitan region. In the state of São Paulo, the ratio between internal movement and entries is 1.5 for those who made their latest move eleven or more years ago, and 2.2 for those who last moved up to five years ago. About 2,680,000 persons made their most recent migratory shift in the last five years within the region comprising Sao Paulo, Rio de Janeiro and Guanabara.

The Brazilian urban system from 1940 to 1970 shows an increase from 60 to 150 in the number of cities with .05% or more of the total population of the country. Nevertheless, whereas in 1940 only 10 of those 60 cities were metropolitan suburbs, by 1970 the number of such suburbs had risen to 46, and 32 were located in the southeast, mainly clustered around São Paulo, Rio de Janeiro and Belo Horizonte. This means that two movements are underway in the country, simultaneous and interlocking: one of population concentrating in the most highly developed regions, and the other of population spreading centrifugally, the former being hierarchically the more important and involving greater masses of population (Geiger *et al.* 1972, 428).

In the areas of immediate metropolitan influence, where farming is a flourishing occupation, highly qualified local elements in the agricultural labour force move on to the cities, and are replaced by migrants from poorer regions. For instance in Jundiaí, a satellite of São Paulo, small farming entrepreneurs embark on urban activities and start employing workers coming from Minas Gerais (Davidovich 1966). In Argentina, Paraguayan migrants take the place of labourers on the Pampas who migrate to Buenos Aires.

In relative terms a recent decline of the population in nuclear regions is to be observed, as in São Paulo, Mexico City and the Santiago–Valparaiso area (Friedman 1971). This is due to the competitive attraction of new regions and secondary poles, including the outflow of people even from the developed region for the purpose of rural and urban settlement in its zone of influence. In the last five years the number of persons leaving São Paulo corresponds to 13.7% of the total for Brazil.

New regions

In the past, the development of new regions has often been associated with international migrations and speculation in a commodity on the foreign market. Built up in successive historical stages, the new regions instituted new socioeconomic structures superior to the older ones, which had become ossified. This afforded a way of expanding the urban and rural middle class.

Continuity in the displacement of the economic frontier was expected to maintain this expansion of the middle class and to meet the following requirements: to drain the population increase and relieve pressure on arable land; to incorporate new riches in the national economy by, amongst other things, the discovery of mineral wealth and the exploitation of forest produce; to promote the development of new cities as central places.

The constitution of new regions under strong demographic pressure, to satisfy the need of extending the subsistence economy to make room for populations not easily absorbed by the metropolises, is one of the differences between the past and present. In Peru, the indigenous populations of the Sierra shift to the Montaña instead of making for the coastal cities. Although the road to Satipo provides better access to the market of Lima and the secondary cities of the Sierra, the road to Apurimac siphons off more people because it opens up more densely populated and more backward areas to outmigration (Wesche 1971, 255).

The new regions contribute to the absolute increase of the rural population. The government not only supports or encourages the spontaneous movement of population by means of infrastructure, roads in particular, but also organizes settlement projects. Nonetheless, alongside the spontaneous peopling of the land by rural workers, there is settlement by capitalist concerns, organizing their own migratory flow.

While the occupation of new areas represents the spread of less advanced methods of farming, extensive economy, low productivity and of forest and soil resources, it is however coupled to certain innovations to meet the growing need for supplies for the big cities, in a process of redistribution of production over the national space. In Brazil from 1940 to 1965 the joint share of the Southeastern and Southern Regions in the production of corn (maize) declined from 88 to 79%; that of beans from 75 to 66%; rice 77 to 60%. Part of this output shifted to the new regions in the west and north. But the former regions began to produce more potatoes, wheat, peanuts, fruit and green vegetables. Upsetting the old patterns, stock raising has taken over forest area in Amazonia, whereas grasslands are being ploughed up for crops in the south and southeast. In Venezuela, the shifting of the outer von Thünen rings is illustrated by the development of cash-crop farming on the western Llanos, corn and rice in particular, accompanying the initial development of beef cattle raising (Miller 1968).

In some countries, instead of supplying the domestic market, farmers in very recently opened regions have turned to export agriculture, as in the case of coffee and bananas in Central America and coffee in the Peruvian Selva. Peruvian farmers with plots of land in the Sierra (food produce) and in the Montaña (coffee) have ended up by settling down definitively in the latter.

In the development of new regions, there are aspects bound up with the cultural patterns of the population. The choice of places for inmigration by the Indians in Peru is more influenced by the preceding settlement. Both the newcomers and the established colonists 'seek security by surrounding

themselves with *conocidos*'. In general, the Indians have a regionally confined spatial perception and the whites and halfcastes a more truly national
spatial concept. Keller has referred to differentiated stretches of land in the
West Central Region of Brazil, marked by distinctive cultural patterns,
traceable to the adjacent areas of the southeast from whence the migration
proceeded (personal communication).

In the rich agricultural region in the north of Paraná, Brazil, prosperity
and identification with the neighbouring state of São Paulo are attributable
to – among other reasons such as rich soils, favourable topography and
location bordering on São Paulo – the massive presence of people from the
state of São Paulo in settlement and inmigration (Graham 1971, 25).

With population spreading to the borders of the South American countries,
overland connection is beginning to be established between a number of
them, presaging a new geographical situation for the near future. Urbanization is reaching the new areas accompanied by higher rates than those
current in traditional farming areas; rural settlement brings urban settlement
in its train. Founded in the 1930s, Londrina, in the north of Paraná, now has
more than 150,000 inhabitants. Of the 2,360,000 migrants in the West Central
Region (Brasília included), 952,000 represent an urban-urban movement
and 312,000 a rural-urban one! The share of Amazonia and the west centre
in the population of Brazil rose from 6.6% to 9.3% from 1940 to 1970. In
the same period, the number of cities concentrating .05% or more of the
national population increased from 6 to 9.5%. Meanwhile, the decline in the
northeast was from 35 to 20.9% in the number of inhabitants, and 26 to
20.9% in the number of cities with .05% or more of the national population.

Conclusion

The migratory process (excluding forced movements) is the result of a large
number of individual decisions, but it is influenced by the regional environmental conditions. Government policies can therefore influence migrations.
The promotion or control of migrations may thus be an instrument of
regional policy, wielded in the form of indirect measures such as distribution
of investments and facilities for access and information.

Interregional migrations should not be condemned, but neither should they
be thought the sole solution for the problem of national and regional development. Nor should the occupation of new regions be condemned, but at the
same time the need for greater modernization in the more developed regions
cannot be ignored.

A migration policy can fulfil the purpose of relieving excessive concentration, as much by stimulating middle-sized cities located in the core region
as by forming new regions. Such a policy should not lead to atomization of

resources nor lose sight of the advantages of the effects of agglomeration. In seeking to reinforce nuclei, planning should be extended to cities, situated around the metropolises but outside the metropolitan region, which are capable of development as growth centres, as well as to the organization of a balanced system of central-places. In new areas, excessively scattered occupation and depletion of natural resources must be avoided. This calls for far-reaching research into the nature of perception and decision of the migrants, if the resources applied are to meet with a suitable response. Similarly there is reason to simulate migrations and their repercussions on regionalization (Faissol *et al.* 1971).

References

Browning, H. L. and Feindt, W. (1971) The social and economic context of migration to Monterrey, Mexico. *Latin American Urban Research*, 45–70.

Cornelius Jr, W. A. (1971) The political sociology of cityward migration in Latin America: toward empirical theory. *Latin American Urban Research*, 95–150.

Davidovich, F. R. (1966) Aspectos geográficos de um centro industrial: Jundiaí em 1962. *Revta. Brasileira de Geografia* 28, 4.

Delavaud, C. C. (1971) Les rapports entre les villes et campagnes dans les départements nord-côtiers du Pérou. *Cah. de géographie de Québec* 15, 35, 233–50.

Faissol, S., Cole, J. P., McCullagh, M. J. (1971) Projeção de população no Brasil – aplicação do método cadeia de Markov. *Revta. Brasileira de Geografia* 32, 4, 173–208.

Frankman, M. J. (1971) Urbanization and development in Latin America. *Cah. de géographie de Québec* 15, 35, 344–50.

Friedman, J. (1971) Urban regional policies for national development in Chile. *Latin American Urban Research*, 217–46.

Geiger, P. P. (1972) *Migrações interregionais e intraregionais no Brasil.* CEDEPLAR, UFMG, Belo Horizonte.

Geiger, P. P., Rua, J. and Ribeiro, M. (1972) Concentração urbana no Brasil, 1940–70. *Pesquisa, Planejamento, Economia* 2, 2, 411–32.

Germani, G. (1961) Inquiry into the social effects of urbanization in a working-class sector of Greater Buenos Aires, in *Urbanization in Latin America*, 206–33.

Gonzalez, A. (1971) Population, agriculture and food supply in Latin America. *Cah. de géographie de Québec* 15, 35, 333–43.

Graham, D. (1971) Algumas considerações económicas para a política migratória no meio Brasileiro. *Migrações Internas no Brasil*, 13–33.

McDonough, P. (1971) *Geographical mobility among Brazilian 'Notables'.* Instituto Universitário de Pesquisas do Rio de Janeiro, Fac. Cândido Mendes (mimeographed).

Martínez, H. (1968) Migraciones en el Perú. *Aportes* 10, 137–60.

Miller, E. W. (1968) Population growth and agricultural developments in the western Llanos of Venezuela: problems and prospects. *Revta. Geográfica* 69, 7–28.

Sahota, G. S. (1968) An economic analysis of internal migration in Brazil. *J. Pol. Econ.* 76, 218–45.

Schwind, P. J. (1971) *Migration and regional development in the United States, 1950–1960.* Research Paper No. 133, Dept of Geography, Univ. of Chicago.

Stevens, R. P. (1968) Spatial aspects of internal migration in Mexico 1950–1960. *Revta. Geográfica* 69, 75–90.

Thomas, R. N. (1970) *Internal migration in Latin America: an analysis of recent literature.*

Valladares, L. do P. and Gaignard, R. (1971) Au Vénézuéla: les villes du diamant. *Cah. de géographie de Québec* 15, 35, 396–402.

Wesche, R. (1971) Recent migration to the Peruvian Montaña. *Cah. de géographie de Québec* 15, 35, 251–66.

Wilkie, R. (1972) Toward a behavioral model of peasant migration: an Argentine case of spatial behaviors by social class levels. *Pop. Dyn. of Latin America.*

12 Internal migration in Southeast Asian countries
R. C. Y. Ng

Introduction

Southeast Asia is a major geographical region of the world, with a total population of almost 270 million in an area of 1.5 million square miles. Although the 11 countries in the area have very different cultural and historical backgrounds, they emerged in the post-war era with much similarity that is relevant to problems of the study of internal migration.

With the possible exception of the Republic of Singapore, these countries are predominantly rural and have extremely uneven population distribution. Population pressure is considered to be high on the alluvial deltas and coastal plains largely because of the relatively low technological levels of agriculture. Outside these congested 'core areas', each country has its rather extensive but sparsely populated 'frontier zones' with high agricultural potentials yet to be fully exploited (fig. 12.1). The growth of settlements until quite recently has occurred largely on the intermediate peripheral belts. Strenuous but often disappointing efforts have been made by the governments to encourage the development of these less densely populated areas. At present, local pockets of denser population away from the major concentrations are associated with centres of plantation development and sites of mineral extraction. This basic disparity of population densities between the 'core' and the 'frontier' zones is one of the primary motivating forces in internal migration. Of Malaysia, for example, it has been said that 'the contrast between close and sparse settlement will be far greater [in the near future], so great indeed that some movement of population to lessen it seems inevitable' (Jones 1965, 50). A similar tendency has also been observed in Thailand (Sternstein 1965, 20–2).

The countries of Southeast Asia are characterized by rapid population increase (table 12.1). There has been a continued decline in the mortality rates while fertility levels have tended to remain high (ECAFE 1970, 218).

Without exception, the governments of these countries have now adopted family planning programmes as a measure for reducing the rate of natural growth. One must, however, recognize the fact that some form of family planning has been going on at the individual level and that policies aim to accelerate the trend of the diffusion of information and the availability of

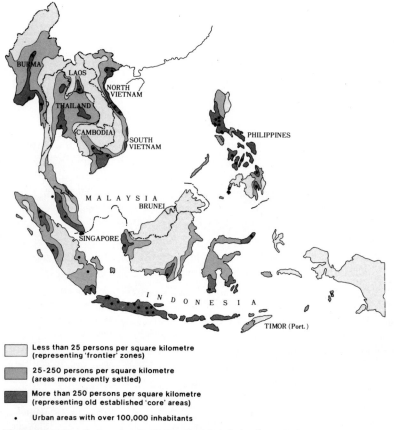

Less than 25 persons per square kilometre
(representing 'frontier' zones)

25-250 persons per square kilometre
(areas more recently settled)

More than 250 persons per square kilometre
(representing old established 'core' areas)

• Urban areas with over 100,000 inhabitants

Figure 12.1 Population density in Southeast Asia in about 1970

contraceptives. This is necessarily a slow process and it is difficult to expect any appreciable decline in the birth-rate to have much effect on the short-term pattern of internal movements. Furthermore, because of the current high rate of increase, the populations of Southeast Asia tend to be rather young (Ward 1960, 208). Vast numbers of youths are entering the labour market every year. The growth of industries and services in the few cities is proceeding at a pace that could not possibly absorb the annual increase

in job seekers. More and more people will have to leave their place of birth
to look for pioneer agricultural land elsewhere.

While pressure of population is building up in individual countries, there
is little prospect of international migration within the region itself. Nations
conscious of the experience of massive immigration of overseas Chinese
and Indians during the pre-independence days are reluctant to accept further

Table 12.1

Population, area and rate of growth of Southeast Asian countries

Country	Population mid-year 1968 (estimated)	Area sq. km	Annual percentage rate of growth 1968 (estimated)
Brunei	112,000	5,765	3.75
Burma	26,390,000	678,033	2.75
Indonesia	113,721,000	1,491,564	2.25
Khmer Republic	6,557,000	181,035	2.15
Laos	2,825,000	236,800	2.40
Malaysia	10,305,000	332,633	2.78
Philippines	35,883,000	299,410	2.73
Singapore	1,988,000	581	1.83
Thailand	33,693,000	514,000	2.67
North Vietnam	20,700,000	155,747	—
South Vietnam	17,414,000	178,090	2.65

Source: ECAFE (1969) *Economic Survey of Asia and the Far East; Far Eastern Economic
Review, Year Book of 1969.*

migrants from even neighbouring countries. The plurality of society which
is so significant in the region tends also to complicate the internal migration
pattern within the countries. Thus with the international boundaries becoming almost entirely impermeable, the rapidly increasing populations
must redistribute themselves within the respective countries.

As there are still rather few studies made of the internal migration
patterns of these countries, this paper attempts to identify and briefly
discuss some of the themes on internal migration in Southeast Asia.

Urbanization and industrialization

Although several Southeast Asian cities have now exceeded the million mark,
the proportion of urban population is still small. The administrative capitals
are invariably the largest cities and the secondary urban centres often fail to

reach a third of the size of these capitals. In these primate cities are concentrated most of the non-agricultural activities, but even so their morpho-
logical, functional and demographic structures show considerable variations
amongst themselves and from the western pattern (McGee 1967, 125).
Apart from in the central business districts and the affluent residential
areas, house structure (Bennett 1970, 53), social organization and general
atmosphere remain indistinguishable from those of their upcountry counterparts. There seem therefore to be little cultural and psychological barriers to
urbanward migration. Sizeable immigrations to the central cities are attested
by their rapid expansion, their predominantly male working age groups and
their slums. The high unemployment levels are good indications that rural-
urban migration is not the result of the economic attractions of the urban
centres which are often exaggerated in the minds of the rural population,
but more because of the 'push' factors operating in the rural areas where
continued population growth is putting much pressure on the cultivated
area. Recent improvements in the transport networks have induced larger
numbers of farmers to travel to the city during the non-agricultural season,
partly for pleasure and partly for seeking some off-season employment as
casual labourers. The latter is more significant in the continental countries
with a monsoonal climatic regime, which means that the halting of agricultural activities in the dry season coincides with the most suitable period
for a variety of construction work.

As far as circumstances allow, almost every country in the region is either
in the process of drawing up or actually executing an economic development
plan. Without exception, these plans call for an accelerated rate of
industrialization. Target rates for industrial expansion, mostly of the
labour-intensive, consumer-import-substitution types, are often set at least
twice as high as in the agricultural sector. The increasing gap between the
per capita income of the industrial workers who are concentrated in the few
urban centres and the vast majority of farmers is likely to provide an added
incentive to potential rural-urban migrants. Experience has shown that for
every job created in the metropolis, several upcountry families have been
attracted. Unemployment, however, usually has a deterring effect on
inward migration, but given the context of the extremely low costs of
living for the indigenous populations in the urban centres, and the assistance
provided by a culture with extended families, the level of unemployment
and urban squalor needs to be much higher than what is generally regarded
as tolerable before any appreciable decline of the massive rural inflow of
migrants is likely to occur.

Urban centres, apart from the primates and their suburban satellites, tend
to have characteristics which are more rural than urban. Their main functions
are the provision of marketing and service facilities for the rural populations
of their hinterlands. In the Philippines, although only half of the manu-

facturing workers are in Manila, industries in the provincial centres are predominantly of the agricultural raw-material-processing types (Luna 1963, 8). These small centres provide only limited employment opportunities and their growth is virtually dependent on the demands of the surrounding countryside, and increase in rural prosperity. There is thus little incentive for the farmers to transfer their residence to these areas and adopt new and often unrewarding skills of trade and commerce. Other non-agricultural centres are associated with the development of mining and plantations. The skills of their inhabitants are so different from those of the capital cities that inter-'urban' migration has not been and will probably not be of great significance in the overall pattern of internal migration in the region.

Population growth and inter-rural movements

The population of Southeast Asia is predominantly agricultural. Inter-rural migration is the process whereby the territories of the region have been settled. By a series of movements overland and across the narrow straits, the original migrants arrived at the present core areas of the deltas of the Irrawaddy, the Chao Phrya and the Mekong, the lakeshore of the Tonle Sap, the island of Java and the Central Plain of Luzon, mostly in the last few hundred years. Population pressure caused by gradual *in situ* growth had led to continuous accretional growth; occasional wars and famine resulted in periodic leapfrogging of settlements. Although wars and famine have largely disappeared since the turn of the present century, mounting population pressure is still being felt keenly in most areas. The peasant solution to this population challenge differs from culture to culture and locality to locality, therefore making it difficult to generalize. In Java it has led to a self-defeating process which Geertz termed 'agricultural involution' whereby the land is cultivated more and more intensively without any appreciable rise in the standard of living or in the *per capita* production of food (Geertz 1963, 80). Countries in continental Southeast Asia are less restricted by the physical limits of the shoreline and there is a tradition of establishing new settlements in the increasingly more marginal areas (Ng 1968b, 205).

Detailed analysis of the pattern of inter-rural migration is not possible for most countries for want of comprehensive information on movements. However, data on birthplace residence and five-year changes in residence reported in the 1960 Census of Thailand provided an insight into the situation of that country. It can be shown that even within the national framework, there is little overall correlation between rural population density and migration flows. Migrants tend to possess very keen perception of their milieu in terms of the cultural, linguistic, environmental and potential land use variations. The myriad of migration streams lend themselves to a distinct system of migration regions which reflects the geographical differences amongst the major component units of the country (Ng 1969, 718). The identity between the regional boundary derived from the changes in residence data and the birthplace residence data in this case opens the possibility of devising migration regions by the use of birthplace data which are more generally available in Southeast Asian censuses.

The necessity for migration in most areas of the region is due mainly to the growth of the local population to levels beyond the carrying capacity of the land at the present level of technology. The increasing inability to achieve the necessary food and cash-crop production is being brought on by mounting pressure on existing agricultural land. National economic development and international assistance programmes include the essential policies of raising rural standards of living by way of increasing productivity through agricultural modernization and environmental improvements. Periodical crop failures brought on by the highly variable seasonal rainfall, so characteristic of the monsoonal climatic regime and such a potent force in inducing inter-rural migration, will disappear. The expected increase in productivity will not only cater for an expanded population, but also raise the *per capita* income of all concerned. Initially, it might lead to the development of these growth points as attractive destinations, but when more of the area will be receiving similar benefits the level of internal migration should decline.

Economic development and land settlement

One of the major characteristics of the population and settlement patterns of Southeast Asia is their highly uneven distribution. Although there is administrative provision in several countries for peasants in the crowded areas to obtain land grants in the more sparsely populated parts, spontaneous pioneering efforts are often stifled by the great difficulties and high costs involved in land clearance and the economic problem of subsistence during the initial period of settlement. State sponsorship and participation in population redistribution schemes seem to be the only solution. As early as the 1930s, 'transmigration', aiming at massive transfer of population from congested Java to the pioneering outer islands, was adopted as state policy of the Dutch East Indies government. Between 1936 and 1940, the number of Javanese colonists in the outer territories rose from 68,000 to 206,000 (Fisher 1964, 294). The scheme was inherited by the independent Indonesian government. Although the density of the province of South Sumatra which received most of the Javanese migrants has jumped from 87.04 in 1930 to 120.58 persons per km^2 in 1961 (Withington 1963, 205), the transfer of 46,096 individuals in 1960, the best year on record, is hardly significant to the problem of pressure on Java where the annual increase of population is in the order of 1,000,000. The programme has thus been more successful in terms of supplying a labour force that is vital to the development of Sumatra than of relieving the pressure on Java itself. With this experience, the current five-year plan calls for a basic change in the official attitude towards transmigration and states specifically that 'the availability of employment activities and opportunities are expected to create incentives for transmigration movement [so that it may] directly contribute to development efforts' (Department of Information, Indonesia, n.d., 18). With this policy reorientation, rigid targets as in the past have become less meaningful and impractical and thus none is set for the duration of the plan.

Malaysia has similar schemes for population redistribution which from inception have had a more definite objective of developing some of the more sparsely settled areas within West Malaysia. Between 1956 and 1964, 61 land settlements, ultimately accommodating 20,000 peasant families, have been initiated by the Federal Land Development Authority (Wikkramatileke 1965, 377). Malaysian projects are on the whole more successful, perhaps because of their greater support for the settlers and of their proximity to the communities whence the settlers originated.

In the Philippines, the settlement of the frontier island of Mindanao seems the logical solution to the population pressure problems developing in the heavily populated islands of Luzon, Cebu, Leyte and Bohol, where the physiologic densities often exceed 5,120 persons per cultivated km^2 (Simkins and Wernstedt 1963, 199). A policy of official encouragement to settle in Mindanao was adopted by the government as early as 1913 and infused with new vigour in more recent years. Migrants in the Philippines are composed of ones assisted by the state to move or those making the passage and establishing themselves on their own. While the policy of the government, like the former Indonesian experience, is directed primarily at the redistribution of population, the non-assisted migrants are entirely economically motivated. It has been observed that this latter category of migrants has always outnumbered their sponsored counterparts and that their combined total is more numerous than the rural-urban migrants in that country (Krinks 1970, 38). During the intercensal period 1948–1960, Mindanao received no fewer than 1.5 million new settlers. As yet, only a third of the estimated 6,250,000 hectares of potential agricultural land has been occupied (Antonio 1963, 18). With the expansion of the road network in the interior, the migration trends focusing on Mindanao will be further augmented. Notwithstanding recent religious conflicts, between migrant Christians and indigenous Muslims, movement towards Mindanao is continuing.

Of more limited scope and on a smaller scale are the self-help land settlement projects of Thailand which are almost solely for settling the landless peasants, particularly those in the Central Plain and the northern valleys, on available public land. The scheme has been in operation since 1940, and there are now forty-eight such settlements in as many provinces (Ng 1968a, 180). At the interprovincial level, the number of 'migrants' involved would not be significant and has often escaped the attention of analysts. Unlike the spontaneously inter-rural migrants, and similar to their peers in other countries in the region, the settlers face the problem of creating a new communal spirit amongst people of very different background, on locations seldom of their own choice. The projects in their present form could hardly be described as popular, but when some of the fundamental problems are solved they can exert considerable influence on the internal migration patterns.

Infrastructural facilities are emerging as new competitors for rural land. Although roads may not occupy more than a minute fraction of cultivated land, and hydroelectricity reservoirs can be sited away from the populated areas, irrigation projects so vital to the future of Southeast Asian countries (Whyte 1967, 141) are usually located near concentrations of population, to derive the maximum possible benefits and least costs of construction and operation. The recently completed projects in northeastern Thailand have caused the displacement of several thousand families. Most peasants in the affected areas chose to collect the monetary compensation and migrate spontaneously to other parts of the country, but the remainder have to be accommodated in specially established settlements. When the proposed projects on the Mekong itself get underway, the number to be displaced in Laos, Thailand and the Khmer Republic will far exceed present levels. The relocation of these people may well be one of the most important forms of internal migration in the areas concerned.

Instability and population drift

Over the past three decades, Southeast Asia has periodically been involved in external conflicts and internal strife which had fundamentally disturbed the social and economic environment of vast numbers of people. Although it is almost impossible to assess accurately the amount of population drift, the significant changes in the pattern of population distribution can be attested by the magnitude of the number of people whose places of residence are distant from those of their birth.

Perhaps the most important single factor inducing internal population movements in the 1940s was the serious ravages of the Pacific war, then thousands of people became refugees in almost every country in the region. The immediate post-war years saw further disturbances as different political factions vied for control of the nascent independent governments (McGee 1960, 49–58). The problems were compounded by the characteristic plurality of society as a result of the massive influx of overseas migrants in the pre-war years. Thus, when the Philippines were repairing the war damage, there was the Hukkabalup uprising which seriously disrupted normal life in Central Luzon and other parts of the country. In Malaya, the refugee squatters in the rural areas during the war had to be regrouped in the numerous 'new villages' set up as a counter-insurgency measure during the 'emergency' period of the 1950s. The more recent conflict with Indonesia necessitated some population movement along the frontier in East Malaysia. Generations have grown up in Vietnam not knowing peace and security of residence. Massive evacuations have recently occurred in Laos, and the end of the internal difficulties in the Khmer Republic is still not in sight. The study of internal migration in these countries will have to await the return of normality.

At times of general insecurity, there is often the tendency for urbanward drift and for dispersion in the rural areas. Population drift caused by in-security serves two important functions in mobility: it tends to break down traditional conservatism by increasing the propensity to migrate; and it helps to increase information on a larger number of destinations. In rural society of the region, temporary disruption of any kind tends to be followed by a period of increased migratory flows and their extension further afield.

Conclusion

Internal migrations are simultaneously affected by a complicated series of interrelated factors. This appears more so in Southeast Asia than elsewhere in the world. Here one has to deal with casual factors of both a transient and more permanent nature. Insight into the patterns can only be gained with intimate knowledge of the country's contemporary history, cultural back-ground, policy orientation and economic development objectives. It is often difficult to separate and isolate any single influence for detailed treatment.

The lack of reliable statistics for analysis is perhaps an even greater problem confronting the student of Southeast Asian internal migration. Most, but by no means all, countries in the region have taken censuses in recent years (table 12.2), but information on population redistribution usually does not go further than tabulations of birthplace and residence. Methods of estimating net population change are not likely to yield significant results as assumptions of uniform rate of natural increase do not normally apply in the face of accelerated family planning programmes in various parts of the countries. The lack of accurate birth and death registrations rules out the possibility of residual methods of estimating migration.

The future of research into patterns of internal migration in Southeast Asia seems to lie in studies of limited scale, in selected localities and with

Table 12.2

Population censuses in the Southeast Asian region since 1900

Country	1970–9	1960–9	1950–9	1940–9	1930–9	1920–9	1910–19	1900–9
Brunei		1960		1947	1931	1921	1911	
Burma		August 1966 inc.	1955, 1954	1941	1931	1921	1911	1901
Indonesia	August 1971	1961	1951		1930			
Khmer Republic		1962	1959, 1958					
Laos								
Malaysia	August 1970	1960	1957	1947	1931	1921	1911	
Philippines	May 1970	1960		1948	1939		1918	
Singapore	June 1970		1957	1947	1931	1921	1911	1903
Thailand	April 1970	1960		1947	1937	1929	1919, 1911	1901
Vietnam, Rep. of		1960						

Source: *Asian Population Programme News*, Vol. 1 (Spring 1971). UN ECAFE, Pop. Div.

restricted analytical aims. Even so, over parts of the region such studies will have to await a return to normality and a re-emergence of the more meaningful basic trends. However, information on patterns and amount of population redistribution is generally considered vital in the planning for economic progress and provides a challenge to the researcher.

References

Antonio, G. E. (1963) Economic development of Mindanao. *Philippine Econ. Rev.* 4, 15–18.

Bennett, D. C. (1970) Some rural and urban housing differences in the Philippines. *Philippine Geogr. J.* 14, 50–3.

Dept of Information, Republic of Indonesia (n.d.) *The first five-year development plan (1969/70–1973/74).* Djakarta.

ECAFE (1970) *Econ. Bull. for Asia and the Far East* 20, 218–20.

Fisher, C. A. (1964) *South-east Asia: a social, economic and political geography* (2nd edn 1967). London.

Geertz, C. (1963) *Agricultural involution: the process of ecological change in Indonesia.* California.

Jones, L. W. (1965) Malaysia's future population. *Pac. Viewp.* 6, 39–51.

Krinks, P. A. (1970) Peasant colonisation in Mindanao. *J. Trop. Geogr.* 30, 38–47.

Luna, T. W. (1963) Manufacturing in the Philippines. *Philippine Geogr. J.* 7, 6–17.

McGee, T. G. (1960) Aspects of the political geography of Southeast Asia: a study of a period of nation-building. *Pac. Viewp.* 1, 39–58.

McGee, T. G. (1967) *The Southeast Asian city.* New York.

Ng, R. C. Y. (1968a) Land settlement projects in Thailand. *Geogr.* 53, 179–82.

Ng, R. C. Y. (1968b) Rice cultivation and rural settlement density in North East Thailand. *Tijdschr. voor Econ. en Soc. Geogr.* 200–10.

Ng, R. C. Y. (1969) Recent internal population movement in Thailand. *Ann. Assoc. Am. Geogr.* 59, 710–30.

Reksohadiprodjo, I. and Hadisapoetro, S. (1960) Trends in population change and food (paddy) production. *Madjadah Geogr.* 1, 15–19.

Simkins, P. D. and Wernstedt, F. L. (1963) Growth and internal migrations of the Philippine population, 1948-1960. *J. Trop. Geogr.* 17, 197–202.

Sternstein, L. (1965) A critique of Thai population data. *Pac. Viewp.* 6, 15–35.

Ward, M. (1960) Recent population growth and economic development in Asia. *Pac. Viewp.* 1, 205–24.

Whyte, R. O. (1967) Monsoon Asia: population and rice – the next 30 years. *Span* 10, 138–41.

Wikkramatileke, R. (1965) State aided rural land colonization in Malaya: an appraisal of the FLDA Program. *Ann. Assoc. Am. Geogr.* 55, 337–403.

Withington, W. A. (1963) The distribution of population in Sumatra, Indonesia, 1961. *J. Trop. Geogr.* 17, 203–12.

13 Patterns of internal migration in India[1]

G. S. Gosal and
G. Krishan

Despite its immense economic, social and political significance, internal migration in India has received inadequate attention from scholars. Basing his observations on the 1931 census data, Davis (1951) noted the general immobility of India's population although the people were free to migrate from province to province, from one princely state to another, from British to non-British India, and even from other countries. Zachariah (1960, 1964) made detailed investigations into internal migration in the Indian sub-continent during 1941–51 and 1901–31 in order to measure and describe its magnitude, assess its contribution to the process of population redis-tribution, and indicate areas of population gain and loss. In collaboration with Bogue (1962), he studied migration to towns in India during 1941–51, with special reference to socioeconomic attributes of migrants. While all these studies are marked for their deep insight into the problem, they lack a sound spatial bias since most of them are based on data by states. The same can be said of Sen Gupta's (1968) and Mitra's (1968) notes on patterns of internal migration in India as revealed by the 1961 census data. By com-parison, Gosal (1961) gave a geographic perspective to the study of this problem by basing his analysis on what emerged in a map of India prepared from district-wise census data (1951) on place of birth. From this and other maps included in the paper, he identified areas of in- and outmigration, and also discussed spatial variations in mobility in detail. The present study is an extension of this work, made possible by the availability of more detailed and more recent data. The main objectives of this investigation are to examine the magnitude of internal migration in India, to discern the patterns of rural-rural, rural-urban, urban-urban and urban-rural migration, to identify areas of in- and outmigration, and to predict likely trends.

[1] *Editors' Note*: The international boundaries shown on the maps in this paper are as recognized by the government of India.

Data on migration and their limitations

The great importance of migration studies in India is countermatched by lack of *direct* data on this vital aspect of population. The main source of information for such investigations is the *indirect* data on 'place of birth' recorded by the *Census of India*. Since the first regular census in 1881, data of this kind have been collected, though the form and detail in which they were gathered and presented varied from census to census. Till 1951, the entire population was classified into categories of those enumerated within the district/state/country of birth along with those born abroad but enumerated in India. It was only in the 1961 census that the number of persons enumerated at the place of birth was also given, making it possible to assess intradistrict migration.

The 1961 census introduced many other improvements. For the first time, it gave rural/urban classification of both birth- and enumeration-places of migrants. Such data facilitate an understanding of the rural-rural, rural-urban, urban-urban and urban-rural patterns of migration. Also, the new data on duration of migrants' residence at the place of enumeration make it possible to discern the temporal-spatial patterns of mobility. Information on the classification of migrants by industrial categories has also been made available. Besides, in the case of cities (places with a population of 100,000 or more), data on age, literacy and occupation of migrants were published. Thus, the data offered by the 1961 census have given new dimensions to the study of migration in India.

According to the Indian census code, a migrant is one who is enumerated at a place other than that of his birth. As such, migrants include persons who migrate for economic reasons, married females who move from their parents' to husbands' places which generally are not the same, children born at places other than those of normal residence of their parents, students getting education outside their birthplaces, families evacuated from new construction sites and rehabilitated elsewhere, persons displaced from Pakistan after partition in 1947 and also those repatriated from other countries, persons on a casual visit to places other than those of their birth for the entire period of census enumeration. The census classifies migrants into four categories: those born elsewhere in the district of enumeration; in other districts of the state; in states in India outside the state of enumeration; and in countries outside India.

Place of birth data are only an indirect tool for an analysis of migration, and for that reason suffer from numerous handicaps. Their first limitation arises from the fact that these do not differentiate between economic, matrimonial, natal, administrative, political, casual etc. migrations. There is no indication available of the number of moves made, the motive behind an individual's migration or the change in occupation which the migration may have caused. Secondly, the smallest areal unit for which these data are available is the district, which with an average area of more than 9,000 km^2 and a population exceeding 1.5 million is fairly large. Data compiled by such large units fail to indicate the distance and direction of local (intradistrict) migration which is very important in Indian areas. Thirdly, the time-to-time changes in district and state boundaries introduce an element of non-comparability of data recorded at different censuses, creating difficulties for conducting temporal studies of migration. The unequal size and irregular shape of these administrative units are other factors which introduce complications.

Above all, the place-of-birth data relate only to inmigration to a particular district but fail to indicate magnitude and direction of outmigration from it since the names of the districts in which migrants were born are not published. There is, however, no difficulty in ascertaining the volume and origin of outmigration at the state level as the names of the states in which migrants were born are provided.

Thus, a population geographer is beset with a number of problems while making use of place-of-birth data for the study of internal migration in India. Nevertheless, the available data, if used with discretion and supplemented by additional information on linguistic composition, population growth and other aspects, can yield approximate if not ultimate results on the magnitude and spatial patterns of internal migration in India.

Magnitude of internal migration

An overwhelming majority of India's massive population spends the entire cycle of life in or near its place of birth. At the 1961 census, 67% of the total population was enumerated at the place of birth, 88% within the district of birth, and 94.5% within the native state (table 13.1). The continuing dependence of most of the people on agriculture, inadequacy of employment opportunities outside agriculture owing partly to a relatively low level of industrialization, high incidence of illiteracy and strong family ties are among the factors accounting for this phenomenon. The increasing availability of local labour arising from accelerating population growth even in potential areas of inmigration, and recent intensification of commuting, especially to big cities, have also been responsible for containing some of the prospective migrants to their native places.

Nevertheless mobility of India's population has gradually been growing, particularly since 1947. In 1921, 24.7 million persons (9.8% of total population) were enumerated outside the district of their birth, the figure rising to 38.5 million (10.8%) in 1951, and to 52.9 million (12.1%) in 1961. The partition of the country in 1947 which displaced several million people,

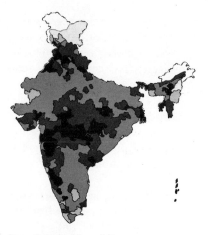

Percentage of total population

16 24 32 40

Figure 13.1 Persons born outside the place of enumeration, India 1961
Source: 1961 *Census of India*

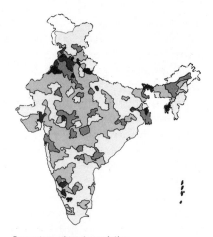

Percentage of total population

8 16 24 32

Figure 13.2 Persons born outside the district of enumeration, India 1961
Source: 1961 *Census of India*

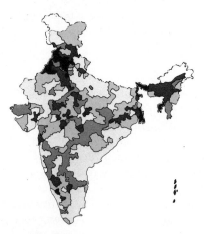

Percentage of total population

2 4 8 16

☐ Data not available

Figure 13.3 Persons born outside the state of enumeration, India 1961
Source: 1961 *Census of India*

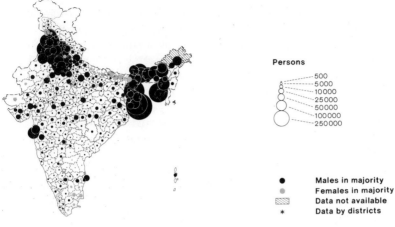

Persons

- - - - 500
- - - - 5000
- - - - 10000
- - - - 25000
- - - - 50000
- - - - 100000
- - - - 250000

● Males in majority
● Females in majority
▨ Data not available
* Data by districts

Figure 13.4 Persons born abroad, India 1961
Source: 1961 *Census of India*

Table 13.1

Population of India according to place of birth, 1961

| Born in | | Percentage of | | |
		Persons	Males	Females
Place of enumeration	A	67.0	79.2	54.0
	R	69.6	84.5	54.1
	U	55.2	56.3	53.9
Elsewhere in the	A	20.9	10.1	32.4
district of	R	22.4	9.7	35.6
enumeration	U	14.1	11.7	16.8
Other districts of	A	6.6	4.9	8.3
the state	R	4.9	2.9	7.1
	U	14.0	13.6	14.4
State in India beyond	A	3.3	3.5	3.2
the state of	R	1.7	1.4	2.0
enumeration	U	10.9	12.5	9.1
Other countries	A	2.1	2.2	2.0
	R	1.3	1.3	1.2
	U	5.7	5.9	5.7

A denotes all areas, R rural areas and U urban areas.
Source: Calculated from 1961 *Census of Indic* Vol. I, India,
Part II-C(iii), Migration Tables, 16.

the implementation of the five-year plans after Independence, a start in diversification of the economy concomitant with the process of new industrialization and urbanization, reclamation of cultivable wastelands in certain areas, rapidly improving means of transport, gradual progress in education, intensifying pressure of population on agricultural land, and the post-Independence emergence of a new zeal for improving standards of living, among other things, are the chief factors underlying this change. The 1961 census revealed that of the total migrants almost half moved during 1951–61 alone. In the case of males, the figure stood at 60% (table 13.2).

Table 13.2

Duration of stay of migrants at place of residence, 1961

Duration	Percentage of migrants		
	Persons	*Males*	*Females*
Less than 10 years	48.9	59.9	43.5
10 to 16 years	14.6	14.6	14.6
16 years and over	33.7	22.3	39.2
Unspecified	2.8	3.2	2.6
	100.0	100.0	100.0

Source: Calculated from 1961 *Census of India*, Vol. I, India, Part II-C(iii), Migration Tables, 90–1.

By the census definition, almost one-third (144.1 million out of 439 million) of India's population was migrant (enumerated at a place other than that of birth) in 1961. Out of the migrants, more than two-thirds (67.6%) were females, this preponderance being associated with their marriage; for under the prevailing system of patrilocal matrimonial residence it is the wife who moves and in the process becomes a migrant. Male migration is, in fact, the true index to economic mobility in the Indian context. In 1961, 79.2% of the males were enumerated at the place of birth, another 10.1% elsewhere within the district of birth. Thus, nearly 90% of the male population was recorded within its native district which indicates the general immobility of India's population. Nonetheless, the 10.7% of the male population which migrated outside its native district and another 10.1% which moved within it together make more than 47 million, a figure which approaches the population of countries like the United Kingdom, France and Italy.

Migration between different categories of settlements

The 1961 census data show that 73.7% of the migrants moved within rural areas. Another 14.6% were involved in rural to urban migration. Urban to urban migrants accounted for 8% of the total and the remaining few were the urban to rural migrants (table 13.3).

Table 13.3

Rural/urban pattern of migrants (excluding migrants from other countries and unspecified persons), 1961

		No. of migrants (in millions)	Percentage of total/male/female migrants
Rural to rural migrants	All	99.1	73.7
	Male	23.5	56.7
	Female	75.6	81.2
Rural to urban migrants	All	19.7	14.6
	Male	10.6	25.6
	Female	9.1	9.7
Urban to urban migrants	All	10.8	8.0
	Male	5.4	13.0
	Female	5.4	5.8
Urban to rural migrants	All	4.8	3.6
	Male	1.9	4.5
	Female	2.9	3.1

Source: Calculated from 1961 *Census of India*, Vol. I, India, Part II-C(iii), Migration Tables, 16.

Thus, as far as magnitude is concerned, rural-rural migration is of exceptional importance, not surprising in a country where 82% of the total population live in villages. A major segment of this migration was, however, the result of marriage of females who accounted for more than 75% of such migrants. Since the practice of village-exogamy of female marriage is less rigid in South India than in North India, the percentage of rural-rural migrants is lower in the former.

However, a more realistic picture of rural-rural migration will be obtainable if only the males are taken into account. Of the total male migrants, 56.7% moved from rural to rural areas. The flow in this type of migration originated largely from the crowded areas with low *per capitum* agricultural productivity, and was directed towards sparsely populated areas with new developmental activities, particularly in the field of agriculture, mining and plantations.

Great economic and social significance attaches to the migration of the rural population to towns. At the 1961 census, nearly 20 million rural-born persons (about 25 million if displaced persons from Pakistan are also inclu-

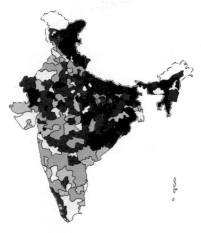

Percentage of total migrants

64 72 80 88

Figure 13.5 Rural-rural migrants, India 1961
Source: 1961 *Census of India*

Percentage of total migrants

8 16 24 32

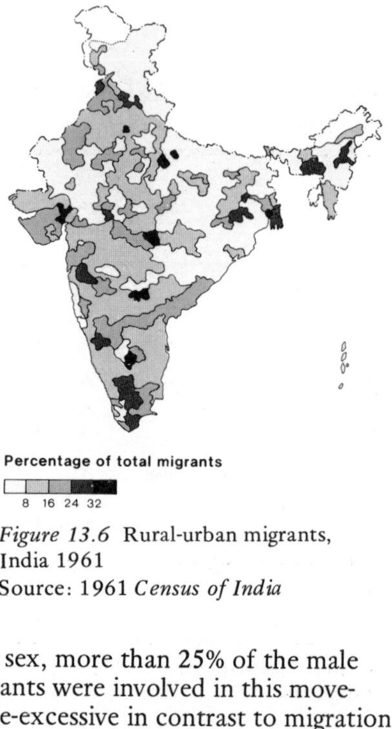

Figure 13.6 Rural-urban migrants, India 1961
Source: 1961 *Census of India*

ded) were enumerated at urban places. By sex, more than 25% of the male migrants and less than 10% of female migrants were involved in this movement. Rural-urban flow was distinctly male-excessive in contrast to migration within rural areas which was dominated by females. The peculiar economic base of urban places in India, still-continuing prejudice (though gradually declining) against female employment and mobility, residential problems in towns and persistence of the joint family system in rural areas account for the excess of males among the rural-urban migrants.

Among the urban places, the big cities have been the major recipient of rural migrants. In Calcutta 77% of the migrants came from rural areas; in Bombay 64%; in Madras 56%, and in Delhi 55%. Broadly speaking, there is a positive correlation between the size of a city and percentage of rural male migrants to it. Several of the large Indian cities have concentrations of textiles and other industries which absorb a multitude of semi-skilled or unskilled labourers from rural areas. The landless agricultural labourers and persons engaged in traditional village handicrafts showed a special tendency to migrate. In correspondence with a higher degree of urbanization in South India than in its northern counterpart, the incidence of this type of migration is greater in the former than in the latter. This is the reverse of more dominant rural to rural movement in the north.

There is an unmistakable trend towards the rapid growth of cities due not only to influx from rural areas but also to considerable migration from

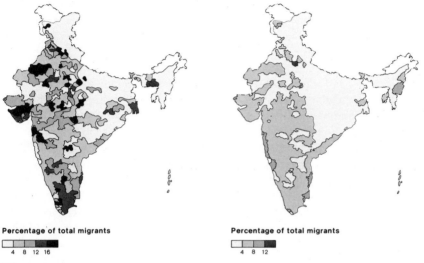

Percentage of total migrants

4   8   12   16

☐   Data not available

Figure 13.7 Urban-urban migrants, India 1961
Source: 1961 *Census of India*

Percentage of total migrants

4   8   12

Figure 13.8 Urban-rural migrants, India 1961
Source: 1961 *Census of India*

smaller urban places. By virtue of their better and diverse employment opportunities, and numerous amenities not available at smaller places, the big cities have become dynamic magnets for economically induced urban to urban migration. The 1961 census recorded 10.8 million urban-urban migrants who made up 8% of total migrants and 35% of migrants to urban places. Confining analysis to cities alone, it is found that the principal administrative (especially capitals of the states), educational (particularly those with universities) and manufacturing centres with highly specialized industries (such as machine tools, heavy electricals, defence equipment, etc.) were the chief recipient of migrants from other urban places. Most of the state capitals recorded the highest percentage of urban-urban migrants as compared with other cities in the same state. In the case of the national capital of New Delhi, 44% of the migrants hailed from other urban places. The corresponding figures for industrial centres like Poona, Jabalpur, Bangalore, etc. were also more than 40%. On the other hand, urban out-migration has been typical of those areas which experienced outmigration of rural population also, lie in the urban shadow zone of big cities, and are situated near the sensitive international border with Pakistan. The small urban places were the worst sufferers in this respect.

The urban to rural migration, which is of growing importance in the Western countries in the form of a 'back to countryside' movement for non-farm enterprises, is of little significance in India. It involved only 4.8 million persons, hardly 3.6% of the total migrants. Females accounted for 61% of such migrants showing that a large part of this migration is the result of marriage of females from small agricultural towns to males in rural areas. The economic segment of this migration is composed of town-born persons serving in rural areas in the field of administration, education, health, defence, etc., and those taking residence or setting up industry in the countryside. In general, the percentage of urban-rural migrants is higher (4 to more than 8%) in South India than in North India, where this percentage is mostly less than 4 and in many cases even less than 2.

The preceding discussion is indicative of sizeable rural-rural, rural-urban and urban-urban mobility in India, though still small when reduced to a percentage of total population. The rate of growth of urban population (205.3%) during 1901–61 has been almost three times that of rural population (69.5%). By a comparative analysis of growth rates of total and urban population during various decades, it has been estimated that 46.3% of the urban growth during this period was contributed by rural-urban migration.

Spatial patterns of internal migration

Viewed in spatial perspective, inmigration has been characteristic of the following types of areas: urban-industrial concentrations; plantations; newly developed agricultural lands; multipurpose project sites, and other areas with developmental activities; mining areas.

The major and minor industrial-urban concentrations proved as strong as magnets for migrants. These include Calcutta conurbation, Bombay-Thana–Poona industrial complex, Gujarat Plain and Saurashtra, Malwa Plateau, western districts of Maharashtra, Godavari–Krishna delta, Western Tamil Nadu, and dispersed industrial districts, such as Delhi, Kanpur and Bangalore. The proportion of long-distance migrants is strongly related to the size and age of an industrial concentration.

Another major flow was directed towards areas which experienced the development of tea, coffee and rubber plantations. Three areas are clearly distinguishable: the foothill zone of the Brahmaputra and Surma valleys in Assam, the Darjeeling–Jalpaiguri tract in West Bengal, and the Southern Ghats in Kerala, Tamil Nadu and Mysore. This migration is only of historic importance as it has practically ceased by now with diminishing demand for labour together with an increasing supply from local areas.

The third flow has been towards the newly developed agricultural lands, prominent among which are the Assam valley, the area served by the Bhakra Canal System in the Punjab, Haryana and Rajasthan, Dandakaranya and Terai of Uttar Pradesh. The Punjabi Sikhs, in particular, have displayed a strong instinct to migrate for agricultural purposes. However, with very little cultivable wasteland left, the frontiers of future agricultural settlement are now practically closed.

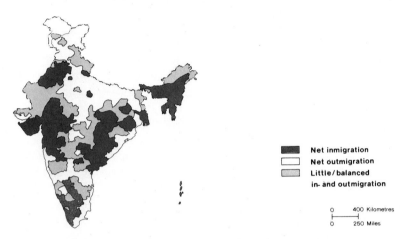

Net inmigration
Net outmigration
Little/balanced
in- and outmigration

0   400 Kilometres
0   250 Miles

Figure 13.9 Areas of in- and outmigration, India 1961
Source: 1961 *Census of India*

The growth of mining activity and the emergence of associated industries led to considerable migration to the Damodar Valley, the North Orissa Plateau and its contiguous area in Bihar, and to southeastern Rajasthan along with adjoining areas in Madhya Pradesh and Gujarat. Migration to mining areas, especially those prominent for coal and iron ore, has been increasing since Independence. Movement to mine-sites was usually of the short-distance type while that to places with major manufacturing (including mineral-based) industries was relatively long-distance.

Independence in 1947 was followed by planned economic development, and a number of multipurpose and minor projects were started and completed. Several developmental schemes were launched, especially in backward areas. Migration to these was marked in the case of construction sites of projects like Bhakra–Nangal, Hirakud, Tungabhadra, the Chattisgarh Plain and Baghelkhand Plateau in Madhya Pradesh, the Eastern Himalayas, and the Andaman and Nicobar islands. Main developments have been in the reclamation of new agricultural land, expansion of mining, growth of industries, and construction of roads.

By contrast the heaviest outflows of migrants have been from those regions where *per capitum* agricultural productivity is low due to high population density, small size of agricultural landholdings, and overdependence on agriculture. These areas include the Ganga Plain in Uttar Pradesh and North Bihar, the North Punjab Plain, northeastern Rajasthan, and the coastal tracts of Tamil Nadu, Orissa and Konkan. Minor outflows originated from the Bundelkhand Plateau (Uttar Pradesh and Madhya Pradesh), the Rayalaseema tract (Andhra Pradesh), the Rarh Plain (West Bengal), the North Mysore Plateau and parts of the Western Himalayas. The excessively populated, overwhelmingly rural and predominantly agricultural Ganga Plain experienced the largest magnitude of outmigration. Here, the existing densities are seldom below 300 persons per km², and in many cases exceed 400. Nearly 90% of the population is confined to rural areas, and as much as three-fourths of the people are directly dependent upon agriculture. Agricultural holdings average barely 1 to 2 hectares. Pressure of population has been very intense and has been relieved to some extent through large scale outmigration. Much the same can be said about migration from the coastal areas of Orissa, Konkan and Tamil Nadu where the pressure of population has been quite acute. The proximity of these tracts to the industrial-urban concentrations of Calcutta, Bombay and Bangalore–Coimbatore–Madurai, respectively, was another potent factor stimulating this process. The agricultural migration from the North Punjab Plain stands in a class by itself as it was impelled not merely by increasing pressure on agricultural land but was also motivated by a strong desire for higher standards of living.

In the context of a predominantly agricultural economy and a consistently fast-growing population, the small (average for India, about 3 hectares in 1961) and declining size of agricultural landholdings has been basic to the process of outmigration, notwithstanding considerable outmigration from areas like the Punjab, where agricultural landholdings are not so small. In both time and space, outmigration was triggered off especially under lean agricultural conditions caused by periodic droughts, floods and low prices of produce. The zeal to improve the standard of living has been another vital consideration which is vivid in increasing migration from small towns to big cities, and the movement of landless agricultural labourers (mostly belonging to scheduled castes) from rural areas to urban places. The proximity to urban-industrial concentrations and major construction sites was a strong pull factor. During the pre-Independence period, the mobility within and between the areas under British rule was strikingly more than that in areas under princely rule. Apart from economic stresses and strains, however, the enterprising spirit of certain communities, such as those of the Punjab, Gujarat and Tamil Nadu, played its own role in migration, not only within India but also abroad. Above all, outmigration from a particular area perpetuated itself. The pioneer migrants not only generated more outmigration from their native areas but also determined the direction and sphere of economic activity of their follower-migrants in most cases.

The history of the existing patterns of economically-induced migration in India can be traced back to the middle of the nineteenth century. This was the period when the process of industrialization was beginning, the first railways were laid out, and plantation agriculture was introduced. The second spurt to the economy and to migration was experienced after the end of the First World War when industries started growing under protection, mining activities were intensified, plantations expanded, and the transport network extended. The developments during and after the Second World War provided an additional stimulus to migration. Lastly, Independence in 1947 was a landmark in the recent history of migration in the country. It resulted not only in the displacement of millions of persons but was also followed by a period of planned development oriented towards a socialistic pattern of society.

What are the prospects for the future? With a consistently staggering increase in population and limited scope for expansion of area under cultivation, the shift of some agricultural population from the rural areas to other activities is inevitable. The operation of prevailing socioeconomic forces is going to accelerate the tempo of migration of the non-agricultural population also. On the other hand, many of the inmigration areas are becoming saturated, the supply of local native labour is increasing everywhere, and regional feelings against inflow from outside the state are getting stronger. Commuting is putting some desirable restraint on influx into cities. The scope of interstate migration on any considerable scale is not too apparent. It is likely, therefore, that the rate of interstate migration may not improve, while that of intrastate migration is likely to rise. The multiregional complex of migration to metropolitan cities is likely to continue.

References

Bogue, D. J. and Zachariah, K. C. (1962) Urbanization and migration in India, in Turner, R. (ed.) *India's urban future*, 27–54. Bombay.
Davis, K. (1951) *The population of India and Pakistan*, 107–23. Princeton.
Gosal, G. S. (1961) Internal migration in India: a regional analysis. *Indian Geogr. J.* 36, 106–21.
Mitra, A. (1968) A note on internal migration and urbanization in India, 1961, in Sen Gupta, P. and Sdasyuk, G. *Economic regionalization of India: problems and approaches*, 251–7. New Delhi.
Sen Gupta, P. (1968) Some characteristics of internal migration in India, in Sen Gupta, P. and Sdasyuk, G. *Economic regionalization of India: problems and approaches*, 79–89. New Delhi.

Zachariah, K. C. (1960) *Internal migration in India: 1941–51.* Bombay.
Zachariah, K. C. (1964) *A historical study of migration in the Indian subcontinent, 1901–1931.* Bombay.

14 Interregional migration in the United States and Canada

D. R. Lycan

A popular book describes America as a nation of nomads, constantly on the move (Toffler 1970, 74–94). One eye-catching (at least to a geographer) subtitle – 'the demise of geography' – suggests that culture is becoming uniform from one part of the United States to another and that there no longer is much attachment of people to place. This aspatial picture does not presently characterize migration in the US and Canada. Migration between regions of North America is characterized by clear-cut inhibiting effects of distance, some cultural discontinuities, and drifts of population toward areas of economic opportunities.

Most of the data used in this paper to describe migration are from the *1960 Census for the US* and *1961 Census of Canada*, though at the time of writing some migration figures from the 1970 census for the US were available and were used for comparison with the earlier data. In both the US and Canada the census respondent was asked the place of residence five years previously for members of the household. In both countries the migration streams are derived from a sample resulting in some sampling error in estimating streams between areas of small populations and distant places. The US census provides some cross-tabulations by socioeconomic characteristics for streams between gross regions, such as between the nine census regions of the US, but only total numbers between finer regions such as state economic areas. Canadian migration data are available on interprovince streams cross-tabulated by age and employment status (see Stone 1969 for a number of special cross-tabulations). Some use is made of migration data for Canada through 1968, based on change of province of registration of family allowance payments which are made to nearly all Canadian families with children. Migration between the United States and Canada is not treated due to its international nature.

Two geographic characteristics of migration in North America are of overriding importance: the pivotal role of urban areas in the migration system and great areal extent of both countries.

The role of urban areas

In Canada from 1955–61 nearly 60% of all migration was between urban areas (table 14.1). Only about 8% of migration was from rural farm

Table 14.1

1956 and 1961 residences for Canada as a percentage of all migration streams

| | Residence in 1956 | | | |
Residence in 1961	All urban	Urban 100,000 and over	Rural non-farm	Rural farm
All urban	58.5	34.9	4.9	8.4
Urban 100,000 and over	39.2	27.6	1.9	3.5
Rural non-farm	14.8	6.7	2.4	5.6
Rural farm	3.0	1.2	1.8	0.7

Source: Adapted from Stone 1969, 55.

residences to urban residences. That a considerable amount of migration is between urban and rural non-farm residences really only suggests that urban areas are probably underbounded from the standpoint of the definition of labour markets. In the United States, if migration which occurs within metropolitan labour market areas is excluded from the total, two-thirds of all migration takes place between metropolitan areas (Adams 1969, 1). For this reason, a study of migration which is not somehow based on movement between urban centres, and on centre-hinterland migration, misses important aspects of the system of population redistribution. This said, it should be pointed out that the magnitude of the US results in complexity so that there are data published for 259,590 separate migration streams between the 510 state economic areas of the US.

Geographic scale

Because Canada and the United States are large countries, the choice of geographic scale used in a study has important effects on the patterns which may be discerned. Most studies of migration in North America are based on highly aggregated data for states, provinces, or multistate regions. Such studies overlook the extensive migration that takes place between different labour market areas within the data regions.

Geographic scale in migration studies, however, involves much more than simply the distance moved. It acts as a spatial filter that presents a very different socioeconomic sample of migrants depending on whether movements are tested between sets of many small regions or a few large ones. Partly for this reason, it is very difficult to integrate the results of studies based on widely varying geographic units. The effects of spatial filtering can be found in the distance bias of the educational composition of migrant streams, using education as a proxy for a number of socioeconomic characteristics. Data on Canadian migration from 1956–61 show sharp differences between the migration patterns of persons with varying levels of education (table 14.2). Movement *within* Canadian provinces of persons with some

Table 14.2

1956 and 1961 residences for males in the labour force in Canada 16 years and older in 1961, by level of education

Educational level in 1961	Total (000)	Percentage in same:			Percentage in different province		
		Resi- dence	Munici- pality	Province	Contiguous	Non-con- tiguous	Immi- grants
Elementary school	1,902	57.7	25.6	11.3	1.1	0.9	3.2
Secondary school	2,022	47.2	28.4	15.8	2.4	2.3	3.7
Two or more years university	398	40.7	25.4	19.9	4.3	3.8	6.5

Source: *Dominion Bureau of Statistics* (1965) *1961 Census of Canada, Population sample,* 4.1–10, *Migrant and non-migrant population in the labour force,* table J6.

university education was at a rate only slightly greater than that of persons with a secondary school education, but approximately twice that of persons with only an elementary school education. However, the proportion of persons with some university education who moved *between* provinces was twice as great as the proportion of moves for secondary education and nearly four times as great as for persons with only an elementary school education. There is a bias in many studies toward analysing the patterns of the more educated socioeconomic classes.

A metropolitan-centred migration system

Because the problems previously described related to questions of scale, a system that bridges both short-distance and long-distance moves is described below. The Portland, Oregon, metropolitan area is used as an example, partly because of personal knowledge of it, but also because it shows some characteristic patterns of loss and gain. Most of the discussion is directed toward a schematic map of the migration streams (fig. 14.1).

During the 1955–60 period the Portland metropolitan area showed an increase in population of 38,000 to total 822,000 in 1960. Most of this increase could be attributed to natural increase. During this period 114,573 persons moved into the metropolitan area and 107,932 departed, with a net gain of only 6,611, a great deal of movement in order to accomplish a small net change of population. There were two main sources of inmigrants: the West North Central states contributed a net of 7,241 and the Oregon settlements surrounding Portland contributed 4,873. The directionality of the stream from the West North Central states was pronounced with 3 migrants to Oregon for 1 in the opposite direction. California was the main area to which Oregon lost population, especially to the metropolitan areas of Los Angeles, San Francisco and San Diego. There was a net loss to California of 12,035, with approximately 3 outmigrants for every 2 inmigrants.

These southward migrants were a better than average educated sector of Portland's population who were seeking possibilites beyond Oregon's slow-growing and technologically unsophisticated economy. By contrast, the movement into Portland was composed of a less educated group suited to the needs of local manufacturing and service industries.

The patterns of migration to and from Portland reflect certain characteristic features of metropolitan area migration: heavy exchange of population with a surrounding hinterland, usually gains from rural areas and nearby smaller cities beyond the suburban fringe; net shifts of population to areas of economic growth in nearby regions as shown by the large net shift to California; and traditional patterns of migration based partly on economic opportunities but also on information flows from friends and relatives who moved at an earlier date, as shown by the moves from the West North Central states.

These migration patterns did not remain constant in the years following 1955–60. During 1960–5 the net numbers of inmigrants to the Portland metropolitan area rose to about 75,000 (from 6,641 in 1955–60) falling to about 44,000 in 1965–70. The origin-destination patterns show that the strong flow to California in 1955–60 reversed to a strong flow from California to Portland during 1965–70. At the time of the reversal of this net stream local and state planning agencies were only partly aware of the turnaround and consequently underestimated Portland's population growth during the 1960s by a substantial amount. The often transitory nature of net migration flows suggests extreme caution in their extrapolation into the future and underlines the need for more frequent data on migration than those provided by a decennial census.

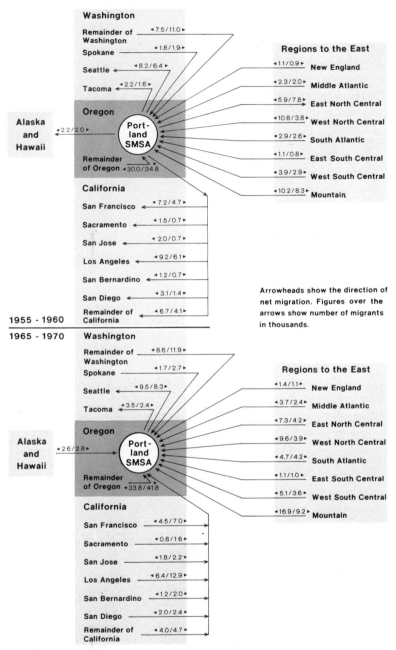

Figure 14.1 In- and outmigration for Portland, Oregon SMSA, 1955–60
Source: *Census of Population.* 1970 Subject Reports, Final Report PC(2)-2E
Migration between state economic areas, 1972. Also see same source for 1960

Gross interregional patterns

At a much grosser scale, the patterns of migration between regions of the US and Canada are reasonably simple in their main dimensions. These patterns can be explained by a special type of cartogram which depicts latent distance and preference patterns (figs 14.2 and 14.3). The diagrams should be visualized as idealized gravity models in which the volume or mass

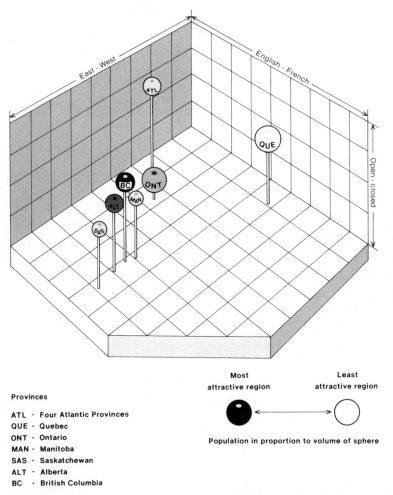

Provinces

ATL - Four Atlantic Provinces
QUE - Quebec
ONT - Ontario
MAN - Manitoba
SAS - Saskatchewan
ALT - Alberta
BC - British Columbia

Most
attractive region

Least
attractive region

Population in proportion to volume of sphere

Figure 14.2 Proximity and attractiveness of Canadian provinces based on 1968 migration streams
Source: Based on transfer of family allowances as recorded in the *Annual Report* of the Department of National Health and Welfare

of the spheres is proportional to the populations of the regions; the gross migration between two regions is inversely related to the intervening distance as depicted in the three-dimensional space of the diagrams; and the direction of net migration is from the lighter to darker shaded sphere with its strength proportional to the difference in shading. While the diagrams only give an intuitive feeling of the relationships, they are based on descriptive factor analytic type models which explain about 95% of the variations in rates of migration between gross regions of the United States and Canada (Lycan 1970, 1–10).

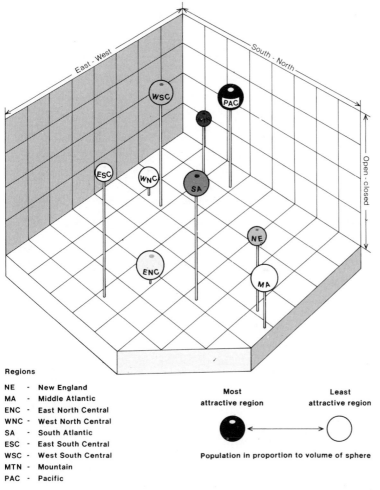

Regions

NE	-	New England
MA	-	Middle Atlantic
ENC	-	East North Central
WNC	-	West North Central
SA	-	South Atlantic
ESC	-	East South Central
WSC	-	West South Central
MTN	-	Mountain
PAC	-	Pacific

Most
attractive region

Least
attractive region

Population in proportion to volume of sphere

Figure 14.3 Proximity and attractiveness of US regions based on 1955–60 migration streams
Source: 1960 *Census of Population*

The pattern for Canada is based on data on the transfer of family allowances during the year 1968. It is a reasonably good characterization since the end of the recession of the late 1950s and early 1960s. There is a distinct east-west distance pattern which can be seen in the alignment from the Atlantic provinces to Saskatchewan (fig. 14.3). This distance effect is generally like that of the arrangements in earth-space except that British Columbia is more central in the migration system than its position on the Pacific fringe would suggest, and Saskatchewan is more peripheral than its location in the Prairies would indicate. Most of the variations in gross migration rates in Canada stem from this east-west pattern of separation. However, a second distinct feature is the offset location of Quebec in relationship to the east-west distance axis described above. The obvious explanation for this displacement is the difference in language and culture between largely French Quebec and most of the other provinces. A third and more subtle pattern is the downward vertical displacement of Ontario which in effect makes it more distant from all of the other provinces. In real world terms, this is probably a result of the large variety of opportunities for migration within Ontario which necessitates less exchange of population with the other provinces.

The shadings applied to the spheres represent attractiveness to residents and migrants. They are the results of a very simple system of locational preferences which permits the scaling of the provinces from the least preferred to the most preferred (Quebec and British Columbia respectively in 1968, although the scaling of attractiveness varies considerably from year to year). The net directional rate of movement between any two provinces is simply proportional to the difference in their attractiveness.

The patterns of gross migration in the US are somewhat more complicated than for Canada, partly because the distribution of population in the US is over two dimensions whereas Canada's is largely east-west linear. Data from the US are for migration between the nine multistate census regions for 1955–60. The two main dimensions that underlie movement during this period are east-west and north-south patterns which are loosely related to the locations of the regions in actual earth space (fig. 14.3). The east-west axis in the diagram can be visualized by the alignment from East North Central and East South Central regions in the foreground to the Mountain and Pacific regions in the background. The ordering departs from that of earth-space in several ways, the most notable being the eastward displacement of the Pacific and Mountain regions and the westward displacement of the West South Central and West North Central regions. The north-south dimension is particularly clear, but the South Atlantic and East South Central regions can be seen to lie to the south (left) of New England and the Middle Atlantic regions. The East South Central region is literally the 'deep south', occupying a very peripheral location due to its low rate of interchange of population with the other regions. The South Atlantic region, on the other hand, is more central than its actual location in earth-space would suggest. The greatest departure of this diagram from actual earth-space locations is that the West North Central and East North Central regions lie in a plane well below that of all the other regions, making them more distant from the other regions. Their location is comparable to that of Ontario in the diagram for Canada. Because they interact less with the other regions, they are isolated in a somewhat unique sense.

As with Canada, a simple pattern of regional preferences governs the net rate of movement between any two regions and hence within the entire system. The Pacific and Mountain regions were the most preferred, producing a strong westward drift of population. The South Atlantic region was also strongly preferred resulting in a southward shift in population along the Atlantic seaboard, particularly from the nearby Middle Atlantic region. While the East South Central region was the least preferred, its isolated location (in the diagram) protected it from heavy rates of population loss.

The causes of the movement patterns

The factors which influence the numbers of migrants between the regions of the US and Canada are often summarized as positively related to populations in the origin and destination regions, and relatively less and more attractive regions. Commonly these factors are expressed in a gravity model of approximately the following form (ter Heide 1963, 55–76):

$$m_{ij} = k \cdot p_i \cdot pj \cdot d_{ij}^{-x} \cdot (a_j - a_i)$$

where m_{ij} is the number of migrants moving from region i to region j in some time period; p_i and p_j are the populations of origin and destination regions; d_{ij} is some measure of distance from region i to region j; a_i and a_j are simple or composite measure of attractiveness of regions i and j; and k and x are parameters which are estimated.

A gravity model similar to that above has been used frequently by researchers studying migration, and many aspects of its performance are well understood. There is not much argument about the effect of the populations of the origin and destination regions on the size of migration streams – it is generally conceded to be positive and strong. The effect of distance is somewhat more controversial, although non-geographers do tend to take it for granted. The last variable, attractiveness, is the one about which there is the most controversy, partly because it has proved difficult to state in operational terms, and partly because it is such a key variable in forecasting the net migration component of population change.

Distance factors

Increased distance nearly always has been found to have a substantial attenuating effect on migration; however, the proportion of the variation in the size of the migrant streams which is accounted for by distance ranges widely (table 14.3). Even within closely comparable analyses, Schwind found that the partial correlation of distance with size of migration streams, holding constant the populations of origin and destination regions, was −.54 between 225 US 'consolidated commuting regions', but fell to −.35 when the same data were aggregated somewhat differently into a set of 133 'consolidated migration regions' (Schwind 1971, 88–91). He provides no answer for this considerable disparity. His experiments with differing mathematical transformations of distance produced only minor variations compared to those resulting from how his data units were aggregated.

Table 14.3

Examples of correlations of gross migration with distance

Source	Region and date	Dist. measure	Correlation
Galloway 1969, 12–17	9 census regions of US, 1957–60	Ordinal measure number of regional boundaries crossed	Partial $r = -.45$
Lycan 1969, 242	10 Canadian provinces, 1956–61	Log. of road distance	Simple $r = -.82$
Rogers 1968, 79	9 California metro. areas, 1955–60	Log. of road distance	Partial $r = -.83$
Schwind 1971, 85–91	133 US consolidated migration regions, 1955–60	Log. of airline distance	Partial $r = -.35$
Schwind 1971, 85–91	225 US consolidated commuting regions, 1955–60	Log. of airline distance	Partial $r = -.54$
Stone 1969, 177–9	10 Canadian provinces, 1956–61	Road distance	Simple $r = -.62$

Perhaps we need to look systematically at the interrelationship between scale and distance. Or possibly this approach is a blind alley, and we need to look more closely at the behaviour of the individual migrants as suggested by Wolpert and others (Wolpert 1965, 159–72). The work of the Survey Research Bureau of the University of Michigan, based on interviews with a sample of the US population, sheds some light on the decision-making process of migrants as it relates to length of move (Lansing and Mueller 1967, 218). One of their findings was that moves of 600 miles or longer were accomplished by longer planning periods, consideration of alternative locations and the use of more information sources. Unfortunately, only a few of the correlates of distance moved were reported in the study; possibly these data should be further exploited.

Economic determinants

Generally, variations in employment opportunities are thought to cause net streams of migrants between regions. Where employment opportunities are stated in terms of new jobs created in the destination region, the correspondence with numbers of inmigrants is very high. Since job vacancies cannot be predicted any better than net migration, this relationship is not very useful. Therefore Lowry (1966) and others have typically formulated their models in terms of unemployment levels, wage rates and amenity factors for origin and destination regions. The composite of these factors constitutes attractiveness as expressed in the ter Heide gravity model above. While this latter type of formulation is theoretically satisfying, few such models have produced practical results. In general, these analyses have produced results which are theoretically consistent, that is, net migration tends to be from areas of lower income and higher unemployment to areas of higher income and lower unemployment. Where the results of such analyses have been theoretically inconsistent, most of these problems could be attributed to problems of multicollinearity in the regression analyses. One of the more interesting studies for the US disaggregated migration by occupation, sex, age, race and education and found clear differences in the responsiveness to regional income differentials, particularly a lower response for black males (Galloway 1969, 105–10). A number of researchers have suggested that income and unemployment variations have more influence in pulling movers to economically desirable destinations than pushing them from undesirable regions. Probably the best evidence for this is in the Survey Research Bureau Study which showed that '. . . economic factors which exert a positive stimulus on in-migration do not have a symmetrical negative effect on out-migration. . .' (Lansing and Mueller 1967, 121–2). The economist Hansen draws heavily on this finding of lack of responsiveness to push factors in migration in explaining the ineffectiveness of migration in clearing labour surpluses from depressed areas of the US. This is one of the keystones of his argument for developing 'growth poles' within and on the borders of depressed areas, rather than encouraging migration to more distant growing industrial areas (Hansen 1971, 256–64).

Amenities

Confronted with an inability to explain very much of net migration by the use of economic indices, many researchers, particularly geographers, have attributed a large part of migration to a drift toward regions of significant amenities. Schwind does precisely this in the conclusion to his monograph on migration and regional development in the US, but does not operationalize the concept of amenities (Schwind 1971, 109–18). In fact, without knowing much more about the decision-making of migrants, it is not really possible to add to the concept of amenities. If personal analyses on the scaling of preference patterns of migrants are valid, the finding of a single dimension of attractiveness means that if both economic and amenity factors strongly influence potential movers, the two factors must synchronize; areas of economic opportunity must also be regions of amenity (Lycan 1970, 12–13).

Again from the Survey Research Bureau study, it appears that movers in post-move interviews rate job considerations strongly first, family ties second, and community preferences a weak third as influencing their decision to move. One interesting observation in this study was that most persons verbalize the role of community preferences in their decision process in positive terms for their new location rather than a dislike for their old location (Lansing and Mueller 1967, 135–9). This coincides with Gould's maps of residential preferences which showed that nearly all persons rated the region where they presently live as better than most other parts of the US (Gould 1969, 32–44).

One thing particularly confusing about the role of amenities in moving decisions is that economic and amenity factors may be confounded if amenities play some role in the location of industries. Particularly relevant here is the expansion of the US aerospace industry in the west and to a lesser extent in the south, and a good example is the shift of the Martin Marietta Corporation from their old aircraft plant in Baltimore to new sites in Florida and Colorado. This shift was made at a point in time when this firm was shifting out of aircraft production and into missiles, space and avionics, with a resulting need to assemble a markedly altered labour force. The choice of Orlando, Florida, and Denver, Colorado, for these new plants must have been an attraction in securing a skilled labour force in a short period of time. The analytical problem illustrated by this example is that while job considerations may have been the major factor for an engineer moving to Denver to work for Martin, amenity considerations may have dictated the location by Martin in Denver.

The time pattern of migration

So far the discussion of migration has been based on single discrete time periods. In fact, the size of migration streams can change greatly during short time periods. For example, various indicators of migration suggest that the stream of migrants to Southern California dried up with the recent decline of the aerospace industry there. Over longer time periods there are distinct patterns of relationship between the performance of the economy and the pattern of migration streams. Migration tends to be greater during periods of high employment with clear patterns of movement toward regions of economic growth. During slack periods less movement occurs and there is a considerable volume of return migration to the economically less advantaged regions (Eldridge and Thomas 1964, 117–22).

The existence of annual data on interprovincial transfers of family allowance accounts for Canada has permitted some interesting analyses of short-term fluctuations in movement patterns. Vanderkamp has shown that the geographical mobility process operates much more effectively under conditions of high employment in Canada, in the sense of moving people from regions of less to those of more economic opportunity (Vanderkamp 1968, 607–8). On this evidence he argues for a full employment policy to alleviate regional unemployment problems.

Using the same data as Vanderkamp, matrices of net migration rates between the regions of Canada for each of the years from 1949–68 have been analysed, using a technique akin to factor analysis. This analysis results in the estimation of characteristic roots of this matrix for nineteen points in time which describe the effectiveness of net migration in redistributing population. The results show a strong tendency for the effectiveness of migration to move counter to unemployment levels; when unemployment is high the effectiveness of migration is low and vice versa. Surprisingly, the total amount of movement does not vary much from one year to the next. This analysis also illustrates some of the difficulties of using census data which describe movement over a time period of several years. For the time period sampled by the *1961 Census of Canada*, 1956–61, effectiveness at the beginning of the period was very high, but by the end of the time period in the census data are unfortunate and probably have resulted in some difficulties in the analysis.

Conclusions

When studying migration between gross regions of the US and Canada, the patterns of migration show reasonably simple patterns, suggesting that they are governed by distances in earth-space and certain types of social distance as typified by the situations of Quebec and the American South. However, the problem is multilayered, since the results of gravity model type formulations based on distance produce widely varying results when the pattern of geographic aggregation of the data is varied.

In a somewhat different way, the studies of net migration and its causes seem to be able to hint at economic and amenity factors, but they do not achieve levels of explanation that would form a basis for a useful predictive model. In spite of painstaking efforts the recent attempt of Schwind (1971) to build a large set of migration regions and to use them in the analysis of gross and net migration does not seem to have moved us much further in the understanding of the economic causes of migration. On the other hand some of the studies of the behaviour and attitudes of individual migrants, as typified by the work of Lansing and Mueller for the Survey Research Bureau, do seem to give reasonably clear results. Another approach which seems to hold some interesting possibilities is the study of the role of migration in the career patterns of various occupations (White 1970, 116–22). In this context migration is given a structural explanation based on the lifetime needs for mobility by individuals.

A newly completed census invites and even demands a certain amount of effort to interpret the recent population history of a nation, particularly since, at least in the US and Canada, shifts in migration streams have been difficult to sense as they occurred. Problems of lack of migration data can and to some extent are being solved by efforts of local and national agencies to tap such sources as driving licences and tax registers to monitor inter-regional migration on a current basis. However, even greatly improved sources of data will not remedy the inconclusive and incomplete body of theory relating to migration. It is imperative that the social scientists concerned with the clarification and extension of this body of theory accelerate their efforts and their dialogue. There is a critical need to extend the tools of the traditional demographer in order to cope with the problems of analysing and forecasting regional population change. It seems that population geographers, more than many other geographers and more than other social scientists, have been guilty of too much individual research with inadequate resources. It should be possible to attack the problems of theory building and to discharge our responsibilities for describing population change by means of a more concerted and cooperative approach.

References

Adams, R. B. (1969) U.S. metropolitan migration: dimensions and predict-ability. *Proc. Am. Assoc. Geogr.* 1, 1–6.

Dominion Bureau of Statistics (1965) *1961 Census of Canada.* Series 4.1 *Population sample, 9, General characteristics of migrant and non-migrant population.* See also 4.1–10 *Migrant and non-migrant population in the labour force.* Ottawa.

Eldridge, H. T. and Thomas, D. S. (1964) *Population redistribution in the United States, 1870–1950, 3. Demographic analysis and interrelations.* Philadelphia.

Galloway, L. E. (1969) *Geographic labor mobility in the United States, 1957–1960.* US Social Security Admin. Rep. No. 28. Washington.

Gould, P. R. (1969) Problems of space preference measures and relationships. *Geogr. Anal.* 1, 31–44.

Hansen, N. M. (1971) *Rural poverty and the urban crisis: a strategy for urban development.* Bloomington.

Lansing, J. B. and Mueller, E. (1967) *The geographical mobility of labor.* Univ. of Michigan Survey Res. Bur.

Lowry, I. S. (1966) *Migration and metropolitan growth: two analytical models.* San Francisco.

Lycan, D. R. (1969) Interprovincial migration in Canada: the role of spatial and economic factors. *Can. Geogr.* 8, 237–54.

Lycan, D. R. (1970) *An analysis of migrants' distance and preference spaces in Canada, 1949–1968.* Paper presented to the Western Regional Science Association, February 1970.

Portland Metropolitan Planning Commission (1965) *Population mobility, Portland metropolitan area.* Portland.

Rogers, A. (1968) *Matrix analysis of interregional population growth and distribution.* Berkeley.

Schwind, P. J. (1971) *Migration and regional development in the United States, 1950–1960.* Univ. of Chicago, Dept of Geography Research Paper No. 133.

Stone, L. O. (1969) *Migration in Canada: some regional aspects.* Dominion Bur. of Statistics Census Monograph, Ottawa.

ter Heide, H. (1963) Migration models and their significance for population forecasts. *Milbank Memorial Fund Q.* 7, 55–76.

Toffler, A. (1970) *Future shock.* New York.

US Bureau of the Census (1972) *Census of Population.* 1970 Subject Reports, Final Report PC(2)-2E *Migration between state economic areas.* Additional data on migration are tabulated in PC(2)-2A *State of birth*, PC(2)-2B *Mobility for states and the nation*, PC(2)-2C *Mobility for metropolitan areas*, and PC(2)-2D *Lifetime and recent migration.* See also same series for 1960. Washington.

Vanderkamp, J. (1968) Interregional mobility in Canada: a study of the time pattern of migration. *Can. J. Econ.* 1, 595–608.

White, H. C. (1970) *Chains of opportunity: system models of mobility in organizations.* Cambridge, Mass.

Wolpert, J. (1965) Behavioral aspects of the decision to migrate. *Pap. Reg. Sci. Assoc.* 15, 159–69.

15 Migration and changing settlement patterns in Alberta

G. R. Lamont and
V. B. Proudfoot

Introduction

While urbanization in Canada has received considerable academic and political attention, certain processes occurring concomitantly with urbanization have been all but ignored. These are, first, the processes leading to, and characterizing, rural depopulation. Such processes where they have been discussed have generally been regarded as an outcome of farm mechanization and increase in farm size (Dawson 1964; Weir 1968). Detailed discussions on such factors as size and age of farm families, length of settlement, the virtual closing of the frontier in western Canada and the price of farm land are needed in order to understand the processes more fully. The second set of processes are those leading to, and characterizing, the decline of the smaller urban centres. These centres are, perhaps, more aptly termed central places than urban centres, for many are small in size with populations less than 1,000, and offer only limited goods and services to the surrounding rural populations. Clearly where these smaller central places are integrated with the agricultural economy and community, as in most of Alberta, the two sets of processes are interconnected.

The present paper discusses some aspects of changing settlement patterns in Alberta and of migration into the smaller centres with populations in 1970 between 500 and 12,000. Data for centres smaller than 500 in size are incomplete, and the larger centres were deliberately excluded from the study on which this paper is based (Lamont and Proudfoot 1972) so that attention could be devoted to the smaller centres which have shown, especially since the Second World War, varied patterns of growth and decline, inmigration and outmigration. Since decline in some centres is occurring simultaneously with growth in others, and since it was feasible to study

only a sample of Albertan centres within the stated size limits, centres were
selected on the basis of their apparent viability, as determined by a consideration of such characteristics as recent population history, value of retail
trade, tax assessment and availability of selected public services.

Information was collected on a sample of those people who had moved
into fourteen selected centres between 1965 and 1970. It is only possible
to collect such data by personal interview or response to mailed questionnaires, for aggregated data such as those available from the Census of Statistics,
Canada, valuable though they may be, do not yield detailed information on
the characteristics of such migrants and of their journeys. Although only
those who moved into the sampled centres during a six-year period are
considered, they represent a significant proportion of the present populations
of the centres, generally greater than 30%.

Patterns of change

There has been little uniformity in the spatial patterns of recent population
change in the province of Alberta, either in terms of minor administrative
units or in terms of individual cities, towns or villages. On a broad scale,
population decline has predominated for the last forty years in the rural
southeastern part of the province, where agriculture initially spread into
physically marginal areas, and since the 1930s the number of farms has
decreased markedly. As the numbers of farms, and farmers, have declined,
so too have the populations of many of the rural service centres. In the
Drumheller area, the collapse of the coal industry 'exaggerated' these
agricultural changes, while in parts of the irrigated areas near Lethbridge
the decline has been less pronounced (Klawe *et al.* 1969).

There has been a northward shift of the centre of gravity of the provincial
population since at least the 1930s, and most of the central places north of
Edmonton with populations over 500 in 1970 have gained population since
1951 more rapidly than the province as a whole (fig. 15.1). During the same
period, there has been an increasing tendency for the populations of central
places along the Edmonton–Calgary axis to increase more rapidly than the
overall provincial population. Especially since 1966, there has been a more
rapid increase in many of the small towns within a radius of 30 kms of
Edmonton and Calgary. Some of these towns seem to have gained population at the expense of similar towns rather further from the two 'metropolitan'
centres, and increasingly function as suburbs of them. Some small towns
and villages near the other, very much smaller cities in the province have
also grown as a result of the development of similar suburban functions
(Ellis 1972; Jankunis 1972).

No general relationship can be observed between population change and
population total, apart from the fact that no centres larger than 3,500 in

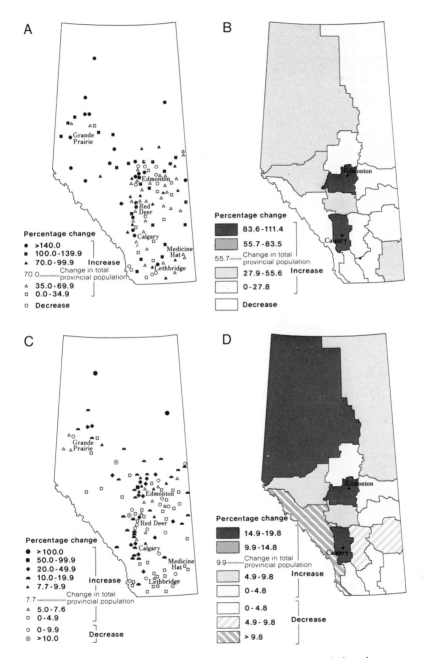

A

Percentage change
● >140.0
■ 100.0-139.9
▲ 70.0-99.9   Increase
70.0——— Change in total
        provincial population
△ 35.0-69.9
□ 0.0-34.9
○ Decrease

B

Percentage change
▨ 83.6-111.4
▨ 55.7-83.5
55.7——— Change in total
        provincial population
  27.9-55.6   Increase
  0-27.8
  Decrease

C

Percentage change
● >100.0
■ 50.0-99.9
◆ 20.0-49.9
◗ 10.0-19.9
▲ 7.7-9.9   Increase
7.7——— Change in total
       provincial population
△ 5.0-7.6
□ 0-4.9
○ 0-9.9
⊗ >10.0   Decrease

D

Percentage change
▨ 14.9-19.8
▨ 9.9-14.8
9.9——— Change in total
       provincial population
  4.9-9.8   Increase
  0-4.8
  0-4.8
  4.9-9.8   Decrease
  >9.8

Figure 15.1 Population changes in Alberta, 1951–70. (A) Population change, 1951–70. (B) Census divisions, 1951–66. (C) Population change, 1966–70. (D) Census divisions, 1961–6

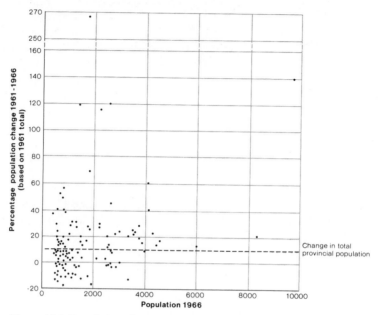

Figure 15.2 Population change and size of small towns in Alberta

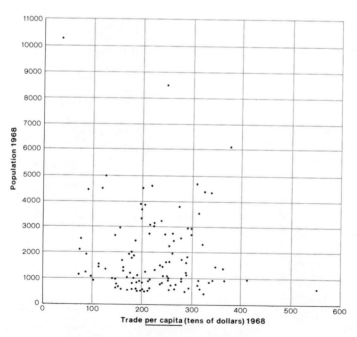

Figure 15.3 Population and retail trade of small towns in Alberta, 1968

1966 had grown less quickly than the total provincial population (fig. 15.2). Of the centres below 3,500 population in 1966, about one-third had grown more quickly than the average, one-third had grown less quickly, and one-third had actually declined. A few centres grew exceptionally rapidly as the result of the development of either suburban functions or natural resources, such as oil or gas. However, among those towns with populations of less than 3,500, size in itself seems to be no indicator of future growth, stagnation or decline.

Since the major function of many small centres in Alberta is to provide services for the centre and its immediate rural hinterland, it might be expected that retail trade figures would indicate significant groupings of centres and provide useful information on small town viability. The volume of total trade increases as population increases, but trade *per capita* shows no simple relation to size of centre (fig. 15.3). The lowest values of trade *per capita* are for resource towns such as Swan Hills, Hinton and Fort McMurray, the highest for centres which serve wide areas across North Central Alberta. During the period 1964–8, the most noticeable spatial feature in changing trade was the low rate of increase, or even actual decrease, in trade *per capita* of many of the small centres along the Edmonton–Calgary axis. It would seem as though the two cities are collecting an increasing amount of trade from these centres, some of which act simply as dormitories for the metropolitan centres.

Classification and sampling

As neither population change in relation to size of population, nor retail trade in relation to population, provided clear evidence for classifying centres into categories which might serve as a basis for studying migration into centres of different types, a principal components analysis was carried out similar to that used by Hodge (1965) in predicting centre viability on the Great Plains. Twenty-seven variables were used relating to population size, recent population changes, retail trade, number of licensed businesses, value of turnover, tax assessment, social and government functions, and spacing of centres. Together, 3 of the components accounted for 56.4% of the variance. The first and major component, accounting for 40.2% of the variance, is an index of the size of the centre. It had heavy positive loadings on the 10 variables indicative of some aspect of absolute size. The second component characterized the centres primarily by the age structure of their populations, and subsequently by percentage population growth and distance to a competing centre. Those places having relatively old populations had generally shown low population growth between 1951 and 1966, and were relatively close to a centre of competing size. Major loadings on the third component were provided by variables related to the number of provincial and federal government offices, and the number of hospitals in each centre. Distance to a competing centre again contributed to the character of the component, which might usefully be described as an index of centrality. As such, high values would be positively associated with viability.

The 3 component scores for each centre were calculated and plotted successively against each other. Five clusters of centres exhibiting some degree of internal consistency of membership could be distinguished, the same centres tending to cluster consistently on all plots. These 5 clusters could be regarded as varying in viability. Resource and new towns, dormitory suburbs and institutional centres lay outside these clusters and they were omitted from the total population for purposes of sample selection since their migration characteristics were expected to bear a different relationship to the development of a centre than would normally be the case. Centres in the Peace River region were also omitted since a similar study of migration had been done for those centres in that area in 1968-9 (Lamont 1970), and 2 centres in Southwest Alberta which were being intensively studied at the same time as this study was being carried out were also eliminated (Kenward 1971).

From the 5 sets of centres, grouped according to their similarities, 14 were selected for study. The number chosen from each group was approximately proportionate to the total membership of that group, and took into account the distribution of members of that group throughout the province.

A sample of inmigrants to each of the 14 centres between 1965 and 1970 was chosen from a list of inmigrants prepared by comparing the Municipal Electors Lists of 1970 with those of 1965. A 100% sample of all inmigrants to the smaller centres was utilized to give a sample size of approximately 80. An equal number of inmigrants to the larger centres was chosen randomly from the lists prepared. A questionnaire was mailed to the sample inmigrants in late 1970. The completed response rate varied greatly, between 24 and 53%. The number of questionnaires returned by the Post Office as 'Moved, Address Unknown' varied from 1 to 32%. These represent people who had moved recently after the Electors List had been compiled. Like the high percentage of inmigrants, varying between 19 and 45% of all household units in the sampled centres, this was an indication of the high mobility rates associated with the populations of smaller centres in Alberta. Responses were weighted because the data were sample-based and the sample design was not a self-weighting one. Varying sample ratios and response rates made the weighting more imperative. Since the sample was selected at 2 levels – the centres themselves and the migrants within the sample towns – the probability of any migrant having responded to the questionnaire was computed on this basis, and on the assumption that the non-respondent inmigrant households within a centre are 'typical' inmigrant units for that town, an assumption validated in the earlier study by Lamont (1970).

The questionnaire was designed to obtain data concerning the migrants themselves, the nature of their move and their reactions towards their destinations. Data were coded and keypunched, then checked for error by an editing program. The Statistical Package for the Social Sciences (SPSS) set of programs was used primarily for analysis of the data, which were considered mainly in terms of frequency distributions, cross-tabulations and means.

The migrants

About 35% of all adult migrants were under 30 years of age, and about 18% were over 60 years. Clearly people are most mobile in the early years of participation in the labour force as they seek to secure and improve their career positions. In later years in a semi-rural prairie environment, however, there is a second peak as rural farm people are no longer able or willing to work their land and migrate into the smaller centres. Significant differences occurred between the 5 sets of centres, grouped according to their assumed viability. Cluster 1, assumed to be the least viable of the 5 sets, had both the lowest proportion of its inmigrants under 30 years and the highest proportion over 60 years. Cluster 5, made up of the larger centres and assumed to be the most viable, had almost twice as large a proportion of its inmigrants under 30, and about one-half the proportion over 60 years. Migrants to the larger towns in Cluster 5 were, therefore, very young relative to the migrants as a whole, to the Canadian population, and to migrants to the other 4 clusters.

Migrants to the clusters also differ in respect to other characteristics associated with age. For example, both Clusters 1 and 5 have higher proportions of migrant households with no children living at home. In Cluster 1 the high proportion of childless migrants is associated with a relatively old population. In contrast, Cluster 5, also with a high proportion of childless migrants, has a larger proportion of younger migrants, a significant number of whom had not begun their families at the time of migrating.

It is often assumed that high levels of mobility are associated with high levels of education. Amongst migrants to the smaller centres levels of education tend to be highly variable. Of the overall group of migrant heads of households, approximately 47% had completed high school; 53% of their spouses had also achieved that level of schooling. However, 26% of the heads completed Grade 8 or less, and these formally less well-educated migrants were dominantly among the older male migrants. Spouses, in contrast to their husbands, had completed Grade 8 or less in only 14% of the cases. The high proportion of high-school graduates among the migrants is reflected in the large number of migrants having professional training, 28% of the heads of households, and 26% of their spouses. The largest proportion of the in-migrants, however, have no additional training – 38% of the heads of households, and 43% of their spouses. To a large extent, these are the older migrants, to whom education was neither so available nor so needed.

Occupation was, as expected, related to the educational characteristics of the migrants. The distribution of migrants through the occupational groupings before moving differed somewhat from the distribution after moving. The largest proportion of migrant heads in any occupation before moving were farmers – 23%. Two other groups were significantly larger than the others – those in professional and technical occupations (16%), and those who were students or unemployed (13%). Only 3% were retired before moving, compared with 20% after. After moving and at the time of the survey only 4% of the migrant heads were farmers; there were 20% in professional and technical occupations and 4% were students or unemployed. A much higher proportion of migrants, both before and after moving, than in the Albertan workforce as a whole, were in professional and technical occupations, suggesting that the propensity for such persons to move is much greater than for clerical workers, for example, who comprise 11% of the Albertan workforce but only 6% of the migrants before they moved and 8% after moving. At the time of moving there were proportionately more farmers among the migrants than among the total provincial labour force, and a much smaller proportion of craftsmen and foremen among the migrants than among all Albertans. It is clear from the data that many farmers retired after moving and that many of those who had previously been students became professionally and technically employed after moving.

Generally the farmers had moved relatively short distances, and at the time of the survey almost one-half of them still owned all their land, although most had retired. Apart from the farmers, the data collected suggest that younger, more highly skilled people are more mobile than those who are older and have fewer skills. There is a concentration of professional and technical people in the younger age groups; one-fifth of these people are 20 to 24 years of age while, before moving, only one-tenth were accounted for in this age category. This implies that a substantial group of 'new' professionals are going to smaller Albertan centres, many of whom when asked about their intentions to remain in such centres clearly indicated that they regarded their current locations as temporary 'stepping stones' in their careers. This evidence is very similar to that obtained by Keown (1971) in New Zealand, who was similarly able to recognize a group of career transients. Of the overall sample, 45% of the migrants fall into four distinctive age/occupation groups indicating the markedly selective nature of migration (table 15.1).

Responses to an open-ended question regarding the motives for moving were coded using 9 empirically derived categories. Most motives for moving were economic and associated directly with employment (except for those who were retiring). About 43% of all migrants moved to take advantage of a job opportunity while an additional 17% moved because of a job transfer. The kind of decision to be made by the potential migrant is quite different

Table 15.1

Major age/occupation groups of migrants

Occupation after moving	Age at time of survey	Percentage of migrants
Retired	Over 60	16
Professional and technical workers	Under 35	13
Craftsmen and foremen	Under 30	9
Clerical workers	Under 25	5

in these 2 situations – the transfer decision being more obligatory or negative from the migrant's point of view and the opportunity decision more positive.

The other major motive for moving was retirement which accounted for a further 18%. Most of those retiring were farmers. About 8% gave the desire for better services and facilities as their primary motive for moving, and about 6% cited nearness to family and friends. Some of this 14% were migrants who had retired.

Migrants were also categorized according to a secondary reason for moving in the 10% of cases where such a reason was given. These reasons included not only the common primary reasons but a significantly larger percentage cited such factors as costs of living, housing, social reasons, improved services and facilities, and dislike of large cities.

Comparisons of reasons for moving with socioeconomic data relating to the migrants indicate that job opportunities are relatively more important as reasons for moving among younger than among older migrants. Better services and facilities and nearness to families and friends tend to be more important reasons for moving among the older and the less-skilled migrants. Those who moved for better services and facilities came predominantly from Albertan centres smaller than those they were living in at the time of the study. Those moving because of their dislike of the big city tended to be young and more highly educated, although most of the migrants from Edmonton and Calgary had moved primarily for job opportunities. When reasons for moving were examined in relation to the assumed viability of the clusters of centres it was found that more migrants moved for job opportunities to more viable clusters than to less viable clusters, although there was considerable internal variation within clusters.

Level of training is reflected in the distribution of reasons for moving by occupational categories. The professional-technical migrants, those in sales, the craftsmen and foremen and the managers showed high propensities to move for reasons associated with employment. Within the managerial group a greater share of moves were by job transfer than in any other occupational group. The remaining group for whom jobs were important motives for moving were those who had been unemployed or students immediately before the move. By contrast, employment motives, whether through job opportunity or transfers, were of low importance to operatives and labourers, who often moved for social or family reasons and to be nearer better services and social facilities.

The actual choice of destination was made mainly in reference to employment, although the roles of familiarity, families and friends and 'town appeal' were all acknowledged by the inmigrants as reasons for the choice of particular centres. Facilities, services and nearness were especially important to the older migrants. The role of employment in the choice of destination appears to become stronger as the distances and differences in size between the places of origin and destination become greater. However, the small centre is attractive to two quite different groups of people: those who already live in such small centres or in the strictly rural areas, and, in absolute terms a very much smaller group, those who live in the largest urban centres and wish to experience life in a small centre, sometimes in the process converting such centres into dormitory suburbs.

Intent to remain

The intention of inmigrants to remain in the centres where they were living in 1970 varied with the age of the migrant upon moving. In total, more than half the migrants, 58%, intended to move to another centre. However, as age at time of movement increased so did the proportion of migrants intending to stay, so that the overall figure of 42% intending to remain masks a wide range of intentions (fig. 15.4). For example, about 15% of those under 50 years of age intend to stay compared with about 90% of those over 60 years. Migrants who were 55 years or older at the date of moving and intend to remain at their destination represent exactly 20% of all migrants questioned, and clearly form a fairly large, older, stable group in the centres to which they have moved. Intentions vary not only with age but also with skills and occupations; inmigrants with professional training exhibited the least propensity to stay and many had already made plans to leave in 1970. Those technically trained had proportionately the greatest numbers whose intentions for moving were uncertain (43%), and potentially this technical group is the most flexible regarding its future in its present locations. Clerical workers, craftsmen-foremen and operatives also have a low propensity to remain. So also do those who have migrated from outside Canada or have moved from Edmonton and Calgary to smaller centres. Those who moved shorter distances within Alberta are more likely to remain than those who moved longer distances.

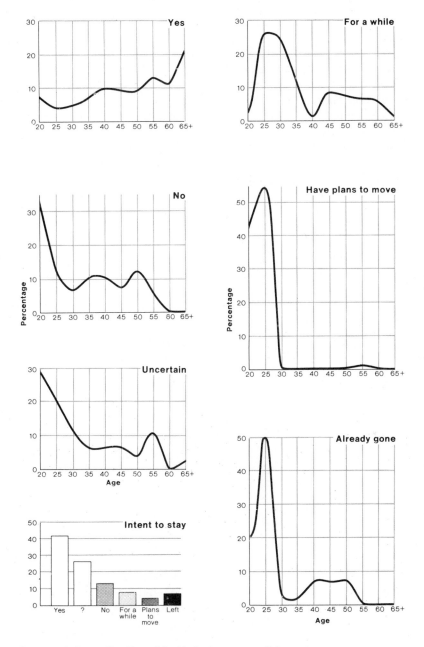

Responses to the question: Do you intend to live here permanently?
Overall response, and distribution by age within each category of response.

Figure 15.4 Age and attitudes of migrants in Alberta

Outmigration

For the discussion of migration patterns in general, it is interesting to note the characteristics of outmigration from the sample centres by those respondents who had already moved away or had planned a move. By size of destination, the largest single proportion, 39%, were going to places of population greater than 100,000, and only 13% were moving to centres smaller than 1,000 population. A second sizeable group of outmigrants, 22%, were going to centres of 5,000 to 24,999 population, while another 8% were going to centres greater than 25,000 but less than 100,000, making a total of almost 70% of the outmigrants going to places larger than any of the sample centres. Those going to places 5,000 to 24,999 population comprise a much greater share of the outmigrants than the share of Alberta's residents now residing in places of that size range, thus indicating a concentration in those centres relative to smaller urban centres.

Of the 39% going to the largest places, some two-thirds were going to Edmonton or Calgary, while 40% of all outmigrants were going to other Albertan destinations. These figures compare with only 14% of inmigrants who had moved from Edmonton and Calgary, and 69% who had come from other locations in the province. Together they indicate an overall movement ultimately towards Edmonton and Calgary.

Conclusions

Selectivity of migrants from the overall population on the basis of age, education and occupation is evident. Migrants to small centres in Alberta are for the most part younger, better educated, and engaged in more highly skilled occupations than the populace as a whole. However, a substantial proportion of the total migrant sample were 65 years or older, many of whom are retired farmers. In general a rise in occupational levels and, therefore, we assume, in economic well-being upon moving is illustrated by the data. This suggests that the most-often-acknowledged goal of migration, increased economic opportunity, is met, to some extent at least, in the migration process. Traditional theories regarding the effect of distance on migration and stepwise migration are also supported by the study data. Distance proved less a deterrent to the younger migrants than the older. Older migrants almost always moved from smaller centres or farms to the sample centres, while most migrants from cities larger than the sample centres are young. Within the sample centres there do appear to be regular differences in the characteristics of migrations to centres exhibiting varying assumed viabilities. The less viable a centre seems to be, the more likely is it to attract older, retiring migrants, and the less likely are the younger, more-skilled inmigrants to remain.

Finally, it must be acknowledged that migration is very much an individual decision, and that the variety of factors affecting a person's motivation to move is highly complex. Nevertheless, broad patterns in the process or urbanization within Alberta can be recognized. All the evidence gathered from the present study of inmigrants to selected small centres suggests that the present patterns will persist. Indeed, migration into the larger centres may well increase, both in terms of volume and rate at which movement takes place, as the levels of education and skills of the total population rise.

Acknowledgements

This paper is based on work carried out for the Alberta Human Resources Research Council. We are grateful to former colleagues at HRRC for helpful comments, and to others for the development of programs to handle our data. However, the opinions expressed are those of the authors.

References

Dawson, J. (1964) *Changes in agriculture to 1970.* Staff Study No. 11, Economic Council of Canada. Ottawa.

Ellis, M. C. (1972) *Local migration in East Central Alberta.* Unpublished M.A. thesis, Univ. of Alberta.

Hodge, G. (1965) The prediction of trade centre viability in the Great Plains. *Pap. Reg. Sci. Assoc.* 15, 87–115.

Jankunis, F. (1972) Urban development in southern Alberta, in Jankunis, F. (ed.) *Southern Alberta: a regional perspective*, 74–85. Univ. of Lethbridge.

Kenward, J. (1971) *Political manipulation and rewards in the Crowsnest Pass.* Unpublished M.A. thesis, Simon Fraser Univ.

Keown, P. A. (1971) Stepwise migration and the career cycle. *N.Z. Geogr.* 27, 175–84.

Klawe, J. J. *et al.* (1969) *Atlas of Alberta.* Univ. of Alberta and Govt of Alberta.

Lamont, G. R. (1970) *Migrants and migration in part of the South Peace River Region, Alberta.* Unpublished M.A. thesis, Univ. of Alberta.

Lamont, G. R. and Proudfoot, V. B. (1972) *Migrants to small towns in Alberta.* Report to the Alberta Human Resources Research Council. Edmonton.

Weir, T. R. (1968) The people, in Warkentin, J. (ed.) *Canada: a geographical interpretation*, 137–76. Toronto.

16   Internal migration in Western Europe

A. J. Fielding

Introduction

This paper outlines recent internal migration patterns and reviews some migration studies in the countries of Western Europe. For these there are major differences in data quality and availability, particularly on internal migration (table 16.1).

Table 16.1

Data sources on internal migration

Country	Annual register	Census question	Residual data as main source
Sweden	✓		
Norway	✓		
Denmark	✓		
West Germany	✓		
Netherlands	✓		
Belgium	✓		
France		✓	
Italy	✓		
Switzerland			✓
Austria			✓
Spain	✓		
Portugal			✓
Eire			✓
United Kingdom		✓	

In every Western European country local and regional net migration estimates can be obtained by the so-called residual method, subtracting natural change (births minus deaths) from total population change. These estimates, however, conflate internal and international migration, are only accurate for intercensal periods and allow no examination of differences between migrants and the population as a whole. Yet these data are the main source of information on regional net migration in four Western European countries, and are the only source of data at the local level in others. Examples of the residual method used to trace trends and patterns of net migration exist for Spain and Portugal (Barbancho 1967; Alarcao 1969). Information on internal migration flows in these countries is usually dependent on birthplace data from the census. These data refer to lifetime migration and are difficult to handle and interpret if interest is focused on recent flows.

For every country in Western Europe other than Switzerland, Austria, Portugal and Eire, migration flow data can be obtained which are an improvement on birthplace statistics. In eight of these ten countries these come from a residence registration procedure, in some cases associated with the maintenance of a full population register. In Sweden, for example, registration has provided an invaluable data base for the study of both gross and net migration; figures of annual net migration by county are published in the following year, making it possible to monitor quite closely the changing pattern of gains and losses. Also, samples drawn from the register are used for longitudinal studies, permitting analysis of sequences of migration decisions and correlations for individuals between the characteristics of the migration and the attributes of the migrants (Olsson 1966). However, delays in registration of migration can reduce the quality of the flow data from registration, as in Italy where many migrants retain their residence registration in their village of origin when they migrate semi-permanently to the industrial triangle of northern Italy, to Switzerland or to West Germany. In Spain, the unequal enforcement of registration means that much of the flow data are suspect. Annual flow data from registration procedures are normally published in the statistical yearbooks, making them an attractive, accessible and up-to-date source of migration data; but they usually suffer from the fact that they include very little information on the social, occupational and demographic characteristics of the migrants.

Flow data from census migration questions do not suffer in this way since responses to them can be cross-tabulated with other data on the census schedule. Comparisons may be made of inmigrant population and employment structures with total population structures (Fielding 1966). However, flow data for France and Britain, which are based on this source, refer only to the intercensal period or to the twelve months prior to the census date. Because the flows are calculated by comparing the locations of residence at only two points in time all intermediate moves are concealed. Furthermore, the information is gathered on a 1 in 10 or 1 in 20 sample basis, which means that it is only worth using at a fairly aggregate (regional) level.

A major factor complicating the interpretation of migration data for Western European countries is the unsuitability of the statistical areas used. West German *Länder* and Swiss *cantons* are probably the worst, but Dutch provinces and Norwegian counties are also difficult. In West Germany, for example, analyses at the *Kreise* level show that large *Länder* (e.g. Nordrhein-Westfalen) contain strongly contrasting migration regions within them, while Bremen and Hamburg are so small that much of the urban expansion of these cities is occurring in the nearby *Länder* of Niedersachsen and Schleswig-Holstein. For England and Wales some of these problems were overcome through the re-tabulation of the 1961 census migration data on a 'city-region' basis (Fielding 1971).

Patterns of net internal migration

The patterns of net migration (wherever possible this refers to internal migration only) are presented at a common scale in figs. 16.1–16.7. In general they fall into three groups. There are those with the industrialization/urbanization/rural depopulation process dominant (Portugal, Spain, Italy, Eire and Austria). They showed migration gains only in their major urban zones and in tourist areas, but these gains were very great and were matched by the heaviest rural depopulation in Western Europe (interior, upland Portugal and Spain, southern Italy and western Ireland).

Secondly, there are the countries in which an agglomeration process has coexisted with an important degree of more local metropolitan decentralization of industry, employment and population (Sweden, Norway, Denmark, Switzerland and to a lesser extent France). In Norway and Sweden the near-empty northern regions were losing through migration to the urban regions of Stockholm – Uppsala, Oslo, Malmö and Göteburg. The transitional status of France is due to its rural exodus having slowed down considerably in recent years and the development of some of the regional industrial decline features of the third group. In this, metropolitan decentralization was dominant and migration losses from old industrial areas also important (France, United Kingdom, West Germany, Belgium and Netherlands). These countries have tended to have only residual elements of rural depopulation, and rates of net gain and loss were characteristically low.

The pattern of net internal migration is not always the same as for net internal and international migration. Countries of net emigration such as Spain tend to lose migrants from specific regions (Galicia), and countries of net immigration to attract migrants to certain regions. In 1962–8, for example, the region centred on Toulouse lost by internal migration but gained overall by migration due largely to the preference of repatriates from Algeria for southern France.

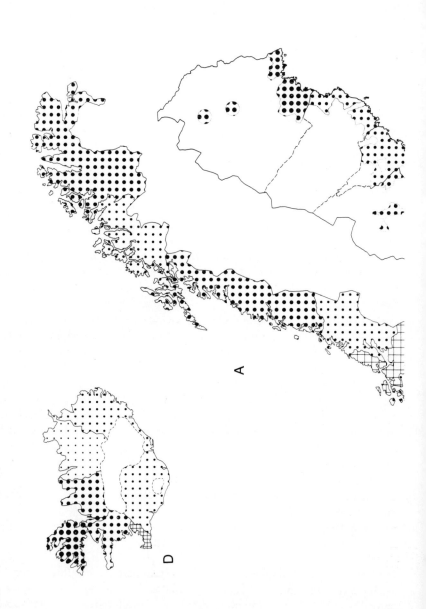

A

D

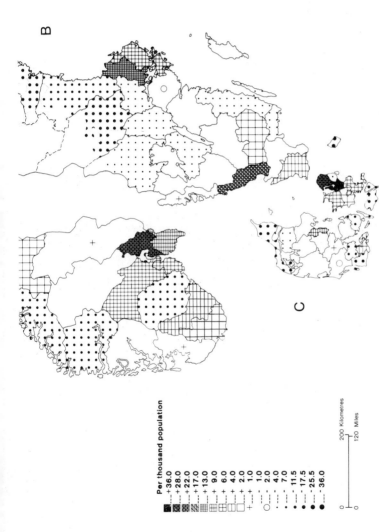

B

C

Per thousand population

+36.0
+28.0
+22.0
+17.0
+13.0
+ 9.0
+ 6.0
+ 4.0
+ 2.0
+ 1.0
- 1.0
- 2.0
- 4.0
- 7.0
- 11.5
- 17.5
- 25.5
- 36.0

0 ___ 200 Kilometres
0 ___ 120 Miles

Figure 16.1 Migration in Scandinavia. (A) Net internal migration, Norway 1970. Source: Statistisk Sentralbyrå, unpublished tables. (B) Net internal migration, Sweden 1969. Source: Statistiska Centralbyrån (1971) *Befolknings förändringar 1969.* (C) Net migration, Denmark 1969. Source: Danmarks Statistisk (1971) *Befolkningens bevaegelser 1969.* (D) Net internal migration, Iceland 1971. Source: Hagstofu Islands (Icelandic Statistical Office) *Folksflutningar aris 1971; Hagtidindi* (Reykjavik) 57, 5 (May 1972), 89–92

Some recent studies of internal migration

The previous section concentrated entirely on total migration and on net migration, but to understand migration processes migration differentials and gross migration flows must be considered. Possibilities of carrying out these analyses are indicated from a review of recent research.

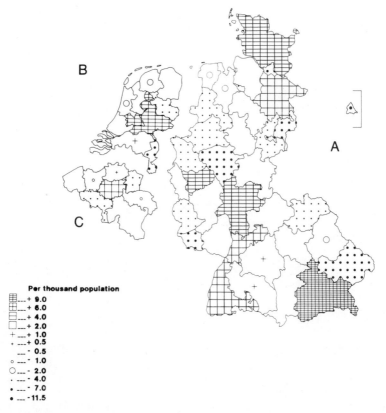

Fig. 16.2 Migration in West Germany and the Low Countries. (A) Net internal migration, West Germany 1968. Source: Statistisches Bundesamt (1971) *Bevölkerung und Kultur: Wanderungen, 1968* Kohlhammer. (B) Net internal migration, Netherlands 1967. Source: Centraal Bureau vor de Statistiek (1971) *Statistiek van de binnenlandse migratie 1966–68*. (C) Net internal migration, Belgium 1969. Source: Institut national de la statistique (n.d.) *Annuaire statistique 1970*

Analyses of migration fields

Jakobsson's monograph (1970) on internal migration in Sweden opens with a review of migration models and of data sources, indicating broad features of migration in the 1950–60 decade and presenting and interpreting details of migration differentials. He then turns to his main focus – the analysis of migration 'fields', fitting the Pareto function ($y = ax^{-b}$, where y is migration rate, x is distance, a is a constant and $-b$ is the distance exponent) to migration distances and achieving close fits between expected and observed values. From these he proceeds to search for systematic changes in the

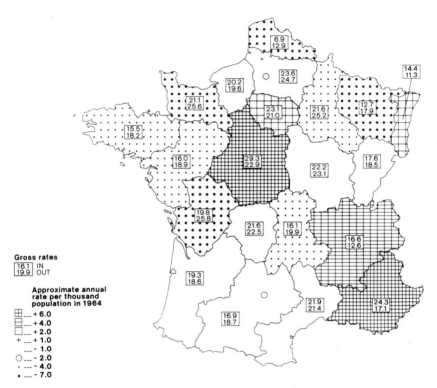

Figure 16.3 Net internal migration, France 1962–8
Source: Institut National de la Statistique et des Études Économiques (1969) *Les collections de L'INSEE D.1.*

distance exponents with changes in urbanization (lower values for urban than for rural places), settlement size, relative location, economic structure. Not the least of the achievements in this part of the exercise is the computerized mapping, made possible by the use of grid square location units. Variations in distance exponents with direction (using 45° sectors) are examined, and median migration distances are calculated for forty subgroups of the population and then compared. People in isolated locations, the young adult (especially men), the unmarried, the educated, the salary-earners, white-collar workers (and especially those with professional and

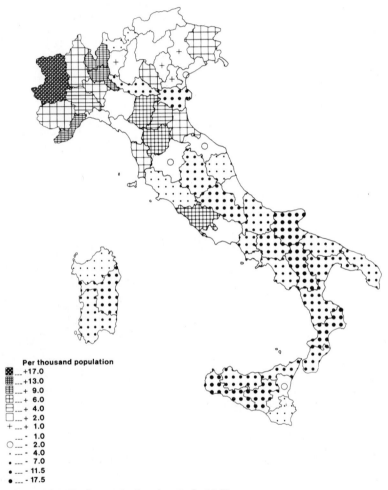

Figure 16.4 Net internal migration, Italy 1968
Source: Instituto Centrale di Statistica (n.d.) *Annuario di statistiche demografiche 1968*

technical jobs), have greater median migration distances than the average, and they also usually have lower values of b.

Similarly, Courgeau (1970) treats migration fields in France. Though with poorer quality data compared with Sweden, he fits Pareto functions to census birthplace and change-in-residence data, and compares the results with an application of Stouffer's intervening opportunity model. The French *départements* are remarkably similar in area and are fairly compact, yet their use in this sort of analysis, combined with the decision to use crude distance bands 60 km wide, inevitably hindered the research. Courgeau noted increased mobility over all distances in the period 1891–1962, and the cases of *départements* whose distance-decay functions differ from the

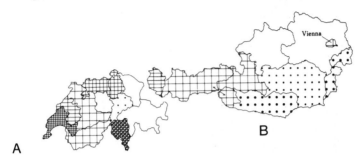

Per thousand population in 1960

▨	...+17.0
▦	...+13.0
▥	...+ 9.0
⊞	...+ 6.0
⊟	...+ 4.0
☐	...+ 2.0
+	...+ 1.0
	...- 1.0
○	...- 2.0
·	...- 4.0

Per thousand population in 1961

⊟	...+4.0
☐	...+2.0
+	...+1.0
	...- 1.0
.	...- 2.0
•	...- 4.0

Figure 16.5 Net migration. (A) Switzerland 1960–70. Source: *La vie économique*, No. 8 (1971). (B) Austria 1961–71. Source: Statisches Zentralamt *Statistisches Jahrbuch 1971* and *Die natürliche Bevölkerungsbewegung im Jahre 1970* (1971)

Pareto norm (with an exponent of −2). For example, some *départements* (especially industrial ones) show indifference to distance for both inmigration and outmigration for distances greater than 250 km. The value of the exponent (−2) was found, surprisingly, to remain fairly constant over time. The *départements* of the Paris region are found to be atypical; in particular the inmigration distance-decay functions differ little (in height) through time and the slopes are very slight. These findings are discussed in the light of the special migration relationships between distant regions and Paris (the information role of early migrants, return migration etc.). Varied results are achieved when the Stouffer model is applied to French data;

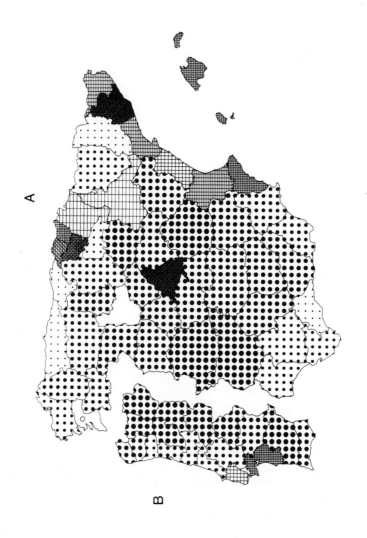

A

B

Percentage population in 1960

+ 22.0
+ 17.0
+ 13.0
+ 9.0
+ 6.0
+ 4.0
+ 2.0
+ 1.0
− 1.0
− 2.0
− 4.0
− 7.0
− 11.5
− 17.5
− 25.5
− 36.0

Figure 16.6 Net migration. (A) Spain 1960–70. Source: III plan de desarollo económico y social (1972) *Estudio sobre la población española.* (B) Portugal 1960–70. Source: Instituto Nacional de Estatística (1971) *Recenseamento de 1970* (preliminary results), and *Estatísticas e Indicadores Regionais 1970* (1970)

the fits of expected and observed values are good on some occasions, but wildly out on others. One of the most interesting parts of the study deals with the effect of the boundary of France and the location of the *département* in relation to this boundary on the distance-decay functions. Courgeau

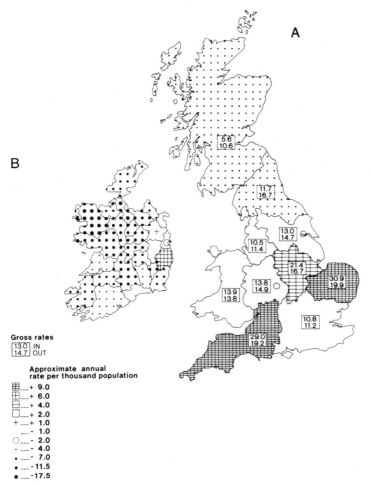

Figure 16.7 Migration. (A) Internal migration, Great Britain 1961–6. Source: *Abstract of Regional Statistics 1970*. (B) Net migration, Eire 1966–71. Source: Central Statistical Office (1971) *Census of Population of Ireland 1971* (preliminary report)

attempts to detach these effects so as to leave a 'true' picture of the relationship between migration and distance. In a second part of the study, the location of foreign-born residents is examined to see if there is a regular decline with distance from the country of birth.

Interaction models of gross migration flows

The studies of migration fields have concentrated on variations in the levels and slopes of distance-decay functions for groups of places and groups of people. Related to this approach, but in a sense more ambitious, are the studies which incorporate 'gravity' variables (population at origin, population at destination and intervening distance), together with economic and social factors as independent variables in linear regression models that try to explain variations in gross migration flows between regions. Two studies of this kind are based on data for the Netherlands (ter Heide 1970; Somermeyer 1970). Somermeyer's was based on a model that included terms for the differences in living standards between region of destination (j) and region of origin (i), and for the 'psychic distance' (dissimilarity in religious composition) between i and j.

$$Mi \rightarrow j = PiPj \cdot (c_0 + c_1(Fj - Fi)) \cdot Dij \cdot (1 - dij)$$

where $Mi \rightarrow j$ is gross migration flow from i to j; Pi and Pj are population at i and j respectively; Fj and Fi are indices of attractiveness for j and i; Dij is geographical distance; dij is 'psychic distance'; and c_0 and c_1 are constants. Urbanization and religious composition were found to be significant, unemployment and underemployment were not important, and the Dij term had an exponent value of -1.67.

Although employing a similar model form, the studies by Masser (1970) and Hart (1970), of intermetropolitan and interregional flows respectively in England and Wales, derived their stimulus from the works of Lowry and Andrei Rogers in the United States. These models use labour-force variables in place of population, and the ratios of unemployment levels and wage levels, Ui/Uj and Wi/Wj, in place of the difference terms in the Somermeyer models. Masser and Hart found that the 'gravity' variables were doing nearly all the work, and that while the R^2 values were high, indicating a strong predictive power, the models were unrewarding as a means of understanding the relationships between migration on the one hand and regional economic structure and change on the other. This was partly because the gravity variables were not independent of the relevant economic variables (distance correlates with difference in economic structure, and several economic variables such as wage rates correlate with population size). Relations between migration and unemployment were again shown to be tenuous and complex. The form of modified gravity model has now been applied to Britain and to other European countries including France and the Netherlands (Drewe 1969; Weeden 1971).

A different approach was adopted by Jansen and King (1968) in a study of internal migration in Belgium. They tested Stouffer's intervening opportunity model, which states that the flow i → j is positively related to the number of opportunities at j, and negatively related to the number of intervening opportunities, and the number of competing migrants. The operational form of the model tested was:

$$M_{i \to j} = \frac{c(M_{i \to q} M_{q \to j})^{\alpha}}{(M_{i \to x})^{\beta} (M_{y \to q})^{\gamma}}$$

where c is a constant; q is 'all other places'; x is the set of areas (excluding j) located in a circle having ij as its diameter; y is the set of areas (excluding j) located in a circle, centred on j, having ij as its radius; and α, β and γ are exponents. Jansen and King also tested a model in which the 'intervening opportunity' and 'competing migrants' terms were replaced by geographical distances, finding that levels of 'explanation' were lower than for a comparable American case study and that the 'competing migrants' term was particularly weak. The distance model was less efficient than the intervening opportunity model. When the models were fitted to flows within linguistic regions, their degree of fit improved markedly to match the American results, underlining the importance of the cultural factor in Belgian migration behaviour. However, the complicated feedback mechanisms that make for the criticisms of 'circularity of argument' levelled against the modified gravity model (especially when employment growth is included as an independent variable) apply in even greater degree to the Stouffer models, and this alone limits Jansen and King's achievement.

Studies of migration differentials

Schwarz (1969), in a study of internal migration in West Germany, brings together analyses of many aspects of migration (historical trends, motivation, modelling and forecasting). The section on migration differentials, while only a small part of the work, does represent its style and provides examples of what can be done with the German register data. For example, it shows that in 1965 the internal migrants included more men than women (70% of the population against 54%), that migrants between *Länder* were predominantly young adults (age groups 21–25, 76%; all ages, 19%), and that the single person was more likely to be a migrant than the married person, though this difference was narrowing over time. The register data did not, unfortunately, permit a comparison of recent migration rates by occupation or industry. On the other hand, Schwarz demonstrates that insights can be provided into the urbanization process. Data for 1958–9 showed that while small rural *Gemeinden* (parishes) had 14.4% of the population, they contributed 16.7% of the total outmigrants and received only 12.9% of the total inmigrants. Small towns (population 5,000–20,000) with 16.4% of the population contributed 19.4% of the outmigrants and 20.3% of the inmigrants, indicating high rates of population turnover. Large cities (over 100,000 population) with 30.6% of the population contributed 22.3% of the outmigrants and 25% of the inmigrants. These are the commonly observed features of low turnover rates for the large city and the tendency, at that time, was for them to be net gainers by internal migration. There is some analysis of migration at the *Landkreise* and *Stadtkreise* level in this work, but often it is only the *Länder* data that are used. More might have been done to avoid the use of these inappropriate areal units. Furthermore, the discussions under several headings (e.g. forecasting and modelling) were very general. It would have been interesting to have seen the ideas and arguments presented under these headings applied to the West German situation in more detail.

Comparisons can be made between the work of Schwarz on West Germany and that of Geary and Hughes (1970) on internal migration in Ireland. Geary is less fortunate than Schwarz in that, in having to use birthplace data from the census to obtain information on migration patterns, he is thus unable to tell precisely when the migration took place, and has no data relating to intercensal years. However, these obstacles have not prevented a number of well-supported detailed statements being made about Irish migration. In contrast to Schwarz, Geary found that women, especially those in the 15–19 age group, were more mobile than men; they were most likely to be moving from rural areas to Dublin. The combined cohort-survival/ birthplace method was applied to data for Dublin which showed that although it gained young adults from the rest of Ireland, it was an overall loser by net migration due to a sizeable emigration, notably to Britain. Taking the country ratios of actual to expected migrants (where the 'expected' migrants were calculated on a *per capita* share-out of the total migrants) for persons born in Dublin residing elsewhere in Ireland and for persons born elsewhere in Ireland residing in Dublin, Geary demonstrated the influence of contiguity and distance. Both were found to be very significant here, and when the exercise was repeated for other Irish counties. For migration differentials in occupation groups, Geary had to use the 1946 census, which showed that the number born in another county as a percentage of non-agricultural socioeconomic groups varied from 60% for the higher professional to 12% for the unskilled manual. Variation in the differences between the inmigration and outmigration ratios could be explained, in large part, by the county '*per capita* income' variable. With a data base presenting so many problems it is understandable that Geary sought alternative information on migration. This explains the inclusion of an interesting section on migration at marriage in which the analyses were based on marriage registration data for the residences of the bride and of the groom.

Migration and regional development

Rodgers (1970) set out to test the hypothesis that the distribution of government aid for regional development explains variations in the net migration rates of provinces in southern Italy. In the period 1951–66 industrial employment in the Italian south increased appreciably in a northern fringe zone extending down to Naples, in the Taranto–Bari–Brindisi zone (Puglia) and in southeastern Sicily and Palermo – that is, in those areas receiving government aid. The pattern of net migration was essentially the same, with large net losses in upland central parts of the peninsula, in Calabria and in central and southwest Sicily; and small net losses occurring only in the Rome–Naples zone, Puglia, southeastern Sicily and Palermo. Regressing net outmigration on changes in industrial employment, a strong negative relationship was found and Rodgers concluded that 'increases in industrial opportunities have helped check potential out movements'. Income growth was similarly related to outmigration, but it was also related to increases in industrial employment. To avoid this multicollinearity in the explanatory variables (not autocorrelation as Rodgers asserts) a principal components analysis was carried out, and the first component was identified as 'socioeconomic health'. A regression of net outmigration on the scores of provinces on this component gave an improved R^2 of .65. The variable 'migration stock' (net lifetime migration, calculated using birthplace/residence data from the census) was then added to help 'sap up' the unexplained variation in outmigration values. This is a dangerous procedure at the best of times, because the time series autocorrelation may be only partly due to the 'information' and 'aid' factors that are invoked here to explain the similarities between present and former migration situations. In Rodgers' work the problem is worse because there was some double-counting of migrants, so that they appeared in both the dependent variable and in the 'migration stock' independent variable. In addition, it is a questionable procedure to run a principal components analysis to obtain orthogonal, non-correlated independent variables and then to add back in a new variable which is correlated with the components. In spite of these technical oddities, the conclusion from this study that much of the industrial growth of the south was influenced by governmental aid is clear and unequivocal.

Termote (1968), for Belgium, treats net migration in a different way and at a different spatial scale, selecting the *arrondissement* net migration of males aged 25–39 as the dependent variable, with the intention of seeing to what degree migration flows can be considered as a response of the population to the characteristics of and changes in the 'economic space' of Belgium. Multiple regression was used to test five hypotheses: that migration is a response to regional income inequalities; that migration is a response to the lack of adjustment between the regional supply of and demand for labour; that migration 'compensates' regions of low natural increase; that migration is due to regional structural change (notably decline of agricultural employment); and that migration behaviour is dependent on location relative to major centres, being affected particularly by the substitution between commuting and permanent changes of residence. Starting with twenty-three independent variables, Termote found that his 'best' model (with an R^2 of .85) was that which regressed net migration on income level, percentage employed in agriculture and change in activity rate, these three variables being not highly correlated with one another. The 'income' and 'structural adjustment' hypotheses were given support while the 'job vacancy', 'natural increase' and 'relative location' hypotheses were shown to be unhelpful. The discussion of the lack of relationship between net migration and unemployment is interesting. Termote points out that the act of migration (the effect) has, for young adult males in particular, the purpose of avoiding the experience of unemployment (the cause), so that the relationship does not get the chance to develop; also, the importance of the 'percentage in agriculture' variable is a partial support for the 'job vacancy' thesis in that it shows that people are leaving areas of 'underemployment'. These examples reflect the thorough and thought-provoking treatment of the net migration/economic growth relationship that characterizes this study.

Conclusion

While the works reviewed in this paper do not constitute the totality of research work on internal migration in Western European countries, they do reflect some of the varied styles and orientations that have been adopted. Little attention has been directed here towards sociological work since this is mostly confined to studies of particular regions and to intra-urban migration. Many of them include questionnaire surveys of migrants' reasons for moving; the 'classic' study of this kind treats the origin, social characteristics and attitudes of a sample of migrants to the Paris region (Pourcher 1964). Nor have the methods been examined by which governments obtain migration estimates for regional population forecasts. For these the Rodgers' matrix formulation is becoming increasingly popular, and this approach has been recently used on British, French and Dutch regional situations. Finally, little account has been taken of the flows between Western European countries. However, with nine of the fourteen countries studied being signatories to the Rome Treaty, with its 'free movement of labour' clauses, there is perhaps need to question traditional notions of what constitutes 'internal' migration.

Short bibliography of recent studies of internal migration in Western European countries

Alarcao, A. de (1969) *Mobilidade geografica da populacao de Portugal: migracoes internas 1921-60.* Lisbon.

Barbancho, A. G. (1967) *Las migraciones interiores españolas.* Madrid.

Boustedt, O. *et al.* (1970) *Beiträge sur Frage der räumlichen Bevölkerungsbewegung.* Hanover.

Courgeau, D. (1970) *Les champs migratoires en France.* Paris.

Drewe, P. (1969) *Interregional migration in the Netherlands.* Phase III Netherlands Economic Institute (unpublished paper).

European Communities (1971) *Regional statistics,* No. 1. Brussels.

Federal Republic of Germany (1971) *Statistisches Bundesamt. Bevölkerungsstruktur und Wirtschaftskraft der Bundesländer 1970.* Stuttgart.

Fielding, A. J. (1966) Internal migration and regional economic growth: a case study of France. *Urban Studies.*

Fielding, A. J. (1971) *Internal migration in England and Wales.* Centre for Environmental Studies, UWP 14. London.

Geary, R. C. and Hughes, J. C. (1970) *Internal migration in Ireland.* Dublin.

Hansen, J. C. (1969) Flyttinger i Norge 1967. *Norsk Geogr. Tidsskr.*

Hart, R. A. (1970) A model of interregional migration in England and Wales. *Reg. Stud.* 4, 279-96.

Instituto Nacional de Estadistica (1968) *Migration y estructura regional.* Madrid.

Instituto Nacional de Estatistica (1970) *Estatisticas e indicadores regionais, 1970.* Lisbon.

Jakobsson, A. (1970) *Omflyttningen i Sverige 1950-60.* Stockholm.

Jansen, C. J. and King, R. C. (1968) Migration et 'occasions intervenantes' en Belgique. *Réchèrches économiques du Louvain* 4, 519-26.

Masser, I. (1970) *A test of some models for predicting intermetropolitan movement of population in England and Wales.* London.

Mossin, A. (1971) *Mobility and equilibrium. A theoretical structure tested on Danish migration data.* Inst. of Statistics and Economics, Univ. of Copenhagen (unpublished paper).

Olsson, G. (1966) Distance and human interaction: a migration study, *Geogr. Ann.* 47, B, 1, 3-43.

Pellicciari, G. (ed.) (1970) *L'immigrazione nel triangolo industriale.* Rome.

Pitie, J. (1971) *Exode rural et migrations intérieures en France.* Poitiers.

Pourcher, G. (1964) *Le peuplement de Paris.* Paris.

Rees, P. H. and Wilson, A. G. (1973) Accounts and models for spatial demographic analysis. *Environment and Planning* 5, 61-90.

Rodgers, A. (1970) Migration and industrial development: the Southern Italian experience. *Econ. Geogr.* 46, 111-35.

Schwarz, K. (1969) *Analyse der räumlichen Bevölkerungsbewegung.* Hanover.

Societa Italiana di Economia, Demografia e Statistica (1968) *Le previsioni demografiche regionale nel quadro della programmazione economica* (ed. Somogyi). Rome.

Somermeyer, W. H. (1970) Multi-polar human flow models. *Pap. Reg. Sci. Assoc.* 24, 131–44.

ter Heide (1970) *Methods and main results of an analysis of Netherlands population register data on internal migration.* Regional Science Association (unpublished paper).

Termote, M. (1968) *Un modèle de migration pour la Belgique.* Louvain.

Weeden, R. (1971) *Models of interregional migration in Britain.* Paper presented to Institute of British Geographers Conference, Liverpool.

17 Population trends and prospects in marginal areas of Norway

J. C. Hansen

The identification and classification of marginal areas

The study of the development of settlement in marginal areas is one of the classic topics of cultural geography, with important Scandinavian examples (Enequist and Norling 1960; Stone 1967, 1971). The delimitation of settlement zones by means of formal criteria (houses, roads, etc.) should be supplemented by a study of population development over time. Identification of economic characteristics of marginality probably would be the most rewarding approach to a problem-oriented study of marginal areas. However, the difficulty with this approach stems from the scarcity of data for the minor primary statistical areas, and the frequent changes of their boundaries.

This paper attempts to clarify problems of marginality with examples at different geographical levels, the smallest being the census enumeration district (*tellingskrets*), the biggest the county (*fylke*) or groups of counties. A further purpose is to identify easily accessible demographic variables describing economic processes and their spatial variations satisfactorily. Material from North Norway is prominent, but the total Norwegian context is outlined, and in conclusion comparisons are made with marginal areas in Sweden and Finland (fig. 17.1).

The importance of urban growth

In Norway, as in most other countries, the development of settlement and population is closely related to urban growth (fig. 17.2). The dominant trend is one of local, regional and national concentration (Myklebost 1968). The general causes of Norway's urbanization are similar to those of most Western countries, perhaps with one important exception; marginal problems are more serious, depressed industrial areas less important.

Development areas

Figure 17.1 Development areas in Norway (*utbyggingsområder*), Sweden (*allmänna stödområder*) and Finland (*utvecklingsområder*)

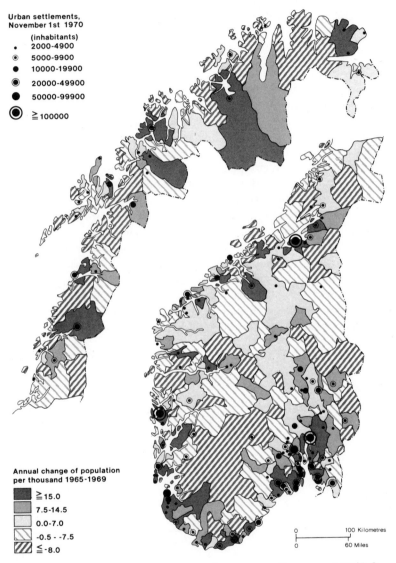

Urban settlements,
November 1st 1970

(inhabitants)

- 2000-4900
- 5000-9900
- 10000-19900
- 20000-49900
- 50000-99900
- ≧100000

Annual change of population
per thousand 1965-1969

- ≧15.0
- 7.5-14.5
- 0.0-7.0
- -0.5 - -7.5
- ≦-8.0

0   100 Kilometres

0   60 Miles

Figure 17.2 Population change in Norway's communes (*kommuner*) 1965–9,
and urban settlement 1970

Population densities are low, and urban settlements widely spaced. Extensive areas of dispersed settlement do not have satisfactory access to elementary services and to work in urban occupations. So far, there have been no exhaustive studies of service accessibility in Norway, but undoubtedly there is a need for a better infrastructure in much of the country.

Commuting – mobility without migration

A recent study (Sandal 1972) of the potential commuting range of Norwegian urban settlements of varying sizes, in which lack of job opportunities within daily commuting distance is taken as an indicator of marginal conditions, gives part of the answer to 'what is marginal Norway?'. On the basis of population data for enumeration districts from the 1960 census, urban settlements have been grouped in different size classes, and the population of the surrounding potential commuting areas within a forty-five minute isochrone has been calculated (fig. 17.3). The commuting range of urban settlements with at least 2,000 inhabitants covers most of Southeast Norway (fig. 17.3 and table 17.1). The urban settlements along the south coast also ensure commuting opportunities for most people, but north of Stavanger the difficult topography and the small number of urban settlements leave sizeable areas outside commuting range. In Sogn county, north of Bergen, only 44% of a total population of 100,000 inhabitants lived within commuting range of such urban settlements in 1960. In the three northern counties, with 450,000 inhabitants, the proportion was less

Table 17.1

Resident population within commuting distance from urban settlements of varying sizes

	Pop. 1960 (in 000)	Pop. 1970 as % of 1960	% of pop. living within commuting distance from urban settlements of		
			>10,000 people (1960)	>2,000 people (1960)	>2,000 people (1970)
Norway	3,591	108.5	63.5	81.5	84.0
Southeast	1,748	111.0	80.5	93.0	94.0
South	425	111.5	71.5	90.5	92.5
West	654	106.5	44.0	66.0	68.5
Trøndelag	328	107.5	49.5	73.5	77.0
North	437	104.0	26.0	58.0	63.5

Sources: Sandal 1972, 31; Kommunal- og Arbeidsdepartementet 1972, 11.

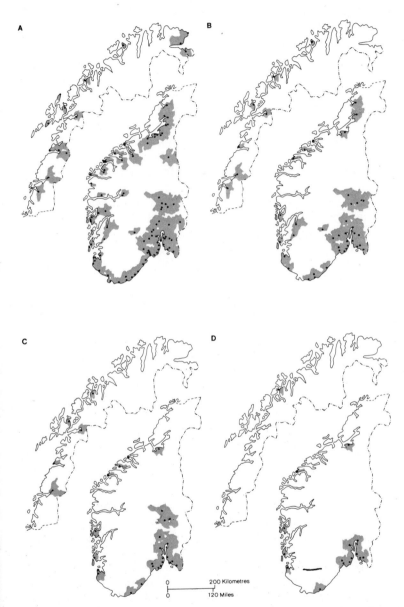

Figure 17.3 Potential commuting regions (1960) of urban settlements of varying sizes: (A) ≥ 2,000 inhabitants; (B) ≥ 5,000 inhabitants; (C) ≥ 10,000 inhabitants; (D) ≥ 20,000 inhabitants
Source: Sandal 1972

than 60%. If new employment could be created in urban settlements right down to 2,000 inhabitants, fig. 17.3 would be the map of commuting in Norway in the coming years. The shaded parts of the maps showing the commuting range of larger centres are smaller (fig. 17.3B–D). On fig. 17.3D, only the Oslofjord area and seven other important city regions outside this core area are left.

Provisional data from the 1970 census have been used for a preliminary updating (Kommunal- og Arbeidsdepartementet 1972) of the commuting areas, and they show an improvement in the intercensal period (table 17.1, last column). This improvement does not necessarily mean that new urban settlements have created new commuting opportunities, but it illustrates that people migrate away from marginal areas into urban settlements and their commuting areas.

Approximately 15% of Norway's population lived in marginal areas in 1970. In Finland the percentage was also in the order of 15 (Hustich 1971, 37); in Sweden the proportion was much lower, in the order of 5% (SOU 1972, 56, 21). Whereas the marginal areas of Sweden and Finland are found mainly in the north, in Norway they are found almost everywhere, except in the southeast (fig. 17.1).

At this macroregional level there is a generalized pattern of gradually increasing marginality westwards and northwards from the southeast.

Marginal Norway: commuting and service hinterlands in North Norway

The marginal position of North Norway can be characterized by important net outmigration to South Norway, and by considerable regional and local redistribution of population within this part of the country. The long-term effects of these migrations have not been fully understood, because the North Norwegian population is still a young one with a relatively high birth-rate, and natural increase has counterbalanced migration losses. Although many communes lost population, the steady increase of the total population of this part of the country served as a tranquillizer to uneasy political consciences. It therefore came as a shock when North Norway had a population decrease during 1969. These problems therefore were given prominent place when research was initiated in 1969 to provide background material for the North Norway Plan, which was presented to the Ministry of Housing and Local Government in October 1972 (NOU 1972, 33).

The main report refers to a study (Kotte 1972) where 3 different hinterlands have been delimited for all urban settlements of more than 1,000 inhabitants in 1970. The belief that urban settlements with only 1,000 inhabitants can serve as adequate centres for work and services may be a piece of wishful thinking, based on an observation that up till now there has been a considerable population growth in most urban settlements of this size. This growth, however, is the result of local migration to the centre from the surrounding countryside, a process which has been going on actively in most areas during the post-war period and unlikely to continue at the same scale during the 1970s, because many of the rural reservoirs of migrants are empty or are drying up now.

The political choice of a lower limit of 1,000 inhabitants for 'basic' centres in North Norway stands in contrast to a limit of approximately 2,500–3,000 inhabitants suggested in recent Swedish research on marginal areas (Bylund and Weissglas 1970), and partial conclusions of the Working Committee for the North Norway Plan.

The commuting hinterland was defined as the area within 30 minutes' travel time by private or public transport from one of the basic centres. According to this definition, 68% of North Norway's population in 1970 lived within potential commuting range of one of these (table 17.2, line 1).

Table 17.2

Resident population in various hinterlands of urban settlements in North Norway, 1970

	North Norway	Nordland county	Troms county	Finnmark county
1. % of pop. 1970 living in urban settlements of >1,000 inhabitants and in their commuting hinterlands (30 min. journey to work)	68	71	63	72
2. % of pop. 1970 within daily travelling distance (by public transport) from urban settlements of >1,000 inhabitants	66	71	57	67
3. % of pop. 1970 within travelling distance (3 times a week by public transport) from regional centres	86	88	87	80

Source: NOU 1972, 36.

Even with such a generous lower population limit for basic urban centres, one-third of North Norway's population live in a non-urban environment with a very limited range of opportunities for work, and migration may be the only alternative. Many of these local communities are dispersed and isolated, and it is difficult to see how an urban environment could be extended to them. When the planned transport development programme for the 1970s is completed the proportion of people living within commuting distance of basic centres will have increased only from 68 to 71%.

Two different kinds of service hinterlands have been defined (table 17.2, lines 2 and 3). One is the local service hinterland, defined as the area where people could go to the basic centre and home again each day by public transport, with a total travel time of not more than two hours, and with a stay in the centre of at least two hours between 9 am and 4 pm. In contrast to the commuting hinterland, only public transport travel times have been calculated, implying that the breadwinners may commute by private transport, but those who go to local basic centres for services often are dependent upon public transport. With this restriction, the section of the total population living within acceptable travel distance of basic centres was slightly lower in 1970 than that living within commuting distance (66 and 68% respectively). On the other hand, the improvements of roads and the extension of public transport planned for the 1970s might lead to a considerable increase in the proportion of the population able to go to basic service centres (from 66 to 75% between 1970 and 1980).

The service hinterland of the regional centres (table 17.2, line 3) is defined as the area from where a person can get to the regional centre by public transport and home again in the course of one day at least three times a week, and with a stay of at least three hours in the centre. In 1970, 86% of North Norway's population were in this position, rising to 96% by 1980. This hinterland, however, is one of infrequent contacts for a small part of the population, as compared to the local service hinterland, and of course the commuting hinterland. Marginal North Norway will be easier to live in for those who demand specialized, infrequent services, but not much better for those who demand daily work.

It has been argued that the important migration from North Norway could be stopped if a policy of 'decentralized concentration' were implemented. This was the policy of the 1960s, but it cannot really solve the problems of the marginal areas outside commuting range, and even within the commuting regions there are many problem areas. The alternatives for the individual may be weekly commuting and seasonal migrations, but these forms of mobility easily turn into definitive migration.

The demographic situation in North Norway

A population increase in North Norway of 4.8% between 1960 (November) and 1970 (January) is a compound of an increase of 14.3% in the commuting areas and a decline of 11.0% in the areas outside daily commuting range. The latter lost 18,000 people, whereas the commuting areas had a net gain of 39,000. Only 4 of the 42 urban settlements with at least 1,000 inhabitants in 1970 lost population between 1960 and 1970, but almost half of the urban settlements in the range 200–1,000 inhabitants lost population in the same period.

In North Norway, 70% of all enumeration districts lost population between 1960 and 1970, and so did 78% of those outside commuting range (table 17.3). Important increases were confined to the commuting areas. There were

Table 17.3

Population changes in enumeration districts in North Norway, 1 November 1960–1 January 1970

	Number of enumeration districts				Population changes (absolute numbers)				
		Rate of change (%)					Rate of change (%)		
	Total	>14	0.1–14	0–÷16	<÷16	Total	>14	0.1–14	0–÷16	<÷16
Total	586	83	89	205	209	20,914	45,051	4,699	−10,078	−18,758
Commuting areas	190	51	36	69	34	38,892	42,124	3,494	−4,574	−2,152
Non-commuting areas	396	32	53	136	175	−17,978	2,927	1,205	−5,504	−16,606

Source: Landsdelskomitéen 1970.

some spectacular increases in certain enumeration districts outside the commuting areas – local service centres in areas distant from basic centres, local communication centres, military settlements and some fishing villages which had received fishermen's families from isolated localities. But a total increase of 4,000 inhabitants in 85 of the enumeration districts outside commuting range should be compared with an increase of 46,000 inhabitants in 87 enumeration districts within commuting areas. On the other hand, heavy population losses characterized many enumeration districts outside commuting range of basic centres – 175 districts out of 396 lost more than 16% of their population is a little more than 9 years. Thirty-four out of 190 enumeration districts *within* commuting range of basic centres also had similar heavy losses. This strengthens the hypothesis that some of the smaller basic centres do not give people within commuting distance adequate job opportunities.

The main trend is concentration in the more important towns. The 5 largest urban settlements (Tromsø 32,000 inhabitants in 1970, Bodø 26,000, Mo 25,000, Harstad 21,000 and Narvik 20,000) contain 27% of North Norway's population, but absorbed 54% of the population increase in the 1960s.

During the last twenty years North Norway's birth-rate has been considerably higher than that of the country as a whole, and the death-rate has been lower, because the population is younger. The natural increase thus has been high, 14⁰/₀₀ in the early 1950s, as against 10 for Norway;

11‰ in the late 1960s as against 7.5 for the whole country (table 17.4). North Norway follows the Norwegian trend, but there is a time lag of about 10 years in the increasing death-rate, and 15 to 20 years in the falling birth-rate. Whereas Norway as a whole has had very little emigration or immigration in the post-war period, North Norway has had a steady increase in outmigration to the rest of the country, so that the increase of population, which was at the national average in the early 1950s, had come to only a little more than a quarter of the national average in the period 1966–71.

Nordland county, the southernmost and most populous, has experienced a more drastic fall in its birth-rate than the two other counties, which have had a steady or even increasing birth-rate in the last decade.

The net migration flows also show clear regional differences. Nordland county was better off in the first half of the 1950s than the two other counties, in part because of the heavy inmigration to the steel town of Mo and the administrative and military centre of Bodø. In the late 1950s the tendency for people from the southern county to move away became stronger. Finnmark county in the far north had a relatively strong out-migration in the early 1960s, partly because of difficult years for the all-important fisheries. In the late 1960s, Nordland and Finnmark alike have experienced a very important net outmigration; the more important urban centres have not been able to absorb the migrants from the rural districts. In Troms county the extremely rapid development of Tromsø in recent years as capital and university town of the north, as well as the military settlements in interior Troms, has given more job opportunities to the county's rural migrants, and outmigration has been less strong here. There have been great variations of demographic structures at the commune level. Only 9 communes have experienced net immigration during the last 6 years; 79 have had net migration losses, exceeding 1.5% per year in more than half of these – a critical evolution, in view of critical population thresholds for services in a marginal area.

A simple classification of North Norway's communes by 6 demographic and socioeconomic criteria (NOU 1972, 33) shows that only 4 communes are rapidly expanding; another 9 are slowly expanding. These communes, with a few exceptions, contain the most important towns of North Norway. Seventeen communes are so-called '*status quo*' communes, whereas the remaining 58 communes are contracting, 34 of them rapidly.

Norwegian population projections

The seriousness of the demographic situation of marginal Norway, of which North Norway has been taken as the most characteristic example, has not been fully understood. Statistisk Sentralbyrå (1969) recently made a

Table 17.4

Norway and North Norway: basic demographic data, 1951–71 (average annual change °/oo)

| Period | *Norway* | | | | *North Norway* | | | |
	Birth-rate	*Death-rate*	*Net migration*	*Pop. change*	*Birth-rate*	*Death-rate*	*Net migration*	*Pop. change*
1951–5	18.7	8.5	-0.5	9.7	22.3	8.1	-4.5	9.7
1956–60	17.9	8.9	-0.5	8.5	20.3	8.0	-6.5	5.8
1961–5	17.5	9.6	-0.1	7.8	20.5	8.7	-6.0	5.8
1966–71	17.5	9.9	-0.6	8.2	20.3	9.1	-8.8	2.4

| Period | *Nordland* | | | | *Troms* | | | | *Finnmark* | | | |
	Birth-rate	*Death-rate*	*Net migration*	*Pop. change*	*Birth-rate*	*Death-rate*	*Net migration*	*Pop. change*	*Birth-rate*	*Death-rate*	*Net migration*	*Pop. change*
1951–5	21.2	8.2	-4.1	8.9	22.4	8.1	-5.0	9.3	25.9	7.8	-5.3	12.8
1956–60	19.4	8.0	-6.9	4.5	20.9	8.1	-6.1	6.7	22.6	7.7	-6.2	8.7
1961–5	19.6	8.9	-5.6	5.1	20.7	8.6	-5.2	6.9	23.1	8.1	-7.3	7.7
1966–71	18.7	9.3	-10.8	-1.4	21.2	9.2	-4.1	7.9	23.7	8.5	-10.5	4.7

Source: Statistisk sentralbyrå, *Folkemengden i herreder og byer, Folketall i kommunene* (annual publications).

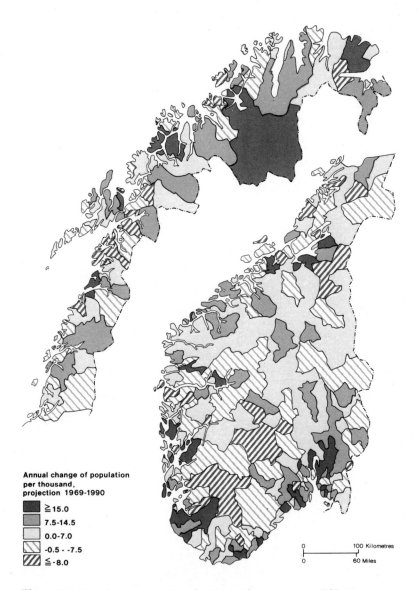

Annual change of population
per thousand,
projection 1969-1990

≧15.0

7.5-14.5

0.0-7.0

-0.5 - -7.5

≦-8.0

0   100 Kilometres

0   60 Miles

Figure 17.4 Population projections for Norway's communes, 1968–90

population projection for Norway's communes up to 1990; the basic data were the 1968 age and sex composition, births, deaths and migrations in 1966–8 (fig. 17.4 and table 17.5).

Table 17.5

Relative distribution of Norwegian communes according to annual rates of population change for the projection period 1969–90 and the observation period 1965–9

	Number of communes	Percentage distribution according to rate of change $^o/_{oo}$				
		$\geqq 15$	7.5–14.5	0–7	−.5–÷7.5	$\leqq ÷8$
Norway: Projection 1969–90	451	16	21.5	28.5	24	10
Observed changes 1965–9		20	13.5	17.5	23.5	25
Urbanized communes: Projection	149	35	31.5	23	10	.5
Observed changes		43.5	25	15.5	11.5	4.5
Non-urbanized communes: Projection	302	6.5	16.5	31	31	15
Observed changes		8.5	8.5	18	30	35

Source: Hansen 1972.

A population decrease was projected for one-third of the communes and for almost one-half of the non-urbanized communes (a commune which did not contain an urban settlement of at least 2,000 inhabitants in 1960). The projections were criticized by politicians, who feared that the sheer existence of a projection showing a negative trend for so many communes would discourage marginal Norway. The actual trend was far more negative than the projection itself (table 17.5; figs. 17.2 and 17.4). Almost one-half of Norway's communes lost population between 1965 and 1969, and almost two-thirds of the non-urbanized communes. An annual decrease of population of more than 15‰ was projected for only 1 of the 88 communes of North Norway, but 23 of them experienced a population decline of this magnitude in the period 1965–9. The main weakness of the projection model was its handling of migration data. The migrants were treated as outmigrants, and the sum total of future outmigrants as distributed to the communes of immigration at the same rate as they had received migrants in the period 1966–8. Such a method does not allow for the real pull effect of the growing urban settlements on the surrounding countryside, and it does not consider that the migration hinterlands of the more important towns may extend as the main immigration reservoirs, closer to the towns, are emptied. Immigration to growth communes was systematically under-estimated and at the same time the ability of the marginal communes to retain their population was overestimated (Hansen 1972).

An analysis has been undertaken of migrations between the 20 trade districts (*handelsdistrikt*) of North Norway and of migrations between trade districts in North Norway and 17 subregions in South Norway during the four-year period 1967–70, for which adequate migration statistics exist. Net outmigration from North Norway during this period was 17,500 persons, or about 9.5‰ per annum. Every one of the 20 trade districts of North Norway had a deficit of migrants to South Norway, varying from 5.7% in Vardø trade district to 1.4% in Tromsø trade district. The Oslo region (Oslo and Akershus counties) absorbed 32.5% of the net migration from North Norway; Southeast Norway as a whole, 61.5%. The 4 main city regions outside Southeast Norway (Bergen, Trondheim, Stavanger and Kristiansand) absorbed another 15.5%.

South Norway was divided into 17 subregions; the migration matrix thus contained 20 x 17 (340) cells or net migration relations. Only 35 of these 340 relations were directed towards North Norway.

Interregional migrations in North Norway

In principle, the trade district is a nodal region, consisting of a group of communes centred around an urban settlement of regional importance. There are 20 in North Norway (fig. 17.5). Delimitation, dependent on administrative boundaries, may in some cases distort the analysis. In this paper migrations between communes within trade districts have not been analysed, but it is assumed that as a rule they are oriented towards the main urban settlements in each trade district (Hansen 1969).

Nine of the 20 trade districts had net inmigration within the closed system of North Norway, the important towns of Tromsø, Harstad and Mosjøen among those with the highest score. Tromsø, receiving migrants from 18 trade districts out of 19 possible, is in a class of its own, the only trade district in North Norway where net inmigration from this part of the country more than counterbalances outmigration to South Norway. The relatively low score of Bodø trade district, with the second most important town of North Norway, is probably related to its shape. The heaviest migration losses within the North Norwegian system are experienced by several coastal trade districts, where the size of the centre is not sufficient for it to function as an intervening opportunity.

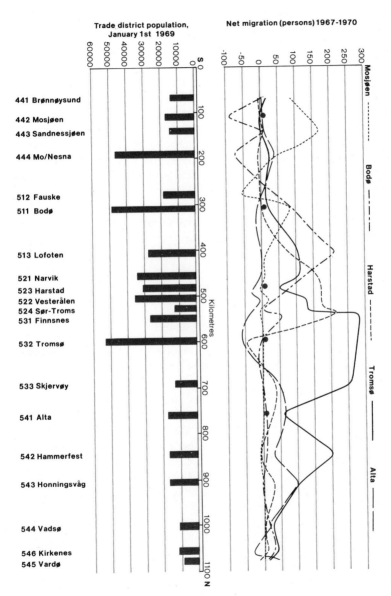

Figure 17.5 Net migration to/from trade districts in North Norway, 1967–70

The centres of the 20 trade districts have been located on an axis, 1,150 km long, from the southern boundary of Nordland county to Tromsø, and from Tromsø to Vardø at the far northeastern tip of North Norway (fig. 17.5). Net migration to and from 5 selected trade districts with important regional centres has been graphically presented in absolute numbers. The spectacular importance of Tromsø clearly emerges. It receives migrants from the whole of North Norway, but its influence wanes faster southwards than eastwards, which is only natural, because of intervening opportunities in the important regional centres south of it and in South Norway. The intervening opportunities of Harstad and Alta south and east of Tromsø show up as wedges in the Tromsø line.

Alta is a centre of much less importance, and the line indicating its migration field shows that it has no dominance over Tromsø in any other trade district (except those of Mo and Vardø, probably due to specific, irregular causes), and that its migration field is asymmetric with more migrants from trade districts east than south of it. Harstad has its own dominant migration field, but its extension is restricted, being effectively limited by Tromsø in the north and Bodø in the south. Bodø's migration field is asymmetric, with a dominance towards the north, and particularly in the Lofoten islands, which seem to be its most important migration hinterland. South of Bodø, other centres take over, and Mosjøen is similar with a north-oriented asymmetric migration field.

The consequences of migration – a cohort analysis, 1965–70

With the 1970 census data not available, the effects of these important migration flows upon the age and sex structure of the population, and the consequences of migrations for the occupational structure of marginal Norway, are difficult to measure. Current population statistics (Statistisk sentralbyrå 1968, 1971) permit a limited analysis of the development of 2 age cohorts between 1965 and 1970. The 15–19-year cohort of 1965 has been assessed again in 1970, and a corresponding assessment of the 20–24-year cohort of 1965 has been made for the 25–29-year cohort in 1970.

In North Norway 9% of the male 15–19-year cohort of 1965 and 17.5% of the female cohort had disappeared in 1970 (table 17.6). The 20–24-year male cohort of 1965 had been reduced by 11% during the 5 years, indicating that young men leave later than young women. The 20–24-year female cohort of 1965 was reduced by only 5% during the second half of the 1960s, but this must be seen in the light of the very strong mobility in the 15–19-year cohort.

The table shows that Nordland county is much worse off than Troms and Finnmark. If the migration in the period 1971–5 is of the same magnitude as that of the late 1960s, one-third of the total 15–19-year cohort of 1965 will have left by 1975. The situation in the 2 northernmost counties is less disturbing, partly because of the high birth-rate, partly because migration is less important in the critical age groups.

Table 17.6

Cohort analysis, 1965–70 (1965 = 100)

	1970 cohort 20–24 years		1970 cohort 25–29 years	
	Males	Females	Males	Females
Norway	98.7	99.8	99.3	99.2
North Norway	90.7	82.3	88.9	95.0
Nordland county	85.9	77.2	83.7	92.2
Troms county	97.7	89.5	94.1	97.8
Finnmark county	93.7	85.3	96.3	95.5

Source: Statistisk sentralbyrå 1968, 1971.

At the commune level the importance of local variations is clear, with few growing cohorts, but many waning ones. For North Norway as a whole, the male 20–24-year cohort of 1965 had been reduced by 11% in 1970, but 61 out of 88 communes had experienced a greater reduction. In 25 communes it had been reduced by more than 30% in 5 years. The female 15–19-year cohort of 1965, reduced in North Norway as a whole by 17.5% during the 5-year period, had been reduced by 30% or more in 50 communes. In 7 communes it had been more than halved.

The development of the 15–19-year female cohort during the 5-year period could be related to the commune classification mentioned earlier. Thirty-one out of 34 rapidly contracting communes lost 30% or more of this cohort in 5 years. The expanding communes, with 1 exception, either had an effective increase of the cohort, or only a relatively slow reduction. It seems that cohort analysis as a means of classifying communes may give good results with little work, compared with the more complex weighting of various demographic and economic criteria used in the North Norway Plan.

The Scandinavian context

Comparisons between Norway, Sweden and Finland have been made for 1969, the latest year for which data were available. Three-quarters of Finland's communes were losing population, one-half in Sweden and in Norway (table 17.7). The Finnish situation is in part caused by very

Table 17.7

Comparative demographic data for communes in Finland, Sweden and Norway, 1969

		Percentage of the total number of communes with			
Country	Number of communes	Population decrease	Pop. decrease >1.5%	Excess of deaths over births	Net out-migration
Finland	521	75	50	38	75
Sweden	848	52	26	49	61
Norway	451	49	17	11	65

Sources: *Suomen virallinen Tilasto* 1972; *Statistiska centralbyrån* 1970; *Statistisk sentralbyrå, Folketall i kommunene.*

significant emigration to Sweden, with 1969 and 1970 as particularly critical years. In the 1960s there has been a net migration from Finland of 170,000 persons, 78,000 in 1969 and 1970 alone (Häggström 1972, Korpinen and Lindgren 1971). In Sweden, the effect of this immigration of Finns is seen in part by the fact that there is an increase of population in one-half of the communes, despite a very low national birth-rate of 13.5‰ in 1969, as compared with 14.3 in Finland and 17.6 in Norway.

In Norway, in contrast to Sweden and Finland, immigration and emigration are unimportant. The national labour market has enjoyed full employment for 30 years. The marginal counties of the 3 countries show a more negative trend than the rest of the country; particularly in Sweden, where 4 out of 5 communes in the 6 northern forest counties lost population in 1969, whereas in the rest of Sweden it was 2 out of 5 communes.

Age-selective migration from marginal areas has been taking place for much longer in Sweden than in Finland and Norway, where it has been important during the last 10 or 15 years only. In Sweden, almost one-half of the communes would be losing population even without outmigration, in Finland almost 40% (but only 26% in 1967), but in Norway only 10%. Generally, the marginal areas closest to the growth areas entered this demographic situation first; the more distant marginal areas kept their vitality longer, partly because migration started later, partly because the birth-rate was higher. In the 2 northernmost counties of Sweden there was an excess of deaths over births in 19 out of 33 rural communes in 1969; in the 4 southern counties of North Sweden there was a deficit of births in 98 out of 115 rural communes. In Finland, 77 out of 81 communes in the 2 northernmost counties had an excess of births in 1969, because the ageing process had not developed as far here as further south. In the 4 counties of Mid-Finland there was an excess of births in 73% of the 154 communes, but in the 6 counties of South Finland, there was an excess of births in only 46% of the 286 communes.

Broadly speaking, there is a zoning from south to north in Sweden and Finland, the most resistant zone being the northernmost one. In Norway, the ageing process does not proceed from south to north regularly, and the pattern is much more complicated (fig. 17.2). Marked growth rates are found in a few core areas. The Oslofjord region is outstanding, with 4 out of the 8 most important city regions of Norway. The 4 others are the regions of Kristiansand, Stavanger, Bergen and Trondheim, which all show marked growth. These 8 city regions had 42% of Norway's population in 1970, but 67% of the national population increase in the second half of the 1960s. Other medium-sized towns with regional service functions also had marked growth in this period, whereas communes with smaller urban settlements had a more complex development: 302 out of 451 communes were defined as rural in having no urban settlement of more than 2,000 inhabitants, and these communes had 29% of Norway's population in 1970, but had no population increase between 1965 and 1969. Such communes are found all over the country, but are most numerous along the west coast, in North Norway, in the Central-South Norwegian mountains and in some forest areas near the Swedish border (Hansen 1971).

Accepting an annual decline of population of more than 1.5% as a sign of a critical depletion process, 50% of Finland's communes were in this situation in 1969, compared with 26% in Sweden and 17% in Norway. This critical development has reached even the northernmost part of Sweden, with 55% of the communes in the 6 northern forest counties in this situation, compared with 35% in North Norway.

The very strong emigration from Finland to Sweden during recent years, and in particular in 1969 and 1970, accelerated the depopulation process in Northern Finland. Recent studies (Häggström 1972) show that in 1969 the 2 northernmost counties of Finland contributed 43% of the 38,500 Finnish emigrants to Sweden; 1.9% of Uleåborg and 3.7% of Lapland county's population emigrated in one year. In 1967, only 36% of Finland's communes had a population decline of more than 1.5%. The diffusion process had not developed as far as in Sweden, since the percentage was highest (40%) in the southern part of the country. In the Mid-Finland counties the percentage was 34, in the 2 northern counties 29. In 1969 the situation was very different; the 1.5% decline or more was attained in 44% of the communes in the southern part of Finland, 58% in Mid-Finland, and 57% in North Finland. A process which took 10 to 15 years in North Sweden has taken only 2 to 3 years in North Finland. The recession of the Swedish economy in 1971 has reduced considerably the emigration from Finland, and many Finns have returned; some to where they came from, but many Finns from

274 *People on the move*

rural areas and small towns seem to have preferred the more important cities of the south.

The critical development in North Norway in the last two or three years has already been described, but it is by no means as critical and comprehensive in North Sweden and North Finland. The advancing phase of settlement and population, characteristic of northern Scandinavia until quite recently, has been replaced by a phase of massive retreat in most rural areas. The drift to the south, national in character in Norway and Sweden with a strong international element in Finland, is a challenge to regional planning in the three countries.

References

Bylund, E. and Weissglas, G. (1970) Glesbygdens servicenät. En preliminär redogörelse (The service structure of marginal areas. A preliminary report), in *Urbaniseringen i Sverige*, 14, section 2. Stockholm (SOU).

Enequist, G. and Norling, G. (eds.) (1960) Advance and retreat of rural settlement. Papers of the Siljan Symposium at the XIXth International Geographical Congress. *Geogr. Ann.* 42, 210–346.

Häggström, N. (1972) *Regionala och demografiska aspekter på flyttbingsrörelserna mellan Finland och Sverige, åren 1968–1970.* (*Regional and demographic aspects of migration between Finland and Sweden, 1968–1970*). Umeå.

Hansen, J. C. (1969) Flyttinger i Norge 1967 (Migrations in Norway 1967). *Norsk geogr. Tidsskr.* 23, 91–103.

Hansen, J. C. (1971) Næringsliv og bosetting i Norge: perspektiver og planleggingsproblemer (Economy and settlements in Norway: perspectives and planning problems). *Bedriftsøkonomen*, 186–93.

Hansen, J. C. (1972) Une critique géographique des perspectives d'évolution de la population norvègienne, in *Géographie et Perspectives à long terme*. Commission de Géographie Appliquée, St-Brieuc.

Hustich, I. (1971) Om avgränsningen av utvecklingsområden i Finland (On the delimitation of development areas in Finland). *Terra* 83, 25–38.

Kommunal- og Arbeidsdepartementet (1972) St. meld. nr. 13 (1972–73). *Om mål og midler i distriktsutbyggingen (On goals and means in regional policy)*. Oslo.

Korpinen, P. and Lindgren, N. (1971) Finland's economy – an outline of a structural analysis. *Skandinaviska Banken Q.* 3, 57–62. Stockholm.

Kotte, P. (1972) Reisetidssoner rundt nord-norske sentra (Travel time zones around North Norwegian centres). *Plan og Arbeid*, 79–83. Oslo.

Landsdelskomitéen for Nord-Norge (1970) *Nord-Norge – folketall og befolkningsendring (North Norway – population and population change)*. Bodø.

Myklebost, H. (1968) Urbanization and regional concentration in Norway in the 1950s and 1960s. *Norsk. geogr. Tidsskr.* 22, 227–44.

NOU *(Norges Offentlige Utredninger)* (1972). *Om landsdelsplan for Nord-Norge (On a plan for North Norway).* Oslo.

Sandal, J. (1972) Det norske bosettingsmønsteret under økende arbeids-plasskonsentrasjon (The Norwegian settlement pattern is dominated by the increasing concentration of jobs). *Plan og Arbeid.* 29–33. Oslo.

SOU *(Statens offentliga utredningar)* (1972) *Glesbygder och glesbygd-politik (Marginal areas and policies for marginal areas).* Stockholm.

Statistisk sentralbyrå (1952–64) *Folkemengden i herreder og byer.* Annual publication Oslo.

Statistisk sentralbyrå (1965–) *Folketall i kommunene (Population in municipalities).* Annual publication. Oslo.

Statistisk sentralbyrå (1967–) *Flyttestatistikk (Migration statistics).* Annual publication Oslo.

Statistisk sentralbyrå (1968) *Folkemengden etter alder 31. desember 1965 (Population by age 31 December 1965).* Oslo.

Statistisk sentralbyrå (1969) *Framskriving av folkemengden til 1990 (Population projection to 1990).* Oslo.

Statistisk sentralbyrå (1971) *Folkemengden etter alder 31. desember 1970 (Population by age 31 December 1970).* Oslo.

Statistiska centralbyrån (1970) *Befolkning 31.12.1969* and *Befolknings-förändringar 1969.* Stockholm.

Stone, K. (1967) *High latitude fringes of settlement.* Madison.

Stone, K. (1971) *Norway's internal migration to new farms since 1920.* European Demog. Monog. I. Den Haag.

Suomen virallinen Tilasto (1972) *Väestönmuutokset 1969 (Vital statistics 1969).* Helsinki.

18 Interregional migration in East–Central Europe

L. A. Kosiński

The present article deals with internal movements of population in a large European region with some 124 million inhabitants. In discussing post-war trends two periods can be clearly distinguished. In the late 1940s internal movements were still influenced by the recent war, territorial changes and transfers of population. Internal migration represented a continuation of external migrations, since repatriation of persons who at the end of the war were located on foreign soil was as a rule followed by internal transfers and resettlement. In some cases repatriation was necessitated by boundary changes, in others by previous forced migration. In Germany new arrivals from lost provinces and from other countries of East-Central Europe created an additional burden for the war-shaken society. In Poland and Czechoslovakia the vacuum created by departing Germans was partially filled by the repatriates coming from lost provinces as well as Western Europe; internal settlers from overpopulated rural regions also participated in these movements to the vacated areas (Kosiński 1962). In Yugoslavia traditional migration, from the less developed mountainous areas to the more fertile lowlands, was accelerated by the departure of Germans from the plains of Vojvodina and by land reform (Djurić 1964).

Only later has a more 'normal' pattern of internal migration developed, accelerated by a drive towards industrialization to which ruling communist parties were so deeply committed.

Data sources

Most countries of East-Central Europe have introduced current registration of internal migration. Statistical data are based on police records (change of address) and are published regularly in standard statistical and/or demographic yearbooks. Only Yugoslavia and Albania do not have this kind of information on the national scale. On the other hand only three countries have consistently utilized population censuses for gathering data on internal migration (Poland, Hungary and Yugoslavia). Recently, however, Bulgaria has also started

Table 18.1

Data on internal migration available for countries of East-Central Europe

	E. Germany	Poland	Czechoslovakia
Census data			
Birthplace	—	1970	—
Prior place of residence	—	1950 (res. in 1939) 1960 (res. in 1950) 1970 (res. in 1960)	1947 (res. in 1945)
Territorial matrix in last census	—	1960: *Województwo* by *powiat* (22 × 419)	—
Current registration since	1953	(1949) 1951	1950
General mobility between (name of a unit given in singular)	*Gemeinde*	*Gromada*	*Obec*
Size of migration flows (published data)			
Between different sized communities	+	+	+
Urban-rural, rural-urban, urban-urban, rural-rural	—	+	—
Interregional matrix (name of a unit given in singular)	*Bezirk* (15 × 15)	*Województwo* (22 × 22)	*Kraj* (13 × 13)
Characteristics of migrants (published data)			
Age	+	+	+
Sex	+	+	+
Occupation and/or social characteristics	+	+	+
Reasons for moving	—	—	+

Hungary	Romania	Bulgaria	Yugoslavia
1949	1966 (date of arrival)		1948, 1953, 1961, 1971
1949 (res. in 1938) 1960 (res. in 1949) 1970 (res. in 1960)	—	1965 (res. in 1956)	1961 and 1971 (last res. and date of arrival)
?	—	1965 (*Okrug* by *okryg*)/(28 x 28)	1961: Demographic regions of the second order (23 x 23)
1955	1955	1947	—
Hely	*Comuna*	*Selo* and *grad*	—
—	+	—	—
+	+	+	—
Megye (27 x 27)	*Regiunea* (18 x 18)	*Okryg* (28 x 28)	—
+	—	—	—
+	—	—	—
+	—	—	—
+	—	+	—

collecting and publishing this type of information in her census. Information on types and general characteristics of available data are assembled in table 18.1. The amount of data collected and processed is greater than can be found in standard publications.

Despite attempts to standardize statistical procedures considerable diversity still persists which makes comparative study extremely difficult. Census questions are different and consequently data cannot be compared directly. Registration data are available for almost all countries and they are theoretically better, but they very much depend on the definitions used. Size of basic reference units influences directly the volume of migration. Hungarian units are by far the smallest (localities or *hely*); Polish, Czechoslovak and Romanian are next (administrative regions of the lowest order) and Bulgarian and German units are the largest (administrative regions of the medium order). As a result Hungarian data tend to overemphasize internal migration rates, while those in East Germany and Bulgaria tend to deflate the rates. Moreover, frequent changes in administrative divisions reduce the internal consistency of data for individual countries. Nevertheless, major trends can be identified and some comparisons can be made.

Migration research in East-Central Europe

Despite the existence of basic data sources and the needs of planned economies, research into internal migration has not been very impressive. Political sensitivity and security restrictions can only partially explain this. Nevertheless, in recent years a number of articles and research monographs have been published (Kuba 1968; Latuch 1970; Minkov 1972). In Poland a special bibliography of migration studies is available (Żurek 1971).

Four basic methods of enquiry based on four types of data can be identified.

(i)   Data from regular censuses and the estimates of population supplemented by vital registration can be used to assess net results of internal migration. The residual method is very useful provided that changes in administrative boundaries are neither too frequent nor too sizeable, and/ or that appropriate adjustments can be made. One such study of the whole area was based on data on 1961–5 (Kosiński 1968) and more detailed studies for Poland, Czechoslovakia and Hungary are also available (Kosiński 1970; Carter 1971; Nováková-Hřibova 1971b; Compton 1972).

(ii) Questions relevant to mobility have been included in the Polish, Hungarian, Yugoslav and, recently, also Bulgarian censuses: they pertained to previous residence in Poland, Yugoslavia and Hungary, and place of birth in Yugoslavia and Bulgaria. Such data provide valuable material for national studies and were widely used, especially in Yugoslavia (Sentić 1968;

Breznik 1968; Yugoslavia 1968, 1972), and also in Poland (Kosiński 1967; Latuch 1970). However, their usefulness for international comparisons is extremely limited.

(iii) The most frequently utilized data are derived from migration registers. A number of national studies have been published including ones for East Germany (Bendemann 1964; Bose 1970), Poland (Kosiński 1967; Poland – GUS 1969; Stpiczyński 1971), Czechoslovakia (Korčák 1959; Kuba 1968; Nováková-Hřibova 1971a), Hungary (Sárfalvi 1964, 1965, 1969; Michaeli 1968; Compton 1969a,b, 1972), Romania (Measnicov and Bîrsan 1962; Cucu *et al.* 1966; Grigorescu 1966; Enache 1967; Measnicov 1968; Mesaroş 1968; Tufescu 1969) and Bulgaria (Rusinov 1965; Todorov 1968; Hess 1969; Popov 1969; Minkov 1972). A number of comparative international analyses are also available (Gerle 1967; Thirring 1967; Kowaleski 1970; Pivovarov 1970).

(iv) Studies based on special surveys have also been carried out. They are usually limited to smaller areas, especially in newly resettled territories of Poland and Yugoslavia.

Simple descriptions of changing temporal trends and their spatial patterns are usually followed by a descriptive explanation of factors involved with emphasis on economic ones. Considerable effort has been devoted to characteristics of migrants, reasons for moving, migration fields and spatial consequences of migration. Regression and correlation analysis has been used in an attempt to relate patterns of internal mobility to several economic and social variables (Kuba 1968; Yugoslavia 1968, 1972). Attempts to construct models were made in Bulgaria (Minkov 1972). An extensive study of Hungarian migration has been made using Markov chain analysis and multiple regression (Compton (1969a, 1972)). Migration research in East-Central Europe has contributed to knowledge of the spatial redistribution of population in the area but has not produced methodological innovations comparable to those made in North America.

Major trends in internal migration

The most important characteristic of temporal trends was the decline of mobility in all countries (fig. 18.1, table 18.2). The annual number of migrants declined from *c.* 3.5 million in 1955 to 2.25 million in the late 1960s (excluding Yugoslavia). The decrease was more substantial in more developed countries – East Germany, Poland and Czechoslovakia, and after 1957–8 also in Hungary. Romania and Bulgaria have experienced less dramatic changes in mobility patterns. The range between highest and lowest rates recorded in any country was greatest in East Germany (32.3 points) and Czechoslovakia (30), followed by Poland (28.6) and Hungary (23).

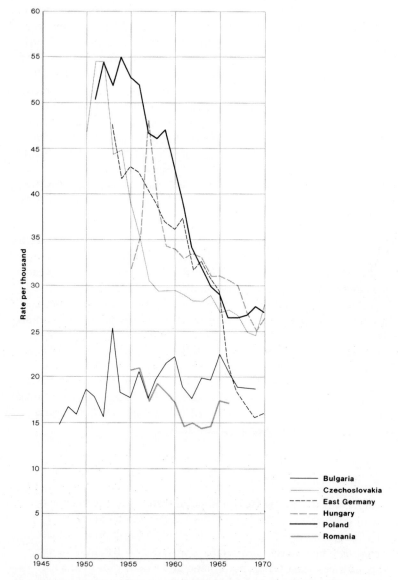

Figure 18.1 Rates of internal migration in East-Central Europe after the Second World War

In Bulgaria and Romania the range was only 10.6 and 6.7 points respectively and the rates much lower than in the remaining countries. While the changing size of basic areal units influences the rates their decline is so striking that the general trend can be unhesitatingly identified.

In an attempt to explain these trends it has been suggested that after early post-war upheavals a new equilibrium is developing (Pivovarov 1970). The following factors seem to have influenced the pattern of internal movements in East-Central Europe.

Table 18.2
Internal migrations in East-Central Europe, 1947–70 (in 000 and rate %00)

Year	German Democratic Republic (Kreis)*		Poland (gromada)*		Czechoslovakia (obec)*		Hungary (hely)*		Romania (comuna)*		Bulgaria (rayon)*	
1947											102.9	14.6
1948											119.9	16.7
1949											114.4	15.9
1950					579.2	46.7					133.8	18.5
1951			1271.2	50.3	682.8	54.5					130.2	17.9
1952			1386.2	54.3	689.8	54.4					112.2	15.5
1953	870.8	47.9	1348.6	51.9	567.4	44.2					185.0	25.2
1954	753.4	41.7	1458.7	55.0	580.3	44.8					132.4	18.1
1955	771.4	43.0	1440.0	52.8	510.9	39.0	312.6	31.8	362.3	20.7	134.7	17.9
1956	749.0	42.3	1444.2	51.9	465.8	35.2	349.7	35.3	367.2	20.9	161.2	20.8
1957	703.4	40.2	1521.9	46.7	408.6	30.6	472.6	48.0	307.2	17.2	131.5	17.5
1958	673.2	38.8	1323.4	46.0	394.2	29.3	383.6	38.8	347.1	19.2	152.7	19.8
1959	638.1	36.9	1372.0	46.9	399.0	29.4	339.4	34.2	331.6	18.2	168.5	21.5
1960	622.4	36.1	1256.2	42.3	401.9	29.4	338.2	33.9	316.3	17.2	176.3	22.2
1961	641.8	37.5	1162.5	38.8	397.9	28.9	330.4	33.0	268.1	14.4	151.8	19.0
1962	544.4	31.8	1034.1	34.1	391.5	28.2	336.7	33.5	277.6	14.9	142.9	17.7
1963	556.4	32.4	986.7	32.1	394.7	28.3	331.2	33.0	267.2	14.2	160.7	19.9
1964	526.1	31.0	932.9	29.9	405.6	28.8	317.9	31.0	274.8	14.5	159.1	19.7
1965	498.6	29.3	914.5	29.0	381.0	26.9	322.8	31.0	329.8	17.3	184.5	22.5
1966	370.1	21.7	840.3	26.5	388.4	27.3	316.7	30.5	327.2	17.1	168.1	20.4
1967	311.3	18.2	842.1	26.4	382.1	26.7	311.1	30.0			156.1	18.8
1968	286.0	16.7	861.5	26.7	357.8	24.9	290.2	27.0			157.0	18.7
1969	266.0	15.6	898.5	27.7	353.7	24.5	273.6	25.0			156.7	18.6
1970	270.5	15.9	881.9	27.2	401.9	27.8	271.0	26.2				

* Name of an administrative unit (in singular) used in migration registration. All changes of residence between these units are defined as migration.

Sources:

Germany – *Stat. Jahrbuch 1972.*
Poland – *Rocznik demograficzny 1967-8* (1951–68); *Rocznik stat. 1971* (1969–70).
Czechoslovakia – *Stat. ročenka ČSSR 1961* (1950–60); *1966* (1961–2); *1969* (1963–8); *1972* (1969–70).
Hungary – *Magyarország népesedése 1961* (1955–61); *Demográfiai Évkönyv 1969* (1960–9); *Stat. Ybk. 1970* (1970).
Romania – Enache 1967 (1955); Mesaroş 1968 (1956–66).
Bulgaria – *Stat. za dvizheneto . . . 1947-1957* (1947–59); *Demografska stat. 1960, 1961, 1964* (1960, 1961, 1964); Todorov 1968 (1963, 1965); Minkov 1972 (1966–9).

(i)   *The presence and size of the uprooted population.* The three northern
      countries were more affected by post-war transfers and had higher
      proportions of refugees and repatriates who tended to be more mobile,
      at least initially. In addition to international transfers of population
      caused by boundary changes, in Poland and Czechoslovakia large areas
      vacated by this German population were resettled by internal
      migrants. The population in the newly settled areas tended to be
      more mobile thus influencing the national averages (Kosiński 1962,
      1967).

(ii) *Transformation of agriculture and collectivization of farms.* These
      reforms were carried on more intensively in the early 1950s and un-
      doubtedly affected the mobility of rural population, especially in
      situations where peasants perceived collectivization as a threat to
      their traditional way of life and economic well-being. Change of
      governmental policies in the late 1950s and the general relaxation
      of the political climate have had a decisive influence upon the attitude
      of peasants and seem to have reduced mobility, especially in Poland
      and Hungary.

(iii) *Industrialization and urbanization.* Forcible industrialization was
      probably most important in communist regimes established in
      East-Central Europe after the Second World War. Growth of industry
      was expected not only to increase military and economic potential of
      the respective countries, but it was also conceived as the most effective
      tool in modernization (Sárfalvi 1964, 1965). One very important
      element of the latter would be the transformation of the society with
      the numerical increase of the urban population in general and the
      working class in particular. Consequently rural-urban migration was
      encouraged and the proportion of urban population jumped from 38%
      in about 1950 to more than 50% twenty years later. However, the
      intake of population into urban and industrial sectors was greatest in
      earlier years when labour-intensive industrial development encouraged
      greater movements of potential workers. More recently capital-inten-
      sive industrialization has tended to reduce the massive demand for new
      labourers. Increased urbanization through large-scale rural-urban
      migration depleted rural population, but in the late 1960s and early
      1970s migration accounted for a smaller proportion of total urban
      growth than in the early 1950s.

(iv) *Shortage of potential migrants.* The sizeable and prolonged post-war
      'baby boom' created a large supply of labour in the 1960s, but the
      decline of fertility which began in the mid-1950s resulted in a drastic
      reduction of working age groups. In fact, several countries are experi-
      encing labour shortages, which developed earlier and are most acute
      in East Germany and Czechoslovakia. The labour shortage can influence

mobility since the potential supply even in areas of traditional surplus tends to be depleted. Additionally, employers make greater efforts to keep the labour force from leaving and try to intensify and rationalize its use since they cannot expect to expand the staff any longer. Besides, changes in age structure reduce the numbers of most mobile age groups.

(v) *Housing policy.* In the early post-war years private ownership was discouraged and only the government provided the accommodation. This arrangement proved to be unsatisfactory and led to drastic housing shortage (funds were easily diverted for other, more 'urgent' matters) and the poor maintenance of the existing housing stock. With the myth of governmental omnipotence tarnished, housing cooperatives, *condominia* and even private individual houses were encouraged, and the distribution of free governmental accommodation greatly reduced. Acquisition of accommodation is still very difficult and in addition places a very heavy financial burden on a household. With limited turnover of apartments and houses new owners tend to be less mobile even if they are very likely to consider a move once the accommodation becomes available.

(vi) *Increasing aspirations of population.* Societies of East-Central Europe are greatly attracted to the consumption-oriented model which results in great importance placed on acquisition. Success in acquiring durables will eventually reduce mobility of households in a situation where new accommodation is almost impossible to obtain without waiting, and moving, especially over a long distance, very expensive and complicated.

Major migration flows

The available data make the analysis of flows between and within rural and urban sectors possible. Rural-urban flows in post-war years have far exceeded the urban-rural counterstreams, resulting in consistent population gains of urban at the expense of rural communities. Urban migration gain has been estimated at 1 million per year in 1951–60 (Pivovarov 1970). Despite rapid increase of urban population its proportion is still not very high as compared with West European countries (the only exception being East Germany). Consequently migration gains accounted for a sizeable share of the urban growth: 43% in Poland in 1960–7, about 50% in Czechoslovakia and Romania in 1956–60 and 1956–61 respectively; 92% in Hungary in 1961–5.

Urban-urban migration has been less important but it will undoubtedly increase as the proportion of urban population reaches a higher level. In Poland it accounted for 22% of the total flows in 1960–7, and in Bulgaria 14% in 1961–5.

Rural-rural migration continues to be important, representing 30% of the total flows in Bulgaria (1961–5) and 36% in Poland (1960–7). Attempts to alter settlement structure and pattern in rural areas by strengthening rural growth points are likely to maintain rural-rural movements at a fairly high level, at least for the duration of this process. However, it is very likely that rural dwellers, if forced to leave their previous residence, may decide to go to urban centres rather than stay in the rural area.

Distance and direction of internal migration

It appears that the proportion of migration between the highest order regions is declining and more people move within them, resulting in decreasing distance of move (Pivovarov 1970). In Poland migration within *województwo* represented 61% in 1960 and 66% in 1967 (Poland – GUS 1969); in Romania migrations within *regiunea* accounted for 58% in 1966 as compared with 48% in 1955 (Enache 1967). A similar trend has been observed in East Germany (Bose 1970).

Nevertheless, interregional migrations do take place. In all countries the areas attracting migrants are restricted to large cities and industrialized regions. On the other hand extensive rural regions are losing population (fig. 18.2). Since a rural colonization frontier hardly exists in East-Central Europe the interregional migration represents essentially rural-urban transfer.

In East Germany southeastern districts and the maritime 'Bezirk' Rostock stood out as areas of attraction between 1953–65 (Bose 1970). These were the major areas of industrial development.

In Poland migration gains were experienced by the *województwo* containing the capital city, two maritime centres, Gdańsk and Szczecin, and a group in the southwest (Poland – GUS 1969). In addition to industrial development the recent demographic history of the area was also important as the western and northern provinces have been resettled after the Second World War.

In Czechoslovakia only four provinces (including the capital city) have experienced migration gains in 1960–70. In the case of the western Czech region (Plzeň) the post-war demographic history, not unlike that in the Polish western provinces, may have contributed to migration gains. More detailed recent study suggests that between 1960–9 areas gaining migrants in Czechoslovakia were restricted to the five largest urban agglomerations, and restricted districts in various parts of the country where industrial development was taking place (Carter 1971).

In Hungary the central region, including the capital city and the northwestern *megyes* as well as the northeastern industrialized area of Miskolc, has gained migrants at the expense of Transdanubia and the great Hungarian

Figure 18.2 Internal migration gains and losses in East-Central Europe (cities, except East Berlin, Budapest and Sofia, are included in surrounding regions)
Sources: East Germany – Bose 1970; Poland – *Rocznik stat.*; Czechoslovakia – Kuba 1968 and *Stat. ročenka*; Hungary – Michaeli 1968 (after Markos); Romania – Cucu *et al.* 1966; Bulgaria – Rusinov 1965; Yugoslavia – *Migracije stanovništva* 1972.

plain. The only region gaining migrants not located in the north was the area of Pécs, where mining and manufacturing was considerably developed after the Second World War.

In Romania the pattern was more diversified, with three areas attracting migrants between 1956–64 – Banat and southern Transylvania, the central

Moldavian district and southeastern zone including the capital city and the
maritime region of Dobrogea (Cucu *et al.* 1966).

In Bulgaria migration gains were not unexpectedly experienced in the
central zone of lowlands and two maritime *okrugs*. In addition the capital
city, Sofia, located in the west, and the quickly developing region of Rousse
on the Danube were also recording gains in 1961–4, whereas migration
losses were spread over mountainous zones.

In Yugoslavia, apart from Macedonia, all areas experiencing migration
gains between 1958–61 were situated in the north, which is generally more
developed and has a higher density of population (Sentić 1968). Bosnia
and Hercegovina, southern Serbia, and most of Dalmatia experienced migration losses. In the late 1960s sizeable emigration from Yugoslavia, especially
from Croatia, has considerably modified the pattern of gains and losses.

Migration factors

Several authors have tried to assess the role of different factors influencing
migration by using correlation and regression analysis. In Czechoslovakia in
1960–4 there was a fairly high correlation between industrial employment
and gross migration (correlation coefficient +.754) but no significant correlation between migration and the size of a community or a settlement (Kuba
1968, 57, 101). In Yugoslavia the coefficient of correlation between net
migration in 1958–61 and percentage of urban population was found to be
+.894 and *per capita* national income +.624 (Breznik 1968). In Hungary
there was a very high correlation between net migration in 1960–70 and
the increase in housing (+.93) (Compton 1972). In the latter case investment
activity is partly a causal factor of and partly a consequence of migration.

In three countries of East-Central Europe data on reasons for moving are
collected by migration registers. In Czechoslovakia housing conditions are
the most important causes, exceeding economic reasons; about 45% and
30% or more respectively in 1966–7 (Srb 1970). It should be pointed out,
however, that the local surveys differ considerably from the results obtained
through official channels (paper by Z. Hájek submitted to 1972 Symposium
on Internal Migration in Edmonton). In Bulgaria, according to the data for
1964, change of work was given as a cause by 37% of respondents, family
reasons by 59% (this included reunification of family, children moving with
parents and marriage), retirement by 2% (*Demografska statistika* 1964).
In Hungary between 1960–8 marriage and dependence on moving breadwinners accounted for approximately 40% of moves, economic reasons
(change of employment and moving closer to the place of work) were given
in 25–30% of cases, change of dwelling in 7–9%, education less than 2%
(Compton 1972).

Classificatory systems differ between the countries and the data obtained refer to different periods, consequently comparison is difficult. However it is surprising and interesting to find that in East-Central Europe the non-economic reasons play such an important role in explaining movement of people.

Conclusion

Internal migrations have played an important role in population redistribution in East-Central Europe and contributed substantially to urban growth. However, since a large proportion of them were restricted spatially they have not changed substantially the macro-distribution of population in East-Central Europe during the last two decades.

The results of the analysis differ from what would have been expected. Increasing mobility is said to accompany economic development and growing urbanization. There is no doubt that both processes have occurred in East-Central Europe contributing to substantial restratification of society. Mobility reached its peak in early post-war years and later was declining, thus contradicting the generally expected trend. The study of relations between migration and economic growth indicates a high degree of correlation in East-Central Europe. However, reasons for moving as reported by individuals themselves indicate that non-economic reasons play an important role. Closer relationships between external and internal movement, so characteristic of West Europe today, existed in East-Central Europe in the early post-war years, even if for entirely different reasons. All through the 1960s, each country represented a closed migrational system with its own pattern of expanding and declining areas. This situation has changed somewhat, especially in Yugoslavia, beginning in the late 1960s.

References

Bendemann, G. (1964) Regionale Besonderheiten der Bevölkerungsbewegung in der DDR, dargestellt am Beispiel des Jahres 1960. *Petermanns Geogr. Mitteil.* 108, 221–7.

Bose, G. (1970) Entwicklungstendenzen der Binnenwanderung in der DDR im Zeitraum 1953 bis 1965. *Petermanns Geogr. Mitteil.* 114, 117–31.

Breznik, D. (1968) Internal population migration in Yugoslavia. *Yugoslav Surv.* 9, 2, 1–10.

Bulgaria. Tsentralno Statistichesko Upravlenie (1960–) *Naselenie*, Sofia. Previous title *Demografska statistika* (1960–6).

Bulgaria. Tsentralno Statistichesko Upravlenie (1961) *Statistika za dvizhenetc na naseleneto v N.R. Bulgaria za perioda 1947–1957.* Sofia.

Carter, F. W. (1971) *The natural and migrational components of population change in Czechoslovakia, 1950–1970.* Inst. Brit. Geogr., Symp. on population change in Eastern Europe (mimeographed).

Compton, P. A. (1969a) Internal migration and population change in Hungary between 1959 and 1965. *Trans. Inst. Brit. Geogr.* 47, 111–30.

Compton, P. A. (1969b) A magyar városok belföldi vándorlási jellemzöinek többváltozós elemzése. *Demográfia* 12, 273–305.

Compton, P. A. (1972) Internal migration in Hungary between 1960 and 1968. *Tijdschr. Econ. Soc. Geogr.* 62, 25–38.

Cucu, V. *et al.* (1966) Conţributii la studiul geografic al migratiei interne a populatiei din România. *Analele Universitaţi Bucureşti Ser. Stiinţele Naturii. Geologie-Geografie* 15, 137–46.

Czechoslovakia. Federální statistický úřad (1957–). *Statistická ročenka ČSSR.* Praha.

Djurić, V. (1964) Współczesne ruchy ludnościowe w SFR Jugosławii. *Przegląd Geogr.* 36, 679–89.

Enache, C. M. (1967) Industrializarea socialistă – baza utilizării eficiente a forţei de munca. *Probleme economice* 20, 119–34.

Gerle, G. (1967) *The demographic and sociological effects of migration from rural to urban areas in the European socialist countries,* 103–17. Pap. of the symp. on the effects of industrialization on the agricult. pop. in the European socialist countries (multilith). Budapest.

German Democratic Republic. Staatliche Zentralverwaltung für Statistik (1965–) *Bevölkerungsstatistisches Jahrbuch der DDR.* Berlin.

German Democratic Republic. Staatliche Zentralverwaltung für Statistik (1955–) *Statistisches Jahrbuch der DDR.* Berlin.

Grigorescu, C. (1966) Rolul utilizării forţei de muncă in repartizarea teritorială a industriei. *Probleme Economice* 10, 35–53.

Häufler, V. (1966) *Changes in the geographical distribution of population in Czechoslovakia.* Praha.

Hess, G. (1969) Probleme der Bevölkerungsentwicklung und Arbeitskräftesituation in der Volksrepublic Bulgarien. *Geogr. Ber.* 51, 81–112.

Hungary. Központi Statisztikai Hivatal. (1956–) *Demográfiai Évkönyv.* Budapest. Previous title *Magyarország népesedése* (1956–64).

Hungary. Központi Statisztikai Hivatal. (1964–) *Statistical Yearbook* (foreign edn). Budapest.

Kassner, G. (1964) Binnenwanderungsstatistik. *Statist. Praxis* 19, 149–50.

Klemenčić, V. (1970) The migration of population and the industrialization of Slovenia, in Sárfalvi, B. (ed.) *Recent population movements in the East European countries.* Budapest.

Korčák, J. (1959) Vnitřní migrace v Československu, in *Sbornik v chest Akad. A.S. Beshkova,* 55–64.Sofia.

Kosiński, L. (1962) Les problèmes démographiques dans les territoires occidentaux de la Pologne et les régions frontières de la Tchécoslovaquie. *Ann. Geogr.* 383, 79–98.

Kosiński, L. (1967) Wedrówki wewnętrzne ludności w Polsce w latach 1945-1965, in *Problemy demograficzne Polski Ludowej.* Warszawa.

Kosiński, L. (1968) Population growth in East-Central Europe in the years 1961–1965. *Geogr. Polonica* 14, 297–304.

Kosiński, L. (1970) The internal migration of population in Poland, 1961–1965. *Geogr. Polonica* 18, 75–84.

Kowaleski, J. (1970) Niektóre konsekwencje demograficzne migracji ludności wiejskiej do miast w europejskich krajach socjalistycznych. *Studia Demograficzne* 21, 81–97.

Kuba, R. (1968) *Racionálny pohyb obyvateľstva.* Bratislava.

Latuch, M. (1970) *Migracje wewnętrzne w Polsce na tle industrializacji (1950–1960).* Warszawa.

Maryański, A. (1966) *Współczesne wędrówki ludów.* Wrocław.

Measnicov, I. (1968) Contribuţii la studiul migraţiei interne în România. *Revista de Statistică* 18, 51–7.

Measnicov, I. and Bîrsan, T. (1962) Unele aspecte ale migraţiunii interne a populaţiei, în corelaţie cu dezvoltarea economică a ţării noastre, in *Studii de Statistică,* 677–88.

Mesaroş, E. (1968) Situaţia demografică actuală a Repùblicii Socialiste România, in *Studii de Statistică,* 628–42.

Mesaroş, E. (1969) Statistica demografică în România în perioada de după al doilea război mondial, in *Studii de Statistică,* 2010–29.

Michaeli, D. (1968) *Les migrations intérieures en Hongrie.* Unpublished thesis, Fac. des Lettres et Sci. Hum. de Paris-Nanterre.

Minkov, M. (1966) *Naselenieto i rabotnata sila v Bulgarii.* Sofia.

Minkov, M. (1972) *Migratsia na naselenieto. Sotsyalno-ikonomicheski problemi.* Sofia.

Nováková-Hřibova, B. (1971a) *Migrace obyvatelstva v moravských krajích.* Praha.

Nováková-Hřibova, B. (1971b) Migration regions of towns in the CSRS. *Studia Geogr.* 21, 137–60.

Pivovarov, J. (1970) *Naselenie sotsialisticheskikh stran zarubezhnoi Evropy.* Moskva.

Poland. Główny Urząd Statystyczny (1947–) *Rocznik statystyczny.* Warszawa.

Poland. Główny Urząd Statystyczny (1967–) *Rocznik demograficzny.* Warszawa.

Poland. Główny Urząd Statystyczny (1969) *Ruch wędrówkowy ludności w Polsce w latach 1960–1967.* Studia i Prace Statystyczne No. 18.

Popov, P. (1969) Statistika migrace a migračních procesů v Bulharsku. *Demografie* 11, 137–47.

Romania. Direcţia Centrală de Statistică (1957–). *Anuarul statistic al RSR.* Bucureşti.

Rusinov, M. (1965) Dinamika i teritorialno razpredelenie na mekhanicheski prirast na naselenieto u nas za perioda 1961–1964 godina. *Planovo Stopanstvo i Statistika* 9, 24–34.

Sárfalvi, B. (1964) Internal migration and decrease of agricultural population in Hungary, in *Applied geography in Hungary*. Budapest.

Sárfalvi, B. (1965) *A mezögazdasági népesség csökkenése Magyarországon*. Budapest.

Sárfalvi, B. (1969) Various mechanisms of internal migration in Hungary, in Sárfalvi, B. (ed.) *Research problems in Hungarian applied geography*. Studies in Geography of Hungary No. 5. Budapest.

Sentić, M. (1968) Some aspects of migration movements in the Yugoslav population, in Szabady, E. (ed.) *World views of population problems*, 321–8. Budapest.

Srb, V. (1970) Důvody vnitřhniho stěhování v Československu v roce 1966 a 1967. *Demografie* 12, 1–12.

Stpiczyński, T. (1971) *Wewnętrzny ruch wędrówkowy ludności (kierunki i struktura)*. Studia i prace statystyczne GUS 32. Warszawa.

Thirring, L. L. (1967) Internal migration in Hungary and some Central and East European countries. *UN world population conference, Belgrade 1965* IV, 527–31. New York.

Todorov, V. (1968) *Migratsionnite protsesi i niakoi sotsialno- ekonomicheski i kulturno-bitovi problemi na seloto*. Sofia.

Totev, A. J. (1968) Naselenieto na Bulgariia 1880–1980 g. *Godishnik na Sofiiskia Universitet* 59, *Yuridicheski Fakultet* 2. Sofia.

Tufescu, V. (1969) Modifications dans la structure de la population en Roumanie, après 1948. *Rev. Roumaine de Géologie, Géophysique et Géographie, Ser. Géographie* 13, 111–27.

Yugoslavia. Institut Društvenih Nauka. Centar za Demografska Istraživanja (1968) *Demografski i ekonomski aspekti prostorne pokretljivosti stanovništva u Jugoslaviji posle drugog svetskog rata*. Beograd.

Yugoslavia. Institut Društvenih Nauka. Centar za Demografska Istraživanja (1972) *Migracije stanovništva Jugoslavije*. Beograd.

Żurek, A. (1971) *Bibliografia polskich prac o migracjach stałych, wewnętrznych ludności w Polsce (lata 1916–1969/70)*. Dokumentacja Geograficzna 1. Warszawa.

Part Four
Migration of specific groups

Introduction

Previously, the need has been indicated for giving greater attention to the mobility of individuals in order better to understand what is most frequently represented in aggregate terms only. There is also the need to give more attention to specific groups of movers who may be identified by the particular nature of their mobility and who may have distinctive characteristics. These specific types of mobility and associated characteristics may be related to one another. The papers in this section are concerned with such specific groups.

Pilgrimage gives rise to a type of mobility that is motivated primarily by non-economic factors, but at the same time has associated socioeconomic and political characteristics and problems. *Birks'* descriptive paper on Muslim pilgrims from West Africa en route overland to Saudi Arabia is concerned with a minority group among the majority of West African pilgrims and among the population of the Republic of the Sudan with whom they must accommodate themselves for varying periods of time. In New Zealand the Maori population are again an ethnic minority among a majority of European settler descent. As *Poulsen, Rowland and Johnston* indicate, they are a minority which has been increasing during the present century and redistributing itself at the same time, particularly in the last three decades. Movement has been away from rural areas over short distances to local urban centres, but also with a more national developed migration system with Auckland as the main destination.

Hawaii has a multi-ethnic population and in this context *Mukherji* has examined, on a micro-scale with a sample from a small community, the differing spatial and temporal characteristics of the various ethnic groups represented. These characteristics are related to varying levels of modernization. The paper is of theoretical and methodological interest with its exploration in relational field theory and canonical analysis of the data collected.

Marriage is everywhere a factor contributing to some degree of mobility, in India of women moving to their husbands' settlements. Analysing census data for 1961 *Libbee and Sopher* estimate the nature and extent of marriage fields in India and discuss their implications for social geography in respect of regional variations which may be identified.

Lastly, for a developed country *Cribier* examines the migration of people when they retire from active life and who may then move greater or lesser distances, dependent upon a variety of influencing factors. For a country with the age structure of France the numbers involved are considerable but the data available for study are limited.

These studies of migrations of specific groups represent only a small sample of those which exist and others which might be undertaken. Traditional pastoral mobility has received very considerable attention, though it is now declining with changing economic circumstances and the settlement of nomadic peoples. At the same time mobility associated with tourism in the developed areas of the world, and increasingly between them and developing areas, is of growing interest and concern.

19 Overland pilgrimage in the savanna lands of Africa

J. S. Birks

Introduction

Pilgrimage is an important element, not always recognized, in total population mobility, though more particularly for those movements which are motivated by non-economic factors. The circulation inspired by religious zeal in turn promotes '. . . secondary flows of trade, cultural exchange, social mixing, and political integration as well as certain less desirable flows, such as the spread of epidemic diseases' (Sopher 1967; see also Alberti 1971; Farid 1956; Prothero 1965). Pilgrim movements have been significant from time immemorial, being inferred for the more distant past, while recorded history abounds with evidence of journeys to the holy places of the major religions of the world and their multitude of sects and subdivisions. In medieval times Santiago da Compostella in Northwest Spain and Canterbury in England, at the present Lourdes in France and Ste Anne de Beaupré on the coast of Quebec, have provided major foci for devout Roman Catholics; the two places of contemporary pilgrimage annually attract millions.

Pilgrim movements are at a variety of scales from local to intercontinental and global. In Hindu India there is '. . . an informal hierarchy of district, region and pan-Indian pilgrim circulation', the latter 'extending to Cape Comorin and Rameswaram in the extreme south to Badrinath and Kedarnath in the Himalayas' (Sopher 1967; Bhardwaj 1972). The literature on pilgrimage is vast but inevitably diverse and much of it difficult of access. That which concerns itself specifically with numbers involved and their characteristics, with source regions, frequency of visits, routes followed and other spatial/ temporal aspects is slight. The pilgrim journey has received literary and artistic treatment but has been given little attention by the social sciences in general (Sopher 1967). There is, for example, an anthropological study of pilgrims travelling on foot in India (Karve 1962), but on pilgrim organization and experience little is known.

One of the pillars of Islam is the duty of the faithful to make the pilgrimage to the holy places in Mecca (and to a lesser extent in Medina) in Saudi Arabia at least once in their lives. The annual pilgrimage represents, both in the past and at the present, one of the major movements motivated by religious adherence. It is notable for its regularity (though the month of pilgrimage varies with the Muslim lunar calendar), for its global attraction (though the source areas of pilgrims are concentrated mainly within the zone extending from West Africa to Southeast Asia), and for the growing numbers of pilgrims associated with increasing numbers of Muslims, increasing affluence and improving means of transport.

The pilgrimage to Mecca has been reviewed recently in its general geographical and historical aspects and reference is made in broad terms to many of the features of pilgrim mobility (King 1972). Many pilgrims to Saudi Arabia nowadays journey by air and sea, but traditional overland movements remain locally important – from the Middle East in general and within the Arabian Peninsula. Though transcontinental travel overland now involves a minority only, the outward and return journeys of Muslims from West Africa along the northern savannas via Chad and the Sudan provide scope for a study of the organization of such movement and of the routes which are followed. In historical and contemporary terms it is of additional interest with reference to social and economic interaction between different ethnic groups.

Characteristics of present-day pilgrimage

It is difficult to determine accurately the number of pilgrims who move along the savanna routes. Estimates from records collected at the quarantine station at El Geneina on the Sudan-Chad boundary, with allowance for illegal movements, range between 3,000 and 4,000 pilgrims per annum. For the most part they originate within the savanna lands of West Africa, from Lake Chad westward to Senegal. The majority come from the areas generally called Hausaland and Bornu in Nigeria and Niger, but in a sample of some 650 pilgrim families in Darfur in 1970–1 all the savanna countries of West Africa were represented. Numbers tend to decrease with increasing distance of origin westward. However, Chad is an exception, for although it is nearer to Saudi Arabia few pilgrims originate there. People in Chad adhere less rigidly to Islam than those in the countries further west, but also as a consequence of a period of unstable conditions the attentions of the population have been turned to more secular matters. The large number of migrants who enter the Sudan from Chad are either refugees or labourers who have a weak pilgrimage intent.

The pilgrims passing overland are predominantly Hausa, this ethnic group making up 55% of the total, and are mainly from the traditional emirates of Kano, Sokoto and Demegaram. A further 20% are Fulfulde-speaking peoples, again largely from Hausaland but also comprising the majority of the pilgrims who come from countries to the west of Nigeria. The remaining pilgrims are drawn from a variety of West African ethnic groups, only the Kanuri being prominent and forming 10% of the total.

Overland pilgrimage takes several years to complete and few make the return journey to Mecca in under three years; for some it may be as long as twenty-five or thirty years, and the average total time taken at present is about eight years. Approximately five years are taken on the journey to Mecca, particularly in earning sufficient money to make the final stage of the pilgrimage which now costs about £75 sterling from the Sudan. On return from the pilgrimage the pilgrims stay approximately a further three or four years in the Sudan before setting off for West Africa.

The lengthy time involved in movement means that few pilgrims travel on their own. Many move in family units which are only slightly smaller in size than those of settled West African families; 4.9 persons per family for the pilgrims as compared with 5.8 for settled families. Over the years but more particularly in the twentieth century a substantial West African population has settled permanently in the Sudan (Davies 1964; Hassoun 1952; Mather 1956). Some are now third or fourth and even fifth generations settled in that country.

The transient and settled West African population in the Sudan is limited in distribution to the savanna, as is their zone of origin in West Africa. Few live in the desert in the north, or in the rainforest in the south of the country. Within the savanna zone the major areas of agricultural production are concentrated, particularly the cotton-growing areas of the Gezira between the Blue and White Niles, and in these the West Africans are a predominant element in both the permanent and seasonal labour force for cotton cultivation (Davies 1964). Further east in Gedaref they are similarly essential for grain production. Relatively few West Africans live in the underdeveloped west of the Sudan, though their number had increased in recent years with the extension of the railway westwards to Nyala and increased opportunities for farming cash crops which have been taken by West Africans.

The system of pilgrim movement

Pilgrims in transit move from group to group of settled West Africans, being thus able to recuperate after covering long distances and to earn money for the next stage of their journey. This they can do while living in the *zongo* which each West African community maintains for their use and where they may stay either free or for payment according to the decision of the *sarkin zongo* who is in charge. Originally the *zongo* was simply a resting place for travellers, but in the Sudan it is now a group of houses set aside specifically for the use of pilgrims temporarily resident. In Chad these *zongos* take the form of large, ostentatious, high-walled compounds, the courtyards of which have cubicles along the walls; in the Sudan a small group of temporary straw shelters is more typical.

Apart from providing a place in which pilgrims live the *zongos* are important in other ways. While in them pilgrims collect information about further stages of their journeys and are isolated from local people who may be to some degree antipathetic to them. Those in charge of the *zongo* are in contact with one another and pass the pilgrims from one *zongo* to the next, making transport and other arrangements. Having entered a *zongo* in northeastern Nigeria a pilgrim need make no further decisions about travel, but can be directed and taken to the east of the Sudan through the *zongo* system. Lack of documentation and language problems would make it very difficult for pilgrims to move without this system. The routes which are followed are largely determined by the agents in this system and not by the pilgrims themselves.

Lengths of stay in *zongos* are influenced by the season (the ease of travel and availability of farmwork), the size of settlement and the consequent amount of employment that is available, the nature of the next stage of the journey to be made, the availability of transport, health, the amount of charity that is forthcoming, attitudes of local authorities and, a most important factor, the enthusiasm of the individual pilgrim to complete the pilgrimage. There are certain jobs in which the pilgrims specialize, in addition to agriculture, which the Sudanese dislike and at which they have not proved particularly proficient, such as barbering, manicuring, tanning and portering. Every member of a family on pilgrimage has a money-making role, and for this reason the family is not necessarily a cumbersome unit in pilgrimage. Even with these activities the pilgrims tend to be an isolated group and indicative of this is the large number of West Africans who cannot speak Arabic even after spending several years in the Sudan.

The development of overland pilgrimage

It has been commonly asserted that overland pilgrimage along the savannas dates from the introduction of Islam into West Africa in about the eleventh century, but this is not the case. Early pilgrimage followed the trans-desert routes along which Islam had been introduced into sub-Saharan West Africa. In this early period the religion was not established among the mass of the people, but was limited to the court and wealthy classes. Thus the number of pilgrims was restricted to those who could afford to travel in style to Mecca. Such pilgrims did not risk their wealth by travelling along routes which were politically unstable, but crossed the Sahara and then travelled eastward from the Maghreb and Fezzan in large caravans of pilgrims and traders. This tradition lasted until the nineteenth century and declined when the European presence in North Africa placed restrictions on this route, with the result that overland movement became more directed along the savannas.

The earliest pilgrimage along the savannas known with any certainty was in the late seventeenth century when a group of Kanuri, led by Sheikh Tylah, arrived in Darfur from Bornu en route to Mecca. The traditions associated with this group indicate the nature of overland pilgrimage at this time. The group moved eastward from emirate to emirate, seeking royal permission and protection on the same basis of travel as in the trans-desert movements where the social and courtly contacts en route were almost as important as the pilgrimage itself. Such travelling was ill-suited to the turbulent conditions of the savannas and the pattern changed to one of clandestine movements of groups passing through areas without the consent of local rulers.

Changes were also associated with the types of pilgrims travelling along the savannas in the eighteenth and nineteenth centuries. They tended to be drawn from the poorer classes who were unable to afford the trans-desert routes. Their small numbers and their modes of travel make it difficult to generalize as to the routes which they followed. Their pattern of movement is best thought of as falling within a zone through the central and southern savannas through which they wandered, avoiding areas of great disturbance and towns in which authority was unfriendly to them. In general terms the route passed through Bornu, Kukawa, Bagirmi, Wadai, Darfur, Kordofan, Sennar, northern Ethiopia to the Red Sea coast in the region of Massawa. However, conditions were so adverse to travel, especially in the eastern areas, that there was always a tendency for some pilgrims to strike northwards across the desert so as to travel in greater security. Pilgrims from Hausaland passed through Kufra and along the 'Forty-Day Road' in order to avoid Kordofan, having travelled the initial stages of their journey through the savannas.

This pattern continued after the Turkish invasion of the Sudan for initially the Sultanate of Darfur remained independent of the Turks, not falling to them until 1874. This meant that the passage of pilgrims to Kobbei, and along the 'Forty-Day Road', was uninterrupted and was swelled both because of the increased numbers setting off due eastward from Nigeria rather than across the desert, and the reluctance of pilgrims to pass through the savannas which were little pacified by the Turkish occupation.

With the Turkish occupation of Darfur in 1874, El Fasher and the northern areas became less attractive to pilgrims and, as a consequence, from Abeche pilgrims struck southeastwards passing through Dar Sila to the Bahr al Ghazal area, and then through southern Kordofan to the Nile Valley. Several West

African settlements were founded in Kordofan, including the important village Kafia Kange. Traditions relating to this period say that by the end of the nineteenth century pilgrims in groups of up to 2,500 were moving along the southern savannas (fig. 19.1).

During the uprising of the Mahdi in the Sudan, pilgrims on their way to Mecca were joined by many West Africans migrating in order to receive the blessings of the Mahdi and the Khalifah. Unstable conditions in the central savannas caused a shifting of pilgrimage routes, travellers passing to the north of Lake Chad. To the east of Darfur pilgrims passed along routes from Jebel Meidob to Omdurman, avoiding populated areas where they were exposed to the risk of enslavement.

European domination of the Sudan came at the close of the nineteenth century, but it stopped short of Darfur where the rule of the last independent Sultanate in the savannas continued for some time. These together influenced the routes along which pilgrims passed. The early twentieth century saw a great expansion in the numbers passing eastwards through the savannas; apart from those who were primarily pilgrims, there were large numbers of refugees from the British occupation of the emirates of northern Nigeria. They were difficult to distinguish from pilgrims and many had Mecca as an ultimate goal. European records and eye-witness reports make it possible to describe these pilgrims in some detail.

After the ending of unstable conditions in the central savannas pilgrims could pass in safety along the direct route via Fort Lamy, Atia and Abeche to the western borders of Darfur; to the east of Darfur the Condominium administration of the Sudan presented no obstacle to their movements. But the presence of the Sultanate of Ali Dinar was a major problem to pilgrims. Those of royal or other distinctive status were well treated, others were lucky to escape with their lives. In the outlying areas of the Sultanate there were continual disturbances which made it difficult for pilgrims to pass through. As a consequence there was a threefold division of the route at Abeche. A small number of pilgrims passed directly through the Sultanate to El Obeid calling at El Fasher. Others went northeastward, passing to Khartoum, or in some instances Fezzan and Tripoli, and founding Hausa-speaking communities in northern Libya. The majority of pilgrims passed southeast from Abeche to Dar Sila and Kafia Kange, which expanded greatly. From Kafia Kange some pilgrims went to Wau, others to En Nahud and El Obeid, these routes then coalescing in the Sennar area.

In the latter days of the Sultanate of Darfur, as its sphere of influence began to contract, the pilgrims, whilst still passing through Kafia Kange, deviated less from the direct route and passed through Adre, through the lower Wadi region of Darfur and then after Kafia Kange through Abu Gabra and Muglad. After 1916, when the Pax Britannica was extended over the whole of Darfur, the Kafia Kange route began to decline. Pilgrims from

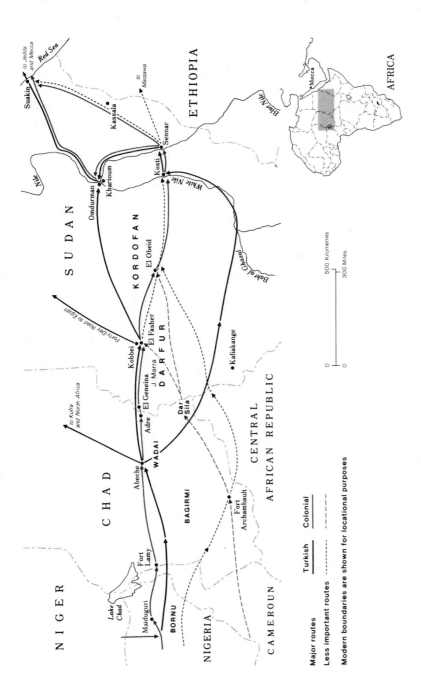

Figure 19.1 Pilgrimage routes during the Sudanese Turkish period, and late colonial times

the west now entered the Sudan in the El Geneina-Foraburange area, passing along a variety of routes mainly to the south of Jebel Marra, to El Obeid. Efforts made by the administration to control the movements of pilgrims in Darfur were largely unsuccessful and relatively few passed to the north of Jebel Marra, the route that was thought best by the British in order to limit opportunities for slaving. In the late 1920s there was still some residual traffic along the Kafia Kange route, but the British division of the Sudan into northern and southern areas brought this to an end and Kafia Kange was destroyed. West Africans moved northwards away from the pagan and Christian populations. The zone of transit in Darfur was limited, but pilgrims still passed along a variety of routes, rather than just that through El Fasher (fig. 19.1).

The eventual concentration of pilgrims' routes through El Fasher was achieved not by government control, but as a result of a revolution in overland pilgrimage caused by the introduction of the lorry as a means of transport. By the end of the Second World War the great majority of pilgrims passed through Darfur by lorry on the route through El Geneina and El Fasher, after which they passed to the railhead at El Obeid. From the point of view of numbers of pilgrims and the facilities made available to pilgrims this period extending into the 1950s was the heyday of overland pilgrimage (fig. 19.2).

It came to an end with the political independence of the savanna countries and the development of the mass transportation of pilgrims by air. Political independence had little immediate effect but there was a steady rundown in the facilities available to help overland pilgrimage. There was also the impact of the extension of the railhead to Nyala in 1958. From El Geneina pilgrims passed via Zalingei to Nyala, establishing a basic pattern of movement that has continued to the present time. When they ceased to pass through El Fasher the West African settlement there began to decline.

Political obstructions to the pilgrimage have gradually increased, though these have affected the routes rather than the number of pilgrims. For example in 1964 the Sudan-Chad border was closed officially and remained so for three years. This had little direct effect, for a system was developed by which pilgrims were helped to enter the Sudan illegally and were assisted in their return journeys. So developed was this system of illegal transit of pilgrims over the border that when it was reopened in 1967–8 few pilgrims entered legally. Most considered that illegal entry was more convenient, particularly as it avoided the payment of border dues.

The second major closing of the border, this time to pilgrims only, was made in 1971, ostensibly because of the outbreaks of cholera in West Africa. Again this action had little effect on pilgrim numbers. However, intensive police action in the east of Darfur province caused further variations in the routes. Pilgrims began to avoid Nyala, where the police were most active,

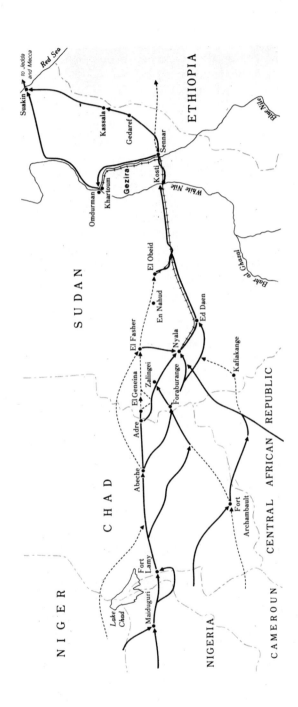

Figure 19.2 Recent pilgrimage routes

and to skirt it to the south, usually boarding the train at Ed Daen along the line to the east. Other pilgrims reopened the route via El Fasher, having entered the Sudan in remote areas away from motorable tracks. An even greater effort is now being made by pilgrims passing along the newly reopened route via Kafia Kange, which had the advantage of being by far the most remote.

Conclusion

Over many centuries various factors for and against pilgrimage have been responsible for considerable deviations in the routes followed, but always there has been motivation for the continuation and furtherance of pilgrimage. Adjustment and adaptation to these factors have come through the *sarkin zongo* who are sensitive to changes and make it possible for overland pilgrimage to continue. In these circumstances there are major difficulties in attempting any control of pilgrimage, though obviously some control is necessary. West Africans have been blamed for perpetrating political unrest and pilgrims have been responsible for the transmission of diseases. For these and other reasons the government of the Sudan might prefer to see overland pilgrimage come to an end completely. But with the expansion of Islam in West Africa pilgrims are likely to increase in numbers rather than to decrease in the near future, and their zeal will continue to be intense. It seems unlikely that the Sudanese authorities will be able to end overland pilgrimage, even with the cooperation of the governments of Niger and Nigeria. As an alternative policy it would probably be better for the Sudan to facilitate the transport of pilgrims who wish to travel overland, so as to minimize the problems associated with their movement and to reap the maximum benefit and advantage of them providing an essential source of labour in the country.

References

Al Nagar, O. (1968) *The influence of the 'haj' on West Africa*. Unpublished Ph.D. thesis, Univ. of London.

Alberti, M. P. P. (1971) *Strutture commerciali di una citta di pellegrinaggio: Mashad (Iran Nord-Orientale)*. Universita degli Studi di Trieste, Instituto di Geografia, No. 8.

Bhardwaj, S. (1972) *Hindu places of pilgrimage in India*. Berkeley.

Davies, H. J. R. (1964) The West African in the economic geography of the Sudan. *Geogr.* 49, 222–35.

Farid, M. A. (1956) Implications of the Mecca pilgrimage for a regional malaria eradication programme. *Bull. Wld Hlth Org.* 15, 828–33.

Hassoun, I. A. (1952) Western migration and settlement in the Gezira. *Sudan Notes and Records* 35.

Karve, I. (1962) On the road: a Maharashtrian pilgrimage. *J. Asian Stud.* 22, 13–29.

King, R. (1972) The pilgrimage to Mecca: some historical and geographical aspects. *Erdk.* 26, 61–73.

Mather, D. B. (1956) Migrations in the Sudan, in Steel, R. W. and Fisher C. A. (eds.) *Geographical essays on British tropical lands*, 113–44. London.

Maurice, G. K. (1932) The entry of relapsing fever into the Sudan. *Sudan Notes and Records* 15.

Prothero, R. M. (1965) *Migrants and malaria.* London.

Sopher, D. F. (1967) *Geography of religions.* Englewood Cliffs.

Sopher, D. F. (1968) Pilgrim circulation in Gujerat. *Geog. Rev.* 58, 392–425.

Willis, C. A. (1926) *Report on slavery and the pilgrimage.* Unpublished memo., Sudan Government.

20 Patterns of Maori migration in New Zealand

M. F. Poulsen,
D. T Rowland and
R. J. Johnston

There were an estimated 125,000–175,000 Maoris in New Zealand at the time of European arrival in 1767 (Pool 1964, 232), but by 1896 there were only some 42,000. The decline is usually associated with the Maori's lack of immunity to introduced illnesses: it was accompanied by a retreat to the least fertile and least accessible areas of the country's North Island. Since 1896, the Maori population has been increasing again, at a spectacular rate since 1926 (table 20.1). The later years of this period of demographic rejuvenation have also produced a large-scale redistribution of the Maori, mainly towards a few urban centres: the time lag was undoubtedly a product of the crippling economic depression of the 1930s. The present paper charts the salient features of this redistribution since 1951, based on census and electoral roll data; both are unsatisfactory sources, but there are none better available.

Maori net migration, 1951–66

The age and sex distribution of the Maori population, by five-year age groups, has been abstracted for a common set of spatial units from the country's 1951, 1956, 1961 and 1966 census tabulations. A variety of methods could be applied to these data to estimate net migration rates during each intercensal period for each area, given that data on births and deaths are not available. The method chosen applied the national Life Table, which gives the survival rate for each five-year age group. This makes certain assumptions about the data and the migration process, some of which were recognized in the formula applied. (Fuller details of the methodology are given in Poulsen 1970.)

Table 20.1

Growth and urbanization of the Maori population since 1896

Census year	Maori	Total	Increase (%) since preceding census		% change to urban residence since preceding census*	
			Maori	Total	Maori	Total
1896	42,113	743,207				
1901	45,549	815,853	8.2	9.8		
1906	50,309	936,304	10.5	14.8		
1911	52,723	1,058,308	4.8	13.0		
1916	52,997	1,149,225	0.5	8.6		
1921	56,987	1,271,664	7.5	10.7		
1926	63,670	1,408,139	11.7	11.8		
1936	82,326	1,573,810	29.3	8.2	1.90	0.07
1945	98,744	1,747,679	19.9	11.0	6.15	3.03
1951	115,676	1,941,366	17.1	13.9	2.60	0.71
1956	137,151	2,176,224	18.6	12.1	4.58	0.45
1961	167,086	2,417,543	21.8	11.1	9.97	0.80
1966	201,159	2,678,855	20.4	10.8	10.38	0.81

* The difference, in percentage points, between the percentage living in urban districts at the two dates: a set of relatively consistent areas has only been available since 1926. Urban districts are the eighteen urban areas, plus all other administrative urban areas.

General features of net migration

Applying the selected method of estimation to the constituent local government areas for the period 1951–66, the following major conclusions emerged.

During the fifteen years there was a net redistribution of Maoris, across local government area boundaries, of some 63,000 persons, or 39% of the 1966 total Maori population. The redistribution rates increased over the three intercensal periods (table 20.2).

Over the period there was a marked increase in the amount of family migration, as indexed by both the sex ratio (percentage of females: table 20.2) and by a dependency ratio (children aged 5–14/males aged 20–59: table 20.2). This parallels Rowland's (1971a) finding concerning migration into the Auckland urban area, and suggests that migration is becoming a much more permanent affair compared to the earlier 'pioneer' period when young males predominated in the migration stream. The earlier pattern may have been similar to that reported in many migration studies, in which the young males move to the towns for a short period and are expected to return with money for their rural family. Metge (1964),

Table 20.2

Maori net migration: numbers and ratios*

	Period		
	1951–6	*1956–61*	*1961–6*
Number of migrants (net)			
Male	7,368	11,616	14,597
Female	6,619	10,475	13,437
Rates (percentage of total Maori population)			
Male	13.0	17.2	18.1
Female	12.3	16.1	17.1
Sex ratio of migrants (females as percentage of total)			
	47.3	47.4	49.3
Dependency ratio (children 5–14/males 20–59)			
Total Maori population	1.398	1.414	1.494
Maori net migrants	0.835	1.129	1.470

* Migration estimate based on Life Table method.

however, suggested that many young Maori males left home against the wishes of their elders, family quarrels being the immediate cause of a 'spur of the moment' decision to migrate.

There were two periods in the life cycle when Maoris were most mobile, the highest rates (net migrations/total population) being among young adults and among elderly persons (fig. 20.1). Because of their weighting in the total population, however, the former group constituted the bulk of the migrants.

Although both sexes had their greatest number of migrants in the 15–19 age group, female migrants were more highly clustered in this group, while a large proportion of males (especially in the later intercensal periods) were aged 20–24 (fig. 20.1).

The areal pattern of net redistribution

According to the estimates of net migration, therefore, most Maori migrants were young, in their teens if they were female and their teens or early twenties if male, and there was a large number of them. To assist in the description of the areal pattern of this net migration, the country has been divided into seven regions to conform with the 1951 distribution (fig. 20.2).

Net outmigration during 1951–6 came mainly from two areas, Northland and Eastland in the North Island. Hokianga County in the far north suffered the greatest net loss, some 1,000 persons or almost 20% of its 1951 Maori population. Inmigration was not entirely to the urban districts, however, although Auckland was the recipient of 25% of the net inmigrants, its Maori population increasing by more than one-third. Rural areas with large inmigration volumes were almost all in the Central North Island; these flows were probably associated with very large forestry developments, which had

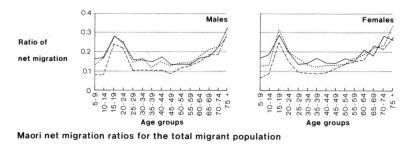

Maori net migration ratios for the total migrant population

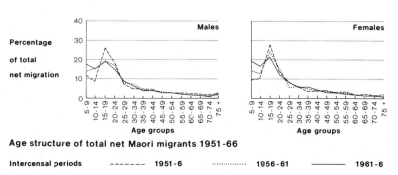

Age structure of total net Maori migrants 1951-66

Intercensal periods   ------- 1951-6   1956-61   ———— 1961-6

Figure 20.1 Age and sex attributes of Maori migration as deduced from census tables

then not produced any large administrative urban agglomerations. Apart from Auckland, the principal urban destinations were Wellington/Hutt, Gisborne and Hamilton, the last two being close to areas of considerable outmigration.

During the following period, 1956–61, the pattern of net migration was much more clearly rural to urban: North Island counties provided 87% of the net outmigrants, and virtually all of the net inmigration was absorbed by North Island towns. Although outmigration was much more widely spread than in the previous five years (36 counties in the North Island lost over 10% of their 1956 Maori population), the major flows again emanated from Northland and Eastland, plus some counties of the Central North Island.

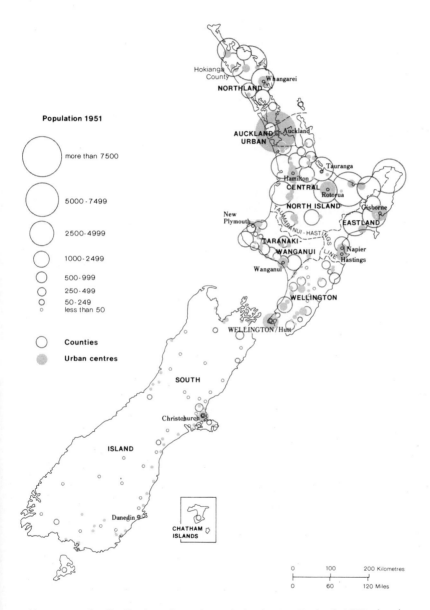

Population 1951

more than 7500

5000 - 7499

2500 - 4999

1000 - 2499

500 - 999

250 - 499

50 - 249
less than 50

Counties

Urban centres

Hokianga
County
Whangarei
NORTHLAND

AUCKLAND
URBAN
Auckland

Tauranga

Hamilton
CENTRAL
Rotorua
NORTH ISLAND
Gisborne

New
Plymouth
EASTLAND

TARANAKI-
WANGANUI
Napier
Hastings

Wanganui

WELLINGTON

WELLINGTON / Hutt

SOUTH

Christchurch

ISLAND

Dunedin

CHATHAM
ISLANDS

0   100   200 Kilometres

0   60   120 Miles

Figure 20.2 The distribution of Maori population in New Zealand, 1951, showing the regions employed in this study, and the places named in the text

Hokianga again lost most (33%), and 3 counties in Eastland lost more than 20%. Auckland was again the principal recipient of inmigrants (almost 30% of the national total, increasing its Maori population by 43%), with the other main centres of the North Island also being major destinations – the Maori populations of Tauranga, Hamilton and Wellington/Hutt increased by 162.5, 66 and 65% respectively, and Rotorua, a major population centre in 1951 with 2,576 Maoris, experienced an increase of 50%. Only 7 North Island counties showed a net migration gain, though there were small net inflows to a number of South Island counties (Heenan 1966).

In the final intercensal period, 1961–6, absolute outmigrant volumes were generally not as large for individual counties; more than 30 lost over 10% of their expected 1966 population, however, and 16 North Island counties lost more than 30% (compared with only 2 during the preceding five years: Hokianga lost 30% during 1961–6). Of the inmigration, 92% was to urban centres, 82% to North Island urban centres, 28% to Auckland and 10% to Wellington/Hutt. Auckland's Maori population increased by 38%

The general pattern (detailed maps in Poulsen and Johnston 1973) is clearly a growing concentration of the net migration of Maoris towards a few places. Nevertheless there have been considerable changes in the migration experience of the seven regions over the three periods (fig. 20.3). The greatest change has been for the Central North Island, the second major destination for net inmigration during 1951–6 but the principal source of outmigrants in the last five years. Of the other main source areas,

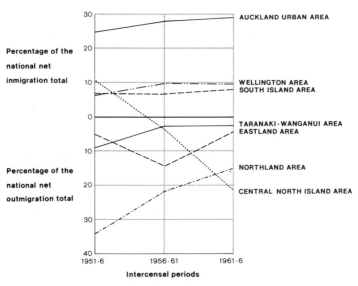

Figure 20.3 The changing pattern of migration flows

Northland's contribution declined over time, while Eastland's rose, only
to be surpassed later by the Central North Island. This suggests a time lag
in migration experience, perhaps accounted for by the greater inaccessibility
of Eastland than Northland relative to the main centres of Auckland and
Wellington/Hutt, and the attractions of the Central North Island forestry
industries during the initial period. Among the three areas of conflux,
change has been virtually negligible, Auckland slightly increasing its share
and Wellington and the South Island each taking just under 10%.

The nature of the net migration streams: a summary

Net Maori migration has clearly been dominated by outflows from the rural
areas of the northern, central and eastern parts of the North Island,
with compensating inflows to the main urban centres. Over time, these
inflows have become more concentrated on a few large and expanding places.
Established migration theory would suggest that these moves were a result
of 'push' factors operating in the rural areas of origin, and 'pull' factors in
the urban destinations. Analyses for the 1961–6 period confirmed this. The
main movement of whole households was from the poor housing, low income,
job opportunity, rural areas and to the North Island towns; subsidiary flows
comprised young, single people moving long distances for high-income jobs
(Poulsen and Johnston 1973).

Migration flows: 1960–9

A basic weakness of the net migration estimates discussed above is that they
give no indication either of the destinations of migrants from areas of net
loss, or of the origins of those who come to live in areas of net gain. And,
of course, as *net* estimates only, they conceal a probably much larger amount
of gross migration into and out of every constituent area. To compensate for
these disadvantages, data have been abstracted from the electoral rolls to give
some indication of the dimensions of the migration streams between the
various parts of New Zealand.

There are numerous drawbacks involved in use of the electoral rolls for
this task. Because only adults may vote, only the migrations of persons aged
21 and over may be studied by tracing their addresses through a sequence
of electoral rolls: this, of course, is most unfortunate because the net migration estimates indicated that the late teenage years were those of greatest
spatial mobility among the Maori (fig. 20.1). It is more difficult to trace
females than males because the former change their name at marriage. Maoris
are apparently very inconsistent regarding electoral enrolment. Mobility
itself may be a part of the reason for failing to re-enrol. In the present study,

only 36.2% of the sample could be traced through all electoral rolls,[1] and of these people only 27.4% were recorded as movers, compared with, for example, 42.5% of those traced through the 1960 and 1963 rolls.

Despite the important limitations of the electoral roll data, they have been employed here in the absence of any alternative, nationwide source. The sample taken was every fifth *male*, beginning with the fourth; thus from about 24,000 males enrolled in 1960, a sample of 4,857 was extracted, with information on address, occupation and tribe. These males were then traced through the 1963, 1966 and 1969 rolls. As already pointed out, 36.2% only could be located in all three of those, though another 27% were located in two of the three rolls. In all, 2,816 moves were identified. Undoubtedly they form a biased sample, but no other source on migration is available at a national scale.

Broad flow patterns

On the basis of established migration theory, one would expect most Maori migration to be directed towards Auckland, perhaps in a number of short steps for those originating from the remote rural fastnesses. Data certainly support the contention of most movement being short distance only (table 20.3). For each of the regions except Wellington (excluding Auckland, which consisted of the urban area only, within which moves were not

Table 20.3

Intra- and interregional Maori migration, 1960–9*

From	To						
	1	2	3	4	5	6	7
1 Northland	191	101	36	5	2	5	6
2 Auckland	39	—	36	13	6	13	7
3 Central North Island	25	85	458	48	18	36	12
4 Eastland	1	9	35	220	4	40	15
5 Taranaki-Wanganui	2	6	26	9	77	18	3
6 Wellington	6	18	12	28	17	74	16
7 South Island	5	3	5	5	1	14	45

* Adult males only. Migration estimates based on electoral rolls. The regional boundaries are shown on fig. 20.1.

[1] Tracing was forwards only, so no attempt was made to locate people listed in the 1963 roll in the 1960, for example. This obviates the problem of whether a person listed for the first time is an inmigrant or has come of age in the preceding three years.

charted), over half of all moves began and ended within its boundaries. This, of course, can mean long journeys (within the South Island, for example), but the hypothesis of short distance moves is also generally supported by the origins and destinations of those who crossed regional boundaries. Thus, for example, over 60% of those who left Northland went to Auckland, no doubt because of the economic and social opportunities there: 'There were already so many kin living there that a prospective emigrant had no worries about accommodation or loneliness on arrival' (Metge 1964, 100). Similarly, most of the migrants into Northland come from either Auckland or the Central North Island region.

Eastland's main connections were with the Central North Island and Wellington regions, as were Taranaki-Wanganui's. Wellington had fairly strong connections with all North Island regions except distant Northland, and the South Island's main connections, especially for outmigrants, were with the national capital and its hinterland. But the Central North Island has the most widespread distribution of migration flows, no doubt related to its centrality and to the ready availability of employment there, especially in the expanding forestry industry. There was considerable movement from this region to Auckland which was not reciprocated, however, suggesting that the industries and towns of the Central North Island may act as a staging-post on many Maori migrations towards Auckland, or as an introduction to the urban way of life.

Movement through the urban system

Well-tested migration theory suggests a common, stepwise process in which moves go from rural area, through local small towns and regional centres, to the national metropolis (Keown 1971). Thus in the New Zealand context, for example, we might expect local towns to be the collecting points for migrants from rural Northland; in turn, migrants from these places would mostly head for Whangarei, the regional capital; and finally outmigrants from Whangarei would head for Auckland. But the previous section has not indicated any mass convergence on Auckland, despite the rapid growth in Maori numbers there.

Many migrants, up to one-third of all those whose move originated in a rural settlement, remained within the rural economy and did not take even the first step up the urban ladder (table 20.4A).[2] Of the movers from rural areas who went either to an urban centre or to a rural area in another region (table 20.4B), the local towns, both large and small, accounted for

---

[2] The following table indicates that the further a person moved, the more likely he was to change his occupation:

at least half in four regions, and 30% in the other two – Northland and
Wellington. The attractions of Auckland clearly drew many of Northland's
rural dwellers direct to the large city: Wellington/Hutt did not similarly
attract local migrants, however, and Wanganui and some of the Central

Table 20.4

Rural-urban Maori migration, 1960–9*

	Northland	Central Island	Eastland	Taranaki-Wanganui	Wellington	South Island
A. Percentage of all migrants staying within same region, moving rural-to-rural						
	21	20	12	15	11	33
B. Percentage of all movers from rural areas who go to						
Local towns	14	37	9	33	28	20
Large towns within region**	16	19	47	16	3	30
Wellington	2	3	9	4	12	10
Auckland	44	15	4	4	7	2
C. Percentage of all movers from local towns who go to						
Large towns within region**	11	14	18	3	0	17
Local rural areas	22	39	27	24	77	25
Wellington	4	1	0	8	0	8
Auckland	52	24	9	8	0	0

* Adult males only. Migration estimates based on electoral rolls.
** The towns were: Northland – Whangarei; Central North Island – Hamilton, Tauranga, Rotorua; Eastland – Gisborne, Napier, Hastings; Taranaki-Wanganui – Wanganue; Wellington – Palmerston North; South Island – Christchurch, Dunedin, Invercargill.

Footnote 2–(*continued*)

	Non-movers	Movers within local region	Movers between regions
% changed occupation	44.4	68.1	77.8

Also movers were more likely to change their tribal affiliation than non-movers
(17.8% among non-movers, 28.6% of movers within local region and 38% of movers
between regions), probably doing this to gain social acceptance among the Maori
residents of their destination (see Hohepa 1964; Kernot 1963).

North Island towns were almost equally attractive to these people. Finally, section C of table 20.4 provides the least convincing evidence in support of the suggested pattern, since in most cases local rural areas were more favoured as destinations for movers from the small towns than were the local or national large cities. In fact, only in the case of Northland did more people head for the 'bright city lights'.

This last finding suggests that much Maori migration takes place within a limited spatial framework of town and hinterland, perhaps in many cases being temporary (if not seasonal the data source would not pick this out). There is little evidence of any national system of migration towards Wellington and Auckland: the major flows from the small towns of Eastland and Taranaki-Wanganui, for example, were to the rural areas of the Central North Island. Moves from the largest regional centres, from which there were enough migrations to suggest a pattern, also indicated this dominance of local rural-urban interaction (table 20.5). Nevertheless, there was consider-

Table 20.5

Maori migration from regional centres, 1960–9*

| | Destination (percentage of outmigrants) | | | |
Origin	Local rural areas	Local small towns	Wellington	Auckland
Whangarei	28	4	4	40
Hamilton	7	21	0	21
Tauranga	38	16	8	15
Rotorua	25	25	8	25
Gisborne	32	12	12	0
Napier	38	13	0	0
Palmerston North	50	0	0	0
Christchurch	31	23	0	8

* Adult males only.

able movement to Auckland from the regional centres of Whangarei, Hamilton, Tauranga and Rotorua, and since the latter three (plus their hinterlands) are also important destinations of migrations from regions further east and south, this suggests that the Central North Island may be an organizational nexus in Maori migrations. Some moves are there and back, many of them perhaps being temporary and based on the high wages of the forestry industry; others may lead to further movement towards the main Maori city, joining there with the migrants from rural Northland.[3]

[3] Rowland (1971a) found that migrants to Auckland from rural Northland and from urban Central North Island tended to locate in different parts of the city.

More detailed analysis of the migration matrix in table 20.3, using the matrix manipulation methods suggested by Brown (1970) and Brown and Horton (1970), were undertaken to establish whether a national system, oriented towards Auckland, existed. This was confirmed: Auckland is the main destination, albeit often after several moves; Hamilton and the Central North Island are important stops en route during the migrant's progress towards the metropolis (Poulsen and Johnston 1973). Thus, while most movement is over relatively short distances, between town and hinterland, these various systems are linked into a national system (fig. 20.4). Each of

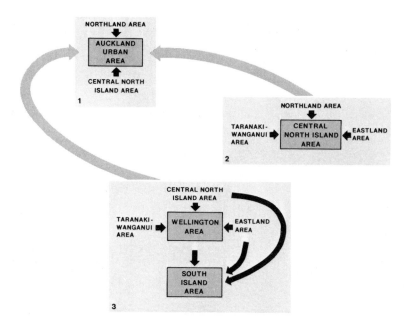

1   Auckland inmigration cell
2   Central North Island inmigration cell
3   Southern inmigration cell

Figure 20.4 Schematic representation of the Maori inter-area migration system

these cells is considerably self-contained and its Maori migration is dominated by short distance rural-rural, rural-urban and urban-rural moves. Inter-cell connection is mainly at the inter-urban level, and is directed towards Auckland, often via the Central North Island.

Migration into and within the city: Auckland

Within cities, low socioeconomic status inmigrant groups very frequently cluster into certain residential areas, especially the poorer housing districts of the inner city (Johnston 1971). In New Zealand, however, such clustering is not a feature of the inner districts only, though it was until fifteen to twenty years ago (Whitelaw 1971). The change results from provision of large estates of subsidized government housing, for which Maoris are eligible, in the outer suburbs. Thus, the spatial patterns of migration of Maoris into and within urban centres are more diffuse than is the case with minorities in many other countries. Auckland urban area has been the main Maori population centre throughout the twentieth century: in 1966 it contained 34% of all Maoris living in cities and boroughs. Each year during the period 1961–6, some 2,800 Maoris were added to Auckland's population; the net total increase for the five years was 8,820 (Rowland 1971a). Electoral rolls were checked to provide information on all adult migrants to Auckland during 1960–6, both male and female. In all, about 590 inmigrants were identified, representing only about 20% of the estimated net adult inmigration and thereby suggesting that a large proportion of Maoris do not re-enrol after a move. Sixty-four per cent of the total came from Northland, 49% from the northernmost counties. Of the 36% coming from south of the city, most originated from nearby areas, though Auckland's influence spread into the area in which it was competing with the economic opportunities offered in the Central North Island.

The locations of the migrants upon arrival do not conform to the general 'port-of-entry' models for the movement of low status groups to the city, which suggests concentration of the new arrivals on the city centre. Indeed, 43% of the arrivals went to Auckland's southern suburbs; only 15.4% were located in the inner city and a further 12.4% in the surrounding collar of central suburbs. Some inmigrants may, of course, have moved to the central areas first before moving on to the outer suburbs, occupying flats or boarding houses in the former, or, more commonly, sharing with a friend or relative[4] while awaiting a suburban home. There were variations in destinations according to origins: 93% of those coming from south of Auckland went to the outer suburbs, compared with only 59% of the Maoris from Northland. This difference seems to reflect the relative ignorance of the urban environment among those from the rural north, and their lack of awareness of the availability of state rental dwellings or housing loans, which together cater for the bulk of those Maoris who do move to the suburbs.

[4] There is a strong tradition of hospitality among Maoris which obliges householders to accommodate homeless relatives on both long- and short-term bases (Metge 1964).

No data are available on the younger migrants (under 21) who do not qualify for electoral registration; their destinations have been inferred from age structures (Rowland 1971b). Most of them apparently gravitate to the inner city and central suburbs, where flats and boarding houses are most frequent. By contrast, migrants to the outer suburbs are mostly in family groups (Rowland 1972).

This distribution pattern of Maoris in Auckland with two poles of concentration – inner city and outer, southern suburbs – has developed during the last two decades, mainly as a result of government policy and of the development of a large industrial node in South Auckland. Maoris are over-represented in a few suburbs mainly because of their economic status and cultural background, rather than any apparent great desire to live together (Ritchie 1961). Few can obtain homes without state assistance because of usually low incomes, large numbers of dependants, and lack of experience in managing household finances. So most are obliged to live in new areas where state flats and houses, Department of Maori Affairs houses and group development homes are found in association in large numbers, to the virtual exclusion of privately built dwellings.

Once in the city, Maoris are a highly mobile group, indirect evidence suggesting that they move twice as often as non-Maoris (Rowland 1972), no doubt partly because fewer of them have home-ownership ties. In general, this mobility emphasizes their bipolar distribution. The electoral roll data yielded information on 509 adult intra-urban migrations. The main source area for these was the inner city, where 47% originated. One-fifth of these remained within the inner city, while 80% of the remainder went to the outer suburbs and just under a fifth to the adjacent inner suburbs. There was also considerable migration (30% of the total) within the outer suburbs, but very little back towards the central suburbs and inner city.

Within Auckland, therefore, the main role of the inner city is as a source for centrifugal movements, mainly to the outer suburbs. It is the major destination for Maoris with little experience of urban life and those whose family situation makes suburban living unattractive. Considerable sorting of the population occurs in this area, as individuals and households constantly search for better housing conditions, but the major moves are into the outer suburbs for home ownership. Households consisting of parents and young children, and possessing either greater knowledge of urban life or friends or relatives in the outer suburbs, are much more likely to move directly to the suburbs. Because of overcrowding, however, they will seek their own home, leading to considerable migration within the outer suburbs, almost all of which takes place within a set of areas which are relatively accessible to the same employment centres.

Conclusions

Over the last forty-five years, and especially the last twenty-five, there has been a very large redistribution of the Maori population within New Zealand. Rural areas, especially those of Northland and Eastland, have experienced considerable net losses, particularly among the younger members of their communities, because their limited land holdings cannot support the rapidly increasing population of working age. This has created great spatial mobility much of it over relatively short distances, as individuals seek employment in the high-wage, low status jobs of local urban centres. In addition, however, a national migration system with Auckland as the principal destination has developed. Within that city, many migrants, especially the young, the single and those with little previous contact with urban life, have moved to the oldest and poorest housing of the inner city. But the growing amount of family migration and paternalistic attitude of the welfare state has resulted in large tracts of low-cost housing being provided for Maoris-in the outer suburbs, and it is to these areas that the majority of cityward migrants now head, along with those moving away from the inner city districts.

References

Brown, L. A. (1970) On the use of Markov chains in movement research. *Econ. Geogr.* 46, 393–403.

Brown, L. A. and Horton, F. E. (1970) Functional distance: an operational approach. *Geogr. Anal.* 2, 76–83.

Heenan, L. D. B. (1966) The changing South Island Maori population. *N.Z. Geogr.* 22, 125–65.

Hohepa, P. W. (1964) *A Maori community in Northland.* Dept of Anthrop., Univ. of Auckland, Bull. No. 1.

Johnston, R. J. (1971) *Urban residential patterns: an introductory review.* London.

Keown, P. A. (1971) The career cycle and the stepwise migration process. *N.Z. Geogr.* 27, 175–84.

Kernot, G. B. J. (1963) *Leadership among migrant Maoris.* Unpublished M.A. thesis, Univ. of Auckland.

Metge, A. J. (1964) *A new Maori migration.* London.

Pool, D. I. (1964) *The Maori population of New Zealand.* Unpublished Ph.D. thesis, Australian National Univ.

Poulsen, M. F. (1970) *Internal Maori migration, 1951–1969.* Unpublished M.A. thesis, Univ. of Canterbury.

Poulsen, M. F. and Johnston, R. J. (1973) Patterns of Maori migration, in Johnston, R. J. (ed.) *Urbanisation in New Zealand, geographical essays.* Wellington.

Ritchie, J. (1961) Together or apart: a note on Maori residential preferences. *J. Polynesian Soc.* 70, 194–9.

Rowland, D. T. (1971a) Maori migration to Auckland. *N.Z. Geogr.* 27, 21–37.

Rowland, D. T. (1971b) Age structures of Maoris in Auckland. *Proc., Sixth N.Z. Geogr. Conf.* 111–17.

Rowland, D. T. (1972) Patterns of Maori urbanisation. *N.Z. Geogr.* 28.

Whitelaw, J. S. (1971) Migration patterns and residential selections in Auckland, New Zealand. *Aust. Geogr. Stud.* 9, 61–76.

21   A spatio-temporal model of the mobility patterns in a multi-ethnic population, Hawaii

S. Mukherji

Introduction

The spatial mobility of people does not exist in a vacuum; it touches life at every point. If individuals are found to have broadly similar behaviour patterns, then we have the beginnings of generalization about the mobility behaviour of a group or a community. An individual's mobility pattern consists of different kinds of moves. The problem is to conceptualize an individual's aggregate mobility behaviour in a logical and organized way, and to identify the basic elements of that behaviour.

We can conceive of a mobility spectrum for each individual consisting of the aggregate of movements for various purposes occurring over different space zones for different time periods. Different kinds of movement can be classified according to this composite 'space-time-purpose of move' concept. Individual movers can be linked and separated in terms of their similar and dissimilar locations within it.

Another basic question is why different individuals vary in their mobility behaviour. An increasingly frequent strategy is to study all those factors found in a particular study area that have some impact upon mobility behaviour, and to analyse them in relation to different mobility patterns. The needs and aspirations of individuals obviously influence mobility behaviour but are extremely difficult to measure. We suggest, for the present, that some of these factors may be reflected through such variables as socio-economic status, roles in the family within the context of the wider community, desire to travel, participation in social-professional-organizational activities, and kinship ties (e.g. Mitchell 1961, 27; Chapman 1970, 220).

A working hypothesis could be that variations in mobility patterns found among the different ethnic groups of a community will be manifest in their varying lifestyles.

The three aims of this paper are to develop a methodology for the micro-level study of mobility, to integrate empirical data about individual mobility behaviour by employing statistical techniques that can group and generalize individual movements on increasing planes of conceptualization, and to attempt to explain why different ethnic groups have different mobility behaviour patterns.

Methodology

Migration is usually defined as a change of residence over the predefined boundaries of a place for a period of one or more years (Mangalam 1968, 8). Field experience shows, however, that people generally do not perceive migration as do demographers. For a community, a person is a migrant if he moves into, or out of, a place for the purpose of permanent residence. If that purpose is absent, then he may be considered simply a mover – a circulator or a visitor.

The study of mobility behaviour requires the collection of fine-grained data free from *a priori* definitional constraints (Chapman 1971, 1). Thus, for this study, movement embraces any territorial transfer of individuals involving a time period from twenty-four hours to thirty or forty years. The classification of kinds of movement (migration, circulation, visiting) was made after and not before the field research. The area for this research was Kurtistown, a small community 10 miles south of Hilo on the island of Hawaii. In 1971, Kurtistown had a multi-ethnic, multilingual and multi-religious population of about 735 persons living in 240 houses. The study area was divided into 4 sampling frames, each containing 60 households and each devised to reflect the main ethnic groups: Japanese, Filipino, part Hawaiian (Chinese-Hawaiian, Portuguese-Hawaiian), and a mixed population of Japanese, part-Hawaiians and Filipinos. Ten households were randomly selected from each sampling frame. The survey covered 233 persons who resided in 40 houses, but the basic unit of observation was the individual rather than the household.

Data were collected on all kinds of movement made in a lifetime, from daily commuting for five or six hours to workplace or school to migration from another country forty years ago. In this paper, moves of less than twenty-four hours are omitted. Territorial shifts varied from a housewife's bi-weekly visit to her ailing mother to a forest-contractor's quinquennial return from Guam to renew his American citizenship; from the exodus of newly graduated high-school students to other islands during pineapple harvesting to the occasional moves of Filipino daughters during

pregnancy from other islands of Hawaii to their mothers. Usually, the
first question asked was the place of birth, followed by: 'To which place
did you move from there? The exact date? Why did you move? By whom
were you accompanied? How long did you stay there? Which places did
you visit for a short or long time? Why did you move to those places?
Did you move to live permanently there?' All moves were recorded and
cross-checked to reduce error. Information was also collected about the
socioeconomic, cultural and demographic characteristics of the movers
(table 21.2), and investigations were made of desire to travel, how soon
people wished to move, and where they wanted to go.

In grouping fine-grained mobility data it is necessary, first, to define
migration and other broad categories of movement; and, second, to
conceptualize within each broad division an endless variety of individual
movement behaviour. Careful examination of the field data led to the
following definitions: *migration* is when a person moves with the purpose
of permanently residing in another place; *circulation* is when a person moves
with no purpose of residing permanently in another place and has the
intention of returning to the place of origin. These definitions closely
approximate those found in African mobility research (*Gould and
Prothero*). As Mangalam (1968, 8) notes, 'The period of time implied by
the term "permanent" cannot be generalized for all instances of migration,
but has to be considered individually in each specific case'; and in the
Kurtistown study a move for 'permanent residence' reflected a person's
expressed intention of having done just that. Circular movements that
involved an absence of more than one year were categorized as long-term
circulation, and those for less than one year as short-term circulation. Hence,
in the first instance, there are three broad categories of mobility: migration,
short-term circulation and long-term circulation.

Grouping movements

A central question is whether broad categories like migration and circulation
capture the essential features of an endless variety of mobility. Is there any
mathematical technique of grouping that can also provide the basis of a
conceptual typology?

Following geometry, the present approach can be termed a 'genetic
definition and classification of mobility types'. In geography we can perceive an individual as a point or a particle within the universe of space
and time, moving for a particular purpose. Obviously, movement geo-
metries cannot be expected to be as neatly defined as a circle or parabola,
nor can such a complex phenomenon as mobility be described by three
elements alone. To these, certain precise spatial and temporal elements
should be added, like distance, direction, frequency, and periodicity of a

move. Such a multidimensional genetic definition of mobility behaviour is very desirable.

The present study attempted to illustrate the approach by considering three major elements as a composite criterion. Certain combinations of space, time and purpose of move will produce distinctive mobility types which may be viewed as bands within the general mobility spectrum of the study population, and such combinations should emerge from the field data. Each individual mobility spectrum may consist of some or all bands of the general mobility spectrum, depending upon a person's movement behaviour and socioeconomic characteristics. Individuals with similar mobility bands or mobility behaviour therefore can be grouped together to indicate the generalized mobility behaviour of a group or a community.

The grouping procedure consisted of four steps. First, all movements of all individuals were listed, together with the distance traversed, duration of absence, and purpose of each move. Secondly, the broad categories of space zones, time domains and purposes of move were identified. Thirdly, all the space-time-purpose combinations of movements were identified and, finally, movements grouped into these combinations according to their inherent characteristics.

For the space dimension, five main zones were isolated within which movements are found to have been bounded in a specific manner. Consequently each movement has one specific space-time-purpose category (STP): for example, familial trips made within the State of Hawaii for a period of less than a week (bottom left corner, fig. 21.1); a movement for marriage from a foreign country that has been followed by forty years' residence in Kurtistown (top right corner, fig. 21.1). Only a few movements are shown for illustration.

Techniques of analysis

To collapse the spatio-temporal characteristics of the movement into fewer and generalized mobility behaviours, we resort to the systematics of numerical taxonomy (Sokal and Sneath 1963, 137). Assuming linearity of the data and making in a few instances necessary logarithmic transformations, the data sets (space, time and purpose of movements and the socioeconomic and other features of the movers) were subject to factor analysis. This systematically explored the many relationships between the space, time and purpose characteristics, from the collapse of which the precise nature and bases of several broad mobility types were identified. Similarly, factor analysis of the socioeconomic and other characteristics of movers identified the precise nature and bases of their 'attributes'. Finally, the underlying relationships between the bases of these two matrices were tested by canonical analysis to specify the degree of interdependence between mobility behaviour and the attributes of movers.

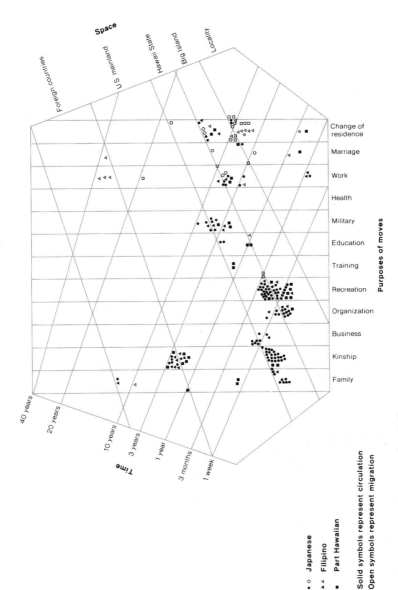

Figure 21.1 Spatio-temporal mobility types

Behaviours and attributes

Two factor analyses were performed on the data sets of the characteristics of movements made and of the movers themselves, to provide a principal components solution and an orthogonal rotation of the factor matrix (see Rummel 1970, 338–94). A set of 6 significant factors or dimensions, with loadings of values greater than .40 and eigenvalues of more than 1.0, was found in each case. In the analysis of movements 6 factors, explaining 76% of the total variance, were identified from 25 spatial, temporal and purpose characteristics of movements (table 21.1). For example, 4 movement characteristics of high loading – area of state, time period of less than one week, a recreational or kinship purpose – collapsed to constitute the first factor, which was identified as 'recreational or kinship move within the State of Hawaii for a period of less than a week'. Similarly variables like locality, time period of 10–20 years, residential change and migration grouped to form the second factor, here termed 'long-term residential migration within the locality'. Thus, all movements were systematically grouped into 6 generalized mobility behaviours.

In the second factor analysis of mover characteristics 6 factors, explaining 79% of the total variance, were identified from 21 characteristics (table 21.2). Variables like occupational prestige and family income constitute the first factor, identified here as 'socioeconomic status'; young age and unmarried status constitute the second; and a high association of education and married status formed the third, called 'educated and married'. These factors systematically collapsed all movers' characteristics into 6 main attribute types (table 21.2).

Relative position of ethnic groups in behavioural spaces

The two matrices of factor scores for mobility behaviour and mover attributes may also be viewed as describing two corresponding sets of abstract space: behaviour space and attribute space (figs. 21.2, 21.3). To plot the factor scores of each mover from the mobility matrix on this two-dimensional behaviour space consequently permits a graphic test of whether different ethnic groups vary in their mobility behaviour. Only 2 out of 15 such graphs are presented here (fig. 21.4) and table 21.3 summarizes their results. In general, there is a significant tendency both within and between ethnic groups towards a particular type of mobility behaviour.

Recreational moves take place mainly within the State of Hawaii and usually continue for one week; residential shifts are confined to a 10 mile radius around Kurtistown and normally occur at 10- to 20-year periods (fig. 21.4). These two kinds of mobility behaviour are completely different in space, time and purpose, as well as in their cyclical/non-cyclical nature, but more importantly the 3 ethnic groups show unique locational

Table 21.1

Factor analysis of Kurtistown mobility data: movements grouped by space, time and purpose of move (STP)

Variables (STP characteristics)	Factors					
	I Short-term state, re-creational move	II Local long-term (10–20-yr) move for residence change	III Island, organizational trip for 1 week to 3 months	IV US mainland business trip usually for 1 week	V 3–10-yr migration for work	VI 1–3-yr trip for military/kinship reason
1 Local	-.05	-.75*	-.07	-.03	.09	.05
2 Island	-.07	.03	.89*	-.01	.11	-.02
3 State	.94*	.12	-.02	-.05	.01	-.05
4 Mainland	-.04	.11	-.05	.78*	-.01	-.05
5 Foreign	-.08	.19	-.10	-.15	-.05	-.09
6 1 week	.84*	.02	.16	.16	-.03	.07
7 1 week–3 months	-.06	.18	.31*	-.08	-.42*	.20
8 3–12 months	-.04	.03	-.06	-.05	-.07	-.11
9 1–3 years	-.01	.12	-.03	-.10	.11	-.63*
10 3–10 years	-.10	.19	.00	-.01	.75*	.16
11 10–20 years	-.04	-.69*	-.03	-.04	.00	.01
12 20–40 years	-.04	-.10	-.01	-.04	.03	.01
13 Familial purpose	.04	.06	-.08	.03	-.01	.27
14 Kinship	.13	.08	-.01	-.05	-.21	-.43*
15 Work	-.04	.18	.01	-.09	.22*	-.07
16 Education	.22	.02	-.02	-.02	.09	-.12
17 Military	-.04	.10	-.04	.10	-.05	-.49*
18 Training	-.01	.03	-.01	-.01	-.10	.04
19 Organization	.15	-.00	.84*	.01	-.10	-.01
20 Recreational	.92*	-.00	.03	-.01	.00	.04
21 Marriage	.06	-.15	.01	-.07	.08	-.01
22 Residential change	.05	-.61*	.01	.01	.11	.02
23 Health	-.03	.06	.02	-.01	.03	.05
24 Business	.01	.01	.01	.70*	.01	-.01
25 Migration	-.13	-.36	.01	-.08	.66*	.13

* Factor loading of value greater than .40.

Table 21.2
Factor analysis of Kurtistown mobility data: grouping of attributes of movers

	Factors					
	I	II	III	IV	V	VI
Variables	Socio-economic status	Young single males	Married and educated	Filipino widower and kinship ties	Japanese in organizational activities	Low income dissatisfied. Wish to move soon
1 Age	-.20	.59*	-.11	.07	-.15	.15
2 Education	.00	.01	.87*	.04	.03	-.12
3 Occupation	.69*	.22	.01	-.10	.05	-.02
4 Family income	.82*	-.12	.04	.09	-.43*	.05
5 *Per capita* income	-.01	-.04	.16	.05	.01	-.57*
6 Married	.09	-.04	.57*	-.04	.01	-.03
7 Single	.07	.36*	-.06	-.01	.14	-.28
8 Widower	.15	.31	.03	-.42*	.12	.11
9 Head of household	.06	-.02	-.21	-.08	-.18	.10
10 Housewife	.45*	.03	.08	-.01	-.08	.06
11 Son	.33	.77*	.07	-.22	.10	.01
12 Daughter	-.09	-.04	.02	-.01	-.06	-.01
13 Organization	-.12	.02	-.01	.10	-.45*	-.09
14 Familial ties	.31*	-.05	.03	.03	.15	-.05
15 Kinship ties	-.08	-.06	.03	-.49*	-.24	.01
16 Japanese	.07	-.06	-.01	-.05	-.70*	-.02
17 Filipino	-.03	-.14	-.03	-.77*	-.07	-.01
18 Part Hawaiian	.08	.23	-.03	.03	.07	.02
19 Wish to move	-.03	.02	-.01	.11	.05	-.51
20 Area to move	.05	-.20	-.06	-.09	.07	.03
21 Year to move	-.01	-.02	-.05	-.12	-.11	-.40*

* Factor loadings of value greater than .40.

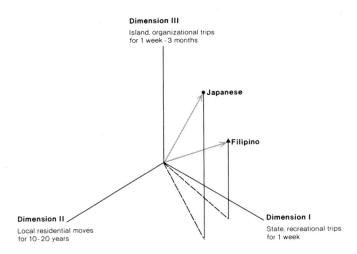

Figure 21.2 Behaviour spaces

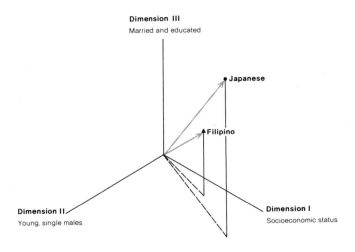

Figure 21.3 Attribute spaces

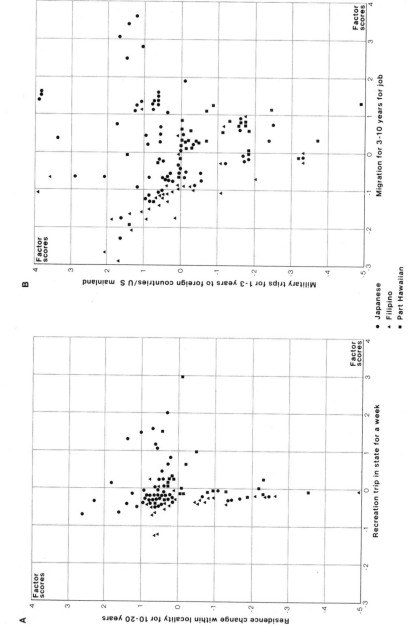

Figure 21.4 Relative position of the ethnic groups on two-dimensional behaviour space. (A) Short-term recreational moves versus long-term residence change. (B) Long-term migration versus long-term circulation

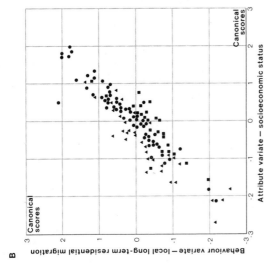

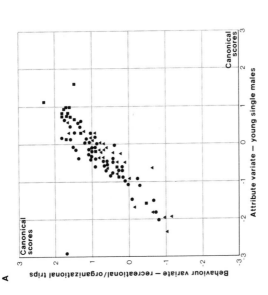

- Japanese
- Filipino
- Part Hawaiian

Figure 21.5 Relationships between pairs of canonical variates. (A) Short-term circulation of young people. (B) Residential migration of high-status people

patterns within the two-dimensional space that they define. Whereas the Japanese tend to make more recreational trips and change their place of residence more frequently, Filipinos register fewer moves for residential relocation and for recreation. The part-Hawaiians, on the other hand, make more recreational trips but are residentially less mobile. Of the ethnic groups, the Japanese migrate more for work and make more military trips that involve absences of three to ten and one to three years, respectively (fig. 21.5). Hawaiians occupy an intermediate position between Japanese and Filipinos; compared with the Japanese they usually make fewer military moves as well as migrate less frequently for work, but migrate more than Filipinos. Filipinos, on the other hand, have a unique position in that they undertake more military/kinship moves but migrate the least of all.

Differential mobility: some generalizations

The findings presented thus far demonstrate distinctive clusterings of mobility behaviour by ethnic groups (table 21.3). In general, the Japanese remain at the top of the scale of frequency of moves made for almost all kinds of reasons, but the position of Hawaiians and Filipinos changes from

Table 21.3

Relative position of three ethnic groups in mobility behaviour space*

Behaviour space		Organizational trip within island for 1-3 months			Business trip to US mainland for 1 week to 3 months			Military/kinship trip to foreign country/US mainland for 1-3 years			Local residential change for 10-20 years		
		Low	Med.	High	Low	Med.	High	Low	Med.	High	Low	Med.	High
Recreational trip in state for 1 week	High		J										J
	Med.	H									H		
	Low	F										F	
Organizational trip in island for 1-3 months	High					J							J
	Med.												
	Low				F	H					H	F	
Migration for job for 3-10 years	High		J						J				
	Med.												
	Low	F	H					H	F				

J = Japanese, F = Filipinos, H = part-Hawaiians
* High, medium and low categories are determined on the basis of factor scores correspnding to each factor on behaviour space. These are considered in relative terms: broadly, high scores above +1.00; medium scores around .0; and low scores below −1.00.

one graph to another, from one kind of mobility behaviour to another. In short-term circulation, Japanese and Filipinos lie on either extreme of the spectrum of mobility and Hawaiians in between. If military and kinship trips are called long-term circulation, then fig. 21.5 shows relative situations with respect to circulation and migration. For each ethnic group the location is unique: the Japanese have more migration and more long-term circulation; Hawaiians less migration and less long-term circulation, and Filipinos less migration but more long-term circulation than Hawaiians, sometimes even more than for some Japanese.

There are three important corollaries to these findings. The graphic technique, first, although lacking a computational algorithm, is based upon linear-system theory and uses the concepts of vector, vector space, and distance vector (figs. 21.2, 21.3). The resultant clusters delineate mobility patterns according to ethnic variations, so that ethnic groups can be distinguished in terms of preferences for certain types of mobility behaviour. Secondly, this technique, used for the first time in a study of mobility systems, may help to develop the required algorithms and to evolve a 'field theory' in mobility and migration studies. Thirdly, although these groups point out the difference in mobility patterns of ethnic groups they do not explain why such variations occur.

Relational field theory: canonical analysis

To understand why different communities vary in their mobility behaviour, a field-theoretic approach was taken and a canonical analysis performed upon the behaviour and attribute matrices specified previously. Field theory, according to Lewin (1951, 25), is simply a method of analysing causal relations and building scientific constructs. It views human behaviour in a total situation and identifies individual behaviour, personal characteristics and the environment as coexisting facts in the psychological field called life space. In a study of commodity flows, Berry (1966, 190) postulated that the spatial patterns of attributes of places and of the interactions among them are interdependent and isomorphic, while in a political conflict situation Rummel (1965, 183) formulated that the dyadic relationship (pair) of one nation to another in behaviour space is a linear function of distance vectors in attribute space that connect the pair of nations and of the proportionality constants (like regression weights). These are dynamic field theories and employ distance vectors on attribute space to explain paired interaction on behaviour space. In the present example a modified version of this approach is taken, which postulates that the mobility behaviour of an individual and his attributes are coexisting facts of the social situation and form a relational field. Instead of relating distance vectors to dyadic interaction, this approach aims to relate a specific attribute vector from attribute space with a specific mobility behaviour vector from behaviour space. The essential postulate of this relational field theory is that only one specific set of mobility behaviour is expected to be related to a specific set of mover attributes, and the central goal is to establish the interdependence of the mobility behaviour and attribute matrices. Since the bases of the behaviour and the attribute spaces are the same, then each can be predicted with the help of the other. Canonical analysis provides the appropriate model for testing the interdependence of these matrix-bases.

At the outset, there are two factor-score matrices, Behaviour (B) and Attribute (A), each n x p dimensions (n is the number of factors, p is the number of movers). Each vector of B provides a measure of an independent kind of mobility behaviour, and each vector of A provides the same for mover attributes. Canonical analysis of these two matrices transforms the vectors from B and A to an independent, uncorrelated pair of vectors, U and V, in both the matrices. Unlike factor analysis, which maximizes the variance explained by individual factors, canonical analysis maximizes the correlations between certain vectors of the B and A sets while reducing other correlations to zero. These correlations are called canonical correlations between each matched pair of variates, U and V (Cooley and Lohnes 1962, 36; Hooper 1959, 25; Berry 1966, 200). Corresponding to these correlations, P_k, are vectors of canonical coefficients, b'_k and a'_k (like factor loadings), which are regression weights that indicate which original sets of variables from B and A are involved in the new canonical vectors U_k and V_k and to what extent they determine variate scores of U_k and V_k. The new canonical vectors consist of standardized, zero mean and unit variance, canonical variates like factor scores (Phillips 1972, 1–22).

Unlike regression analysis, where there is a single solution because of only one dependent variable, canonical analysis yields a set of solutions as large as there are orthogonal patterns in B and A matrices. Since there were six patterns in our B and A matrices, six pairs of vectors, U_k and V_k, are extracted successively from B and A with decreasing order of predictability, in the same manner as in principal components analysis. Consequently the 'b' types of mobility behaviour and the 'a' types of attribute patterns are linked, and the canonical correlations between the pair of vectors maximized.

Results from this canonical analysis are presented in table 21.4. The trace correlation is high, .769, indicating a significantly high overlap in the two spaces described by the original behaviour and attribute variables, which in turn explain 64% of the variance in the behaviour indicators. The interdependence of the attribute and behaviour matrices is proven not only by such a high value for the trace correlation but also by the amount of total variance in behaviour explained by the attribute variables. Successive canonical correlation between pairs of canonical variates also provide five statistically significant measures of interdependence of the bases of the behaviour and attribute matrices. The largest canonical correlation is .969, showing a high interdependence between the behaviour and attribute sets of standardized variables in the first independent pair of variates. Corresponding

Table 21.4

Canonical structure matrix

A. *Behaviour variables*	Canonical variates					
	Separate patterns of relationships between variable					
	1	2	3	4	5	6
1. Short-term, state, recreation trips	.63	−.34	−.32	−.26	.46	.28
2. Local, long-term residential moves for 10–20 years	.40	.77	.23	−.03	.33	.07
3. Island, organizational trips for 1 week to 3 months	.78	.18	.46	.20	−.21	−.20
4. US mainland business trips for 1 week	−.11	.42	−.12	.79	−.43	−.05
5. Migration for work for 3–10 years	−.27	.26	−.59	.29	.14	−.58
6. Trips for military/kinship purposes for 1–3 years	.38	−.39	.77	−.42	.42	−.45

B. *Canonical correlation*						
(Statistical dependence between each matched pair of variates)	.969	.926	.882	.792	.585	.04

C. *Attribute variables*	Canonical variates					
1. Socioeconomic status	.30	.66	.35	.06	.58	.01
2. Young single males	.73	.46	.25	.34	−.33	.09
3. Education and married	−.56	.24	.11	.11	−.67	.38
4. Filipino and kinship	−.05	.36	.81	.29	.15	.28
5. Japanese in organizational activity	−.11	.35	−.20	.80	−.33	−.25
6. Low income dissatisfied	.17	.10	−.14	.36	−.18	−.87

D. *Proportion of total variance*							
(Percentage of variance among all variables involved in particular variate pairs)	100.00	19.58	17.25	16.81	16.47	15.23	14.62

Notes:

1. Trace correlation (general overlap between attributes and behaviour) −. 769.
2. Figures in parts A and C represent canonical loadings: degree and direction of relationships of variables with this pattern.
3. Variables most highly related to a particular mobility behaviour underlined.

canonical loadings describing the correlations of the variables with the variates are also given for the behaviour and attribute matrices. Comparison of the loadings for all variables with the pair of variates permits the identification of those attribute variables most highly related to particular mobility behaviour(s) (underlined in table 21.4).

In the first pair of variates, short-term recreational trips within the State of Hawaii and organizational-participational trips within the island (behaviour variate) are highly correlated with young single males (attribute variate). Since each behaviour and attribute variate are linear combinations of the vectors of earlier behaviour and attribute matrices, the interpretation of such relationships of mobility types to attribute patterns becomes difficult. The following kinds of relationships can, however, be written for new canonically-transformed scores on the first behaviour and attribute variates:

u_1 = .63 (short-term recreational trip) +.40 (local long-term residential moves) +.78 (island, organization-participation moves for less than 3 months) −.11 (US mainland business trips) −.27 (migration for work for 3–10 years) +.38 (military-kinship trips for 1–3 years).

v_1 = .30 (socioeconomic status) +.73 (young single males) −.56 (educated and married) −.05 (Filipino and kinship) −.11 (Japanese in organizational activity) + .17 (low income dissatisfied).

This can be interpreted that, for the first set of canonical analysis, the attribute 'young single males' is a more important variable than socio-economic status, education, desire to move or ethnicity in explaining the short-term moves for recreational and organizational-participational purposes. Such is, of course, to be expected, but this attribute alone can explain 50% (loading of .73 squared and multiplied by 100) of the variation involved in the first pair of canonical variates (19.58% of the total variance).

Successive canonical correlations, canonical loadings and corresponding patterns of relationships between the behaviour and attribute sets can be interpreted in like manner. The second set of variates links socioeconomic status with residential migration; the third, Filipinos who have stronger kinship bonds with kinship-oriented or military trips for 1–3 years; the fourth, Japanese who participate more in organizational activities with business trips to the United States mainland; and the fifth pair of variates, socioeconomic status with recreational trips. The sixth pair of variates, in which low-income, dissatisfied people are linked with migration to work for an absence of 3–10 years, has a very low, statistically insignificant correlation and is of doubtful value. In fact, the one pattern of movement for which the canonical analysis could not provide a satisfactory explanation was migration to work. Otherwise the structural relationships between mover characteristics and patterns of mobility behaviour have been specified and a quite satisfactory test of relational field theory thereby achieved.

Relative position of ethnic groups in canonical space

Canonical scores for each mover are calculated for each pair of canonical variates in the same way as detailed above: the sum of the weights (canonical loadings) times the data products for each mover for all variables in a specified matrix (behaviour and attribute). This gives one score each for two variates, behaviour and attributes. Canonical scores are plotted for each of six pairs of canonical variates producing six diagrams, of which only the first two are presented here (fig. 21.5).

In each case, only the most important attribute type that links the most important mobility behaviour type is labelled in the diagram, even though both dimensions are vectors or linear combinations of variables. In fig. 21.5A there are no distinguishable ethnic variations for short-term, recreational-organizational movements. This is again to be expected: young single males of all three ethnic groups show an almost equal tendency for such short-term circulatory behaviour. Fig. 21.5B, on the other hand, indicates a causal relation between differences in socioeconomic status and long-term residential moves within the Kurtistown locality. A greater number of Japanese register higher socioeconomic status and also make frequent changes in their residences. Part-Hawaiians rank next, followed by Filipinos, but the difference between them reflects less the frequency of residential moves and more the lower socioeconomic status of the Filipinos. In both the diagrams individuals are highly clustered along the least-squares lines, thus confirming the almost one-to-one relationship between the attribute and behaviour types. Increasingly diffused patterns are to be found in the second and subsequent diagrams because of 'random noise' due to other variables involved in the attribute and behaviour variates. The main variations among the three communities on the canonical spaces are summarized in table 21.5 and indicate that they are probably due to varying levels of cultural adaptation.

Mobility patterns and modernization: a generalized model

Which, of the many factors discussed here, really underlies the mobility behaviour of different communities? Can variations in mobility patterns be explained in terms of a generalized concept like economic development or social change? At the present state of knowledge in the social sciences, there can be no decisive answers to these questions. Therefore by way of conclusion this paper attempts to relate differential spatial mobility to a tentative concept like the varying lifestyles of different communities.

Table 21.5

*Relative position of ethnic groups in canonical spaces**

Canonical space	Behaviour variate			

ATTRIBUTE

1 — Short-term recreational-organizational trips — Young single males

	Low	Med.	High
High			H, J
Med.		F	
Low			

2 — Long-term residential migration in the locality — Socio-economic status

	Low	Med.	High
High			J
Med.		H, F	
Low			

3 — Military/kinship moves for 1–3 years — Filipino and kinship

	Low	Med.	High
High			F
Med.		H	J
Low			

VARIATE

4 — US mainland business trips for 1 week — Japanese in organizational activities

	Low	Med.	High
High			J
Med.		F	H
Low			

5 — Short-term recreational trips — Socio-economic status

	Low	Med.	High
High			J
Med.		F	H
Low			

6 — Migration for jobs for 3–10 years — Low income dissatisfied

	Low	Med.	High
High			J
Med.		H	
Low			

J = Japanese, H = part-Hawaiians, F = Filipinos

* High, medium, and low categories are determined as indicated in the footnote to table 21.3.

Zelinsky offers some clues about the evolutionary nature of spatial behaviour, believing that: 'There are definite, patterned, regularities in the growth of personal mobility through space-time during recent history, and these regularities comprise an essential component of the modernization process' (Zelinsky 1971, 221). This suggests an association between spatial mobility and modernization, the precise nature of which is not clear. Modernization, to one authority, is 'the process by which individuals change

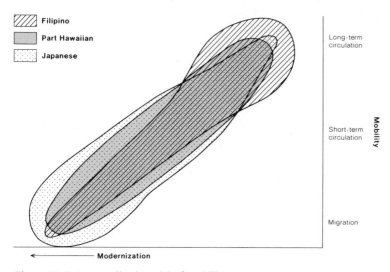

Figure 21.6 A generalized model of mobility patterns

from a traditional way of life to a more complex, technologically advanced, and rapidly changing style of life' (Rogers 1969, 14), and it may be postulated that such changes will be reflected in more education, higher standards of living, improved socioeconomic status, greater information, and wider and more complex organizational activities. Yet it is not currently known which, if any, of these variables best indicates or measures the stage of modernization for a specified population.

The present study on the island of Hawaii took a different strategy, for there was no attempt to measure modernization *per se.* However, some variables have been identified that have, as the foregoing analysis demonstrates, an appreciable impact upon the movement behaviour of individuals and that can be viewed collectively as aspects of modernization with particular revelance to mobility.

Stimulated by Chapman's (1970, 242) recent work, each of the two-dimensional spaces previously discussed has been superimposed and smoothed into a composite diagram (fig. 21.6). On the X-axis, modernization denotes the sum total of mover attributes previously identified, while the Y-axis depicts the three generalized mobility categories of migration, short-term circulation and long-term circulation (the Y-axis is not to scale and long-term circulation is placed first as a matter of convenience in illustration). Migration includes moves for residential relocation and long-term absence for work; short-term circulation subsumes recreational, organizational and business trips; and long-term circulation refers to kinship or military moves.

The diagram portrays a definite and unique location for the Japanese, Part-Hawaiian and Filipino communities of Kurtistown in terms of different mobility patterns and varying phases of modernization. The Japanese have high socioeconomic status, more education, greater participation in formal organizations, looser kinship ties, and more desire to travel; as such, they are placed high in terms of 'modernization'. They have a higher rate of migration and short-term circulation but indulge relatively less in long-term circulation. Filipinos are characterized by stronger kinship ties, less education, fewer organizational activities, and lower socioeconomic status. Compared with the Japanese, they evidence less modernization and their mobility is most often long-term circulation, with comparatively little migration and even less short-term circulation. Part-Hawaiians, on the other hand, are between, having strong familial and kinship ties, less education, average socioeconomic status, and a higher incidence of recreational and organizational activities. They are placed midway along the scale of modernization. Part-Hawaiians have a strong propensity for short-term circulation but, compared with the two other communities, have no clear-cut tendency to either migration or long-term circulation.

Conclusions

Each ethnic community within the larger population has its own mobility patterns that indicate differing levels of modernization at a particular point in time. Naturally such patterns may alter over time. Following Zelinsky (1971, 221) this process can be termed the 'mobility transition', wherein mobility systems change over time with different phases of modernization. Some ethnic groups, even some societies, may pass to a new phase of transition quickly, others may take longer. Over time some groups may manifest more migration than long-term circulation; some others more migration and short-term circulation but little long-term circulation. When and how such changes might occur at what point in time is a fundamental but as yet unanswered question. The present paper has had the more limited objective of attempting to show that mobility transitions do exist. The idea of transition is very new, and very few empirical or theoretical tests are available. A major future venture in population geography should be to select from Zelinsky's hypothesis and test with data from the real world.

The present paper raises more questions than it answers. It indicates the need for a genetic definition of mobility types, for evolving conceptual constructs through inductive research strategies, for successive approximations in generalizing from micro-level data of individual mobility behaviour, and for the increasing use of mathematics for the more powerful integration of concept, technique and theory in mobility and migration research. Mobility behaviour must be viewed as an integral part of life; we need to known more precisely what underlies the widely ranging mobility behaviour of individuals.

No matter how small-scale nor how preliminary, studies such as this serve two useful purposes: in the development of concepts and models, and in the area of prediction, for mobility and other kinds of spatial behaviour. The more accurate are such predictions, then the greater their value in all kinds of social planning.

Acknowledgements

I am most grateful to Professor Murray Chapman, of the University of Hawaii and the East-West Population Institute, for all kinds of help without which this study would not have been possible. My thanks are also due to Professors Rummel, Riddell, Sang-Woo Rhee, Murton, Earickson and Schwind. Fieldwork was done under the Human Ecology Program of the University of Hawaii and financed by the National Science Foundation.

References

Berry, B. J. L. (1966) *Essays on commodity flows and the spatial structure of the Indian economy.* Chicago.

Chapman, M. (1970) *Population movement in tribal society: the case of Duidui and Pichahila, British Solomon Islands.* Ph.D. dissertation, Univ. of Washington.

Chapman, M. (1971) *Population research in the Pacific Islands: a case study and some reflections.* Working Pap. No. 17, East-West Pop. Inst., East-West Center, Honolulu.

Cooley, W. W. and Lohnes, P. R. (1962) *Multivariate procedures for the behavioral sciences.* New York.

Hooper, J. S. (1959) Simultaneous equations and canonical correlation theory. *Econometr.* 27, 25–50.

Lewin, K. (1951) *Field theory in social sciences.* New York.

Mangalam, J. J. (1968) *Human migration: a guide to migration literature in English, 1955–1962.* Lexington.

Mitchell, J. C. (1961) The causes of labour migration, in *Commissions for technical cooperation in Africa south of Sahara* (eds.) *Migrant labour in Africa.* Abidjan.

Phillips, W. R. (1972) *Introduction to canonical analysis.* Behavioral Sciences Laboratory, Ohio State Univ. (mimeographed).

Rogers, E. M. (1969) *Modernization among peasants: the impact of communication.* New York.

Rummel, R. J. (1965) A field theory of social action with application to conflict within nations. *General Systems, Yearbook Soc. Gen. Sys. Res.* 10, 183–211.

Rummel, R. J. (1970) *Applied factor analysis.* Evanston.

Sokal, R. R. and Sneath, P. H. (1963) *Principles of numerical taxonomy.* San Francisco.

Zelinsky, W. (1971) The hypothesis of the mobility transition. *Geogr. Rev.* 61, 219–49.

22 Marriage migration in rural India*

M. J. Libbee and
D. E. Sopher

Geographers concerned with the spatial organization of society have been
giving increasing attention to the marriage field, outlined by the location of
affines. As a contribution to comparative spatial studies of social interaction,
this paper identifies variation in the size of marriage fields in rural India by
utilizing census data dealing with population movements.

The rural marriage field in India

In India, where the almost universal custom is for brides to move to the
groom's home, often located in a different village, the village marriage field
is a composite of distinct 'caste' fields, each related to a discrete distribution
of potential partners within the circle of an endogamous group. But marriage
to many such within this circle is in some regions prohibited as having an
incestuous character. In the Western Gangetic Plain, in particular, the pro-
hibition extends to otherwise permissible caste partners who reside in the
same village and, sometimes, in contiguous villages. An associated effect
seems to be a pushing out of the 'bride-shed' much farther than the actual
distribution of permissible partners would seem to require.

The result is both a crater effect in the curve of distance-decay and a gentle
slope of decay for tens of miles beyond the village (fig. 22.1). The method
used to standardize marriages is Perry's (1969), modified slightly here in order
to make different marriage fields directly comparable. Although bus and
bicycle have been less generally available in India, and rural population
density in the Indian districts involved is many times greater than in Dorset,
the Indian fields are spread much wider than the English ones. It is estimated
that the combined affinal ties of an Indian village of this kind will link it with
between 200 and 400 villages, a potential information field of perhaps a
quarter of a million persons. Marked variation in the size of marriage fields
may therefore have significant implications for other kinds of social circulation,

* The notes for this chapter will be found on pp. 357–9.

for the spread of ideas, the range of group loyalty, and other elements of the spatial structure of society.

Materials for the construction of an all-India map of average marriage distance have hitherto been wanting. Village monographs that provide reliable measures of marriage migration distances are rare, and even sound estimates of average distances are scarce in village studies. Such data, moreover, are not available for many linguistic-cultural regions within India.

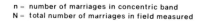

n = number of marriages in concentric band   D₁ = radius of inner edge of concentric band
N = total number of marriages in field measured D₂ = radius of outer edge of concentric band

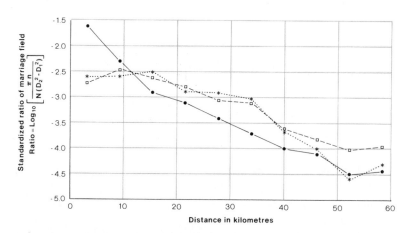

• Dorset (Perry 1969), median distance: 9.0 km
* Aligarh District (Marriot 1951-2), median distance: 22.5 km
□ Saharanpur District (Mahar 1966), median distance: 23.0 km

Figure 22.1 Marriage fields: India and England

Nevertheless, scholars have been able to gain some sense of the general pattern from the diffuse ethnographic literature and the intuition acquired through fieldwork in different Indian locales. Although her work has not gone unchallenged, Karve (1968) undertook to divide India into five 'kinship regions', grouping linguistic regions according to her impression of the level of village exogamy and the size of the marriage field, among other criteria (fig. 22.2).

Until 1961, *Census of India* place-of-birth data differentiated only persons born within a district (an administrative unit with a median area of about 9,000 sq. km) from those born outside it, outside the state, or outside the country. Even at this scale, a large number of females were recorded as having migrated across district boundaries in many parts of India between birth and date of enumeration. This movement has long been attributed in part to marriage migration. It was also recognized that the ratio of such

Karve's hypothetical
'zones of kinship organization'

☐ Northern zone

▨ Central zone

▨ Southern zone

▨ Eastern zone

0   250   500 Kilometres

0   150   300 Miles

Figure 22.2 India: reference map

female migrants to the female population of a district would vary inversely with the size of a district, making it difficult to identify variation in marriage practice. And then most students of migration have used the same data to answer questions about population movement in relation to economic trends; marriage migration, largely a balancing migration, was if anything to be screened out from the statistics.

Estimating the marriage field from census data

The 1961 census published additional place-of-birth data: statistics from rural places of enumeration, henceforth called 'villages' for convenience, were separated from urban data and the former category 'born within the district' was further differentiated into 'born in place of enumeration' and

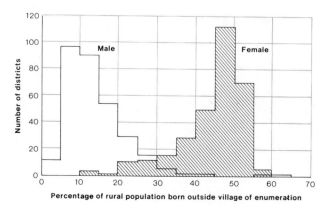

Figure 22.3 Village immigration: male and female

'born elsewhere in the district'. The rural place of enumeration is the 'revenue village', which is not always characterized by the predominance of a single agglomeration. Even when not, the revenue village is likely to represent a social entity and it is assumed here that census villages are social units within which distance has no significance.

The new material showed for the first time the full extent of female migration between villages, the only available explanation for the great bulk being that it is marriage migration. From data for almost all districts, the following relationships have emerged. The percentages of rural males and females who were born outside the village of enumeration show virtually no correlation with each other ($r = +.001$) and have different frequency distributions (fig. 22.3). There is fair correspondence ($r = +.69$) between the proportions of females enumerated in the village of birth and of those never married; the best-fitting regression line has a slope close to unity. Some degree of village exogamy thus appears to be widely practised in India. As expected, the ratio of females born elsewhere within the district to all those born outside the village shows a moderate positive correlation with district area. It appeared reasonable to suppose, then, that with correction for the area of the district, the 1961 data could provide an index of the average marriage distance: with district size and shape held constant, it would follow that the larger the ratio of within-district marriage migration to all marriage migration, the smaller must be the marriage field.

Subsequent investigation showed that use of the numbers of female migrants alone led to very large anomalies in certain districts, such as Dehra Dun and Naini Tal in the northern *tarai* and foothill zone, which had experienced substantial rural colonization in recent decades. These had abnormally high proportions of male inmigrants, and an estimate of the associated pull on females was made by examining the data for districts in Uttar Pradesh and Bihar. The assumption was made that each male migrant to a village or district is accompanied by .75 females, and this number (.75 x number of male migrants) was subtracted from the female migrants, the remainder being considered as migrating brides. Similar difficulties arose in several districts bordering Pakistan because of the large refugee component in their rural populations, and it was decided to omit from computation persons recorded as having been born outside the present national territory. Hereafter, the number of female migrants to village and district should be understood to have been corrected in these ways in all cases.

Libbee derived a formula to predict in effect the probability that any straight line of fixed length, D, taken at random and having at least one end within a circle of radius R, will lie completely within that circle (Libbee 1971). The apparent simplicity of the problem is deceiving and in the end an approximate formulation was obtained for the probability value, G.[1] Only a graphic solution could be found for the next step, the calculation of D, given G and R. G was then replaced by the ratio of females born outside the village but within the district to all females born outside the village (the number of females being corrected as above), and R by the value $\sqrt{A/\pi}$, A being the district area. The corresponding value, D, read from the derived probability tables, was taken as the *estimated median marriage distance*.

This procedure requires the additional assumptions: marriage migration is random in direction; district boundaries have no effect on marriage migration; the population is evenly distributed; every female who has migrated for marriage has moved the median marriage distance; a district is generalized as a circle of area equal to the district area. Note that the median distance does not include the zero travel distances of intravillage marriages.

Estimated marriage distances for all districts were divided into five classes of equal size and these were mapped (fig. 22.4). While the assumptions

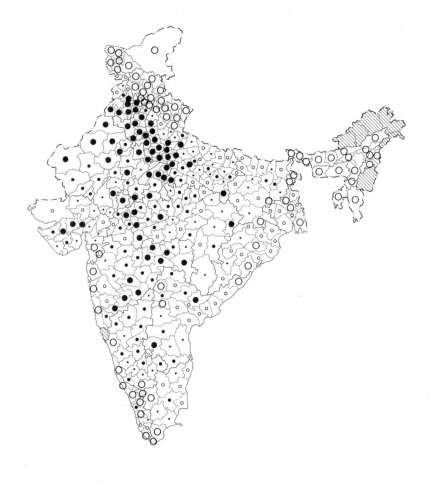

Kilometres (approx.)		Miles
under 7.50	◯	under 4.50
7.50 - 14.90	◦	4.50 - 9.49
15.00 - 19.90	·	9.50 - 12.49
20.00 - 29.90	•	12.50 - 18.49
30.00 and over	●	18.50 and over
▨	Data not available	

Figure 22.4 Estimated median marriage distance

underlying the estimates are clearly not altogether realistic, they provide
the basis for a relative measure of areal changes in marriage distance. Thus,
before the distribution pattern is discussed, evidence bearing on the validity
of the estimates will be considered.

First, there is a low correlation between estimated marriage distance and
district area, indicating that a satisfactory correction for a major source of
difficulty has been made. Secondly, it is intuitively satisfying that the
pattern does not seem to be the result of random processes. There is marked
spatial clustering of like values, with some clusters appearing to correspond
to conventionally recognized cultural-ecological areas. Note particularly the
distribution of high and low values in the northwest, which corresponds to
the pattern of plain and highland.

From the few available estimates of rural marriage fields for a single village
or a small group, fourteen median distances were approximated and correlated
with the corresponding district estimates, giving a coefficient of +.78. The
best-fitting regression line suggests that the estimated marriage distances may
underestimate actual low values and overestimate high ones.

For Bihar alone, the census provides a full interdistrict rural migration
matrix. Analysis of this was undertaken, assigning district values to the
district centroids to ascertain whether distance-decay rates of female
migration correspond inversely to the estimated marriage distances. This
approach was unsuccessful chiefly because of the large intercentroid
distances (mean and median approximately 230 km) and the very small
numbers involved in long-distance transactions. There are other difficulties :
Bihar has only seventeen districts; nine of these border other states; there
has been agricultural colonization in the northeast and mining and industrial
development in the southeast, some in dispersed or suburban locations
classed as 'rural'. Some regularities appear in the distance-decay equations,
which have high correlation coefficients, but the slopes and residuals show
little correspondence with the estimated marriage distances. It is surmised
that such marriage migration as is involved in movements of more than
75 km is associated with a small, specialized stratum of the rural population.
Intuitively interpreted, the patterns show two-way exchanges between the
more literate districts of the western plains and the southeastern area of
economic dynamism; the apparent prestige of marriage ties with Shahabad
District in the west; a powerful barrier effect exerted by the Ganges river
on marriage transactions between the northern and southern plains. This
may be reflected in moderately low estimated marriage distances in the
northwestern districts.

From the correspondence between the proportions of unmarried females
and those enumerated in their birthplace, a measure of local endogamy was
sought in the expectation that it would vary inversely with marriage distance.
Correcting the female population as before for male-associated economic

**Percentage (estimated) of married females
born in village of enumeration**

■	under 21.5
▪	21.5 - 27.4
·	27.5 - 32.4
▫	32.5 - 45.4
☐	45.5 and over
▨	Data not available

Figure 22.5 Estimated local endogamy ratio

migration, an estimated endogamy ratio, ER, was computed,[2] this being
the estimated ratio of females marrying within the village to females ever
married (fig. 22.5). A moderate correspondence is seen (figs. 22.4 and 22.5),
although the correlation coefficient is somewhat low (r = −.38). A scatter
diagram discloses a closer correspondence in that an apparent marriage-
distance 'ceiling' decreases regularly as the village endogamy ratio increases;
high levels of village exogamy may, however, be associated with short
marriage distances. The two variables are virtually independent statistically
since the estimate of marriage distance does not incorporate the zero distances
of cases of village endogamy. Large residuals appear in separate clusters, large
negative ones being found chiefly in the northwestern highlands and spottily
in the northeastern wet-rice region, large positive residuals mostly in a wedge
of semi-arid to arid open plains in northern Rajasthan and adjoining districts
in the Punjab and Uttar Pradesh. Ecological factors and associated differences
in 'surface friction' seem to be involved. The coherence of the regional pattern
of endogamy, its general correspondence to gross estimates of village endogamy rates derived from some twenty-five case studies, and its relationship
to the pattern of marriage distances, lend considerable intuitive support to
the validity of the latter.

A final test was made, using these endogamy ratios to derive from the
1931 census data a crude estimate of marriage distances for that period, and
these were compared to similarly derived 1961 values.[3] Only districts whose
territory had remained virtually unchanged could be compared, and of these
a set of sixty-eight, comprising all such districts in Uttar Pradesh, Bihar and
Tamil Nadu (Madras), was used. Although total district population had to be
used in place of rural population, this did not introduce much distortion: this
set of 1961 marriage distances correlated closely with the first set. When
these crudely computed 1961 estimates were then correlated with the comparable 1931 values, a correlation coefficient of +.93 was obtained. Clearly,
areal *differences* in the flows of females that are being interpreted as marriage
migration were stable over the thirty-year period. Since this is to be expected
of marriage migration, given the stability of rural social institutions in India,
the interpretation is further supported. The range of individual movements
did not stay the same; the regression equations predict a 50% increase in
the marriage distance, which can be explained as a consequence of the
increase in local transportation facilities between the time of the generation
preceding 1931 and the following one.

Implications for the social geography of India

If one accepts the general validity of the areal variation in these census-derived
patterns of marriage distance and village endogamy, what are the implications
for the social geography of India? Critical features of the so-called 'northern'

kinship structure are confined to the northwestern plains and plateau margins, with a conspicuous southward extension through Malwa to the central Deccan. Conventional extension of the region eastward through eastern Uttar Pradesh and Bihar (Karve 1968, 104–5; Mandelbaum 1970, 101) is called into question, so far as these criteria are concerned.

The contrasting pattern of a high level of local endogamy and short marriage distances, usually associated with a 'southern' kinship type, is well developed in Kerala and some adjoining districts, but it is not predominant throughout the southern, Dravidian-speaking zone. The Keralan pattern represents an exceptional situation, since much of the population is matrilineal. The combination of fairly high local endogamy with medium-sized marriage fields, such as is found in Karnataka (Mysore), suggests a mixing of kinship structures. This is far south of the conventional north-south transition zone, usually placed in Maharashtra and Gujarat (fig. 22.2). The combination of small field and high endogamy that occurs in Kerala is also found in predominantly Muslim Kashmir, another exceptional area because of the prevalence of the North Indian Muslim preference for cross-cousin marriage and local endogamy. The same combination of traits appears on the maps in much of the northeastern wet-rice zone. Within the Indian Himalayan system – Kumaun and Himachal Pradesh – and in the Konkan and some northeastern districts, marriage distances are short, but the level of village exogamy varies from high to medium. This may be a consequence of severe 'surface friction' imposed by terrain, drainage patterns, and the character of the agricultural landscape; an alternative possibility is that boundary interference causes the estimate of marriage distance to contract, for example, in the Konkan, and this possibility merits investigation.

In general, local exogamy and the fetching of brides from some distance seem to be more widely practised *throughout* India than is generally acknowledged in the literature, although by no means as universally in the north as is supposed. The average Indian field, while less extensive than those measured by Mahar and Marriot, is well above the rural European range indicated by Perry's data (fig. 22.1).

The two distributions mapped would seem to give some support to speculation (Karve 1968, 251–2) that the 'northern' principle of extended exchange may be associated with a tradition of pastoralism, i.e. large-scale cattle pastoralism, while the territorially more closed 'southern' system of immediate exchange may be associated with an agricultural society that lacks such traditions altogether. The impression is strong that some variation in the pattern is related to ease or difficulty of local surface movement. Whether there is a relationship also with population density and with the size and spacing of settlements, separate from the possible effects on these of different degrees of surface friction, is a question that needs to be pursued.

Before such speculation can be carried much further, one must test these results against more data from the literature and from additional village studies. A sampling of villages by region would provide data for a strong test.[4] Modifying some of the necessarily crude assumptions of the predictive model might wait until then. As a first approximation of variation throughout India of a surrogate for the mean information field, it may, even at this stage in its development, find use in comparative studies of regional social networks, innovation diffusion, patterns of caste solidarity, and the like. At the very least, it should suggest fruitful lines of enquiry to the social scientist and the social historian concerned with India, while adding something to our understanding of circulation associated with marriage.

Notes

1. In a circular district, X, of radius R (fig. 22.6), if every one of an evenly distributed population (of brides) migrates a distance, D, in a straight line, what is the ratio, G, of the population that will find new homes within the district? All brides originating within circular area A, i.e. at a distance D or greater from the circumference of the district, will find destinations within the district, but only a portion of those originating in annulus B will do so. This proportion is estimated by the probability, K, of within-district migration from any point on the circle, radius P, which bisects annulus B. The probability of within-district migration at the circumference of the district is assumed to be sin Q/2, and this increases to 1 at the circumference of A. K is found by proportioning this increasing probability according to the ratio to D of the distance of the circumference of circle radius P from the circumference of the district, i.e. $R - P$. Then, $G = (A + KB)/X$, or

$$G = \frac{(R - D)^2 + K[R^2 - (R - D)^2]}{R^2},$$

where

$$K = \frac{\sin Q}{2} + \left(\frac{R - P}{D}\right)\left(1 - \frac{\sin Q}{2}\right),$$

$$P = \sqrt{\frac{(R - D)^2 + R^2}{2}},$$

and sin

$$Q = \frac{\sqrt{R^2 - \left(\frac{2R^2 - D^2}{2R}\right)^2}}{D}.$$

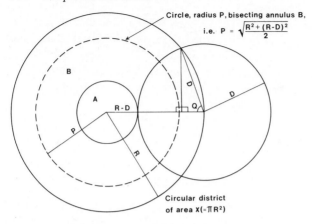

Figure 22.6 Method of estimating proportion of migrants crossing boundary of a region

2.

$$ER = \dfrac{\dfrac{FBIV}{RF - .75\ MBOV} - \dfrac{RFUW}{RF}}{1 - \dfrac{RFUW}{RF}},$$

where FBIV = females born in village of enumeration; RF = rural females; MBOV = rural males born outside village of enumeration; RFUW = rural females never married.

3. As before, D, the estimated marriage distance, is extrapolated from the computed table, giving G, the ratio of female marriage migrants from within the district to all female marriage migrants, for all combinations of D and X, the district area. G is now estimated thus:

$$G = \dfrac{(FP - FUW)(1 - ER) - (FBOD - .75\ MBOD)}{(FP - FUW)(1 - ER)},$$

where FP = total female population; FUW = females never married; ER = district endogamy rate as computed for 1961; FBOD = females born outside the district; MBOD = males born outside the district. Considerable variation in ER, such as might result from using a standard endogamy rate for each state, would not change G by much, and would have hardly any effect on the correlation of the 1931 and 1961 values.

4. Further research, including some fieldwork in India, has suggested some useful adjustments to the model. Rural male migration shows remarkable

regional variation, indicating the presence of some sort of non-economic mechanism. Tentative recalibrations of the models point to an increased marriage distance estimate and a decreased endogamy ratio in the area of northern Maharashtra and Madhya Pradesh. In Uttar Pradesh and elsewhere in northern India, it is customary for girls to go through the initial marriage ceremony, *shādī*, and to wait at home for several years before *gaunā*, that is, moving to the husband's home and consummating the marriage. Census enumeration during this period will record the girl as married and living in the village of birth, although she will no longer do so after *gaunā*. Some experiments with the data on marital status by age classes suggest that this factor may have been inflating the endogamy estimates in eastern Uttar Pradesh, Bihar and northern Madhya Pradesh.

References

Karve, I. (1968) *Kinship organization in India* (3rd edn). Bombay and New York.

Libbee, M. J. (1971) *A model estimating marriage distances in India.* Unpublished M.A. thesis, Syracuse Univ.

Mahar, J. M. (1966) *Marriage networks in the Northern Gangetic Plain.* Unpublished Ph.D. dissertation, Cornell Univ.

Mandelbaum, D. G. (1970) *Society in India* (2 vols). Berkeley and Los Angeles.

Marriot, M. (1951–2) Unpublished field survey data, used here by kind permission of the author.

Perry, P. J. (1969) Working-class isolation and mobility in rural Dorset, 1837–1936: a study of marriage distances. *Trans. Inst. Brit. Geogr.* 49, 121–40.

23 Retirement migration in France

F. Cribier

Introduction

While an interest in the age structure has been considerably to the fore in
the study of developing countries, the human sciences in the last two decades
have directed interest to the age structure of developed industrial societies.
Geographers may follow demographers, sociologists and psychologists in
paying attention both to age and generation, to the temporal dimension
of the life cycle and to its spatial aspects (Rochefort 1965). Geographers
have shown some interest in the ageing of population in the rural areas of
Europe caused by the exodus of young people and a consequent decline in
birth-rates, but they have paid little direct attention to the elderly and to
their behaviour. In urban areas more attention has been paid to socioeconomic
groups than to age groups.

There are general problems relating to the spatial behaviour of different
age groups. The older population is particularly interesting because an
important element in this population must choose whether or not to
remain in the places where they have lived during their working lives.
Many people change more or less their relationship with space as they
grow old. The place of the elderly in a regional population and the relationships between the places where the elderly live and their way of life need
to be studied.

The spatial distribution of the elderly, in France as in other industrial
countries, is becoming more and more complex and varies between regions
and communes. The proportion of the elderly in the population of a region,
which used to be a function only of the birth-rate and the exodus or inmigration of young people, today depends also on the actual behaviour
of the elderly. The majority do not move, but in France 13% of the
population of 65 years of age and over moved between the 1962 and 1968
censuses as against 27% for the total population. Most of the elderly move
at the time of their retirement or a few years later to another commune
and often to another region. Among the 9 million retired persons in France,

it is estimated that more than 2.5 million and probably nearer 3 million have moved at least once since the end of their working life to another place to live. Some of them moved a few years before retiring and found another job in their proposed place of retirement; this behaviour is not unusual among some types of civil servants and may be called 'pre-retirement migration'.

Few studies of these phenomena have been made because they concerned an unproductive part of the population. Furthermore, the aged migrants are a minority within a minority. They are a minority amongst migrants of whom 90% are under 60 years of age. They are a minority amongst old people, since the majority remain where they lived during their working life. In the period 1962–8, 6 out of every 7 elderly persons remained in the same commune.

Attention is now being paid to the problems of the older population, because of its growing importance, its particular characteristics, and because of the general problem of the more elderly section of the population for society and the economy. At the present time 40% of the population of France is 65 years of age or more. The social and economic system is itself a great burden for the aged. Investigation of problems associated with this situation involves truly interdisciplinary work among the social sciences. It provides an opportunity for geographers to share in social action with those working to improve the conditions of life for retired people. It provides an opportunity for a critical view of existing socioeconomic organization, an essential function of the social sciences.

Table 23.1

Changes in residence in France by age group, 1962–8

Population	Percentage in 1968 in the same commune as in 1962	Percentage in 1968 in another commune	
		Total pop.	Inactive pop.
55 years and over	86.5	13.5	14.5
55–64	85.9	14.1	16.8
65–74	87.1	12.9	13.8
75 years and over	87.0	13.0	13.3

Source: 1968 census.

For the same period as the table above the absolute numbers of migrants still alive over 55 years of age was 1,635,000, of whom about 1,200,000 were inactive or retired, and 860,000 were aged 65 years and over. This is a major phenomenon presenting original features, as the reasons for moving and the choice of new places of residence are in most cases different from those of migrations of people still at work. The phenomenon is becoming increasingly important in absolute terms. In a comparison of the number of migrants over 55 years, over 60 years and over 65 years of age between the 1954 and 1962 censuses and the 1962 and 1968 censuses, there was an increase of 35% for the whole of France and 50% for Paris.

Nature of 'retirement migration'

Some migrations of the elderly are not specific but are just a part of general mobility as when they move with other members of their families. But two types of migration are specific and constitute the greater part of the migration of the elderly. One occurs when people are no longer self-dependent and have to go to a nursing home, to a hospital or to their children's home at the end of their life. Many of these migrants are over 70 and the majority over 75 years of age. The other accompanies or follows retirement from work: this is 'retirement migration' which generally involves people under 70 years of age. It is the more important in terms of the numbers involved and in the changes which it brings about in regional distribution. This retirement migration has been studied in terms of the 'push-pull' hypothesis, observing the relationships between the characteristics of people (social class, income, background, lifestyle), the places they have left and the places to which they move. This phenomenon is a complex one as every region, town or city and nearly every commune have seen old people move away or arrive, and as the older population is socially and culturally diversified.

The information required to study this mobility may be obtained in the first instance from the census, which defines as 'migrants' those people who arrived in the enumeration area since the last census and who are still alive. However, the census tells little about the individual migrant, because no question has been asked about reasons for moving, or the conditions or characteristics of the previous residence. On the other hand, the former economic activity of those who have retired is indicated briefly and the census distinguishes only four broad categories of previous occupations. Of these only one, 'agricultural', is really meaningful for purposes of study. Moreover the census data of 1968 have been computed on a 25% sample only for migrants. Even if access could be obtained to gross tabulated data these would be for aggregate conditions only. Access to the data for individuals is not possible. Data that have been obtained about individuals from other sources (e.g. pensions fund data) have provided information on many thousands of moves and have presented the problem of then finding meaningful categories of migrants and of regions which they had left and to which they had come. The most useful concept has been a distinction between two main groups of people who move at the time of retirement.

First, those who go back to the area from which they originate; this is called 'return migration'. Secondly, those who move to another place than that from which they originate. The socioeconomic characteristics of migrants were related to the types of area which they had left and those to which they were moving. Two topics are examined here: the propensity to leave or not to leave, according to differing socioeconomic and geographical characteristics; the choice of new place of residence.

The propensity to migrate on retirement

The national average of 13% of people aged 65 years and over who moved between 1962 and 1968 masks important social and regional differences. The propensity to migrate depends on social characteristics and place of residence.

For people over 55 years of age living in a household whose head is retired, according to his former employment and age group, the position is as follows:

Table 23.2

Percentage of migrants, population 55 and over, living in a household whose head is retired

Head of the household	Over 55 years	65 years and over	55–64 years	Number
Formerly in agriculture	8.6	7.3	14.0	76,000
Formerly self-employed	15.2	13.0	23.0	76,000
Formerly civil servants (state and local)	15.0	11.4	21.0	234,000
Formerly in salaried private sector	11.5	10.6	14.3	254,000
Unemployed women	8.5	8.1	15.6	68,000

Source: 1968 census: unpublished tabulations.

The personal characteristics of retired migrants related to age and type of education show a relationship between higher education and higher mobility. These concern those who are employed other than in agriculture. Mobility of the retired is higher for the younger ones, 38% of the retired movers are less than 65 years of age.

Table 23.3

Percentage of migrants in the retired population, 55 years and over, excluding former agricultural workers, 1962–8

Educational status	Over 55 years	55–64 years	65 years and over
Little education	13.0	13.0	13.2
With 6 years of school	16.4	22.6	14.4
With 10 years of school	21.0	28.2	18.2
With 13 years of school	24.3	35.2	19.3
University education	25.5	39.2	22.1
Total	15.14	17.8	14.2

Source: 1968 census: unpublished tabulations.

There are also important differences related to social status. Education is the best indicator of this in terms of data from the French census. The more educated are on average more mobile because they are wealthier, and because they are more urbanized. The outmigration of the elderly is lower in rural areas than it is in cities and somewhat higher in Paris than in any other area.

But the national average for age groups, social groups, types of places according to size is made up of very important regional differences for outmigration as well as for inmigration. If the 375 urban units of over 10,000 inhabitants in France are considered, the number of migrants aged 60 and over per 100 people in this age group in 1968 gave the following values – a median of 7.5, a standard deviation of 4.2, a minimum of 3.4 and a maximum of 21.4. A very clear, although at the same time complex, regional pattern emerges, with at least 15 different regions. For inmigration the median value is 11.4 (inmigration includes movers who arrived from foreign countries, and since 1962 from Algeria), the standard deviation is 5.3, the minimum 8 and the maximum 31. Again the regional pattern is clear, high, middle and low values giving rise to many different regions. Clearly most regions are more or less attractive than the average for retired migrants, more or less able to keep their population at the end of their active life. This depends not only on presence or absence of amenities (climate, landscape, quality of housing, social amenities) but also on regional, social and economic conditions. For example, in the industrialized and urbanized regions of northern France and Alsace the elderly are inclined to be tied to their region or city and there is no tradition of 'going back to the country'. There is a long history of urbanization in these areas so that most city dwellers have been born in an urban setting, and as the countryside has a high density there are few houses available and land prices are high.

The differences in the intensity of outmigration amongst the retired are linked with the characters of the places which are left, the characteristics of city dwellers and also with the characteristics of places that can be chosen, according to the location of the previous residence and according to income. The whole range has to be considered in order to discover the underlying factors which provide an explanation. Of those retired who ended their active life in Paris, those who are well-off move away less than workers. For example, in automobile factories it was found that 20% left Paris in the two years following retirement, and among office workers, especially those in government services (e.g. postal clerks), the proportion was the same. The explanation is complex. The elderly who have to live on small pensions cannot remain in Paris; the majority are tenants and the rents which they have to pay, although low compared with the average in Paris, are too high for them to meet after retirement. Three out of 4 of those with modest incomes leave Paris for a rural setting compared with 1 in 3 of those who are well-off. Those with lower incomes have more links with the rural areas and small towns from which they originate as compared with the educated and wealthy. For example, more than half of the metal workers in Paris were born in a rural setting, in contrast with only 5% of engineers. In most cases the rural settings from which they came can still accommodate them, with good houses which are often inherited or which may be purchased at low prices.

A further important factor in the spatial behaviour of the retired is to be found in the urban social structure. Many lower-class citizens are poorly integrated into urban society, even after 40 years of residence in the city, and profit little from it. In contrast the well-off retired are more often integrated into urban society, are willing to remain and benefit from the social and cultural amenities. The higher emigration rate among the recently retired Parisians is therefore to be found among the lower middle class who may have houses in the provinces to which they can retire, or who have money to purchase accommodation and information about possible areas of retirement. The upper middle class moves less than the average; they benefit more than others from the amenities of the capital, living in the best central districts or in the better suburbs. Many of the latter have second homes around Paris or in resort areas and are able to stay during the winter on the Riviera and spend the summer at the seaside or in the country as substitutes for permanent migration.

Of the retired who lived their active lives in small towns and in provincial cities it is the richer who move away more frequently than others. They originate more often from outside the region in which they have worked, they have wider geographical horizons and also they have a means to choose another region. They are especially numerous in northeastern France, north of the line from Normandy to Lyon.

Choice of place of retirement

The study of places of residence reveals interesting relationships between people and places. The results justified the categories proposed for analysis, the 'return migration' and the other, as they seem to follow different patterns both for the location of retirement places according to the previous one and in terms of the social and economic characteristics of retired migrants. This results in different spatial patterns for the choice of place for retirement. Low-income people, who form the majority, are involved in 'return migration', and there is a small minority of well-off people involved in this also.

Four points may be made. First, there are important contrasts between the French regions according to the retired migrants which they attract. Each region can be characterized by the number of older migrants – for example, their density is high on the Riviera, in the countryside of the Paris basin, west, south and southeast of Paris, and low in most mountainous areas and in the eastern provinces of Champagne and Lorraine; the proportion of retired migrants among the older and the total population; the proportion of natives among retired migrants – for example this is high in Brittany, in northern and northeastern France, and low in the Midi, especially east of the Rhone; the social characteristics of the retired – for example in the Massif Central, in Brittany (except on the coast) and in northern and northeastern France most retired migrants are of the low-income group, but the average income is higher immediately around Paris, in the Midi and in the best resorts; and the distribution of elderly migrants between the countryside, the town, the cities, which varies according to regions.

Figs. 23.1 and 23.2 give an idea of the density of the retired and the varying importance of 'return migration'. Around each city there is a zone of retirement which coincides partly with the zone of origin of its population and with the dispersion during the summertime of its holidaymakers. (Cribier 1969). The extension of this retirement and recreation area depends little on the size of the city, in contrast to other zones of urban influence, but much on location. The retirement settlement rings are more constricted in the west, the southwest and in the Midi, whereas the retired city dwellers of northeastern France, except for Alsace, are distributed over a much wider area.

The retirement areas of Parisians do not resemble any others as they involve almost the whole of France (fig. 23.3). Nevertheless, the same rule applies to

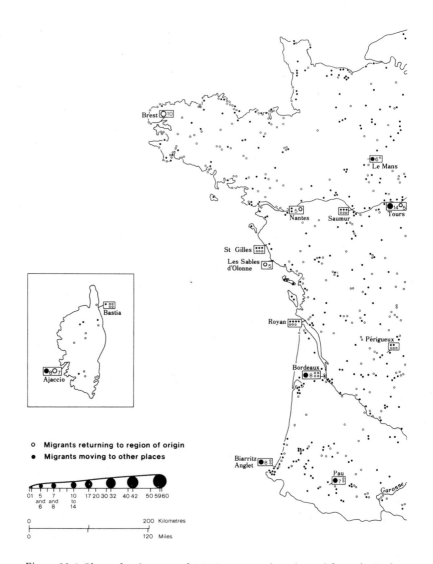

Figure 23.1 Place of retirement of 2,500 persons who migrated from the Paris

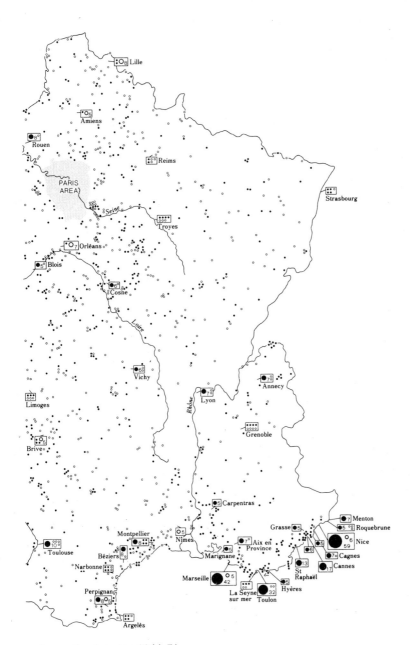

agglomeration between 1966–71

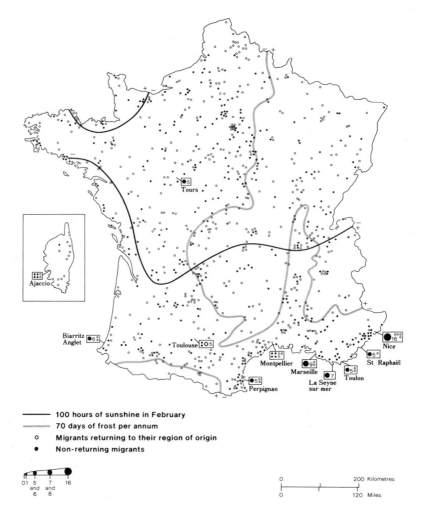

Figure 23.2 Place of retirement of 1,000 postal employees who changed residence on retirement in 1969–71

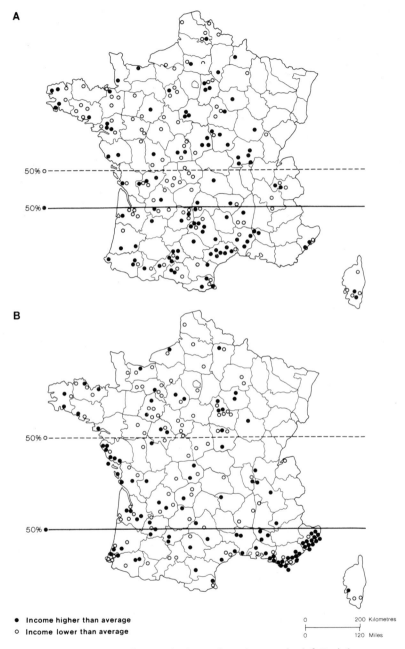

A

B

50% ○
50% ●

● Income higher than average
○ Income lower than average

0 ————— 200 Kilometres
0 ————— 120 Miles

Figure 23.3 Location of 200 retired postal employees who left Paris between
1969–71 and (A) returned to their native *département*; (B) migrated to places
other than their *département* of birth

the migration of retired people: thus places chosen by the less well-off are more evenly distributed; those who are more comfortably off are more selective, they are more numerous close to Paris but are also found at more distant places. Well-off Parisians are three times more likely than the lower class to retire in an area from which they do not originate, and settle more often in the 'second homes belt' around Paris, in resort towns of the Atlantic and Mediterranean coasts and in the foothills of the Mediterranean mountains. They are particularly numerous also in the favoured regions of the middle Loire, in the Basque country and more recently in Perigord. Even when they return to their region of birth, those who are comfortably off behave very selectively. Only 1 in 10 who originate in Northeast France returns there, but 1 in 2 of those originating in the Midi returns there for retirement.

If the differences between types of regions appear very distinct, the differences between types of commune are less clear and have to be analysed according to regional location and social groups. However, some general patterns appeared when it was calculated in 1968 that in rural communities 6% of all retired people had arrived during the previous six years, 15% in towns under 5,000 inhabitants, 11% in towns of 20,000–50,000 inhabitants, 5% in cities with 200,000 to 1 million inhabitants, and less than 3% in the Paris metropolitan area which has a population of over 8 million inhabitants. The notion of an attractive place and community is central to our study, even if most of the retired have not really chosen the place to which they move, or have been restricted in their choice. In any case, migration poses two interesting questions for consideration: the type of community to which the elderly have been attracted; and the relationship between the place to which people come and their style of life. To understand more of these, data from individual pensioners' forms are being analysed, together with interview surveys.

This unequal attraction for different types of places and regions leads to an unequal distribution of the elderly, in both quantitative and qualitative terms, leading in some instances to something in the nature of age and/or social segregation. This in most cases reinforces the pre-existing segregation. The more climatically favoured regions, the more privileged districts of the cities, the best resort towns, and the more desirable places around great cities, attract or retain a wealthy retired population. The old poor are more likely to be found in the less climatically favoured regions, in the depressed areas of central cities, in the less favourable and declining areas of the countryside where they are less likely to make demands upon social amenities. Most rural settings are less able to provide necessary services, and some retired workers who ten years ago retired from industrial areas to their places of origin have seen the decline of these services in terms of the closure of local shops, the departure of doctors, the closing of postal and bus services.

Conclusion

'Retirement migration', in contrast to any other form of permanent migration in industrialized countries, is not linked to the labour market. While moving from places where they have worked, those who retire may move to places chosen for a wide variety of reasons. The places chosen for retirement may be important in the future pattern of settlement. Important aspects of the organization of sociogeographic spaces are involved.

References

Cribier, F. (1969) *La grande migration d'été des citadins en France.* Paris.
Cribier, F. (1970) Les migrations de rétraite en France: materiaux pour une géographie du troisième âge. *Bull. Assoc. Geogr. Franc.* 381.
Rochefort, R. (1965) Pour une géographie sociale du troisième âge. *Rev. Geogr. Lyon* 1, 5–33.

Conclusion

The Preface and Introduction to this volume pointed to the interest which has been directed to the study of migration and to the contributions which have been made to it by various disciplines. The papers presented illustrate the interest and contribution of geographers to this study. They range widely both in topic and in area but represent nonetheless only a small part of the geographer's contribution to the study of migration. To this must be added the contribution of demographers, statisticians, sociologists and economists. It is a paradox that though these various contributions are in total so considerable, migration remains the most neglected of the components of population change. It is not difficult to explain why there should be this neglect.

Compared with fertility and mortality, the other variables in population change, migration is much more elusive to define, measure and understand. The events of birth and death are absolute and specific and there are no problems in defining their occurrence. Being specific in place and time they may be recorded by systems of vital registration set up for this purpose. Where these systems operate there are data for analyses of rates and trends in fertility and mortality.

Movements of population are generally not so specific either in place or in time. They are difficult to define in the first instance and range greatly in scale both spatially and temporally as the papers in this volume illustrate. Even if acceptable definitions can be worked out, many movements of population are difficult to record and measure. From censuses the data on migration, whether these are of a direct or of a surrogate nature, are inevitably highly aggregated. Many data used in the study of migration, for example those derived from age/sex structures, are not time-specific even with reference to intercensal periods. When sophisticated systems exist for the continuing registration of movements, there are problems in the subsequent handling and analysis of the data collected. Difficulties of analysis also arise when data are collected for individuals whose migration histories have been recorded, assuming that these are reasonably accurate despite problems of recall. Altogether the collection of data on migration by any means and their subsequent analysis present formidable and complex problems.

However, the relative neglect of migration study has been due not solely to conceptual and operational difficulties involved in its undertaking. Within the broad field of population studies, and particularly among demographers, fertility has received much greater attention for reasons which are readily apparent. Fertility is a more important determinant of population growth. With rates of growth being experienced at the present time, particularly in the developing world associated with decline in levels of mortality, it is necessary to understand the rates and determinants of fertility in order to proceed with greater awareness to devising and applying means which may reduce fertility. There has been considerable achievement in understanding the nature and determinants of fertility but to date there has been relatively limited success in promoting satisfactory means of control. Fertility rates remain high in the developing world in general and the impact of family planning as a means of control has been only marginal. There are grounds for at least some reappraisal and possible reorientation of approach to the factors influencing population change.

While the study of fertility must remain a top priority there is some indication of more appreciation of the need to pay attention to migration than has been so previously. If it is not possible in the short term to achieve stability, or preferably reduction, in the size of populations through fertility control, then consideration must be given to the possibility of a better ordering of population in relation to available resources. This requires some redistribution of population through planned or through spontaneous movement. Planned movement may involve very direct, specific and possibly drastic official action in order to attain desired ends. Spontaneous movement is not literally spontaneous but is influenced by degrees of pressure, encouragement and incentive applied indirectly by environmental, political, social and above all economic forces. The studies in this volume are concerned largely with examples of movements of a spontaneous nature.

The redistribution of population, whether directed or spontaneous, can do no more than alleviate problems in limited areas and for relatively limited numbers of people. Transferences of population on sufficiently large scales to make major impact are logistically impossible. To the problems of logistics must be added political factors which would prevent massive movements of population. The era of great intercontinental mobility that characterized the nineteenth and early twentieth centuries has passed and is not likely to be revived. There are now limited major pioneer frontiers to be advanced, and few of these are in the developing parts of the world. Those that remain, particularly in Canada, Latin America and Soviet Asia, require major investments of capital and technological skill for their development. These will be provided from within the countries concerned and with benefits accruing from them reserved for their nationals.

However, benefits of a limited but worthwhile nature can be achieved through the redistributing of population within countries – through the development of empty or sparsely populated areas, in the concentration of population in areas which offer the best potential for economic development, and by adjustments in the balance between urban and rural sectors. These apply variously to countries in different stages of economic development. There is no part of the world at the present day without some problem or problems relating to its population to which migration would not give some relief, even if it was not able to provide a solution. Among official bodies at international, national, regional and local levels this fact needs to be increasingly recognized. To then achieve something effective requires a much better knowledge and understanding of migration, its nature and processes, than exists at the present time.

This need to concentrate greater attention on population movements relates not only to the possible redistribution of population involving permanent moves. There is also the fact that throughout the world, at various levels of social and economic development, people are involved in increasing mobility of a circulatory nature as individuals and in groups. They move over varying distances and over varying but for the most part limited spans of time. These various forms of circulation are poorly understood and cannot be accommodated in conventional concepts of migration. The fault is in the conventional concepts and not that circulation is intrinsically different.

Movements, whether they result in the permanent redistribution of population or are of a circulatory nature which causes only temporary displacement, demand greater consideration than has been given to them previously. Theory on mobility is limited in absolute terms. It is mainly derived from experience in Europe and in North America where most empirical work has been done and where most data exist to make this possible. These data are far from ideal but they highlight the deficiencies elsewhere in the world. As yet relatively little account has been taken of mobility experienced in the less developed parts of the world. In these, empirical studies have been restricted by major data deficiencies. Those which have been made need to be related to existing theory, to determine to what extent they can be adequately accommodated within it. This will be of value not only for greater comprehension of mobility in the developing world, but for the light that this comprehension may cast upon past mobility in the now developed parts of the world.

This volume points out some of the directions in which major thrust in the future is required. An increase in empirical studies, improvements in data and extensions of theory must come together to enhance understanding of the spatial and temporal dimensions of population movements and of their economic and behavioural aspects. This is required not only for academic purposes, it is also of practical importance. Population movements are influenced by social, economic and political developments. Social and political organization, employment, education and health are only some of the many elements in contemporary life which are vitally affected by people on the move.

List of migration
bibliographies
List of periodicals
and serials
Index

Migration bibliographies[1]

Alzate, B. (1972) *Emigración de profesionales: bibliografía.* Bogotá.

Aquino, C. (1971) *Migrations: bibliography.* UN Social Research Institute Documents.

Ascolani, A. and Birindelli, A. M. (eds.) (1971) *Introduzione bibliografica ai problemi della migrazioni.* Rome. Includes a supplement by G. Marbach *Sugli aspetti della criminalità fra i lavatori migranti.*

Bertelli, I., Corcagnani, G. and Rosoli, G. F. (1972) *Migrations. Catalogue of the Library CSER* [Catalogo della Biblioteca del Centro Studi Emigrazione]. Rome. In English and Italian.

Beyer, G. (1963) *Rural migrants in urban setting.* The Hague.

Beyer, G. (1972) *Brain drain. A selected bibliography.* European Demographic Monographs No. 3. The Hague.

Brooks, T. R. (1970) *Labor and migration: an annotated bibliography.* Brooklyn College Center for Migration Studies. Brooklyn.

Canada, Department of Manpower and Immigration (1969) *Immigration, migration and ethnic groups in Canada. A bibliography of research 1964–1968.* Ottawa.

Daniel, R. E. (1969) *Local residential mobility: a selected and annotated bibliography.* Council of Planning Librarians. Monticello, Illinois.

Europäische Gemeinschaft für Kohle und Stahl, Hohe Behörde (1958) *Bibliographie über die ausländische Beweglichkeit und die internationalen Wanderbewegungen der Arbeitnehmer.* Luxemburg. In German, French, Italian and Dutch.

European Society for Rural Sociology (1959) *Bibliography on rural migration in 10 European countries.* Bonn.

Gould, W. T. S. (1974) *Bibliography of population mobility in tropical Africa.* African Mobility Project, Dept of Geography, Univ. of Liverpool.

Gutierrez de MacGregor, Ma. Teresa *et al.* (1972) *Sintesis bibliografica sobre migracion interna en America Latina.* Inst. of Geography, Univ. of Mexico.

[1] This list includes only bibliographies and review articles devoted specifically to migration. In addition, general demographic bibliographies, usually published for individual countries, should be consulted.

Horna, J. (1972) Brain drain: a bibliography. *Internat. Newsletter on Migration* 2 (3), 1–25.

International Labour Office and Food and Agricultural Organization of the United Nations (1968) *Bibliography of rural migration for selected developing countries (1960–1967).* Geneva. Duplicate text in French.

Kosiński, L. (1972) Bibliography on Yugoslav migration. See Tomović, V. I.

Kosiński, L. (ed.) (1972) *Education and rural-urban migration: a bibliographic analysis.* Manuscript in UNESCO. Paris.

Laquian, A. A. and Dutton, P. (1971) *A selected bibliography on rural-urban migrants' slums and squatters in developing countries.* Exchange bibliographies No. 182. Council of Planning Librarians. Monticello, Illinois.

Lavel, C. B. and Schmidt, C. (1956) An annotated bibliography on the demographic, economic and sociological aspects of immigration, in Tracy, S. J. (ed.) *A report on world population migrations.*

Macisco, J. J. (1971) *Bibliography on internal migration.* UN CELADE. Santiago.

Mangalam, J. J. with the assistance of C. Morgan (1968) *Human migration. A guide to migration literature in English, 1955–1962.* Lexington.

Myers, G. C. and Macisco, J. J. (1972) *Selective bibliography on migration and fertility.* Center for Demographic Studies, Duke Univ., Working Paper No. 6. Durham, NC.

Newbury, G. E. and Newbury, C. W. (1971) *Bibliography of Commonwealth migration, the tropical territories. Vol. 1: Africa. Vol. 2: Asia, former British dependencies and independent states.* Oxford.

Organization for Economic Cooperation and Development (1969) *Bibliography. International migration of manpower.* Paris.

Price, C. *et al.* (eds.) (1966 and 1970) *Australian immigration: a bibliography and digest.* Australian National Univ., Canberra. 2 vols.

Pryor, R. J. (1971) *Internal migration and urbanization.* Geography Dept, James Cook Univ. of North Queensland, Monograph Series No. 2. Townsville.

Scobie-de Maar, M. J. A. (1970) *Bibliography about the migration and future of professionals.* Norwegian Inst. for Studies in Research and Higher Education. Oslo.

Simmons, J. W. (1968) Changing residence in the city: a review of intra-urban mobility. *Geogr. Rev.* 4, 622–51.

Thomas, B. (1961) *International migration and economic development: a trend report and bibliography.* Paris (UNESCO).

Thomas, D. (1938) *Research memorandum on migration differentials.* Soc. Sci. Res. Counc. Bull. No. 43. New York.

Tomović, V. I. (1972) A selected bibliography on migration in Yugoslavia. *Internat. Newsletter on Migration* 2 (1), 3–6. Supplement by L. Kosiński, 2 (3), 3–5.

United Nations, Dept of Social Affairs (1949) *Problems of migration statistics.* Population Studies No. 5. Lake Success – New York.

United Nations, Dept of Social Affairs (1953a) *International research on migration.* New York.

United Nations, Dept of Social Affairs (1953b) *Sex and age of international migrants: statistics for 1918–1947.* Population Studies No. 11. New York.

United Nations, Dept of Social Affairs (1955) *Analytical bibliography of international migration statistics, 1925–1950.* Population Studies No. 24. New York.

United Nations, Dept of Social Affairs (1958) *Economic characteristics of international migrants: statistics for selected countries, 1918–1954.* Population Studies No. 12. New York.

United Nations, Economic Commission for Asia and the Far East (1968) *Family planning, internal migration and urbanization in the ECAFE countries: a bibliography of available materials.* Asian Population Studies Series No. 2. Bangkok.

Welch, R. (1970) *Migration research and migration in Britain.* Univ. of Birmingham, Centre for Urban and Regional Studies, Occasional Paper No. 14. Birmingham.

Żurek, A. (1971) *Bibliografia polskich prac o migracjach stałych, wewnętrznych ludności (lata 1916–1969/70).* Dokumentacja geograficzna No. 1. Warsaw.

Current bibliography can be found in the following periodicals:

Eur. Demog. Inf. Bull. Quarterly published by the European Centre for Population Studies. Martinus Nijhof, The Hague.

Geoabstracts Ser. D. Social Geography and Cartography. Bi-monthly. Norwich.

Internat. Bibliography of the Soc. Sci. Docmn. Four annual vols. incl. one each on Sociology and Economics. UNESCO, Internat. Ctee for Soc. Sci. Docmn. London.

Internat. Migration. Quarterly published by the Intergovernmental Committee for European Migration and the Research Group for European Migration Problems. The Hague and Geneva.

Internat. Migration Rev. Three numbers per annum. Center for Migration Studies of New York. Staten Island, New York.

Pop. Index. Quarterly published by the Office of Population Research and the Population Association of America. Princeton.

Periodicals and serials exclusively or partially devoted to migration[1]

PERIODICALS AND SERIALS APPEARING CURRENTLY
Old titles – series that have ceased to appear or have changed titles
Non-English titles of parallel linguistic versions OR
    secondary titles if given in a different language

ACIM DISPATCH (1952–). Quarterly. American Committee on Italian Migration, New York.
AMERICAN NEAR EAST REFUGEE AID NEWSLETTER (1972–). Bi-monthly. Washington.
Ausländerarbeit → MIGRATION TODAY.
AWR BULLETIN (1963–). Quarterly. Association for the Study of the World Refugee Problems, Vienna. Supersedes **Integration** (1954–62).
BILTEN CENTRA ZA ISTRAŽIVANJE MIGRACIJA (1974–). Monthly. Centar za Istraživanje Migracija, Sveučilište u Zagrebu, Zagreb. Supersedes **Bilten Odjela za Migracije** (1972–3).
Bilten Odjela za Migracije → BILTEN CENTRA ZA ISTRAŽIVANJE MIGRACIJA.
Cahiers Nord-Africains → HOMMES ET MIGRATIONS. ÉTUDES.
CIME Notizias → **ICEM News.**
CIME Nouvelles → **ICEM News.**
CIME Réalisations → ICEM REVIEW OF ACHIEVEMENTS.
CIME Realizaciones → ICEM REVIEW OF ACHIEVEMENTS.
COMPTES RENDUS DE RECHERCHES ET BIBLIOGRAPHIE SUR L'IMMIGRATION (1974–). Irregular. Société des Amis du Centre d'Études Sociologiques, Paris. New series separately numbered supersedes old series (1960?–73?).

---

[1] This list does not include government sponsored series: statistics, reports, bulletins of counselling series etc. Some of these can be found in 'Special Bibliography – a checklist of current government serial publications containing vital or migration statistics' in *Population Index* 39 (1973), 4.

DEMOGRAPHY (1964–). Quarterly. Population Association of America, Washington.

Documents Nord Africains → HOMMES ET MIGRATIONS. DOCUMENTS.

EMIGRATIE KOERIER (1949–). Semi-monthly. Christelijke Emigratie Centrale, s'Gravenhage.

Etudes Migrations → STUDI EMIGRAZIONE.

France Migrations → MIGRATIONS ET PASTORALE.

France Vie → MIGRATIONS.

Hombres para el Progreso → PEOPLE FOR PROGRESS.

HOMMES ET MIGRATIONS. DOCUMENTS (1965–). Semi-monthly. Paris. Supersedes **Documents Nord Africains** (1950–65).

HOMMES ET MIGRATIONS. ÉTUDES (1965–). Irregular. Paris. Supersedes **Cahiers Nord-Africains. Main-d'oeuvre nord-africaine** (1950–64).

ICEM News → MIGRATION BULLETIN.

ICEM REVIEW OF ACHIEVEMENTS (1972–). Annual. Intergovernmental Committee for European Migration, Geneva. Appears also in French and Spanish.

IMMIGRATION BAR BULLETIN (1970–). Quarterly. Association of Immigration and Nationality Lawyers, Brooklyn.

IMMIGRATION HISTORY NEWSLETTER (1969–). Semi-annual. Immigration History Society, East Lansing.

Integration → AWR BULLETIN.

INTERNATIONAL LABOUR REVIEW (1921–). Monthly. International Labour Office, Geneva. Appears also in French (*Revue Internationale du Travail*).

INTERNATIONAL MIGRATION (1963–). Quarterly. Intergovernmental Committee for European Migration and the Research Group for European Migration Problems, The Hague and Geneva. Supersedes **Research Digest ICEM** (1955–60), **Migration** (1961–2), in 1962 merged with **REMP Bulletin** (1953–62). Formerly parallel French version, *Migrations Internationales* (1963–7) superseded **Migrations** (1961–2), and Spanish version, *Migraciones Internacionales* (1963-7).

International Migration Digest → INTERNATIONAL MIGRATION REVIEW.

INTERNATIONAL MIGRATION REVIEW (1966–). Quarterly. Center for Migration Studies of New York, Staten Island, New York. Supersedes **International Migration Digest** (1964–6).

INTERNATIONAL NEWSLETTER ON MIGRATION (1971–). Quarterly. Dept of Sociology, Univ. of Waterloo.

ITALIANI NEL MONDO. Rivista quindicinale dell'emigrazione e del lavoro italiano all'estero (1944–). Semi-monthly. Rome.

Les Hommes du Progrès → PEOPLE FOR PROGRESS.

Menschen Unterwegs → MIGRATION NEWS.

MIGRACIJE RADNIKA. MIGRATIONS OF WORKERS (1970–).
Irregular research monographs. Centar za Istraživanje Migracija,
Sveučilište u Zagrebu, Zagreb.

MIGRANT (1930–). Quarterly. Elizabethton.

MIGRANT ECHO (1972–). Quarterly. San Francisco.

MIGRANTS FORMATION (1973–). Semi-monthly. Centre de Documentation pour la Formation des Travailleurs Migrants, Paris.

Migration → INTERNATIONAL MIGRATION.

Migration → MIGRATION TODAY.

MIGRATION BULLETIN (1974–). Quarterly. Intergovernmental Committee for European Migration, Geneva. Published in English, French
and Spanish. Supersedes **ICEM News** (1969–73). Quarterly with
occasional special issues in English, French, Spanish and German.

MIGRATION. INFORMATIVE SERIES (1958–). Irregular. International
Catholic Migration Commission, Geneva. Most issues appear only in
French as *Migrations. Série Informative.*

MIGRATION NEWS (1956–). Bi-monthly. International Catholic Migration
Commission (ICMC), Geneva. Supersedes **News ICMC** (1952–5).
Parallel versions with different layout and content appear in French as
Migrations dans le Monde, 1956– (**Nouvelles CICM**, 1952–5), and in
German as *Menschen Unterwegs,* 1956– (**Nachrichten**, 1952–5). There
was also an earlier series in Spanish, **Noticiario.**

MIGRATION TODAY (1963–). Semi-annual, recently irregular. Secretariat
for Migration, World Council of Churches, Geneva. Appears also in
French as *Migrations,* 1973– (**Migrations**, 1963–72), and in German as
Ausländerarbeit.

MIGRATIONS (1963–). Monthly plus one special issue per annum. Ed.
Lafayette, Paris. Supersedes **France Vie.**

Migrations → INTERNATIONAL MIGRATION.

Migrations → MIGRATION TODAY.

Migrations (1952–3). Bi-monthly. International Labour Offices, Geneva.
Later it was attached as a monthly appendix to *Informations Sociales*
(1953–60). Appeared also in English.

Migrations dans le Monde → MIGRATION NEWS.

MIGRATIONS ET PASTORALE (1969–). Quarterly. Commission
Épiscopale des Migrations, Paris. Supersedes **France Migrations**
(1957–68).

MIGRATIONS. FACTS AND FIGURES (1956–). Irregular. International
Catholic Migration Commission, Geneva. Appears as a supplement to
MIGRATION NEWS. Parallel French and German versions.

Migrations Internationales → INTERNATIONAL MIGRATION.

Migrations rurales → QUOI DE NEUF.

Migrations. Série Informative → MIGRATION. INFORMATIVE SERIES.

Migrations of Workers → MIGRACIJE RADNIKA.

Nachrichten → MIGRATION NEWS.

News ICMC → MIGRATION NEWS.

Noticiario → MIGRATION NEWS.

Noticias CIME → **ICEM News.**

NOTIZIE, FATTI, PROBLEMI DELL'EMIGRAZIONE (1955–). Monthly. Associazione Nazionale Famigle Emigrati, Rome.

Nouvelles CICM → MIGRATION NEWS.

PALESTINE REFUGEES TODAY (1961–). Bi-monthly. United Nations Relief and Works Agency for Palestine Refugees in the Near East, Beirut. Appears also in French and German.

Papers on Migration and Mobility in North East England → PAPERS ON MIGRATION AND MOBILITY IN NORTHERN ENGLAND.

PAPERS ON MIGRATION AND MOBILITY IN NORTHERN ENGLAND (1966–). Irregular. Dept of Geography, Univ. of Newcastle. Supersedes **Papers on Migration and Mobility in North East England** (1964–6).

PEOPLE FOR PROGRESS (1966–). Semi-annual. Intergovernmental Committee for European Migration, Geneva. Appears in two bilingual editions, English-French (*Les Hommes du Progrès*) and English-Spanish (*Hombres para el Progreso*).

POPULATION (1946–). Bi-monthly plus one supplement per annum. Institut National d'Études Démographiques, Paris.

POPULATION INDEX (1935–). Quarterly. Office of Population Research and Population Association of America, Princeton.

POPULATION STUDIES (1947–). Three times a year. Population Investigation Committee, London School of Economics and Political Science.

QUOI DE NEUF (1964–). Syndicat des Migrations et Etablissements de Ruraux de la Vienne, Poitiers. Supersedes **Migrations rurales.**

Rapport du HCR → UNHCR REPORTS.

RAZPRAVE O MIGRACIJAMA (1974–). Irregular. Centar za Istraživanje Migracija, Sveučilište u Zagrebu, Zagreb.

REMP Bulletin → INTERNATIONAL MIGRATION.

REMP BULLETIN. SUPPLEMENTS (1953–). Irregular. Research Group for European Migration Problems, The Hague.

REMP REPORTS (1951–6). Irregular research monographs. Research Group for European Migration Problems, The Hague.

Research Digest ICEM → INTERNATIONAL MIGRATION.

Revue Internationale du Travail → INTERNATIONAL LABOUR REVIEW.

SELEZIONE CSER (1969–). Monthly. Centro Studi Emigrazione, Rome.

STUDI EMIGRAZIONE. ETUDES MIGRATIONS (1963–). Quarterly. Centro Studi Emigrazione, Rome.

STUDIES AND DOCUMENTS ON IMMIGRATION AND INTEGRATION
IN CANADA (1962–). Irregular. Jewish Immigrant and Aid Services
of Canada, Montreal.

UNHCR REPORTS (1951–). Monthly. United Nations High Commissioner
for Refugees, Geneva. Appears also in French as *Rapport du HCR*.

Index

Note: In order to prevent a long list of items under *migration,*
frequently occurring items, e.g. *data*, are listed separately in
alphabetical order.